Praise for *Vertigo: The Rise and Fall of Weimar Germany*

'From women in the workplace to traffic lights, from yo-yos to dance culture, Jähner tracks the 15 chaotic years of the Weimar Republic with his characteristic verve and attention to detail. This is one of the most gripping accounts of an era spanning war defeat, humiliation and failed revolution in 1918 to the violence, intimidation and propaganda of the Nazis' rise to power in 1933. It contains many lessons for the world now'
– John Kampfner, author of *Why the Germans Do it Better*

'*Vertigo* is outstanding. Harald Jähner's gift for illuminating the big picture with telling detail gives the reader an uncanny sense of what it was actually like to be present in Germany during the Weimar Republic. This is history at its very best'
– Julia Boyd, author of *Travellers in the Third Reich* and *A Village in the Third Reich*

'Wonderfully written and compulsively, electrifyingly readable. The Weimar Republic and its chilling fall is – like Shakespearean tragedy – an enduringly fascinating, profoundly human story. And with consummate skill and a rich breadth of research, Harald Jähner makes us look again at what we thought we knew and gives this history new, extraordinary depth. Taking us through the neurotic violence of the 1918 German revolution, and the neon flowering of Weimar art and culture, thence to the dark rise of Hitler, Jähner deftly overturns many old assumptions about economics and politics along the way. And against this backdrop, he also invites us to explore everything from nude gymnastics to modernist architecture, fast cars to dance halls and, fundamentally, love and loss and the cold horror of hate'
– Sinclair McKay, author of *Berlin* and *Dresden*

'Any decent centrist will shiver at this wonderfully illustrated account of how Weimar's heady metropolitan progressiveness failed to cope with loss of national pride, technological modernism, social change, early globalisation and financial crash. The confidence of the middle classes was lost, readying them to accept wild conspiracy theories: a new fusion of hard left and hard right, National Socialism, was swept to power by Germany's flyover country, with disastrous results which the traditional elites only saw too late. A priceless lesson for anybody interested in Germany then – or the world today'
– James Hawes, author of *The Shortest History of Germany*

Praise for *Aftermath: Life in the Fallout of the Third Reich*, also by Harald Jähner

'Magisterial, fascinating, humane – a brilliant book of the greatest importance and achievement'
– Philippe Sands, author of *East West Street* and *The Ratline*

'What does total defeat mean? Germany 1945–55. Ten years of poverty, ruins, fear, violence, black markets, manic hard work, inventive sex – and always, always, silence about the murdered millions of the Third Reich. A fascinating read'
– Neil MacGregor, author of *Germany: Memories of a Nation*

'Exemplary [and] important . . . This is the kind of book few writers possess the clarity of vision to write'
– Max Hastings, *Sunday Times*

'This panoramic journey through Germany in the ruins of the Third Reich is unforgettably thought-provoking [and] intensely moving'
– Dominic Sandbrook, *The Times*

VERTIGO

THE RISE AND FALL
OF WEIMAR GERMANY
1918–1933

HARALD JÄHNER

Translated by Shaun Whiteside

WH
ALLEN

WH Allen, an imprint of Ebury Publishing
20 Vauxhall Bridge Road
London SW1V 2SA

WH Allen is part of the Penguin Random House group of companies
whose addresses can be found at global.penguinrandomhouse.com

The translation of this book was supported by a grant from the Goethe-Institut

First published in German by Rowoholt, Berlin in 2022
This translation published by WH Allen in 2024

www.penguin.co.uk

A CIP catalogue record for this book is available from the British Library

ISBN 9780753559963
Trade Paperback ISBN 9780753559970

Typeset in 11.75/14.75pt Dante MT Std by Jouve (UK), Milton Keynes
Printed and bound in Great Britain by Clays Ltd, Elcograf S.p.A.

The authorised representative in the EEA is Penguin Random House Ireland,
Morrison Chambers, 32 Nassau Street, Dublin D02 YH68

Penguin Random House is committed to a sustainable future
for our business, our readers and our planet. This book is made
from Forest Stewardship Council® certified paper.

For my brother Uli, who didn't get the chance to read this book

Contents

Preface: The New Life

History is sometimes made with a camera. In 1925, in her studio on Kurfürstendamm, Berlin, the photographer Frieda Riess posed the young boxer Erich Brandl naked in front of her lens. His trained body was lit with a sophistication usually reserved for female nudes. When the art dealer Alfred Flechtheim published the full-page pictures from the shoot, showing the boxer nude from the front and from behind, in his trendsetting magazine *Querschnitt* (Cross-Section), both photographer and editor had a sense of being ahead of their time. Boxing had exploded in popularity in America and was now causing a stir on the German cultural scene. There was much to be learned from boxing matches; the prominent left-wing poet and playwright Bertolt Brecht thought an evening in the theatre ought to be like a boxing match. He installed a punching ball in his study, and the author Vicki Baum trained regularly in a boxing club. The word *Körperkultur* (body culture) did the rounds; the immaculate, fully trained body became an obsession of the age. The picture-hungry Weimar Republic had a particular weakness for women photographers and the female gaze; the most interesting, innovative creators in this new craft were women.

Frieda Riess had directed Erich Brandl to look at the floor. That way he appeared more like an object than if he had shown his face and looked at the viewer. Riess also forbade him to pose in the usual challenging boxing stance. Rather than covering himself with raised fists, Frieda Riess asked him to raise his right arm a little to make his body appear less shielded. This added vulnerability emphasised the radical and challenging way in which the usual roles of men and women had been swapped. Even in the provocative 1920s, a woman reducing a male body to the status of object as lovingly as Riess did in this picture (p. 225) wasn't something that happened often. It would have consequences, that much was certain.

Using scenes like that photo-shoot in Frieda Riess's celebrity studio, this book tells the story of a time that in many respects looks like a blueprint for our own. Viewed from the perspective of the present day, the Weimar Republic appears like a lenticular image – a picture printed to look different at different angles – surprisingly contemporary at one moment, weirdly alien the next. At times it seems almost more modern than we are – as if we're looking back at something that is still in front of us – and then again it looks as far removed from us as the black-clad, rigid figures in the family portraits of our great-grandparents.

How euphorically it had begun in 1918, with the fall of the kaiser and the proclamation of the first democratic republic on German soil. 'The old world is rotten, all its joints are creaking. I want to help to demolish it,' the young expressive dancer and pioneering performance artist Valeska Gert proclaimed. 'I believe in the new life. I want to help to build it.'¹ In every area of life a new age seemed to be dawning; there were expectations of the 'New Man', the 'New Woman', the 'New Building' – even a new art movement, *Neue Sachlichkeit* (New Objectivity). The architect Bruno Taut, soon to be famous for the restrained functionality of his large housing estates, was not a man given to overreaction, yet he celebrated in almost religious ecstasy in 1920:

Our tomorrow gleams in the distance [. . .] Up with transparency, clarity! Up with purity! Up with crystal! And up and higher up with the fluid, the graceful, angular, sparkling, flashing, light – up with the eternal building!²

As cool as our responses today might be to the cubic buildings and the plain furniture of the 'New Building', we can barely imagine the dizzying, vertiginous excitement with which they were designed at the time. And the aggression. Taut, the architect, raged against stuccoed nineteenth-century buildings with a violence that called for dynamite and wrecking balls:

> Away with the gravestone and cemetery facades outside four-storey junk stores and bric-a-brac markets! Smash the shell-limestone Doric, Ionic and Corinthian columns, smash all the ludicrous fakery! [. . .] Oh! Our concepts: space, homeland, style . . . ! God alive, those concepts stink to heaven! Tear them to bits, dissolve them! Let nothing remain! [. . .] Death to all that's musty![3]

How does it fit together? How did this stirring proclamation result in the unadorned modern architecture that seems so sober and cool to us today, almost well-behaved in its balanced elegance? The deliberately dramatic radicalism, typical of these years in many fields, led me to enquire into the emotional state of the Weimar Republic. Very few moments in German history have prompted such intense emotions as these. Born out of the torment of war, the enthusiasm of revolution was overshadowed by the humiliations of defeat and a sense of intellectual homelessness, along with the risks of unfamiliar freedom. It was a time of extreme fluctuation: 1923 saw the madness of hyperinflation, with its billion-mark notes that even a street beggar would have refused. Inflation called into question centuries-old notions of value, obliterated traditions and prepared people for a turbulent decade that, in the words of the historian Detlev Peukert, 'played breathlessly and extravagantly through all the positions and possibilities of the modern age, explored them all and rejected them at almost the same time'.[4]

This book deals in the feelings, moods and sensations produced by the political attitudes and conflicts of the age; emotional manifestations such as unease, confidence, anxiety, ennui, self-reliance, a desire to consume, a desire to dance, a hunger for experience, pride and hatred. How did people feel in the Weimar Republic? Impossible to generalise, of course. But amidst the different, contradictory perspectives it is a question that needs to be asked. How did it feel to be young, to be a woman, a city-dweller or a farmer? How did the Freikorps soldiers feel in 1918, when they couldn't understand why the war was over? What did the revolutionaries feel? Whence the widespread hatred of soft plush, of decoration and ornament? How did young women see their future when inflation reduced their dowries to nothing and instead, in huge numbers, they received something fundamentally new: secretarial work? How did people feel when the cities grew and grew and no one knew, unlike us today, whether they would ever stop? And why was the melancholic Austrian writer and journalist Joseph Roth, of all people, so enthusiastic about city traffic that he cried: 'I am devoted to the Gleisdreieck [a railway junction in Berlin]'? Why did the young author Ruth Landshoff-Yorck plant a kiss on the radiator of her car when she parked it in the garage at night, and why did she urgently recommend that her readers do the same?

The story of the Weimar Republic is best told in the places that shaped its intellectual development: whether it be the dance hall, the Bauhaus dwelling, the open-plan office, heavy traffic, the photographic studio, the sports hall, the beer tent at election time or the edge of the street when the fighting gangs were marching. We also catch a glimpse of the villages and small towns in which a yearning for the city was growing, supposedly turning people's heads, inspiring young women to run away, leaving many disappointed bachelors behind. In the countryside, everyday struggles contrasted with the promises of the beautiful new modern world of consumerism, whose siren call was heard loud and clear coming from the cities. Is there a danger that we ignore life in the provinces if we focus on the glamorous urban scene of the 1920s, and by doing so are we guilty of repeating an error that Berlin cultural elites were accused of committing at the time? And conversely, what are we to make of the Weimar Republic's nostalgia for the countryside, of the fanatical 'settler' movement, which called young people into the fields, a forerunner of today's ecoculture and rural communes?

The momentum of the cultural upheavals that were taking place would be unthinkable without jazz, which inspired and intoxicated people, sending them into raptures. The gramophone record created pop culture, which violently cranked up the intensity of life. The fact that one could dance the Charleston alone had consequences for the self-empowerment of the individual; to be able to join in solo on the dancefloor was nothing less than revolutionary. But then we adjust the image slightly and see the elegant people still standing on the sidelines. Those young decommissioned officers who now served in the dance halls of the Republic and were paid for by independent women who had no time to sit around for ages waiting until someone asked them to dance – how did they feel? Haus Vaterland (Fatherland House), a pleasure palace in Berlin, even provided childcare when mothers wanted to dance in the afternoon.

This book tells the story of the highly charged politics of the body, exciting new developments in masculinity and femininity, about the need to be both more affectionate and more sexually ambiguous, while at the same time toughening up and engaging in self-improvement in every area of life. Crucially, this was true of the armed combat groups formed of disaffected men that marched down the streets in close formation and gave the individual the intoxicating feeling of superior strength. This book will describe the attempts of rapidly changing governments to ride on the tiger of public disorder, but it is that very disorder that deserves the greatest attention: the pre-political states of mind that formed people's values, attitudes and convictions. It was no coincidence that journalism enjoyed a stylistic and perceptive heyday. The intellectuals of the Republic, whatever their politics, developed a particular sensitivity to the political content of apparently quite unpolitical everyday phenomena.

Wanting to know what it felt like in the Weimar Republic means not always interpreting historical events from their endpoint. Unlike us, people at the time didn't know how things were going to turn out. In view of the monstrous and horrific development of National Socialism, we might be tempted to see the Republic only as the prehistory of its conclusion, and constantly search for early clues to its downfall. But even mass unemployment was not a compelling reason to vote for Hitler, and many of the unemployed didn't. So who did?

Why did a woman such as Luise Solmitz, who was happily married to a Jew, sympathise with the NSDAP? Who did people at the time see when they saw Hitler? The same person whom we see today, after two generations of processing? Why could so many Germans no longer hear one another? Why did so many of them see the debates in the Reichstag as so much empty noise, and the newspapers that reported on it as propagating nothing but lies?

During the global economic crisis of the late 1920s and 1930s, the balance of German emotions alternated between hatred and a longing for unity. The exhilarating diversity of the 1920s often came to be seen as a burden, and by many as a curse. These people felt that their society was torn, split into irreconcilably opposed worlds that would never be mutually comprehensible. Inevitably, this dissatisfaction invites comparison with the present day. Around 1930, democracy lost one of its most important and most fragile resources: confidence. Much that had, during the boom times, felt like liberation and high-altitude flight, now came to be seen as exploitation and betrayal. From 1930 onwards, the attitudes of many Germans changed in ways that fed deeply into tastes in fashion, the sense of the body, tonal register and musical preference. The mood plummeted, the desire for salvation rose, new kinds of vertiginous intoxication were sought, more thrilling, aggressive and menacing than ever.

Any historical narrative implicitly asks questions concerning individual responsibility. The march towards National Socialism was not inevitable. Weimar democracy was not so weak that any other outcome was unimaginable. People had a choice, each for themselves, including in the polling booth. At the time, they couldn't see exactly how important that choice was.

When the War Came Home

Café Vaterland is brightly lit. I go in briefly. Even though bullets could strike at any moment, the Viennese Orchestra is playing.

Harry Graf Kessler

The first few days

The Weimar Republic begins with a paradox: no sooner was the war over than it reached Germany. From November 1918, one step at a time, it came home.

For the four years of the world war the German army had managed to keep the conflict outside the door. While large stretches of France and Belgium had been laid waste in ways never seen before, in Germany not a single roof tile had been destroyed. Though Germany was physically unscathed, the monarchy was done for, and the people were done with war. Before the armistice to end all hostilities had even been signed, strikes paralysed production and citizens' committees (called workers' and soldiers' councils) assumed power in the towns and cities. Revolution seemed to be winning as soon as it began, with an admirable lack of bloodshed. Soldiers ran away from their officers, there was a mutiny among the sailors of Kiel, who refused orders to launch a last-ditch naval attack on the British, and the regime, already bled dry by the war, was afflicted by collective revolts. First, the monarchy fell in the Kingdom of Bavaria, with the deposition of King

Ludwig III followed two days later, on 9 November 1918, by the abdication of Kaiser Wilhelm II, Emperor of Germany and King of Prussia. The government under Max von Baden, who had only been in office for a month – at the head of the first cabinet in German history to include members of the centre-left, reformist Social Democratic Party (*Sozialdemokratische Partei Deutschlands*, SPD) – had announced His Excellency's abdication, even though Kaiser Wilhelm II had not declared himself ready to go. A defenestration of the first order. The following day, the kaiser would quietly flee to Holland.

Now a massive crowd assembled in Berlin between the Kaiser Wilhelm Palace and the Reichstag building, the home of government. Nervous, unsettled, enraged, ready for adventure. There were surprisingly many women among them, mostly in groups of friends or colleagues. Clerks in office suits, workers, also affluent citizens in elegant clothes. They were united by the certainty of experiencing something great, something potentially violent. They felt that they were standing on the brink of a new era whose outcome no one could predict. Happiness or just more anxiety? Anarchy, mob rule, fratricidal warfare? A dictatorship of the proletariat? Bourgeois order for everyone? Or at least a return again to simple, pre-war pleasures?

Who would guide them through it? Germany without a kaiser – for many people that was unimaginable, a frightening idea. Who would grasp the sceptre?

It was taken up by one Philipp Scheidemann, who was having his lunch in the Reichstag canteen as the mob congregated. The 53-year-old author and journalist from Kassel, a member of the German Social Democratic Party since 1883 (when it was still illegal), appointed himself secretary of state just five weeks after the fall of the kaiser. He had been able to do so because the collapsing German Empire needed a Social Democrat as part of its hastily assembled emergency government, although only in the back row. This was to ease the mood among the enraged workers. The opposite happened.

Scheidemann, a famously cheerful soul who regularly wrote satirical articles in Kassel dialect under the pseudonym Henner Piffendeckel, understood on 9 November that the disorder outside the palace was going to become worse and worse. Germany, which had only been without a kaiser for a few hours, urgently needed a sign of some kind – and a respectable leader at the top again. Scheidemann saw this leader in the burly Friedrich Ebert, the affable, melancholic head of the Social Democrats, a man known for his willingness to compromise. So, 'between soup and dessert', as he later jokingly said, Scheidemann stepped out on to one of the Reichstag balconies, and in his characteristic singsong voice, without having discussed it with anyone, proclaimed the Republic: 'The German people have been victorious all down the line. The rotten old order has collapsed; militarism is at an end! The Hohenzollerns have abdicated! Long live the German Republic! The member of parliament Ebert has been proclaimed Reich chancellor. Ebert has thus been appointed to assemble a new government. All socialist parties will belong to this government. [. . .] Our task now is to ensure that this brilliant victory, this complete victory by the German people, is not sullied, and therefore I ask you to see to it that there be no disturbance to security! We must be able to remain proud of this day for all time to come! Nothing must exist that would later bring reproaches upon us! Peace, order and security is what we need now!'

And that – a feeling of peace and security – was exactly what Scheidemann gave the furious crowd. His spontaneous address was a piece of political bravura that ensured that the Social Democrats, who had successfully led the uprising against the monarchy, kept the reins in their hands, and that they would not immediately be taken away from them again by the left. How easily the mood could have escalated in that heated situation, and the balance have shifted from the Social Democrats, who held sway in the workers' and soldiers' councils, to the more radical communists, who were trying, with blazing speeches, to transform the still bourgeois revolution into a communist one on the Russian model.

Karl Liebknecht, future founder of the German Communist Party (*Kommunistische Partei Deutschlands*, KPD), took action two hours later and proclaimed the Republic for a second time, from another balcony of the City Palace. This was not as ridiculous as it might have seemed. While the Social Democrat Scheidemann had invented some facts and depicted the revolution as successfully completed when it had only just begun – so successfully that he insisted on the immediate importance of establishing peace and stability – Liebknecht informed his listeners that they were standing at the beginning of a long battle. It would be a tough fight. First the 'state order of the proletariat' had to be established, then the global revolution completed: 'Hail freedom and happiness and peace!' This was a slogan that anyone could subscribe to, as well as an excellent battle cry.

So far the fall of the German Empire had cost 60 human lives, 8 of them in the capital. That wasn't many given the strength of the establishment, and the many armed clashes that it took before the military representatives of the old regime stepped aside. To that extent it was a peaceful revolution, and 9 November seemed like a good day both to the media and to the public who lined the street, heads bowed, a day that might eventually go down in German history as a real jewel. On 10 November the liberal editor-in-chief of the *Berliner Tageblatt*

Revolutionary sailors in Wilhelmshaven fire signal rockets and emergency ammunition – a big firework display to celebrate the proclamation of the Republic on 9 November 1918.

hailed the victorious revolution on the front page in almost hymnic terms. Theodor Wolff praised Ebert's desire to re-establish peace and order, to secure the food supply and to offer the old civil service a role in the new state. Difficult as it might be, the 'devotees of the new' and the representatives of the old now had to work together 'out of love of the people'. Wolff presented the desired new order as a community based on communication and compromise:

No one who lays claim to free thought will be allowed to get too close to and wound those whose hearts ally them to a different divine cult. It is not always the worst who are unable to learn new things each time the wind turns and new powers arise. A people that has achieved independence honours itself by also honouring a sincere attitude, even in those whose rights it has advanced beyond.

Wolff must have written his exhortation to mutual respect in great haste on the very evening of the day of revolution, and he took a great step back and included the whole people in his wide embrace. We can imagine him writing, taking hasty drags on his cigarette, marching agitatedly around the desk after each line – an editor in an emergency. Every word was so important to him that the text clumsily continued for a further two lines on the next page. There he ended with the appeal to disarm anyone who wished to disavow this happy achievement by violence.

The war was lost; now it was time to bring it to an end. Two days after the proclamation of the Republic the representatives of the new provisional government signed the armistice in the Forest of Compiègne and thus created the precondition for what most Germans dreamed of, even if they had only very recently begun to do so: the establishment of a democracy based on peace and freedom, in which everyone could live on the fruits of their labour and pursue their private happiness untroubled by war and brutal violence.

That was the plan, the opportunity that lay within people's reach. But not everyone yearned for freedom and democracy. Even among the ordinary citizens there were many who couldn't imagine anything

other than the Empire. Without the magic triangle of their identity –
God, Honour, Fatherland – they felt homeless. For that reason, the
war that had been so furiously fought for Empire and Kaiser could
not be stopped so simply with a line from a pen. It came home with
the demobilised troops and turned itself against the very people who
had brought it to an end. Rather than being fought out in blood-
drenched battlefields in France and Belgium, it continued in German
streets and railway stations; it was discharged in isolated flashpoints.
Soldiers were alert to what they perceived as betrayal, and every now
and again they took revenge entirely at random.

At Wanne station near Bochum on 30 November, a guard battal-
ion returning home frustrated from the war, on a stopover on the
platform, ran into a unit of a workers' and soldiers' council. After
violently insulting the 'mob without a fatherland', the former
frontline soldiers, still loyal to the kaiser, knocked down a station
guard. This escalated into a shootout with both sides using machine
guns. Four soldiers were seriously injured. Their comrades then
roamed through the city and stormed an official building. A nine-
year-old boy was killed and another railway guard injured. Once
their rage had subsided, the gang of soldiers continued on their
journey by train. So commonplace were such occurrences that this
one merited a mere five lines in the issue of the *Berliner Tageblatt*
for 1 December 1918.

There were countless such incidents in which soldiers of the
returning army took revenge for the armistice. They felt deprived of
an honourable end to the war, which would have made the sacrifices
of the previous years of battle worthwhile. Whenever the opportunity arose, they picked fights with the sentries of the new government.
Small groups of soldiers hunted down individual passersby whom
they suspected of being revolutionary workers and intellectuals, draft
dodgers and traitors.

At the request of the provisional Reich government, the army high
command in Berlin issued a proclamation headed 'An end to senseless
shooting!', which hinted at who was broadly responsible for these
outrages, namely the army itself:

Fellow citizens! In scattered parts of the city bodies of the present Reich directorate and citizens in civilian clothes and uniform jackets are still being fired upon. The rumour is circulating that this gunfire is coming from individuals who believe they must defend the old regiment. In this context it should be noted that the order is given to support the present Reich directorate by all available means.

Appeals were printed and widely distributed for the maintenance of the virtue most favoured by the Germans, and which they now so painfully missed: discipline. It was the workers' and soldiers' councils, spontaneously established bodies of a civil society that was yet to be formed, who urgently appealed for peace and order. 'Workers' and soldiers' councils' – to present-day ears these sound wildly radical and revolutionary, but in fact that impression is far from the reality. Most councils consisted of solid citizens, craftsmen and skilled workers – people brave enough to take personal control of things in the chaotic power vacuum, to get things working again in the agitated country as quickly as possible. Almost all of the councils were packed with centre-left Social Democrats. They wanted democratic rights along orderly lines.

Typical of the councils' thinking was a proclamation published on 14 November in the north German *Bütower Anzeiger* under the headline 'Self-Discipline and Order are Required':

Only a people capable of maintaining voluntary discipline is mature and capable of self-determination. Are we capable of that? Is our people capable of governing itself? The government believes it is. It is confident that the people are capable of self-discipline. Let us prove that we are worthy of this confidence. Let us prove that we are ripe for political freedom. Let us prove that we can practise self-discipline. Then order will prevail. And the army and the people need order to achieve peace. Signed Krahn, Fitzner and Reserve Lieutenant Voss.

It was people such as these who shaped the peaceful face of what came to be known as the November Revolution, but also earned it the contempt expressed in the much-quoted judgement attributed to Lenin, to the effect that a German revolution wasn't worthy of the name: 'Revolution in Germany? It'll never happen. If those Germans wanted to storm a railway station they'd buy a platform ticket.'

If only that had proved to be the case. The proclamation of these three committed citizens gives a sense of the chaos that began to spread in the wake of the successful revolution. Away from the main arenas of the revolution, there was a tangle of minor conflicts in which determined citizens, foremen, sailors, officers and council chairmen, but also adventurers and criminals, had a say in whether or not blood was to flow. Alongside the many skirmishes between 'army and people', between moderate and radical socialists, between left and right, white and red, there were the anarchic actions of countless opportunists who cooked their personal little pots of soup on the fires of political disturbances. On the first day of the revolution, for example, a decommissioned sailor, Otto Haas, stole a car and put himself, as the later trial recorded, 'at the disposal of the new government'. Demonstrating the randomness of things, he was given the post of chauffeur by one of the newly appointed people's representatives. He also drove around privately in the car, a Wanderer W3. The *Berliner Tageblatt* reported:

> He also came to Potsdam, when a hospital train had just pulled in. He made use of this opportunity. He presented himself as a law enforcement officer and had the leaders of the train, an accountant and a deputy official, arrested, confiscated everything that the train contained in the way of food – bacon, ham, sausages, eggs – and had it brought to Berlin, where he sold it.[1]

Criminal acts such as this, dressed up as state activity, were frequent events. A pimp presented himself as a representative of the people, grabbed a couple of sentries from the workers' and soldiers' council who were standing on the nearest street corner, and brusquely ordered them to execute a wicked traitor. The sentence was obediently carried out on the spot. What the dutiful marksmen didn't know was that the victim was not a counter-revolutionary, but a former associate of the criminal, who had become too dangerous for him.

In most cases this kind of official assistance wasn't required, because after the end of the war there was no shortage of weapons. The soldiers who had deserted in their hordes had simply taken their weapons with them, either keeping them or selling them for a pittance over the pub counter. Shady sections of society were armed to the teeth. People masquerading as Volkswehr security officials plundered passersby or confiscated supplies from warehouses and shops. In Berlin-Buchholz a group presenting themselves as law enforcement officers tied up the mayor and made off with the community cash box.[2] And the violence was always at its worst when the Social Democrat-led government called in the army for help.

Unholy alliance

The morning after the proclamation of the Republic, Friedrich Ebert – who must have had a sleepless night – put a call through to the most powerful man in Germany, Wilhelm Groener. Via a secret telephone connection, Groener, head of the German army and based in Spa in Belgium, assured Ebert of the army's loyalty and promised to stand by him in maintaining public order. In return, the general expected the new leaders to ensure the continuing existence of the army and the broad recognition of the old officer corps. The victorious revolutionaries and the generals of the Reich seemed to have made peace.

Ebert probably slept better that night. Any kind of upheaval was anathema to the man who had been swept to power and to the cabinet provisionally installed until the planned election. The fact that they owed their fantastic careers to a revolution did nothing to reduce their abhorrence of it – quite the contrary. The very thing that had catapulted them to the top could bring them back down to the bottom just as swiftly.

It is hard to overestimate the insecurity of this group, completely unpractised in politics, which suddenly found itself at the head of the Reich. At the very top was Friedrich Ebert, a former saddler and landlord, who had run the 'Zur guten Hilfe' pub in Bremen with his wife Louise. Temperamentally, Social Democrats were still close to the Reich and many of its values, but they were also resolved to squeeze a fair deal for the working class from society: an eight-hour day, the right to strike and the right to assembly, the recognition of trade unions, and universal suffrage, including votes for women. Private property remained sacred, and they did not consider the nationalisation of the big key industries as an urgent goal. They did, on the other hand, acknowledge the vital importance of swiftly re-establishing internal security, preserving economic life and keeping the civil service in operation. It was the freedom that the liberal editor of the *Berliner Tageblatt*, Theodor Wolff, had so emphatically stood up for. That freedom might easily have been dismissed as a petty bourgeois fetish, but the chaos that swept the country did endanger life and limb. Food supplies were at stake. The Social Democrats were aware of the fragility of modern infrastructure, and wanted to demonstrate at all costs that they were capable of government – not least to the world. They feared that the victorious powers might still invade if the new government proved incapable of supplying peace in the country, and for both Ebert and the victors that meant above all preserving it from the Russian model of communism.

For the communist revolutionaries it seemed far too early to have internal peace. Hardly a day went by without the leaders of the far-left Spartacus League, Karl Liebknecht and Rosa Luxemburg, demanding that the revolution be taken to its conclusion. With repeated provocations and strong-arm tactics, they tried to goad their supporters into keeping the widespread disturbances going. The intention was to blind people to the fact that the radical left was in a hopeless minority even in the workers' and soldiers' councils. Even so, the Spartacists were able to demonstrate intimidating strength. Combat groups such as the Red Soldiers' League appeared in the streets heavily armed, and rumours whizzed

A new era. Back to back with 'Old Dessauer', Leopold I of Anhalt-Dessau: 'Long live freedom and happiness and peace'. Announcement of the Ebert–Scheidemann government on 6 January 1919 in Berlin.

constantly around the cities that the Russian Bolsheviks had armed them to the teeth.

Many Spartacists were, at heart, gentle souls. But behind the typewriter they developed an aggressive radicalism that worried many people, and, in their words, the 'rotten supports of society trembled'. Within the small bubble of their like-minded followers they lost all sense of reality. Drunk on the fantasies that his resounding speeches produced in the crammed meeting halls, Liebknecht demanded that all military weapons be handed over 'to the proletariat'. A ridiculous proposal. Who was going to hand them over? After the weapons had been received, 'the revolutionary proletariat should not hesitate for a moment before removing bourgeois elements from all of their political and social positions of power' and 'taking all the power into their own hands'.[3] Liebknecht could not have been surprised that even sympathetic 'bourgeois elements' might have been horrified by this prospect. 'We don't want a lemonade revolution,' he cried, meaning that he didn't want anything soft or half-hearted, 'we want to raise the iron fist against anyone who stands in our way. The Ebert–Scheidemann government is the deadly enemy of the German proletariat!'[4] The deadly enemy took his threats seriously and sought refuge in the protective arms of the military.

Admittedly, the provisional government also had its own troops, but they were weak and unreliable and also in competition with one another: the 'Voluntary Auxiliary Service of the Social Democratic Party', the hastily assembled 'Republican Soldiers' Defence' and the 'Greater Berlin Security Troop' under police president Emil Eichhorn were still overwhelmed by the amount of patrol and guard duty needed to suppress chaos and anarchy in the streets day and night, and to protect the public buildings, government offices and banks. Attempts to win additional volunteers for the Republic's protection squads failed for lack of interest. So Ebert and his army and navy minister, Gustav Noske, entrusted the delicate first shoots of the Republic to a defeated and demoralised army that was itself in the process of disorderly dissolution. Once the message of revolution and armistice had reached them, any soldiers still in their right minds had long since quit the service and made sure that they had made it home under their own steam, just in time for Christmas. There were constant calls in the newspapers to hand over any military munitions, but many deserting soldiers ignored them. A large number of rifles were simply kept and stored under beds and in wardrobes. Most of the remaining soldiers, who were regularly demobilised and returned home in close formation, also longed for nothing more than peace and recuperation. Only a proportion of them was inclined to continue in armed service and push for 'peace and order' within the country. But that proportion was still considerable. Paradoxically, the voluntary units that were supposed to be ensuring stability in the new Republic contained some of the Republic's worst enemies.

The irregular right-wing Freikorps (Free Corps) volunteer units assembled by individual army officers developed into a collecting point for the former frontline solders whose taste for war had been ended too soon. They felt not so much defeated by the enemy as betrayed by their own homeland. There were also disoriented secondary-school pupils who were stupid enough to believe that they'd missed something uplifting when the war came to an end, embittered students who feared that they wouldn't be able to have a career in a 'workers' republic'. Then, finally, there were thugs who liked the idea of being paid for their passion. They formed wild gangs of mercenaries, which took their names from their leaders: Marine-brigade Ehrhardt, Freikorps Epp, Freikorps Hacketau, Freikorps Von Petersdorff, Sturmabteilung Rossbach and so on. Overall there are thought to have been a total of 365 of these right-wing volunteer Frei-korps units, one for each blood-soaked day of the year. For these unruly groups, love of the fatherland meant eliminating everyone in the fatherland who didn't, as they saw it, share their love.

Some Freikorps units headed east to continue fighting even though the war had officially come to an end. In Poland, where according to the terms of the Versailles Treaty plebiscites and negotiations on the future border were imminent, they believed that they had to go on defending the fatherland. Nationalists on both sides were reluctant to wait for the votes and talks, so for several years the Freikorps fought a bloody 'fight for the death on the Eastern Marches' – with ambushes, terrorist attacks and fierce partisan battles.

But the main thrust of the Freikorps' energy was directed inwards. Just what these troops were capable of became apparent in Berlin on 6 December 1918, St Nicholas's Day, a day that had already begun in a strangely agitated atmosphere. Just before 6pm there was a blood-bath at the busy intersection of Chausseestrasse and Invalidenstrasse, not far from the place where the Federal Intelligence Service stands today. A group of soldiers, Guard Fusiliers in fact, who had only been 'back from the field' and in the city for a day, sprayed the area with bursts of machine-gun fire. One account related that a number 32 tram, whose driver had driven to the scene unsuspectingly, also came under fire. The passengers fought for the doors, shoving each other out of the way.

People ran along the pavement screaming for their lives, knocking each other to the ground. In all of the buildings the residents had turned out the lights and moved back terrified to the rooms at the rear. When the soldiers had stopped firing, for a while there was almost complete silence. Then the first people ventured out of the houses and looked at the battlefield.[5]

The horror only lasted a few minutes, but 12 people died, the youngest of them, who bled to death in the tram, a 16-year-old girl. Over 80 people were injured.

It was never explained how shots came to be fired at peaceful passersby in rush-hour traffic. On the morning of St Nicholas's Day some soldiers led by an officer by the name of Spiro had attempted a kind of coup d'état in the Reichstag, proclaiming Friedrich Ebert 'President of the German Social Republic', but at the same time had called for the arrest of the 'Executive Council of the Workers' and Soldiers' Council' – the provisional Parliament to which he was subordinate, and which was assembled in the Prussian Landtag. The affair was a complete failure but may have further intensified the overstrung mood of the day.

The following day Spartacists and Social Democrats blamed one another for the massacre, while the bourgeois newspapers claimed that the 'all too understandable' fear of a communist seizure of power had found expression in a panicky overreaction on the part of the soldiers. Furthermore, two lines of demonstrators had approached the intersection from different directions and caused confusion. It is more likely that it was simply the hatred of frustrated frontline soldiers for their supposedly traitorous homeland that was being vented here, as it was elsewhere – a hatred that would in future degenerate from manageable minor disturbances into dramatic acts of terrible brutality.

The suppression of the Munich Soviet Republic – the Republic declared by the workers' and soldiers' councils in Bavaria – involved extreme excesses of Freikorps violence. Late in April 1919, right-wing Freikorps units and regular government troops besieged the Bavarian capital on the orders of the Berlin government. In fact, its picturesque

'Republic of Dreamers' had already been finished for some time. After a failed putsch, power had been seized by a communist clique that only enjoyed the sympathy of a minority of the population of Munich. This explains the rather disparaging tone with which the scholar Victor Klemperer made fun of the civil war in which the 'free state' of Bavaria imagined itself to be. Klemperer, who wrote a collection of gripping diaries around this time, also worked as a correspondent for the newspaper the *Leipziger Neueste Nachrichten*:

> While Franz Maier [a term meaning an everyman] is shooting pheasants in the English Garden, Hubert Xavier at Feilitzschplatz believes the Whites [the counter-revolutionary forces] are holding a putsch and shoots as well, and already the sentry is sounding the alarm of an attack on the nearby Savour's Church, and now the whole area is rattling away. It's very gratifying.[6]

But soon even Klemperer was less than gratified. On 1 May 1919 the Empire's guardians of order stepped in: the Eppsche Freikorps, the Württemberg Security Troops and regular Reichswehr troops from Prussia. The 'carnival of lunacy', as the Social Democratic minister of defence called what was by now a genuinely self-destructive attempt at revolution, was to be brought to a swift end. These men, some of them gloriously fitted out in Guards Corps uniforms, were celebrated by most local people in a festive spirit.

It all looked like a folkloric procession. But then hatred and vengefulness spilled out in a way that deeply shocked this respectable part of Munich. Rather than peace and order, the Freikorps spread terror on the streets, with the support of members of the petty bourgeoisie who were also eager for a scrap. They went in search of hidden subversives in working-class areas of the city. The author Oskar Maria Graf, who had himself been part of the Soviet government until a short time before, reported:

> A terrible spree of denunciation began. Anyone with an enemy could now send them to their death with a few words. Now all of a sudden

the citizens who had previously been invisible were back, busy running behind the troops with rifles over their shoulders and white and
blue civil militia armbands. They looked around eagerly, pointing here
and there, running after someone and bawling as they rained blows
down upon them, spitting, shoving them crazily and dragging their
half-dead victim to the soldiers. Sometimes it happened faster than
that: the unsuspecting person would be standing there frozen, then
the mob would charge over and surround him, a shot would ring out
and that was it. The people would spread out again, laughing and
satisfied.[7]

The soldiers sometimes fired on anything that moved. Graf saw an
old woman hobbling across the road, being caught in the crosshairs
and shot to the ground. The same fate awaited a little boy who ran to
help the dying woman.

The hatred of civilians – women and children included – had a history that dated back several months and originated in Berlin. For
Freikorps and Reichswehr soldiers the 1918 Christmas holidays held a
humiliation that unfortunately taught them a great deal. The task
was to drive a group of revolutionary soldiers calling themselves the
Volksmarinedivision (People's Navy Division) out of Berlin Palace.
The division was a proud if somewhat rogue element of the revolutionary November days. Just six weeks previously they had been
asked by the Social Democrats to protect important government
buildings against looting, and were installed in the city palace for this
purpose. But when it came to removing them from the building, they
were discovered to have been radicalised. On 23 December, the People's Navy Division had even taken Berlin's city commander Otto
Wels hostage and engaged in a wild gunfight with an armoured car
outside the Berlin Opera, just as audience members were leaving the
building in their fur coats. Now they were threatening to arrest the
whole government. Ebert himself contacted army supreme command and asked for the sailors to be driven from the palace.

The operation was entrusted to one General Arnold Lequis, who
had acquired a dubious fame in the brutal genocide of the Herero

people in German South West Africa. Lequis formed his troop of Guards on the morning of 24 December among the architectural glories of Berlin's Museum Island. The main entrance to the Hohenzollern palace came under heavy artillery fire, and the balcony from which Kaiser Wilhelm had delivered his famous *Burgfrieden* speech (calling for a truce between political parties during the war) in August 1914 was among the parts of the building that were struck. Machine guns also fired numerous salvos at the palace from the roof of the arsenal. Standing in the immediate vicinity was the city's tall Christmas tree, festively decorated for the first peaceful festive season since the war. Then Lequis gave the order to charge but was halted by a barrage of gunfire delivered by the sailors of the People's Navy Division, who had also taken up position with machine guns on the palace roof. Four soldiers were left dead in front of the building and a further ten were seriously injured. Lequis interrupted the charge on the palace and the Guard division retreated in humiliation.

From a military point of view the skirmish was insignificant, one of countless small battles fought out during those months. But in terms of its symbolic effect on the mood of the soldiers, the disaster could not be overestimated. At the centre of the Prussian monarchy, once so glorious, the remains of the army, loyally devoted to God and fatherland, had been forced to retreat by a violent gang of unruly sailors. Waldemar Pabst, an officer heavily involved in the right-wing Kapp Putsch attempt to oust the government in the spring of 1920, described the defeat as 'the most shocking moment of their military lives for all members of Prussia's proudest regiment'.[8]

Undefeated in the field, but vanquished by women

On the day of the defeat in front of the palace, General Lequis gave an interview to the *Vossische Zeitung*. Events, after all, were played out under the very close eye of the press. The photographers had been only a short distance away from where the guns were fired, and they waited with their unwieldy tripods for a shot that might suggest a civil war. The general explained to the *Vossische Zeitung* how things had got quite so bad. He came up with an explanation for the defeat that would have serious consequences: a horde of civilians headed by women and children had surrounded his soldiers during a 20-minute ceasefire that had been previously negotiated. 'My soldiers don't fire on women and children. That was where the mistake was made. A rank of my troops was driven back, they laid down their arms, and the rest went back to the university.' The message that the campaign to liberate the palace had been derailed by women's resistance spread swiftly around military circles. The refusal to fire on civilians was seen as the cause of this unparalleled disgrace. From now on there would be no more 'humanitarian poppycock': in February 1919 troops were instructed to open fire at any encounter with a hostile mob.[9]

Whether the story of the women and children who had defeated a division of the Guards on Christmas Day is true or was in fact invented by Lequis as an excuse, it certainly led to mindboggling rage among the humiliated soldiers. The claim that it was women above all who had caused the defeat of the army would be a sore point in the new Republic, and one that we will come back to: the dramatically changing relationship between the sexes. In Lequis's version the soldiers became victims of the chivalry that traditionally prevents men from firing on unarmed woman. The more reactionary warriors saw such inhibitions as old-fashioned – women had long ago ceased to be in need of protection and were henceforth to be seen as fierce adversaries.

Even the decade before the war had supplied many examples of the demonisation of women. Symbolist paintings swarmed with Furies, witches and 'wind brides'. The new workplaces in offices, department stores and telephone exchanges granted women more and more autonomy and independence. And the fact that they had successfully assumed traditionally male occupations during the war had strengthened their self-confidence, which had turned into open militancy: many working-class women had taken part in demonstrations in the cities against the wartime shortage economy. During the days of the revolution and the strikes that followed, they often bravely confronted martial military squads – a challenge that mutated in the minds of many soldiers into delusional phobias.

In his ground-breaking study *Male Fantasies*, the cultural scholar Klaus Theweleit investigated the literature written during the Weimar Republic by and about Freikorps soldiers. He found a misogyny that was so insanely unbridled and so obviously paranoid that it takes the breath away. The books are filled with uninhibited '*Flintenweiber*' ('rifle women') who want to devour, emasculate and kill courageous soldiers. Woe to the man who falls into the 'filthy claws of the scandalous women of Hamborn'; there will be literally nothing left of him, the writer Tüdel Weller warns in his novel *Peter Mönkemann – Freikorpskämpfer an der Ruhr* (Peter Mönkemann – Freikorps Soldier on the Ruhr).[10] One of his Freikorps colleagues, the author writes, was repelled and 'scratched to bits' by working-class women with their bare hands.

The author Ernst von Salomon, member of the Freikorps Maercker and Berthold, the right-wing terrorist Consul Organisation and the Ehrhardt Brigade that took part in the 1920 Kapp Putsch, describes an anti-militarist demonstration against his uniformed gang of thugs as an apocalyptic encounter with brides of Satan:

Shaking their fists, the women shriek at us. Stones, pots, fragments begin to fly. [. . .] They hammer into us, hefty women dressed in blue, their aprons soaked and skirts muddied, red and wrinkled faces hissing beneath wind-whipped hair, with sticks and stones, pipes and dishes. They spit, swear, shriek. [. . .] Women are the worst. Men fight with fists, but women also spit and swear – you can't just plant your fist into their ugly pusses.[11]

In *Ruhe und Ordnung – Roman aus dem Leben der nationalgesinnten Jugend* (Peace and Order – Novel from the Life of the Nationally Minded Youth) Ernst Ottwalt relates how General Maercker instructed his Freikorps soldiers and short-term volunteers in their treatment of women loyal to the government during the Kapp Putsch:

'It's a well known fact that women are always at the head of these kinds of riots. And if one of our leaders gives the order to shoot and a few old girls get blown up, the whole world starts screaming about bloodthirsty soldiers shooting down innocent women and children. As if women were always innocent.' We all laugh.

'Gentlemen, there's only one thing to do in cases like that. Shoot off a few flares under the women's skirts, then watch how they start running. It won't really do much. The magnesium in the flares will singe their calves or behinds, and the blast flame may burn a few of the skirts. It's the most harmless device you can think of.'[12]

The soldierly chivalry that General Lequis cited in his interview with the *Vossische Zeitung* in order to explain the defeat in front of the Palace of Berlin at Christmas 1918 had clearly dissolved within two years. Either that or it had been an invention from the outset.

'You can't dance the shame from your body'

The woman upon whom this pathological hatred was most concentrated was called Rosa. Red Rosa. The strikingly small, often elegantly dressed woman might have had a delicate appearance, but she was always determined and energetic, an extremely clever, quick and original debater who persevered with her argument until her adversary retreated into exhausted silence. Rozalia Luksenburg had grown up as the child of an affluent Jewish family in Poland, and to the distress of her parents was a convinced socialist even as a school student. A poem by the girl has survived: 'I demand punishment for those / who are sated now, who live in lewdness / who do not know, who do not feel / the torments under which millions earn their bread.'[13] Even at the age of 6 she worked on a school newspaper, and at 16 she was a member of one of the illegal 'self-education youth circles'. Since the police already had her in their sights, when she was 17 some older colleagues smuggled her over the border, from where she reached Zurich. Here Rosa Luxemburg – as she was now known – studied everything, from zoology via law and administration to philosophy, that her endless thirst for knowledge was able to absorb. In the end she graduated with a dissertation on the industrial development of Poland, naturally getting top marks. In Germany (she moved to Berlin in 1898) she quickly became one of the most prominent voices on the left wing of the Social Democrats. She broke with the party at the outbreak of the First World War when the SPD reached a political truce (*Burgfrieden*) with the Reich government and the kaiser, and agreed to war credits. She paid for her courageous anti-war position with several prison sentences. From the start of the revolution onwards she was editor-in-chief of *Rote Fahne* (Red Flag) and the face of German communism.

It is a face that still enchants people today. Even the serious-minded historian Ernst Piper describes his 2018 Luxemburg biography as the result of a 'serious liaison'. Rosa Luxemburg painted, drew, wrote poetry, had wild and passionate love affairs. No one could agitate more vividly, condemn more forcefully, inflame an auditorium with greater Shakespearean eloquence, certainly not standing on the chair that she needed to be seen. Her verdict that social democracy was only a stinking corpse was unforgettable. But Rosa Luxemburg was not unambiguous – she was a Sphinx, a Marxist chameleon that was almost impossible to pin down and pigeonhole. In her nine-volume collected works you can find evidence for every ideological variant of Marxism. Because of her famous quotation that freedom is always the freedom of those who think differently, posterity wrongly honours her as a representative of radical democratic socialism. Rosa Luxemburg was not, whatever people think, an ardent democrat who wanted to persuade people rather than fight them.

In the weeks of the revolution, there was nothing that she hated more than democracy, supposedly fetishised by the Social Democrats. She saw it – quite rightly, in fact – as the grave of communism. Over a million SPD members faced a thousand-strong Spartacus League. In terms of sympathisers the figures were quite similar. So in a leading article in the *Red Flag* she stubbornly refused to allow the development of the revolution to be voted on by elections or majority decisions at the National Assembly: 'We will not talk with the guardians of the capitalist cashboxes either at the National Assembly or through the national assembly.' Working until she dropped – sometimes she had to be dragged from her desk and carried home – she recommended that her readers do exactly what she herself had practised for a long time: surrounding herself with like-minded people only, she said, 'It is our duty to break down every bridge with the present government.'[14] Shortly before her death she thought a dialogue between her peers was appropriate, but otherwise she recommended the deployment of raw force: 'Socialism doesn't mean sitting down in a parliament and making laws. For us socialism means overthrowing the ruling classes with all the brutality that the proletariat can muster.'[15]

That brutality would explode early in 1919. Between 5 and 12 January, Berlin held its breath as it watched a new revolt that would soon be given the exaggerated name of the 'Spartacist Uprising'. The spark for this was the dismissal of the Berlin police chief Emil Eichhorn, who had always been on the side of the radical left. In the course of the resulting protests, armed and predominantly communist demonstrators and so-called 'Revolutionary representatives' occupied the building where the Social Democrat daily newspaper Vorwärts was printed. The offices of the publishing companies Scherl, Ullstein and Mosse were also occupied, as well as the Wolffsche Telegraphenbüro and the editorial office of the Berliner Tageblatt – an attack on the bourgeois press that clearly signalled how the radical left planned to deal with the freedom of opinion they had fought for only two months previously.

At first the occupations were somewhat random, which is why the term 'Spartacist Uprising' is misleading. After some delay, Karl Liebknecht and Rosa Luxemburg put themselves rhetorically at the head of the revolt and tried to make it bring down the Ebert–Scheidemann government. 'The Berlin proletariat now stands and fights for itself, for Germany, for the proletariat of the world. Never was a struggle more beautiful, never one more just, never one of greater value in history,' the Rote Fahne cheered on 10 January.

Wild rumours circulated in Berlin once again: a thousand Russian Bolsheviks were about to arrive, disguised as German soldiers, to stand by their comrades. The Spartacists already had over 20,000 rifles at their disposal. Much of the press saw Germany sinking into chaos if the Social Democrats failed to deal with the rebels. In fact, neither the 'Volunteer Auxiliary Service of the Social Democratic Party' nor the *Republikanische Schutztruppe* (Republican Protection Troop), also close to the SPD, proved strong enough to clear the occupied buildings. Once again Ebert and naval minister Noske sent in the Friekorps via army command, but also the regular Potsdam Regiment. Civil war raged for several days in the Berlin newspaper district. 'They used aeroplanes, flame throwers, armoured cars, machine-guns and hand grenades against revolutionary insurgents, who were generally fewer in number and only in possession of rifles and machine-guns.'[16] The rebels took up position on the street behind large rolls of paper and bundles of printed newspapers. The free word served as a dense barricade. There were men in smart suits and men in wornout uniforms, all with rifles at the ready.

Straßenkämpfe in Berlin.
Zweifronten-Barrikade in der Schützenstraße.

Shielded by newsprint: rebellious Spartacists who had occupied the Mosse publishing house in Berlin, taking refuge behind bales of paper. 11 January 1919.

Past the bales of paper they peered out from under their hats and steel helmets. The combatants here were not only individual workers and revolutionary soldiers but – perhaps even predominantly – members of 'the intelligentsia', as they were known in left-wing parlance. The factory workers, on the other hand, were mostly dumbfounded by the spectacle. They also demonstrated in the Berlin districts of Spandau, Lichtenberg and Wedding against the bloody 'fraternal war' that was being fought out there between hot-headed radicals and government socialists. In vain, the workforces of various large companies established a 'fraternisation committee' consisting of members of the Social Democratic Party, the Independent Social Democratic Party (*Unabhängige Sozialdemokratische Partei Deutschlands*, USPD) and the German Communist Party (*Kommunistische Partei Deutschlands*, KPD), and issued the slogan: 'Proletarians united, if not with then over the heads of your leaders!'[17]

Each of the attacks during the battles of January led to multiple casualties, including innocent passersby. *Freiheit*, an organ of the USPD, reported that even near the Reichstag and Unter den Linden hardly a quarter of an hour passed without a machine gun starting to rattle: 'A number of people have fallen victim to this mischievous shooting, and many have been wounded.'[18] 'A number' – no more precise than that. The reports turned quickly into rumours and vague suppositions. People said to each other in the street that government troops were using dumdum bullets that left terrible injuries.

At dawn on 11 January government shock troops advanced on the *Vorwärts* building. Under heavy shell fire the central facade of the editorial building collapsed, burying part of the rebel machine-gun positions. But one machine gun, not far from the corner of the building, caused the soldiers severe problems. It took them 45 minutes to take the position, which they were convinced was held by the 'shotgun woman' Rosa Luxemburg.

Many of the rebels underwent physical abuse as they were taken to the Dragoon Barracks in Kreuzburg. Once there, they were subjected to appalling torture before being shot. The 20 or so women among the 250 arrested occupiers were treated just as badly as the hateful fantasies from the Freikorps novels would lead us to imagine.

Rosa Luxemburg and Karl Liebknecht were arrested four days later, on 15 January. But rather than take them to jail, the 38-year-old Captain Waldemar Pabst, leader of the Freikorps troop undertaking the arrest, decided to kill the pair. Rosa Luxemburg was beaten unconscious with a rifle butt before being thrown into the Landwehr Canal. Pabst served up a story to the press that Liebknecht had been shot while trying to escape, and Luxemburg had been lynched by a furious mob. The claim, still encountered today, that the murder of the two Spartacist leaders had been ordered by the Social Democrat Gustav Noske has been thoroughly debunked. It seems quite likely that it was tacitly believed and tolerated by the public at large.[19]

★

The events of the January uprising, which strongly resembled those of a civil war, were fought out amidst ordinary people. Normal everyday life was relatively unaffected by the fact that there were occasional skirmishes in the streets. Friedrich Schiller's play *The Robbers* was performed in the Schauspielhaus on 11 January, the bloody finale of the Spartacist Uprising; *Stars that Shine Again* was playing at the Berliner Theater, and in the Theater am Nollendorfplatz *The Imaginary Baron*. At the Urania scientific society a large audience heard a lecture on 'The Beauty of the German Landscape', and in the side room an introduction to 'The World of the Planets'. Within a few days postcards were printed of the half-ruined building of the *Vorwärts* office for Berliners to send to their relatives in the provinces. There were also souvenir postcards of the fighting on the barricades. One of these, for example, showed a committed bourgeois behind the barricade, in collar and tie, rifle at the ready – an impressive picture to display on a kitchen shelf.

The cameras were always there to capture images for those who were unable to witness the exciting events themselves. Passersby stood shaking their heads, worrying that the French would soon invade if this chaos didn't stop: 'First they bring the bones safely home, then they beat each other to death.'[20] Even the elegant, endlessly curious collector of art and experiences Harry Graf Kessler didn't stay at home in his drawing room while all this was going on. During the Spartacist Uprising he strolled about central Berlin day after day: Neue Wilhelmstrasse, Friedrichstrasse, Leipziger Platz, Potsdamer Platz. Everywhere he went he heard individual rifle shots and the rattle of machine guns, while city life continued, just more agitatedly than usual:

> The street traders with cigarettes, malt bonbons and soap still selling their wares in the street. Café Vaterland is brightly lit. I go inside briefly. Even though bullets could strike at any moment, the Wiener Kapelle is playing, the tables are quite full, and the lady in the cigarette kiosk smiles at her customers as if deeply at peace.[21]

In the cabarets and on the dancefloors people were partying wildly as never before. The dance halls that were closed during the war had only opened again a week before, on New Year's Eve 1918. 'With the relaxation of the ban on dancing the people fell on the pleasure so long denied them like a pack of hungry wolves, and nothing can strip them of their desire to party,' the *Berliner Tageblatt* reported after a foray through the New Year's Eve festivities.

> And what is the Berliner celebrating? He's celebrating the second that is giving him today what it may not be able to grant him tomorrow, the unboundedness of the word, the drinking before the drowning. [. . .] Never before has Berlin danced so much and so furiously.[22]

On the advertising pillars there were posters showing a skeleton and a girl dancing. 'Pause, Berlin! Reflect. Your dance partner is death,' was the caption. It was supposed to have been printed by 'the government', whoever that was these days.[23] There was so much wild dancing that it even became too much for some showbiz stars. In 1920 the revue composer Friedrich Hollaender took the poster as inspiration for a song that his wife Blandine Ebinger, the 'tubercular Madonna' (Erich Kästner), sang at the cabaret Schall und Rauch, an establishment that the couple had founded along with Kurt Tucholsky, Klabund (nom de plume of Alfred Henschke), Joachim Ringelnatz, Walter Mehring and Mischa Spolianky:

> Berliners, your dance partner is death!
> Berlin, pause you are in trouble.
> From strike to strike, from swindle to swindle,
> Whether dancing nude or tapdancing,
> You need to enjoy yourself tirelessly!
> Berlin, your dance partner is death!
> Berlin, you're rolling in the mud with pleasure
> Take a pause! Leave it! And think a little:
> You can't dance the shame from your body,
> Because you're boxing and jazz-dancing and foxtrotting on a
>   powder barrel.

The chanson ends with the line: 'Under the earth, that's where the fuse glows, take care!/In the middle of your foxtrot there'll be a *bang* and then it's night.'

And with that they made the sound that would go on to characterise the whole of the Weimar Republic. But for now there was no *bang*; instead there was an election.

★

A week after the end of the Spartacist Uprising, on 19 January 1919, a Sunday, Germany held its first fully democratic election, with no restrictions of sex or class. Eighty-three per cent of those eligible to vote did so, an astonishing turnout by today's standards. The SPD was the strongest party by some way, with 37.9 per cent of votes. The left-wing breakaway party USPD received 7.6 per cent. The Communists didn't even take part, because the result would have been too pitiful. The conservative German National People's Party

(*Deutschnationale Volkspartei*, DNVP) received 10.3 per cent, the liberal parties 22.9, the Catholic Centre Party 19.7.

The Ebert–Scheidemann government that had been brought to power by revolution had now been democratically legitimated. In spite of the frightening chaos in the country it seemed to be inhabited by a majority of order-loving, sensible, balanced, progressively minded people. Things could only go upwards. The 423 elected parliamentarians, including 37 women for the first time, came together on 6 February 1919 – not in the Reichstag in Berlin, but in the National Theatre in the city of Weimar, some 300 kilometres southwest of Berlin, which had been specially hired for the purpose. Given the continuing disorder, the Reich capital Berlin did not seem safe enough. In the months that followed they agreed on Germany's first democratic constitution. Because of the location of its first parliamentary sessions, the new state was called the Weimar Republic.

Friedrich Ebert, now the Reich president, signed the constitution, in line with his undramatic style, at the breakfast table in his holiday resort of Schwarzburg in the central state of Thuringia. Article 1 announced: 'Political authority emanates from the people.' That was true in law but, shockingly, not always true in reality.

'Day labourers of death'

A month after the assembly in Weimar that determined the constitution, the situation in Berlin escalated again, this time more brutally than ever before. After insurgent workers had occupied a police station and the post office in the district of Lichtenberg, and there had been many instances of looting and rioting, Gustav Noske, now responsible for internal security as Reich defence minister in the Social Democrat government, had the district violently cleared. According to official figures, 1,200 people died, but the number was probably greater than that. Most of them were executed on the spot by Freikorps soldiers deployed for the purpose. Their 'legal basis' was Noske's order to shoot anyone who was caught fighting with a gun in their hand. The self-appointed bloodhound of the SPD had issued this order after the rumour circulated that the rioters had murdered 50 policemen in the occupied station. The Freikorps soldiers had extended the order to mean killing anyone who even owned a gun. They combed the buildings of Lichtenberg for rifles and pistols, and shot anyone with a gun found in their apartment. They even shot members of the revolutionary People's Navy Division who were standing peacefully in line by a military depot to hand over their weapons and collect their demob cheques.

The people of Berlin were strangely casual, almost unmoved, in their response to the massacre in the east of their city. The doctor and author Alfred Döblin, who lived in Lichtenberg, and whose sister Meta was killed by shrapnel during the fighting when she went to fetch milk for her children, reported on the events in a pointedly hard-nosed style. But he did at least report on them, in the *Neue*

'Day labourers of death': Freikorps soldiers used as government troops against the Spartacists. The gun on the tank had been removed to comply with the disarmament terms of the Versailles Treaty. Taken at Tempelhofer Feld, Berlin.

Rundschau under the pseudonym Linke Poot, while many of his colleagues registered the horror in silence:

> As I am about to go to the Allee, a patrol comes up the street, march-
> ing powerfully, twenty-strong, rifles shouldered, steel helmets wedged
> on their heads. What do they want, we've got enough soldiers here.
> They're led by a man as tall as a tree, pale, brave, serious face, strange
> that they're all wearing steel helmets and he's in a cap. [. . .] And when
> I turn round, the tree-sized patrol leader is climbing the steps to the
> cemetery, and they're all whispering: then someone else gets shot.
> And in the blink of an eye a salvo rings out. I see, I see. That was
> once. And now what there once was is lying outstretched in a black
> coat. That was once a human being and is now an object. The idea is
> a hard one to deal with. One is undeniably horrified. One has seen a
> lot of people die – but this is something special. It's the extent of the
> planning, the idea would make your head spin. [. . .] I'm not bothered
> by one or two deaths, it comes to us all. But this nonsense is unbear-
> able, boundlessly repellent.[24]

Once again it was the Freikorps who had perpetrated these shocking
massacres, and calls to dissolve these uniformed mobs proliferated.
The few dedicated republicans in the ranks of the executive, such as
the former officer and now police major Hermann Schützinger,
demanded a republicanisation of the police and the army. Police tasks
such as the suppression of unrest could no longer be placed 'in the
hands of a military apparatus that was a law unto itself'.[25] Instead, it
was argued, they required more barracks-based police trained in de-
escalation strategies, 'capable of adapting to the various stages of
mass agitation'. They were no longer allowed to act according to the
military principle that the adversary was to be destroyed at all costs,
but had to 'force the insurgent compatriots under the law with a minimum of casualties'.[26]

Only a year after the massacres in the east of Berlin, in March 1920,
Noske tried to dissolve several Freikorps brigades, including the
notorious Ehrhardt Brigade. He didn't decide to take this step out of

some inner conviction, but because the Versailles Treaty required a reduction of the army to 100,000 men. But the army was far from keen on the idea of allowing itself and its irregular comrades to be decimated as simply as that, and showed its true face to the ministers that it had been struggling to endure.

The highest-ranking Reichswehr general, Walther von Lüttwitz, resisted the order and marched into Berlin with Freikorps Ehrhart, who as always wore swastikas on their helmets. The government district was occupied, and the government fled to Darmstadt and Stuttgart at the last minute. The Reichstag deputy Wolfgang Kapp, a duelling-scarred, grim-faced 62-year-old estate owner from western Prussia, declared the Ebert–Scheidemann cabinet deposed and appointed himself as the new chancellor. The Reichswehr refused to halt the putschists. The Republic seemed to be over after only 17 months.

However, the German people showed Wolfgang Kapp that he had barely any followers. The biggest general strike in German history completely paralysed public life. Nothing worked. No mail was delivered, no trains ran, there was no electricity, the telephone service was on strike, the department stores were closed. After five days Kapp and Lüttwitz gave up – like riders of horses that simply lie down in the mud rather than trotting on. The Ehrhardt Brigade retreated embittered from Berlin, but not without firing off a few rounds at the curious onlookers by the Brandenburg Gate who were bidding them farewell with mocking cries. Twelve people died, 30 were injured.

The determined resistance to the putschists could be among the happiest and proudest moments in German history had it not been overshadowed a short time later by events in some Communist strongholds. Instead of ending the general strike after the overwhelming victory and the retreat of Kapp and Co., the KPD and other radical left-wing groups saw the overheated atmosphere as a chance to lay their hands on power. They just went on striking. The situation escalated dramatically in the Ruhr, whose workers had put up the most determined resistance against the putschists and inflicted devastating losses on the Freikorps. The confiscated weapons joined the old holdings of the civic guard, and soon the 'Red Ruhr Army' had armed forces numbering around 50,000.

The Red Ruhr Army deserves every sympathy for their victorious battle against the putschists, but it too was not a collection of noble humanitarians and freedom fighters. In paragraph three of one of their many service regulations it states bluntly: 'Cowardice in the face of the enemy is punishable by death.'[27] And the Executive Council of the city of Duisburg, where particularly chaotic conditions prevailed, issued the ruling: 'Anyone loitering behind the front without permission will be shot. That also applies to female persons of dubious character.'[28] The Red Ruhr Army occupied town halls and prisons, requisitioned food from private individuals, punished insubordinates as they saw fit and sent armed censors into editorial offices. In Duisburg, power was seized by radical anarcho-syndicalists who tried to push every strike into political, violent riots, from whose violent rule even the KPD distanced itself.

In the states of Saxony, Thuringia and Hamburg the KPD hoped for a revolutionary shower of sparks that would take hold of the whole of Germany and sweep parliamentary politics away. In view of this prospect, Ebert and Noske opted against imposing discipline on the army, which was needed more than ever after the putsch. The pattern was always the same: the more furious the radical workers became with the government, the less inclined the government became to weaken the military – and once again the greater the fury of the oppressed. But after the putsch even the bourgeois press called for the 'eradication' of enemies of the Republic from the ranks of the army. The left-liberal *Berliner Volks-Zeitung* even argued for the renunciation of the 100,000-strong army that the victorious powers still permitted Germany to have, instead strengthening the police: 'The best thing would be to put the security men into a kind of sporting uniform, and in place of the sabre give them a rubber truncheon.'[29]

Instead, more Freikorps units moved into the Ruhr, this time with the blessing of the government, to 'calm' the situation that had got out of control there. The inevitable happened: instead of obeying police instructions, the Freikorps took their revenge for their defeated comrades by holding bloody criminal trials that alienated many workers from the Ruhr from the Republic for ever. The Oberjäger (first huntsman) of Freikorps Epp, a student in civilian life, wrote to his 'dear sister' about the killing party:

> We made our first charge at one o'clock in the morning. There is absolutely no mercy. We shoot even the wounded. The enthusiasm is great, almost incredible. Our battalion had two casualties, the reds 200 to 300. Everyone that falls into our hands is finished off first with a rifle butt and then with a bullet.

Ten Red Cross nurses, each of whom was supposedly carrying a pistol, were shot immediately, however much they wept and prayed. His proud conclusion: 'We were much more humane towards the French in the field.'[30]

Frontline experience, domestic misery

Who were these Freikorps soldiers? What was the source of the unappeasable hatred with which they converted their law enforcement duties into bloody excesses? The answer to this question leads back into the war that still raged in the heads of these men. If we believe their stab-in-the-back legends, they would 'happily have gone on fighting for their lives'.

That's all the more surprising since it would be natural to assume that the often described battles within the war of annihilation would have left them utterly demoralised. Why were many Germans not as weary of fighting at the end of the First World War as they would be after the Second? In terms of experiences at the frontline, the First World War is in fact considered by many to have been even more terrible than the Second.

The '1914 War', as it was known in Germany, was marked by a horrific escalation of military killing. Tanks, artillery technology, unimaginable quantities of ammunition and finally poison gas turned what was once known as 'the art of war' into a competition of pure military capacity. Fighting was no longer carried out face to face; the enemy was invisible across no-man's land, their covered position being held with a hail of shells from a great distance. The two fronts held one another in place, while the troops dug themselves into their trenches and tried to send each other mad with endless drumfire. A shift of the frontlines by only a few metres cost countless thousands of human lives, all of them consumed as cannon fodder. Whole divisions were 'burned to clinker', as war reporters liked to put it.

Most front soldiers returned to Germany in a spectral state. In his 1929 anti-war novel *All Quiet on the Western Front*, Erich Maria Remarque wrote of a 'lost generation'. In the first weeks after publication the book sold an astonishing 450,000 copies. So many people recognised themselves in the novel that it became one of the most successful German books of all time.[31] The novel, peppered with cruel scenes of battle, follows its 18-year-old protagonist Paul Bäumer into the war that finally takes his life, on a day that was unusually so quiet and peaceful that the war report could be reduced to the single sentence of the title.[32] But in fact Paul Bäumer died long before. 'We are dead men with no feelings,' he observes, 'who are able by some trick, some dangerous magic to keep on running and keep on killing.'[33] Zombie-like, as a result of his countless incommunicable experiences, he is lost to his loved ones. During a brief visit home he establishes that he has become so alienated from his family and friends that he's glad to be back at the murderous frontline. His comrades are the only ones with whom he feels any kind of connection. It's a 'brotherhood on a large scale'[34] in which the individual no longer has a part to play. They were no longer fit for life in peace: 'Even if someone were to give us it back, that landscape of our youth, we wouldn't have much idea of how to handle it.'[35] Anyone who felt alien and out of place in the Weimar Republic, anyone who couldn't find their feet in the maelstrom to which the 1920s would lead, could feel that this book at least understood them.

But the overwhelming majority of soldiers in the Republic did feel very much at home, insofar as one can feel at home in such a new construction. After all, they were the ones who had risen up against the old order by disavowing their own officers. They were glad that the war was over, whether it had been a victory or not. It was no coincidence that the biggest veterans' association, the Reichsbund der Kriegsbeschädigten und Kriegsteilnehmer (Imperial Association of War Veterans and War Wounded), which had 820,000 members in 1922, was dominated by Social Democratics and still felt loyally connected to the new Republic even when it was riven with crises.[36] However, these considerable numbers gradually fade from the focus of memory simply because they didn't cause anybody any problems – unlike the component of their comrades who felt betrayed by the revolution and hated the Republic from the very first day.

The right-wing counterpart to Remarque's bestseller is the book *In Stahlgewittern. Aus dem Tagebuch eines Stoßtruppführers* (Storm of Steel) by Ernst Jünger, 25 at the time. This work, which remains famous today in spite of contradictory critical responses to it, shows marked similarities with Remarque's novel. Both stress the fraternal relationship of the front soldiers, the fact of their being lost to bourgeois life, their matter-of-fact response to monstrosity. 'We don't have any choice but to be pragmatic. So pragmatic, in fact, that I sometimes shudder,' Remarque writes.[37] 'The degree of objectivity of a book such as this is the measure of its inner value', says Jünger.[38] Even Jünger sees that the modern battle of attrition no longer really provides a setting for the actions of the war hero of former times: seldom did the 'laurel wreath adorn the brow of the worthy winner'.

> And yet this war also had its men and its romanticism! Heroes, if that word has not become trite. [. . .] They stood alone in the storm of battle, when death, a red rider with flaming hoofs, galloped through swirling mist.[39]

In Jünger's book the assault with which the soldiers, holding out in the trenches for weeks, tried to break out at last, becomes the hour of the birth of an entirely new type of fighter:

Seldom were they granted the salvation of looking the enemy in the eye, after everything terrible had been heaped up to the highest summit, hiding the world from them behind blood-red veils. Then they loomed up to a brutal magnitude, agile tigers of the trenches, masters of explosives.[40]

The theory that industrialised war, with its long-distance weapons and trench warfare, was unsuited to individual heroism and left behind a uniform army of traumatised men is not entirely applicable in Jünger's book. He finds literary garlands even for the mass of cannon fodder, the ones who were never going to be seen as storm-troop tigers of the battlefield. The slow dispiriting decline in the dankness of the muddy trenches is intensified into a kind of hyper-proletarian mass martyrdom:

They spent their days in the bowels of the earth, enveloped in mould, tormented by the eternal clockwork of the falling drops. [. . .] They worked and fought like that, ill-fed and ill-clad, as patient, iron-laden day-labourers of death.[41]

In this trench-mysticism the abysmal treatment of frontline soldiers twists itself into a cult of meaningless servitude. Books such as Storm of Steel did their part in helping the experiences on the 'battle-fields of madness' to bring the frontline soldiers together into a caste of initiates, even once the war was over; they saw themselves as a grubby elite, however low their status in the eyes of the rest of the world. A fraternity, just as destructive as the war that had produced these same confused men.

The fact that they were no longer fit for civilian life, that they didn't fit in with the modern world and failed in the face of its demands, did nothing to diminish their arrogance, filled as it was with a contempt for life. For the pacifist-minded Remarque, their fraternity was cruelly imposed upon them, a shrunken form of being that was all that these spent and burned-out soldiers had at their disposal. To Jünger's heroes, on the other hand, it appeared as the supreme fulfilment. They could not summon the courage required to acknowledge and admit their internal wounds. They interpreted the fact that they could only deal with their peers as a sign of their membership of an elite, which was not and could not be understood by those who stood outside it.

Many soldiers did not experience the end of the war as the result of a battle that had been dramatically lost, or as an imprisonment. They were spared the idea of having to surrender with arms raised, as millions of Wehrmacht soldiers were obliged to do just 30 years later. Unlike their generals, who had a panoptic view of the hopeless situation, the end of the war came as a complete surprise to them. The guns fell silent overnight as if on their own initiative, and the people who had fired them retreated just as devotedly as they had once marched on the enemy. The war was not ended by a dramatic defeat, there was no roar of joy, no incisive caesura, just a listless agony, ended unexpectedly by orders from above. The stab-in-the-back legend fell on fertile ground where many soldiers were concerned. The historian Gerd Krumeich, who has engaged intensely with the trauma of war, estimates the number of anti-Republic front-line soldiers to be around 3 per cent of participants in the war, or 14,000 in all.[42]

In the coming years, however, this sense of betrayal would be crucial, because a large proportion of Weimar society had also failed to anticipate the defeat. While many may also have been glad that the Great War was over, the idea that it had actually been lost was not something that they could grasp. Thinking back to 1917, surely they had been so victorious on the Eastern Front that they had been able to impose a negotiated peace on Russia the following spring? One which contained just as many excessive reparation requirements as the later Versailles Treaty?

As we have suggested, for the defeat to be processed, an important ritual was missing: no enemy had invaded, no one had occupied the country. The occupation of territory that usually ends a war was absent. And in contrast with the Second World War, every stone was still standing. Certainly, everyone was drained and war-weary. But wasn't that true of the enemy as well?

Unlike in 1945, the defeat remained abstract and the capitulation a far-away procedure that the German people read about in the newspapers. At first, they were grateful that the war was over, but when they experienced the heavy burdens of the Versailles Treaty, many people felt as if they were suffering as the result of a mere chimera, as though the defeat were only a notional one, a stitch-up between the 'November criminals' (as many Germans labelled the government leaders who had signed the armistice) and the hostile powers. Conspiracy theories did the rounds, such as talk of the Elders of Zion, who had got together in a Prague cemetery to plan the fall of the monarchy and the military capitulation, to make Germany disappear from the face of the earth once and for all. There was suspicion and ill-will towards anyone who thought themselves 'stateless'. That meant anyone with global inclinations: the communists who identified with an international proletariat; or speculators on the global stock market. This toxic conspiratorial delusion would be particularly directed against the Jews, who were accused of using 'world Jewry' to achieve 'world domination'.

*

Born out of an almost incomprehensible defeat, the Republic remained a chilly homeland, associated with shame and betrayal. The frontline soldiers had been deprived of the joy of returning home victorious. Many, however, still had a need to receive the returning men as proud warriors and to feel a sense of triumph beyond any sense of shame. But how was that to work? Homeland dignitaries ground out embarrassed formulaic greetings that were supposed to comfort the defeated men while covering over the truth.

When the soldiers passed through the Brandenburg Gate, onlookers sat and watched like crows in the autumnally leafless linden trees. 'No enemy has vanquished you!' Ebert declared, before immediately continuing: 'It was only when the enemy's superior power in terms of men and material became increasingly oppressive that we gave up the fight.' In Ludwigshafen, in the southwest of the country, the mayor managed to shoehorn lies and truth into a single sentence: 'You were not granted the chance to be victorious, the enemy's superior power in terms of men and material was too great, but you return upright and unbeaten, and the homeland greets you.'[43] And on 19 November the *Frankfurter Zeitung* tied itself up in knots to come up with the following sentence: 'We greet you, German soldiers! Germany has lost its war; but you have won yours!'

All of these distractions were pointless. The embittered soldiers spotted them for the hollow nonsense that they were, and felt 'spat upon from head to toe and assailed by falsity and posturing'.[44] They received confirmation of their conviction that they had not been defeated by the enemy, but betrayed by their homeland. 'With a bitter smile they read the trivial newspaper drivel, the empty words about heroes and heroic death. But they didn't want that gratitude, they wanted understanding' – in the words of Ernst Jünger.[45]

The guard troops of the defeated German Army passed through the Brandenburg Gate on 10 December 1918, past the People's Commissar Friedrich Ebert: 'They didn't want that gratitude', Ernst Jünger wrote two years later in his book Storm of Steel, *'they wanted understanding'. What that might have meant, he left open.*

The soldiers were even embittered about the welfare treatment of injured veterans, generous by European standards, because they were categorised on the same level as victims of civilian accidents, as if they had been run over by a tram. While in victorious France or Britain the war wounded were seen as heroes, and didn't attempt to hide the loss of their limbs, their German counterparts felt despised because of their disabilities and made great efforts to cover them up with prostheses and special clothes. Artists such as George Grosz and Otto Dix liked to show reactionary conformist types on crutches and with scarred faces in their caricatures. The fact that a private soldier with a pig's head hung from the ceiling in an art exhibition by the Berlin Dadaists will not have done much to increase the soldiers' feeling of being welcomed home with honours.

Many frontline fighters didn't return to the bosoms of their families, their businesses, their friends and associations, instead seeking a continuation of their humiliated comradeship in the Freikorps brigades; their hatred was unquenchable. Arnolt Bronnen, one of the most gifted wordsmiths among the Freikorps writers, put it like this:

> Nothing floated on the surface but the sour, lamentable, handwringing, terrified, sweating, nauseating atmosphere of the paper republic – with appeals to the world's conscience, protestations of rightness, bent backs and exaggerated hand gestures. But vibrating in the depths, as if in enormous steam kettles, was the energy of the nation that had been banished from the surface: waiting for the call of the hidden men who felt the destiny of the Reich within them.[46]

Servants of state in the crosshairs

A bloody trail of political murders runs through the Weimar Republic, most of them committed by the right. Among the best-known victims was Matthias Erzberger. The former finance minister was murdered by members of the Consul Organisation in August 1921, while on holiday in the Black Forest, for signing the Compiègne armistice that had ended the war. Foreign Minister Walther Rathenau, hated for his policy of reconciliation with France, was murdered in the street in the Berlin district of Grunewald on 24 June 1922. That same month the former prime minister Philipp Scheidemann (who had resigned from the post in 1919 over the terms of the Versailles Treaty) narrowly survived a cyanide attack; a gust of wind meant that he wasn't hit by the full charge. The well-known journalist Maximilian Harden was also lucky to survive an attack outside his house in Berlin-Grunewald. But the perpetrators did achieve their goal: Harden abandoned his often controversial magazine *Die Zukunft* and fled to Switzerland.

These attacks, which attracted global attention, form only a tiny proportion of the attempts at intimidation to which the people of the Weimar Republic were exposed. In 1922 the statistician Emil Julius Gumbel investigated all the known political murders that followed the foundation of the Republic.[47] He reached a total of 354 assassinations by far-right extremists. On the other side there were 22 carried out by members of the left. But they were the ones who met the full fury of the law, while right-wing murderers were treated with great leniency. On average, left-wing perpetrators were sentenced to 15 years' imprisonment, while the right-wingers got away with an average of four months each. The Social Democrat-led Justice Ministry confirmed the results of Gumbel's research but did not consider itself to be in a position to influence the practice of the courts.

The attacks were intended to intimidate local politicians, mayors and senior officials. 'County Commissioner, don't worry, it won't be long now,' in the words of a song that right-wing activists spread among the farmers of the Rural People's Movement.[48]

Let's take a closer view at one of the murdered men, the aristocratic landowner and former lieutenant captain Hans Paasche, in 1920 candidate for the city council of Deutsch Krone, now in west Poland. It was as good as certain that he was going to win the election, because in matters of land reform the landowner was on the side of the agricultural workers. The scion of a wealthy and very conservative parental home, he wasn't necessarily what one would associate with a man of his standing. He does, however, give us an idea of the enormous range of lifestyles to be found among the upper class.

Paasche had, under the impression of his four-year period of service in Africa, developed into a romantic 'friend of the Black Continent'. He returned to Germany as a passionate critic of Western civilisation, campaigned for the protection of the environment and was active in the *Wandervogel* (Wandering Bird) hiking movement. In many of his writings he had harsh words about the inhuman leadership of the war and described his learning processes in discussion with the African population. In 1912 he wrote a proclamation that today reads like an early ecological manifesto for the Green Party:

> While a single gazelle whose hide has value on the global market still lives, or a whale in the Arctic Ocean, or a bird of paradise in the jungle of remote islands, then business activity will not rest, coupled with inhuman thoughtlessness and short-sightedness.[49]

Paasche won fame with a fictional travel story by an African from whose perspective the peculiarities of German growth-driven society appear wonderfully abstruse and ludicrous. His book *The Research Trip of the African Lukanga Mukara into the German Interior* became a bestseller in 1912, and later inspired the international hit *Der Papalagi* by Erich Scheurmann, first published in 1920. This book sold 1.7 million copies in its German-language edition alone, and in 1968 became a cult book of the anti-authoritarian movement. It can hardly be denied that Paasche was extremely influential. His book, a head-shaking critique of the strange practices of German natives from the perspective of an intellectually superior Black man, was received as a provocation by the supposedly civilised nation. Nothing characterises Paasche better than the gesture that he made during the war to the French forced labourers working on his farm at Waldfrieden on their national day. He hoisted the Tricolore, right in the middle of the German state of Farther Pomerania.

The last straw for his opponents came in 1918 when Paasche tried to enter politics in Berlin, joined the Workers' and Soldiers' Soviet and energetically demanded that the Ebert–Scheidemann government arrest and punish the Supreme Army Command – in vain, as we know. Disappointed by the realities of politics, Paasche quickly retreated to Waldfrieden. His wife Ellen, daughter of a well-to-do banker and niece of the journalist Maximilian Harden, died of Spanish flu on 8 December 1918, only nine years after their honeymoon, which had taken them across East Africa. Now the landowner set about bringing up their four children on his own. On an unusually warm day in May 1920 he was swimming with them in the lake when a village policeman ordered him to come home. He followed him wearing only his swimming trunks and dressing gown, but turned around when he caught a glimpse of some of the 60 soldiers who had surrounded the farm. Their hail of rifle fire struck him in the back. When Harry Graf Kessler heard of Paasche's murder he noted in his diary: 'The safety of political dissidents in present-day Germany is worse than in the most notorious South American republics or in the Rome of the Borgias.'[50]

Hans Paasche and Ernst Jünger – the two decommissioned officers/authors were worlds apart. In between there is room for the most exciting social tableau that Germany has ever seen.

Ebert, a man despised

If we were to amalgamate the many different aspects of German society in a single individual we might end up with Friedrich Ebert, a great pan-Germanist – the ideal composition of a president, in fact. Although by 1924 his image had been delivered many millions of times over on postage stamps, cheap stamps which, even decades after his death, survive in children's collections, it's fair to say Ebert did not leave a great mark on posterity. His was a bullish face with a bushy moustache and inexpressive eyes, a face marked by bitterness, bile and an unsatisfied yearning for power. And this was supposed to be the man 'who rode the tiger'? Who took the reins of the revolution and in defiance of all resistance transformed Germany into one of the most modern, turbulent and experimental societies on earth? Yes, that was him, the man known as 'Ebert the traitor'.

His career was a modern fairy tale; the dream of rising from dishwasher to millionaire is as nothing in comparison. Born in 1871, the son of a Heidelberg tailor, Ebert left education after secondary school, trained as a saddler, was the tenant landlord of a pub in Bremen, an expert in matters of social insurance, and since 1919 suddenly president of the Empire. By his side stood Louise Ebert, née Rump, former label-sticker in a cigar factory. Friedrich Ebert, a smart young man, who could deliver long speeches at public festivals and gatherings in public halls, had married Louise, of humble origins, in 1894 when she was four months pregnant. As soon as the child was born, she helped in the inn where they had just become tenants, happy with her relative independence, because Ebert himself didn't enjoy serving behind the bar. In her childhood, she said later, she 'had to endure very, very much that was difficult and gloomy'.[51] As first lady of the Republic, the former label-sticker was the successor to the Kaiserin Auguste Viktoria.[52] She performed her role to perfection. She hosted receptions in the presidential palace on Wilhelmstrasse with 'such natural grace and unforced courtesy' that even one Baroness von Rheinbaben confessed herself delighted.[53]

Ebert himself also had a talent for hospitality. He had always paid attention to manners. And he always advised the more rough-and-ready customers in his pub to wear a frock coat at their next visit. He ran his local as a kind of advice centre. Ebert the pub landlord had excellent knowledge of legal matters and guided his customers through the jungle of the new social laws – an activity that he later used in his professional life as permanently employed 'workers' secretary' in his party's advice office.

Ebert was what might be called a right-wing social democrat. Socialism for him meant not so much the nationalisation of key industries and more a society aiming for equality, one in which workers could in future aspire to the lifestyle of the middle class. He

Saddler, pub landlord, President – Friedrich Ebert in February 1921, not yet marked by illness and disappointment. When he died in 1925 people had a sense of what they had lost.

himself had made the same move, after all; he comfortably celebrated the hobbies of high society. He went sailing in a white suit, hunting in a green loden jacket.

But bourgeois though he might have appeared – and however presidential his manner in the end – for the conservative pillars of society the parvenu remained beyond the pale. The *Tägliche Rundschau* called him 'Friedrich the Temporary':

> The squat, short-necked figure, the Van Dyke beard, the roll of fat at the back of his neck. Even today he emanates the fresh, sharp scent of Russian leather, which he previously worked. Oh, if only he had stuck to that occupation! He has the horizon of a cheese-dome.[54]

The diatribes were unrestrained. In August 1919 an image of the president swimming was even published: he and Gustav Noske appeared half-naked on the front page of the *Berliner Illustrirte Zeitung*. The head of state and his defence minister stood in the Baltic Sea, grinning for the photographer. Today the picture might be used to demonstrate how close to the people the two men were, but in those days it prompted near-universal horror and revulsion. To many, the half-naked president looked like the symbol of an unarmed fatherland. The photograph might have made Ebert appear human, but most people wondered whether the revolution hadn't led to an entirely unsuitable person becoming head of state. Postcards were printed showing the representative of the new regime looking a bit like a cartoon character in his ill-fitting swimming trunks and next to him, by way of comparison, the dignified representatives of the old regime: Kaiser Wilhelm and his field marshal, Paul von Hindenburg, both in full dress uniform with rows of medals. The caption above the picture: 'Then and now'.

The undistinguished Ebert had a tough time in the new world of mass media. He exercised his duties without charisma or drama, without wit or humour, opting instead for a cautious tone of balance and moderation. This was unwelcome in an age accustomed to boldness, with an appetite for excitement and spice. The widespread feeling that something exciting was afoot made Ebert look like a timid slowcoach. There was much talk of 'the New Man', and a yearning for danger and thrills. Many people cultivated a brash, supercilious style, which meant that everything left them unimpressed. At such a time, with everyone wanting to reach for the stars, Ebert couldn't have come across as anything but shockingly mediocre. For the writer Kurt Tucholsky he was 'an average citizen, the worst mixture imaginable: personally clean and actually dirty'.[55]

Left and right came together in the conviction that Ebert was guilty of betrayal. Some saw him as a traitor to the revolution, others as a traitor to the fatherland and his brave soldiers. Later, the journalist Sebastian Haffner had no qualms about borrowing the stab-in-the-back legend from the right and reshaping it for the treacherous assassination of the revolution, to which Ebert was guilelessly committed.[56] In 1968, Haffner wrote that the fact that they weren't rogues on the grand scale but respectable citizens doesn't make Ebert and Noske any more likeable. The monstrosity of their historic deed isn't reflected in their private character. If we look for their motives, we don't find anything demonic or magnificently satanic, just banalities: a love of order and a petty-bourgeois over-achievement.[57]

Ebert's image really doesn't have much of a chance against the posthumous charisma of Liebknecht and Luxemburg. Their hideous murders, their status as victims, the humanity they demonstrated in rejecting the First World War, lead posterity to overlook their share of responsibility for the bloody course of the post-revolutionary months. Had they accepted democratic rules rather than constantly threatening to seize power for themselves, it would have been easier to democratise the forces of order and put the Reichswehr on a chain.

Today, Ebert has the thankless reputation reserved for those given to moderation and balance, undervalued qualities in the period under discussion. 'There is a lack of flaws, a lack of catharsis,' his biographer Walter Mühlhausen writes; Ebert, in his view, lacks the special aura 'that so strongly fascinates historians and the interested public about big historical personalities in general'.[58]

History prefers more gripping protagonists. At the same time, the mediocrity that Ebert embodies was arguably suited to what was an essentially risky programme. In contrast with the churned-up passions of the post-war era, the attempt to reconcile a divided society was on a scale that required a titan – even though titans would have been entirely unsuited to the task of peacemaking. So was the phlegmatic Ebert perhaps the right person after all? He was only granted six years in office. He died of appendicitis on the last day of February 1925, already quite frail. Much of the public felt orphaned when they heard the news of his death. A huge crowd, over a million, came to watch the funeral procession pass by the Tiergarten park in Berlin. Although rather muted and quiet, the crowd did 3,800 Reichsmarks worth of damage to monuments and flowerbeds. With familiar fury, members of parliament on both the far left and the far right opposed the bill being paid by the taxpayer.

For all its diversity, the intellectual world united in its mockery of the order-loving Ebert during his lifetime. Out of their ranks, it was no less an observer than Thomas Mann who defended Ebert most stoutly. That's hardly surprising. The 'poet with the ironed trousers', as Alfred Döblin somewhat contemptuously called him, had thought with greater subtlety and ingenuity than anyone else about what was appropriate, about the path between the decorous, the deviant and the authentic, in aesthetics, the erotic and politics. Thomas Mann confessed in 1925 that his sympathy for Ebert was 'boundless'. He saw in him 'the fate of a man that the age impelled into something initially quite incredible, fantastical', but which was quite unable to 'twist the personality into eccentricity, but a fate that was borne and implemented with simple dignity and relaxed reason'.[59]

Still shaken by the murder of Foreign Minister Walther Rathenau, in 1922 Thomas Mann wrote an essay for young academics defending the German Republic. A short time later he delivered his declaration to predominantly anti-democratic students in Berlin. He tried to persuade them, taking extravagant detours via German romanticism, Friedrich Nietzsche and Walt Whitman, that the new state could also be theirs. Just as people would later call Angela Merkel 'Mutter' or even 'Mutti', at first contemptuously, then almost as if in a need for protection, Thomas Mann adopted a familial vision of the president: 'Father Ebert is known to me', he assured the students, who at first followed the words of the revered Nobel laureate respectfully: Ebert was 'a fundamentally pleasant man, modestly dignified, not without cunning, relaxed and humanly solid. I have seen him a few times in his black tie and tails, the gifted and incredibly sly child of fortune, a bourgeois among bourgeois, perform his high office calmly and amiably at festivities; and as I was also able to observe the late master [the kaiser], a decorative talent without a doubt, engaged in some dealing or other, I gained the insight, which I should like to present to you here, that democracy can be something more German than an imperial opera gala.'[60] Loud foot stamping followed in protest, grumbling among the upper-class youth, who wanted something grander. Even if it was only not losing their privileges in a 'workers' republic'.

2

When Money Dies

The dollar is rising, let us fall!
Why should we be more stable than our currency?

Klaus Mann

Loser pays all

For most people, the new age started with big hopes. Many people who had emerged from the war unscathed looked for a job and quickly found one. Others simply carried on where they had stopped four years before. Craftsmen, doctors and owners of small businesses announced their return to civilian life via small ads. The newspapers were full of reports of survival: 'Back from the field. Dr Zuckermann, ear, nose and throat. 42 Grunewaldstrasse' – 'Back home. Alois Feilchenfeld. Accept all kinds of bricklaying work' – 'Released from military service, I have resumed my consultations. Dentist Karl Feuker, modern tooth replacement specialist.'

The advertisements proliferated endlessly. And not just the advertisements. Even though the war was lost, and in spite of the unrest in the country, the economy revived surprisingly quickly. All over the place, people were making plans, developing business ideas, imagining a new life for themselves. The newspaper small ad pages were filled with people seeking and finding each other. After four years of mayhem the economy needed to pull itself together again and establish connections. In the *Vossische Zeitung*, manufacturers sought wholesalers, offering 2,600 scythes, 4 wagons of pickling jars or 10 tons of metal screws. People with ideas sought people with money: 'Large-scale capitalist sought for the exploitation of an extremely profitable import article. Guarantees available.' And conversely, money looked for brains: 'Capitalist seeks lucrative business, cinema and cabaret included.' In the *Berliner Tageblatt* alone investors often found as many as 30 requests for capital per issue: 'Silent partner sought with ca. 100,000 marks worth of capital outlay for the rational exploitation of profitable invention.' Factories sought new functions: 'Factory seeks businessman to manufacture its own articles. Also takes manufacture into account. Good location near Frankfurt-Bebra express train station. Extended storage space for raw materials and connecting platforms for 20 railway goods carriages available.' Travelling salesmen sought manufacturers to take their products on tour. Meanwhile one manufacturer also sought a 'long-distance transporter with own convoy'. Businessmen sought salespeople abroad, even overseas, in Mexico, the Dutch East Indies or the Portuguese colonies. Germans living abroad sought residents who could use their local knowledge and contacts.

Trade even resumed with countries with which Germany had recently been at war. Suddenly people were speaking French again, in spite of the lasting tensions, and practising an accent that had been frowned upon during the war. While the Dujardin cognac company had only recently felt the need to assure consumers that in spite of its name it was in fact 100 per cent German, French dictionaries were now advertised ('Bad pronunciation is an embarrassment!') along with foreign language courses.

Small ad markets are a true reflection of social needs and opportunities. Someone requested information about the precise location of a grave in Aleppo, seeking the bones of a fallen soldier by the name of Eugen Hounchericher in order to bring them home. In the advertisement below that, a woman asked if anyone had found a moleskin muff that she had lost outside the Philharmonie. Countless companies needed workers: cleaning company directors and models (sometimes called mannequins), foremen, head clerks, publicists, buyers, drivers. Some people who found such tasks too laborious looked for a capable wife instead, ideally a war widow who now had something to bring to the marriage:

> Seek dark-complexioned, dark-haired lady, with cheerful tempera-
> ment and heart full of love, who will find joy in my five-year-old
> daughter. As I am keen to boost my business and I am in a position to
> provide a useful outlay of capital, considerable assets are required,
> even though I would never marry for that reason. Photograph desir-
> able, I could never be indiscreet. The more open we are, the sooner we
> reach our goal.

Others wanted to settle down comfortably straight away: 'Twin brothers want to marry into well-run grain business.' That sounds a bit direct today, but it might not have been entirely senseless at the time. The war had cost 2.4 million German soldiers their lives and skewed the marriage market in favour of the remaining men. The fact that they were fewer in number made the men look more valu-able than they perhaps were.

The country took an upturn that surprised the victorious powers. While the mood in France and Britain was darkened by pressing economic concerns, the Germans had full employment – in spite of the fact that they had lost the war, in spite of the reparations imposed upon them. How was that possible? The answer lay in the printing trade. The Reichsbank simply printed out more money. They had become accustomed to this simple method of increasing the money supply during the war. In order to finance the essentially unaffordable battles of attrition, in 1914 they had opted for two strategies: first, they borrowed the money from German citizens in the form of gov-ernment bonds; and second, if they were still short of anything, they simply went back to the printing press. In 1913 there had been 2 billion marks in circulation; in 1919 it was 45 billion. In the meantime the state had put itself in debt 30 times over, from 5 billion marks to 153 billion.[1] This inflationary practice was commonplace in all the warring nations, and insufficient thought had been given to the question of how the borrowed money might be repaid to the country's citizens and the economy brought under control once the war was over. All nations were equally convinced that they were going to win the war, and that whoever lost would have to pay up in the end. In 1915 Karl Helfferich, secretary of state in the Treasury, had promised the Germans that they would be able to saddle the losers with 'this terrible burden' after the inevitable victory: 'The instigators of the war have earned the lead weight of the billions; *they* can carry it down the decades, rather than us.'[2] While the sons were fighting in the field their fathers were giving credit to the state. It didn't occur to them for a moment that they wouldn't get the money back. 'The Frenchies' would have to pay up in the form of interest and interest on interest.

Their enemies were thinking in exactly the same way. They too acted according to the motto 'loser pays all' when they dictated the peace conditions to the Germans in Versailles. In one of the first instalments of reparation payments for the war damage suffered by the victor states, Germany was expected to pay 20 billion gold marks. Faced with such rosy financial prospects, the British and the French looked at their books and switched from an inflationary war economy to a thrifty peacetime budget. They cut back on all social spending, saved wherever they could and relied on money from Germany. The prospect of reparation payments emboldened them to undertake the necessary economic fasting cure. For the Germans, on the other hand, this kind of economic realism was rendered impossible by their hopeless situation. Their mountain of debts was unimaginably huge. The state was still 98 billion marks in the red, even without the victors' demands. With debts on that scale, the very idea of saving was out of the question. On that logic, the coalition governments of the first years of Weimar simply continued with the inflationary policy of the war economy.

Instead of weapons they were now producing social welfare payments. The Social Democrats, the strongest party in the coalition, were under particularly enormous pressure to provide a successful and legitimate government. If they didn't just want to defeat the communists militarily, they had to prove that the revolution had been worth it for the country's citizens. Large-scale social packages, as they would be called today, were pulled together. The social services, grants and work creation measures further inflated the state budget, but for a while it looked as if the inflation rate might actually fall. State intervention created workplaces. Things looked brighter, particularly for the industrial workforce and for low- and mid-ranking clerical workers. As the value of the Reichsmark declined, with the printing presses churning out new notes, German products abroad became cheaper. Exports rose, unemployment fell. In spite of patriotic appeals to their governments, the British and French bought up more than affordable quality goods from Germany in enormous quantities. For now, the fact that the mark was constantly losing value was no concern for people who had no savings; the main thing was that wages were rising to the same extent or even a bit faster. The mad times of hyperinflation were yet to come.

The biggest losers in all of this weren't the have-nots, but the middle class, the savers. The security-conscious members of the cultured middle class had traditionally put any excess income into savings and now, month by month, they were watching their assets lose value. To make matters worse, they were the ones who had bought the most bonds and patriotically helped to finance the war. Inflation dramatically devalued the claims they could make on the state: in the end, the 98 billion marks of debt that the state had incurred among its citizens weren't worth much more than a sack of potatoes. Small wonder that everyone who had lent money to the kaiser in good faith now felt cheated by what was known in many circles as the 'Republic of the November Criminals'. What was being played out quite openly was what John Maynard Keynes had recognised in 1919: 'By a continuous process of inflation, governments can confiscate, secretly and unobserved, an important part of the wealth of their citizens.'[3]

A second pillar of the recently affluent middle class also fell away: rental income. Doctors, professors and senior civil servants regularly boosted their livelihoods with rental properties. For reasons of social policy, however, the new state imposed a rent freeze, which helped tenants to survive during the period of inflation, but also deprived landlords of an income that they desperately needed.

While some employers adjusted their workers' wages to reflect the devaluation of the currency on a weekly basis, the state went in the opposite direction. People who worked for the state came to see their employer as a swindler. It paid their wages every three months in the form of an advance. The higher inflation rose, the faster the prepaid money lost its value. As a result, a professor with ten years' service at a university could end up earning half the amount of an unemployed worker, simply because unemployment benefit was paid out on a monthly basis.[4]

Live for the moment

Inflation was whipping out the ground from under the feet of the very people who saw themselves as pillars of society, and who had for that reason long felt protected by the state. The main beneficiaries of inflation, on the other hand, were debtors. Apart from the debt-ridden state itself, these included businesspeople who had invested in credit, landowners whose farms were heavily in debt, speculators with borrowed capital – they all had cause for celebration. They had only to recalculate their debts into dollars or loaves of bread to see that their burdens were miraculously getting smaller. The winners were anyone who lived on tick; the losers, anyone who economised in the traditional way. Honest people were made to look like fools – the conviction was rife among socially conservative citizens that they were living in a republic of rogues.

Anyone who was unable or unwilling to speculate, anyone tied to a system of fixed incomes and who had to work their way gradually up established hierarchies, quickly came to see themselves as losers. Many senior officials who had easily been able to afford a maid and a gardener before the war now found themselves mowing their own lawns and cleaning their own kitchens. Maidservants now demanded

The daily rise of the dollar was usually the most important news of the day.

the same wages as secretaries – and their employers worried about how long they would be able to afford to pay them.[5]

From June 1922 the value of the mark against the dollar had fallen monthly by 50 per cent; early in 1923 it went into freefall. Two developments were crucially responsible for hyperinflation: the withdrawal of foreign investors after the assassination of Walther Rathenau and another rise – an incredible one this time – in state spending after the French occupation of the Ruhr.

The murder of the foreign minister, who was highly respected abroad and always determined to achieve fair play, was just one of many acts of far-right violence. But this attack attracted a great deal of international attention, and confirmed many foreign investors in their fear that Germany was turning into a banana republic and was liable to sink into political chaos. They became increasingly hesitant to invest, even though the falling value of the Reichsmark made economic commitments very enticing. The loss of foreign capital meant the loss of many jobs and further inflated the state budget by raising the cost of social services.

With the occupation of the industrial Ruhr in January 1923, inflation spiralled completely out of control. A hundred thousand French soldiers invaded the region on the grounds that Germany had deliberately fallen behind with reparation payments. To reinforce their demands, the French wanted to cut off German industry from its raw materials and redirect the coke, coal and steel into their own country. In spite of brutal attempts at intimidation, however, the workers refused to go to the smelting furnaces or down the mines for the occupying forces. Over 150,000 people, not only workers but officials and office clerks, were violently expelled from the Ruhr. The rest went on striking or, sometimes with the help of Freikorps members, engaged in acts of sabotage.

For a while the German public pulled together, as they had during the domestic political truce (*Burgfrieden*) declared during the war. It was only on the far right that people went on mocking what was known as the 'policy of fulfilment' – an agreement to repay reparations with a view to renegotiating the deal in due course. But there was little sign in government of its supposed submissiveness towards the victorious forces. On the contrary: in order to maintain resistance against the occupation, the state went on paying damages to the Ruhr companies and wages to the approximately 2 million striking workers. These strikers were known as 'Cuno pensioners' after the acting non-party-aligned Wilhelm Cuno, President Ebert's sixth chancellor. To keep them fed, the government went on printing money for almost nine months – in vast quantities. More than 5,000 printing works were now churning out notes on behalf of the Reichsbank. New bills were constantly being designed to make the money manageable, in terms of weight at least, so that people didn't always have to go to the baker's with a wheelbarrow full of notes. In November, a pound of rye bread cost a thousand billion marks. In February 1923 the 100,000-mark note entered circulation. This was followed within eight months by the 50-million mark note, the 200-billion and finally the 100-trillion note.

The Germans might not have had much of an idea what was going on, but they could still count. Never again were they such masters at calculating numbers with 12 zeros as they were in the autumn of 1923. It took some people a matter of seconds to work out how long they could survive on the trillions they had in their pockets. But the 100-trillion note marked the end. It was the largest denomination ever printed on a German banknote. As if this record had been predicted, the 100-trillion mark note was particularly fine to look at – a masterpiece of the money-maker's art. It was truly heart-rending that such trouble should have been taken with such a debilitated currency. On the right-hand edge of the note, there was a symbol of German culture: Albrecht Dürer's portrait of the humanist Willibald Pirckheimer. The watermark was a row of thistles; a complicated braiding of lines artfully made the note difficult to forge. But who would have wanted to forge it? This absurd level of accuracy didn't enhance the note's value. According to a widespread story, some thieves stole a whole laundry basket full of money. They threw away the money and kept the basket.

*

The faster hyperinflation rose the more difficult it became to do business. But many people had become rich and richer, not in spite of hyperinflation but because of it. Hugo Stinnes, a major industrialist from the Ruhr known as the 'Inflation King', exploited it on a grand scale. Unlike most other classic steel barons, Stinnes was a deft financial juggler, who swiftly converted the profits he had made in foreign currencies into Reichsmarks, to buy companies which were, on paper at least, now more valuable than they had been shortly before. When Stinnes died at the age of 54 in 1924, he owned 1,535 businesses with 3,000 factories and different branches. These included 81 mines, 56 iron- and steelworks, 57 banks and insurance companies, 37 refineries and oilfields, as well as 389 trading and transport companies. Thirty ships sailed under the Stinnes flag between Hamburg and Central America, and in the seas around East Asia.[6]

There were many businessmen like him, on larger and smaller scales. They sold their products abroad and bought up one company after another back at home with their increasingly valuable dollars. With this flight into material assets, the important thing was to be even faster than inflation. These new investments allowed them to borrow large sums, on the assumption that these would have greatly declined in value when it came to paying them back. Consequently it was possible to get richer and richer on the never-never – a route from which less creditworthy people were, of course, excluded.

Even during hyperinflation things looked good for the asset-rich. The cars became sleeker, the magazines glossier. Horseracing enjoyed a boom, and sailing regattas continued to be held. Many people had a sense that the Social Democratic Republic had become the plaything of a tiny elite.[7]

The more cunning among the well-to-do were joined by a new species: 'Raffkes' and 'Schieber' – spivs and money-grubbers – who put their wealth even more visibly on display. They made huge profits on black-market deals and currency speculation. In the afterword to his novel *Raffke & Co.*, the bestselling author Artur Landsberger identified the 'Schieber' as 'a new genus that learned to walk' during the war:

> Someone who goes against the grain! With brushes on his teeth. Who soaps himself with whipped cream and makes mincemeat with his razor blade. A gibbon whose arms are as long as his conscience is broad. [. . .] With a fine-tuned sense and a completely new attitude. Who has nothing in common with the people of former times but his language.[8]

The state of the economy could be read from the dollar exchange rate. The dollar was rising hourly; the new rates were announced at midnight every day, delivering a judgement about the value, or lack of it, of people's remaining assets. Anyone who had been paid in

Reichsmarks had to convert them to a stable currency as quickly as possible. All over Berlin there were 'dollar booths', 'glass booths in the middle of the street where foreign currency can be changed'.[9] Particularly notable was the way in which deals on the 'black stock market' in Düsseldorf were conducted. Here, on the border with the occupied Ruhr, foreign currencies were exchanged openly in the street – US dollars or French and Belgian francs. On Kaiser-Wilhelm-Strasse the black stock market was formed of a dense knot of people that moved back and forth whispering exchange rates to each other. 'Mingling with the crowd of very dubious, criminal figures were exhausted women, old men, young lads offering clothes and bedlinen for sale,' wrote the author Joseph Roth,[10] shocked that he was supposed to pay more there for his lunch – 50 billion marks – when he would rather have had wurst and sauerkraut standing up in a Berlin bar for 20.

Anyone who didn't join in with the currency devaluation game slipped into penury. Bankruptcies accumulated, and the numbers of unemployed people and beggars soared. They now defined the cityscape, panhandling in cafés and waiting outside factory gates and office blocks. One outraged Munich beggar threw back a bundle of 100-mark notes: 'You can keep that crap for yourself.'[11]

Because many people who were still in work knew how quickly they too might lose their jobs, poverty shed some of its stigma. Donation-funded soup kitchens sprang up all over the place. Reporters strolled through the waiting rooms of the starving. Egon Erwin Kisch, for example, had himself locked up in a night shelter. Hans Fallada brought poverty closer to his readers by having his protagonists rise and fall through the social strata as if in a lift. Social mobility accelerated at a dizzying pace, like everything else during those years. Careers that had been on the rise suddenly took a tumble. While there were food riots, and grocers' shops were looted, some people had enough money to go to the theatre at a cost of 2 trillion marks. But it was also possible to pay with two eggs. The play *My Cousin Edward* by Fritz Friedmann-Frederich was running at the Komödienhaus in Berlin. The premiere coincided with the height of hyperinflation. 'There has often been a lot of laughter,' the *Lokal-Anzeiger* reported, 'but never as much as this. You really can't stop laughing.'

You didn't need much in the way of funds to enjoy inflation. A smart student from Heidelberg made the best of his family's financial collapse. Shortly after the start of hyperinflation, their savings, originally totalling 800,000 marks, had shrunk to a value that was just enough to buy a ticket to Holland. With that money he travelled to Limburg and worked in the coalmine there until he had saved 50 guilders. Back in Heidelberg he used the 50 guilders as security for a short-term bank loan, which he soon paid back with devalued money. Then he took out a new loan, and so on and so on. In the end he still had in his pocket the 50 guilders, with which he had financed an entire year of study.[12]

Little billionaires, 1923. The bundles of notes lost their value so quickly that they were given to children to play with.

Only people relatively uninhibited by traditional ideas of value were capable of that kind of resourcefulness. Anyone who stuck with the old German maxim that 'begging is better than borrowing' soon found themselves facing destitution. Inflation rewarded the resourceful, not the virtuous.

Old people couldn't keep up. Things were easier for the young and quick-witted, who weren't overburdened with traditional notions of thrift. Reliance on past experience was punished with hunger, impulsiveness with enormous wealth, the journalist Sebastian Haffner, 16 years old in 1923, would recall. In a memoir written in British exile in 1939 he reports on the astonishing transformations in his comrades, only a little older than himself:

> The twenty-one-year-old bank director appeared, as did the sixth-former who followed the stock exchange advice of his slightly older friends. He wore Oscar Wilde ties, organised champagne parties, and supported his impoverished father. Beneath all this suffering a feverish, hot-blooded youthfulness, lasciviousness and a general carnival spirit flourished. Now all of a sudden it was the young and not the old who had the money.[13]

And it was money that kept its value only for a few hours: 'It was spent like never before or since; and not on the kind of things on which old people spend money.'[14] Inflation fed the cult of youth typical of the Weimar Republic, and confirmed the young in their arrogance and the old in their insecurity. Among affluent school students it became the fashion to invest pocket money in shares. The author Georg Hirschfeld described these young people, brought up by inflation, as 'world citizens without a world'. They 'laugh their way through terrible pointlessness' and want to travel far 'on the corpses of yesterday'.[15]

Haffner experienced the effect hyperinflation had on the life of his father, a senior Prussian officer, and the family in general. On the first of the month, when his father's salary arrived, they had to spend the entire monthly allowance on non-perishable goods all at once. The whole family ran back and forth buying up huge cheeses, hams and hundredweights of potatoes. The maid brought the things home in a wheelbarrow. Monthly tickets for the underground were bought the same day before they went up in price again the next. Speed was vital, not least when it came to spending money; quick, get rid of the bills before they become even more worthless. 'Quick, my wife, here's another ten thousand marks, buy something with it. It doesn't matter what, a pound of carrots, shirt buttons, the record "She Wants Bananas from Me" – or a rope to hang ourselves with . . . But be quick, run, fast!'[16] With these words a man in Hans Fallada's novel *Wolf Among Wolves* spurs his wife on to keep pace with the currency's devaluation. But money lost value faster than anyone could run; 'flight into real goods' was almost physically impossible.

The pace required to keep up with hyperinflation meant faster communication in every area of life. In 1923 Siemens came up with a special stock-exchange telephone for currency trading, with which companies could conclude their transactions more quickly. While a currency purchase was being negotiated by telephone, the employee could consult the boss on a second line without interrupting the original conversation – an early form of modern conference switching.

The experience of the creeping death of money even altered people's neural circuits. There was a widespread sense of unreality, and any kind of monetary transaction put people's nerves on edge. Those undaunted by money's tendency to evaporate were gripped by a weird feeling of boldness, a sense of the impossible, of enormous changes in fortune that lurked behind the new threadbare reality. There was talk of 'starving millionaires' – an incongruous phrase that captured the ridiculous nature of everyday life. There were people with billions in their pockets and nothing in their bellies. Things were worsening by the day. The only miracle was that not everyone had already hit rock bottom.

Friedrich Nietzsche's 'revaluation of all values' was constantly being cited. The whole system of cultural values had gone into decline along with the value of the currency. Parents were worried about their children's morals. Love seemed to be following the example of money: the more its importance was affirmed, the more its value dropped. 'The young people who learned to love in those days skipped romance and embraced cynicism', Haffner wrote.[17] Older generations have always tended to believe that respectability is on the way out, but now young people themselves believed the same thing

> Everyone is a match for everyone, it doesn't matter. This girl is a match for this boy just as much as the next. [. . .] The dollar is rising, let us fall! Why should we be more stable than our currency? [. . .] millions of underfed, corrupt, desperately lewd, furiously pleasure-seeking men and women twist and stumble away in a jazzy delirium.[18]

It was in these terms, in his autobiography *The Turning Point*, that Klaus Mann, the son of Thomas, described the capital's bohemian crowd into which he had fallen as an 18-year-old. And in the Munich district of Schwabing things were no better. It was not without reason that the Bavarian Oskar Maria Graf, who for a time organised glamorous parties in return for money, invented the term 'sexual democracy'.[19]

The faster money lost its value, the faster people danced. Ecstatic dancing on a busy dancefloor dispelled all cares for now. The dance style that went with inflation was the almost rule-free shimmy, which had arrived in 1920; it involved ecstatically shaking the shoulders and hips in a very contemporary-looking way. It was danced in a very tight space, with no touching between partners. You could only shimmy as part of a crowd; critics saw it as the end of social dancing: a whirling monument to loneliness.

Inflation, new freedom and moral collapse – Otto Dix & Co. see the Republic as one big brothel

One of the social dividends of inflation was greater independence for women. It's no coincidence that the locus for this was on the dancefloor. The dance-hall clientele now included a type of customer who had never been seen before: unaccompanied women. Most of these were young shorthand typists and secretaries who visited the clubs alone or with girlfriends. To the puzzled observer from more conservative circles, or indeed from the provinces, this type of behaviour was unheard of, and seemed dangerously close to prostitution. Many girls came from the provinces to Berlin, eager to breathe the balmy air of freedom. If, as often happened, they didn't find a regular income as quickly as they might have wished, they at least wanted, like the famous 'artificial silk girl' in the novel of the same name (*Das kunstseidene Mädchen* in German) by Irmgard Keun, to enjoy some kind of night-life glamour, and act like proud, independent women who 'are their own environment' and can switch themselves on 'like electric light-bulbs, and no one can get at them through the beam'.[20]

Certainly, money played a part in the style with which young women conquered the city's nightlife. During hyperinflation, there was effectively no aspect of life in which money didn't play an important part. Many of these women could more or less find their feet thanks to their new office jobs. But the ones who didn't have that kind of independence in mind, and who instead had their eyes set on marriage, had their plans scuppered by hyperinflation, which had ruined the dowry system. From rich family's elder daughter to simple housemaid, some kind of dowry was seen as an economic requirement for marriageability. Even many single housemaids had set aside everything they could in order to increase their chances on the marriage market. Now those savings were basically liquidated. The prospect of marriage wasn't completely ruled out – sometimes love outshone the bride's lack of means – but it had become more unlikely. Many young women saw themselves thrown back on their own devices, forced to recognise a potential for emancipation in the loss of their dowries. They took control of their own fortune, and played an active and independent part in the search for a partner. Without a dowry, parents had no say in the matter. The idea associated with the dowry that one was supposed to 'save oneself' for the wedding night was further battered by hyperinflation. Once again the same principle applied: saving is pointless. Don't think of tomorrow, all that matters is today.

Just as hyperinflation accelerated all social trends in swirling counter-currents of fresh liberation and new constraints, it also gave an almost explosive boost to female emancipation. Tough and athletic, quick-witted and sparklingly intelligent, the 'new woman' became a new social role model. Starting with the very highest social strata, where the fashionable attributes of tennis playing, car driving and writing counted for a lot, the rebellious daughters fought their way downwards. Praised and photographed a thousand times over in the illustrated magazines, the 'new woman' also impressed the girls who had to earn their money at typewriters in the cities, and in many respects created a hypermodern type of woman pointing far into the future, who found her goal in self-determination.

One of the more regrettable aspects of inflation was the rise of prostitution. It had nothing to do with emancipation but was ideally placed to bring the notion into disrepute. Sudden poverty forced even upper-class women on to the street. 'Now only amateurs practise prostitution, and in broad daylight,' Egon Erwin Kisch wrote from Berlin in August 1923:

> When I was leaving the café yesterday, a woman addressed me and told me that her husband was an interior designer, but that he had had no commissions and was ill. Could I go with her? I hadn't even answered when a girl stepped between us and tried to push the woman away. 'I have fabulous hair and a beautiful body . . .'[21]

There was an abundance of information on prostitution in the years of inflation, including tips and travel guides. Today, in Mel Gordon's *Voluptuous Panic: The Erotic World of Weimar Berlin*, one can read about which Berlin street offered which kind of prostitutes, from minors to pregnant women to the disabled.[22] How much of this was factually accurate and how much was lewd and voyeuristic exaggeration – widespread even at the time – is hard to tell.

Prostitutes acted as a handy real-life metaphor to contemporaries who were inclined, understandably enough, to see inflation as a moral decay in every respect. Left and right outdid one another in their scorn for a society that they saw as selling itself. Prostitutes can hardly have been painted as frequently in any age as they were in the interwar years, usually in a shockingly ugly way. They strut like greedy seagulls through the paintings of Otto Dix and George Grosz – overweight coquettes in the company of paunchy provincials. Others, cat-eyed and sharp-clawed, snuggle up to their black-tie-and-tailed patrons, playing the role of vulnerability. In the watercolours of the painter Jeanne Mammen, sarcastic gold-diggers eye the dancefloor in search of prey. Ferrety and pig-headed faces can be seen in Elfriede Lohse-Wächtler's pub paintings. These pictures contained a great deal of social criticism, a love–hate feeling for ugliness, but there was also a subliminal current of contempt for the Republic, particularly in the work of George Grosz, a mixture of arrogance and revulsion, a degree of disappointed idealism, but also a secret fascination with the perverse dressed up as critique. The bad ones were always other people. Everyone else was just looking.

The prostitute became an essential part of the scene in the 1920s; many people saw her as the face that lay behind the seductive mask of the 'new woman'. In Alfred Döblin's novel *Berlin Alexanderplatz* or Fritz Lang's film *Metropolis*, as the Great Whore of Babylon, she became the incarnation of the city, the symbol of a capitalism that had ended up in the moral gutter.

In his 1931 *Moral History of Inflation*, Hans Ostwald, a tireless observer of Berlin nightlife, assembled a series of set-pieces to form an image of the decadent 1920s. He described how, evening after evening, nocturnal strollers met up in the station waiting room of Berlin's Bahnhof Zoo – caught off guard by the closing time, they still wanted to spend the rest of the evening in the stylish way it had begun:

In lace and silk dresses, fur coats and tuxedos, the party crowd sat among the few weary travellers who didn't have enough money to spend the night in a hotel bed. The others, guests from Dollarica, the Dutch land of the Guilder, Russian émigrées dripping with jewellery, mingled stars from stage and screen, beside cheeky young inflation profiteers, banking apprentices and dollar spivs. Nearby, the heavily made-up dregs of the street jostled, most of them underage girls. It produced a noisy, shrieking image that had never been seen before in Berlin, and which has luckily disappeared again since.[23]

Does this 'deeply intertwined confusion of avarice, playfulness, lust for life and superficial pleasure' not recall the pictures of nightlife painted by Otto Dix and Gorge Grosz? And as if to emphasise the similarity with Dix, the cripple who is an inevitable part of the stereotype appears when Hans Ostwald continues:

> While the party raged under the railway arch, the war-wounded stood outside in the street offering matches or shoelaces for sale. Miserable street-corner tarts strolled around, unable to make enough to get them through the next day even by giving up their own bodies.[24]

The revulsion that many Germans felt at the sight of this tumultuous nightlife and partygoing had also to do with the dubious power of foreign currencies. For the British, the Americans or the French, Germany became a discount sale for prostitution. Some people came specially for the nightlife, particularly Americans tired of the strict rules of prohibition at home. Others bought their cut-price pleasure as an afterthought once they had done their business deals during the day. Germany was on sale in every respect – or that was what many shocked observers thought. Whole hordes of foreign shoppers came to buy up goods and take them away on a grand scale. Under the heading 'German export trade', the Berlin *Vossische Zeitung* – in October 1923 it was 5 million marks a copy – published two pages of small ads directed at foreign importers, sorted alphabetically by products, from A for Abziehbilder (stickers) to Z for Zeitschaltuhren (timers).

In the city centre alone, foreigners who could afford at best a two-room apartment on the outskirts of town became billionaires when they stepped off the train at Berlin's Anhalter Station and rented whole suites at the Excelsior Hotel. Newspapers published shocking depictions of their luxurious lives – 'glitzy parties, feasts, masquerades, balls, dance parties', at which the lady guests ostentatiously displayed their cheaply purchased pearls and furs.[25] The Viennese journalist Alfred Polgar, head of the features section of the left-liberal newspaper *Der neue Tag*, reported from Berlin on the foreigners' bad behaviour, including an American in the dining room of a luxury Berlin hotel practising his habit of whisking egg whites at a provocatively high volume: 'For ten or twenty minutes his spoon strikes the plate. The room shakes with the noise. And the pallid locals keep their heads down. It's as if the noise of victory is roaring above their heads.'[26] Humiliated, journalists wrote about how the foreigners gorged themselves at copiously laden tables, got drunk on the most expensive champagne and then availed themselves of the newly unemployed shorthand typists, now known as 'currency girls'.

The maelstrom of devaluation seemed to drag down with it everything that had once been cherished and expensive: loyalty and faith, morals, dowries, innocence, honour – it all disappeared down the drain of time. In an ecstatic trance, wildly shaking to the shimmy, in endless columns of now absurd zeros, Germany seemed to be hurtling towards the end like an out-of-control steam engine.

And then it juddered suddenly to a halt.

The turning point: 20 pfennigs = 120 billion marks

In November 1923 hyperinflation came to an end. Not overnight, and not as efficiently stage-managed as the 1948 currency reform 25 years later. But the 1923 forerunner of that intervention was effective and halted the decline surprisingly quickly. The decision was made by the second cabinet under Chancellor Gustav Stresemann, in the ninth government of the Weimar Republic (which was fast changing, driven by the social and economic turbulences of the previous years). One of the 'engineers' of the currency reform was the former bank director Hjalmar Schacht, who was appointed 'Reich currency commissioner' in November 1923, and a short time later president of the

Reichsbank. By establishing a second bank of issue, the 'Rentenbank', the government sensibly imposed a straitjacket on itself. From now on the Reichsbank and the Rentenbank, as the supreme financial authority, were able to oppose the printing of new money according to the wishes of ministers.

The Rentenmark, as it was known, was first issued on 15 November. On that day a single copy of the *Berliner Tageblatt* cost 50 billion marks. Two days later the paper was more than twice as expensive; but the crucial innovation was different. At the top of the front page of the daily newspaper, where the price always appeared, there was a second number: 'issue 20 pfennig = 120 billion mark'.

It was still little more than a claim, a hope. But it would be fulfilled. The whole secret of the Rentenmark was its rarity, strictly protected by the new Rentenbank. The Rentenmark was guaranteed by a series of mortgages on agricultural, industrial and commercial real estate. That cover was far from transparent, but the assurance that the sum was limited and controlled by the independent board of the Rentenbank gradually ensured a minimum degree of confidence, without which no national economy can flourish. That confidence took hold, even though the end of hyperinflation was as incomprehensible to most Germans as its origins. It was a confidence in credit, borrowed from misery. Hardly enough in itself to ease the general sense of insecurity.

On 20 November 1923 the fixed exchange rate was announced: for 1 trillion in paper marks, the Germans received 1 Rentenmark. The unit betrays the randomness of the measure; the plan was to make it easy for people to calculate. Now they only had to delete 12 zeros from the old currency and they had the sum in new marks. That clearly showed what people had known for a long time: they were poor and their financial assets had gone up in smoke. But the freefall seemed to have been halted. From now on people would have to learn to calculate using small sums and even take care of pfennigs.

Calculating became easier, but at the same time it was harder to keep an eye on the political situation. The Social Democrats still emerged from the Reichstag elections in December 1924 as the strongest party, but they were in opposition when the government was formed. A right-wing bourgeois block, including the ultra-conservative German National People's Party, the DNVP, formed the government. The election result reflected real shifts in power. The fact that bankers had gained considerably more power over the government as a result of the currency reform signalled a transfer of political weight in favour of the old elites. They enforced a tough course of austerity. Many civil servants were dismissed, and social welfare spending was cut. It was another few months before the economy recovered to a degree that everyone could see. Politically, though, the Republic did stabilise, albeit with chaos never very far away.

A putsch in Munich by Hitler, now the leader of the National Socialist German Workers' Party (*Nationalsozialistische Deutsche Arbeiterpartei* or NSDAP), was defeated in November 1923; in spite of its 20 victims it still had a folkloric ring to it, with its beery origins in the smoke-swathed Bürgerbräukeller, and with Hitler's call to 'march on the sinful Babylon of Berlin', which was halted by the police only a few hours later at Odeonsplatz. In the rest of the Reich the excitement subsided after a day, and the Munich disturbances (later known as the Beer Hall Putsch) came to seem like only one uprising among many. A month before, communist putsches had been attempted in the states of Thuringia and Saxony, as part of the wider plan of the 'German October', a plan by the Executive Committee of the Communist International to attempt a revolution across the Weimar Republic; in Saxony revolution had only been averted when the Reich government proclaimed a state of emergency and deposed the head of the regional government.

Against this background of chaos, Gustav Stresemann, who was chancellor for three and a half months from August 1923, managed to launch the initial phase of currency reform during his brief time in office. The main reason for this accomplishment was his gift for foreign policy. Currency reform was only possible as the result of a change in the relationship with the victorious powers. Stresemann persuaded the majority of Germans to abandon their passive resistance against the occupation of the Ruhr and convinced them to tolerate his intention to seek dialogue with the French. At the same time he talked the French into reducing reparation demands to something approaching a realistic level. When the victorious powers abandoned their impossible requirements, a willingness to engage rationally in economics increased – and with it the chance to break the spiral of hyperinflation through drastic economising measures.

While Stresemann was only chancellor for those few turbulent months, he was foreign minister in the cabinets that followed. He was striking and unforgettable in appearance –unsettlingly large, rather staring eyes, a bullish yet sensitive physique. The 'tree frog', as the centrist politician Matthias Erzberger called him, became the face of a new Germany that was ready for peace. Hated by far-right extremists as a compliant *Erfüllungspolitiker* – literally 'fulfilment politician' – less obstinate political commentators saw him as one of the Republic's very few figures capable of achieving integration.

Stresemann, the son of a Berlin pub landlord (or *Budiker*) who ran a small wheat beer company, soon became a clerk with the Association of German Chocolate Manufacturers after writing his dissertation on 'The Development of the Berlin Bottled Beer Business', and proved to be a cunning political tactician as well as an inspiring speaker. Having become chair of the liberal *Deutsche Volkspartei* (German People's Party) soon after the war, Stresemann became a master at forging coalitions, an art that was looked down upon by most Germans, even though in view of the government's fragmented majority it was urgently needed. Among hardliners a willingness to compromise was seen not as a virtue but a weakness; Stresemann, on the other hand, made it his passion. Personally somewhat conservative, he was among the 'rational republicans' who derived a great deal from pluralism even though their hearts really beat for the monarchy. His forms of communication were as elegant and pragmatic as his clothes. The 'Stresemann' look – striped trousers, black jacket, waistcoat, turned-up short collars – replaced the traditional need to switch from business suit to formal evening wear: you could now hurry from office to party without changing your clothes.

Gustav Stresemann, Chancellor in 1923 and then Foreign Minister until his death in 1929, suffered under the widespread contempt for diplomatic activity: 'We cannot be polite and loveable without immediately coming under attack from our own people'.

Stresemann liked to break down hardened attitudes by putting himself in the shoes of his adversary and aligning their perspective with his own. For militarists this was seen as high treason. Stresemann tacked back and forth between different attitudes and knew how to present himself as an ally to opposing forces. It didn't always go well, but he managed to win back trust, loosen the stranglehold of the Versailles Treaty and bring Germany back on to the diplomatic stage.[27] Few people thanked him. He explained to his party: 'I have a sense that we Germans have too little understanding or none at all for what the French call fine gestures. It doesn't come naturally to us at all, and it does us great harm internationally. We cannot be polite and loveable without immediately coming under attack from our own people. We cannot practise global politics with the idea that nobody is to associate with those other fellows in any way.'[28]

It was only when he died of a stroke in 1929 that the hole he left became apparent. 'More than a loss: a disaster!' was the headline in the *Vossische Zeitung*, followed by four pages of mourning. Stresemann embodied the communicative virtues that were threateningly lacking from the Weimar Republic. To that extent he was an exception, a 'lonely man', as the historian Arthur Rosenberg rightly said, who had neither a clique nor a mass organisation behind him, and who was constantly losing the support of his rightward-drifting party. Nonetheless he managed to put the pieces in place for Germany's consolidation.

The victorious powers and Germany negotiated a moderate payment plan for reparations – the Dawes Plan, named after Charles Dawes, the American chair of the international Reparations Commission. This allowed Germany to re-join the circle of stable and creditworthy nations. The French withdrew from the Rhineland, foreign investors gradually returned and long-term business planning began once more. The temporary Rentenmark could be jettisoned and replaced by the Reichsmark, which was now backed by gold and foreign currencies. From mid-1924 the economy enjoyed another boom, an incredibly powerful one from 1925 onwards. Germany became a member of the League of Nations; in 1926 Stresemann was awarded the Nobel Peace Prize along with his French colleague Aristide Briand.

Hurtling again, but upwards this time

With the end of hyperinflation the Republic entered a phase of prosperity. The period between 1924 and 1929 forms the core of what has gone down in history as the 'Roaring Twenties', the 'Années Folles' or the 'Goldene Zwanziger'. The upheavals they went through were a phenomenon common to the whole Western world, but in Germany they enjoyed a special heyday, a myth that has been endlessly retold and re-examined because of its terrible ending.

What would it bring, the new money, the new age? On New Year's Eve 1924, by which time the upturn had become impossible to ignore, the *Berliner Tageblatt* drew up a provisional balance sheet. About 50 per cent of what was possible had already been achieved, the leader writer Erich Dombrowski wrote: 50 per cent of pre-war perform- ance, 50 per cent of export, 50 per cent of trade tonnage. And, he continued, matters were advancing quickly: 'With the Zeppelin mir- acle that surprised America, and with the rotor ship that heralds a revolution in energy utilisation, the German spirit has achieved great conquests all around the world.'[29] But all of that was still not enough. The article closed with the mysterious words: 'Of greater import- ance are moral conquests in the world. With those it is best to start closer to home.'[30]

Moral conquests? The liberal *Tageblatt* saw the young Republic as being in a moral vacuum. Leader writer Dombrowski feared above all that a strengthening of conservative forces might intensify the class struggle once again, via unbridled egoism from above. 'Quiver- ing with excitement', the Junkers (large landowners from Prussia) and big businessmen would make a grab for power: 'The purses of the big landowners and heavy industrialists, left so thin after inflation, are now on the way to being filled once more, at the expense of the rest of the population.'[31]

The article expressed the concern among liberals that after the end of the great coalition of the SPD and the Centre Party, the narrow layer of citizens loyal to the state might be crushed in the conflict between capital and labour. But the concept of 'moral conquest' rep- resented something even bigger than that. Hyperinflation had left an empty, uncertain terrain in people's understanding of their own lives, one that needed to be explored, measured or 'reconquered'. Many people felt that this was the case, but they did so in different ways. How was that vacuum to be filled? Theories of salvation were at a premium. Obscure theses and conspiracy theories went flying around. Clairvoyance boomed, along with experiments in psycho- kinesis and esotericism. New crazes constantly appeared on the horizon, promising miracles out of nothing.[32]

Some people expected lasting peace to come from international stamp collecting, others fought furiously for shorthand reform, which was bound to revolutionise the notion of efficiency. Far Eastern religions were studied, itinerant preachers travelled the land calling for a change in behaviour, for naked bathing, for a national rebirth, a spiritual revolution, a herbal diet and a return to the innermost German spirit. 'Saints of hyperinflation' such as Friedrich Muck-Lamberty, the 'Messiah of Thuringia', collected thousands of young followers in his *Neue Schar* (New Flock), moving like the pied piper of Hamelin from town to town, setting up camp wherever they went. Muck-Lamberty's huge wandering commune practised arts and crafts and free love, and gained enormous publicity. Another guru, Louis Haeuser, the 'Saviour of Bönnigheim', mocked his sinful disciples as 'travelling toilets' and 'rotting charnel-houses'[33] – but still didn't get rid of them. Robert Musil identified an 'inspiring fever' as a symptom of the age, one that euphorically heightened the emotions and expectations associated with improving the world:

> Something went through the thicket of beliefs in those days like a single wind bending many trees – a spirit of heresy and reform, the blessed sense of an arising and going forth, a mini-renaissance and reformation, such as only the best of times experience; whoever entered the world then felt, at the first corner, the breath of this spirit on his cheek.[34]

The bottomless plunge in the value of money had swept away the last certainties that remained after the abdication of the kaiser and the overthrow of the old world. A question mark hung over every tradition, and nothing offered stability apart from the hope associated with the future and large-scale plans.[35] Unrestrained by any kind of certainty, both worries and feelings of joy were wildly over-dramatised. A destructive zeal and a feeling of vertigo went hand in hand: 'The old world is in decay, its joints are creaking. I want to help to smash it. I believe in the new life. I want to help to build it,'[36] cheered the dancer Valeska Gert. And how was she going to do that? By dancing, more eccentrically than anything anyone had ever seen before. That too was viewed as a contribution to the changing times:

Valeska Gert 'dances out the unbornness of the present day, its wild, fantastical and exaggerated sensitivity', an enthusiastic critic wrote in *Sport im Bild*.[37]

The Germans were seized by a profound desire for renewal. It gripped every area of life and was directed equally at waste management reform and the renewal of critical epistemology. Everything needed examination, even the structures of thought and feeling themselves, of concepts, of reason. The impulse towards extreme radicalism lived in everything from barefoot prophets to the religious fervour of the members of the Bauhaus group of designers and architects, from the earth-shaking challenges of psychology and nuclear physics to the logical abysses in the philosophies of Ludwig Wittgenstein and Martin Heidegger: rethink the world! Or pull it down: the author Wolfram Eilenberger accurately describes Heidegger as a 'conceptual wrecking ball'.[38] Heidegger was one of many with that particular enthusiasm; the next chapter, which deals with demolition and rebuilding, will show as much.

The economy took a powerful upward turn in 1925, but the uncertainty remained. Hyperinflation had erased internal traditions, deleted established certainties in people and liquidated their collected troves of experience. By laying waste to people's identities, it made room for the various concepts of the 'New Human Being'. Whatever one imagined the term to mean, one was free to express and imagine it as one wished. So insecure were most people about their experiences that they put up little resistance to even the boldest visions. The decade belonged to the young, to high spirits, to thoughtlessness. They were the ones who had seized their chance during hyperinflation, not older people with their traditional virtues such as caution and thrift. As the value of the currency rose, the worth of experience declined. People could no longer rely on themselves, but they had nothing else.

When Walter Benjamin looked back on those years in 1933, he dressed up the most important possession that human beings possess in the language of the stock exchange:

Experience has fallen in value. And it looks as if it is about to fall into bottomlessness. With the First World War a process began to become apparent which has not halted since then. [. . .] And there was nothing remarkable about that. [. . .] For never has experience been contradicted so thoroughly as strategic experience by tactical warfare, economic experience by inflation, bodily experience by [hunger], moral experience by those in power. A generation that had gone to school on a horse-drawn streetcar now stood under the open sky in a countryside in which nothing remained unchanged but the clouds, and beneath these clouds, in a field of force of destructive torrents and explosions, was the tiny, fragile human body.[39]

So frail and yet heroic, so falsely humble and falsely modest, the projection of a future that was either gloomy or a bright new dawn; that was how the artists of the *Neue Sachlichkeit* (New Objectivity) movement painted the New Human Being, how the communists dreamed of them, the technocrats imagined them and racists fetishised them. The New Human Being became an idée fixe, in various styles of clothing and with various kinds of equipment. And the New Humans repeatedly divested themselves of everything. Naked gymnastics became the fashion, naked dancing, physical exercise in the open air. Inspired by a will to sobriety, stripped of all décor, modern human beings wanted to have a sense of themselves in all their vulnerable physicality.

The chair that corresponded precisely to this sense of self was about to be invented. The cantilever chair would become the symbol of the age.

3

Extreme Living

Let us want, dream, create together the new building of the future, which
will be everything in one form: architecture and sculpture and painting,
which will rise towards the heavens from millions of hands of craftsmen,
the crystalline symbol of a new coming faith.

Walter Gropius, 'Bauhaus Manifesto', 1919

In the Bauhaus house

'Death to everything fusty!' the architect Bruno Taut proclaimed in 1920. The 40-year-old was not yet the famous builder of large-scale Berlin housing estates, but he had already been able to erect a garden city for ordinary people in Magdeburg and the 'Tuschkastensiedlung' – Paint-Box Estate – in Berlin, so called because of its bright colours. Bruno Taut had bigger dreams, but in the meantime he had to pay the rent with second jobs, for example by designing stage sets or publishing the journal *Frühlicht* (Morning Light). In the magazine, he published visions of the 'New Building', and gave free rein to his revolutionary energy: 'Away with the sourpusses, the dopes and the miseries, the always self-important frowners!' Away with the 'gravestone and cemetery facades outside four-storey junk stores and bric-a-brac markets! Smash the shell-limestone Doric, Ionic and Corinthian columns, smash all the ludicrous fakery!'.[1] With puritanical rage, these words were directed at the historical stucco facades of the *Gründerzeit* ('the age of the founders' in the 1870s, when an economic boom at the beginning of the German Empire led to an ornate triumphalism in architecture), the 'buffonery', which shaped the face of cities at the time. Taut wanted those facades knocked from the walls as soon as possible: 'Down with the elegance of sandstone and mirrored windows, smash to pieces the marble and fine wood junk, on the rubbish heap with all the trash!'[2]

And he wanted to chuck the thinking that had led to such monstrosities on the rubbish heap as well:

Oh! Our concepts: space, home, style! Ugh! How those concepts stink! Tear them up, break them down! Nothing should be left of them. Scatter their schools, send the professorial wigs flying, we'll play catch with them. [. . .] Death to everything fusty! Death to everything that means titles, dignity, authority!

Impossible not to think of the slogan of the anti-authoritarian revolt of 1968: 'Under the gowns the mildew of a thousand years.' But we mustn't imagine that Bruno Taut and his comrades-in-arms didn't have positive things in mind as well – his treatise ends with a lot of cheering: 'Our morning gloss in the distance. [. . .] Hail to transparency, to clarity! Hail to purity! Hail to crystal! And hail and hail again to all that is flowing, graceful, angular, sparkling, flashing, light – hail to eternal building!'[3]

That's Bruno Taut in a state of euphoria. Taut was actually a man of moderation and the middle way who wanted to make 'big architecture for little people' and – unlike many of his colleagues in 'New Building' – was able to take into consideration what might be seen as the petit-bourgeois need for comfort. He saw himself with his pickaxe at the front of a historic battle for architectural authenticity, borne aloft on a sparkling, flashing upcurrent of enthusiasm. The new was to come into the world as something eternal: detoxified, pure, liberated from all superficial trappings.

The functionalism of the Bauhaus was also celebrated with religious fervour. In 1919, a year after the end of the war, the architect Walter Gropius, supported by the painter Lyonel Feininger, formulated the founding manifesto of the Bauhaus:

Let us want, dream, create together the new building of the future, which will be everything in one form: architecture and sculpture and painting, which will rise towards the heavens from millions of hands of craftsmen, the crystalline symbol of a new coming faith.[4]

'Rethink everything from the ground up' – Gropius relied on the fundamental radicalism of so many innovative movements in the 1920s.

His appeal to found a new kind of learning community ignited. Reprinted in many newspapers, it was followed by painters, architects, sculptors, designers, typographers and photographers – famous artists who had no interest in teaching *ex cathedra*, but instead wanted to shape the future with their students in workshops: Johannes Itten, Gerhard Marcks, Paul Klee, Oskar Schlemmer, Wassily Kandinsky, and later followed by László Moholy-Nagy, Josef Albers and many others. They weren't just concerned with making a clearly designed lamp or a contemporary chair, but with a renewal of lifestyles, developed out of a community that wanted to live together almost as intensely as a commune. Their sense of mission was aggressive, their range of subjects all-encompassing. They were concerned with the entire building, from the whole down to the tiniest detail, seen as a unit, from the ground plan to the door handles, the coffee cups and even the chess set that stood on the plain table – everything was reduced to its elementary function. The knight in the Bauhaus chess set was no longer a gorgeously carved horse, but an angular lump that visibly showed what moves could be made with it: forward and then off to the side at a right angle. The bishop wasn't a slender messenger, but an X-shaped lump that represented its diagonal paths. Reduced to the geometrical distillate of their movement, the Bauhaus chess figures dismissed centuries of history of precious carved figures as knick-knacks – the sublime, they argued, was always simple.

Collaboration between the individual arts in the Bauhaus was what we would call 'interdisciplinary' today; the Bauhaus members strove for 'spiritual unity', based on a shared understanding of good crafts and the willingness to respond to mutual influence and criticism. Such fundamentally different characters as the ironic dreamer

Paul Klee, the advertising designer Herbert Bayer, the dogmatic esoteric colour theorist Johannes Itten and the dance-machinist Oskar
Schlemmer made common cause: the individual arts should find
their way back 'from their lonely separation into the lap of the all-
encompassing art of building'.[5] The prospect of coming close to the
spirit of the new in a community of students and teachers, and the
certainty of being able to shape the changing times, led all these
avowed artists to break away from the spheres of their previous lives
and come together in Weimar. The city was open to them, because
the Academy of Art and the College of Applied Art (devoted to the
avant-garde under the direction of Henry van de Velde), both closed
in the war, were in need of revival.

The initial idea was almost a redemptive one: the Feininger drawing that decorates the 1919 Bauhaus manifesto shows a church in the
middle of an electric storm of lines and stars – the cathedral of the
future as a glorious building of flashing thoughts. In spite of its
delight in the future, the Bauhaus philosophy also yearned for the
past, for a pre-bourgeois time in which the biggest building projects
were undertaken communally by the best craftspeople and artists.
Like the medieval site hut in which builders had once gathered for
the pious intention of cathedral building, similarly minded people
were now to come together in living and working communities to
'prepare the cathedral of freedom of the future'.[6]

So high the tone, so sober the result. It's therefore entirely consist-
ent that the cathedral of freedom should have looked very cubic in
the end, quite bare and at first glance quite monotonous in appearance. The maxim of thinking anew from the ground up led to a
return to the fundamental forms of design. When it worked, the
results could be entirely breathtaking. The Haus am Horn, the MT8
lights of Wilhelm Wagenfeld, Marianne Brandt's silver teapot or
Josef Albers's nest of tables were quintessential: in their simplicity
they went straight to the heart – their reduction, balance and harmony were enchanting. The editors of the journal *Uhu*, when they
saw a *Neue Sachlichkeit* chair by the Rasch brothers, were reminded of
a poem by the nonsense poet Christian Morgenstern: 'When I sit, I

don't want to sit as my bottom might wish, but as my sitting-mind might, should it sit, weave the chair.'[7]

The best Bauhaus pieces, which have rightly been remembered, look almost alive, spiritually charged in spite of their ascetic coolness. 'Ever bolder means of design' were Gropius's goal, 'in order floatingly to overcome the earthbound in effect and appearance.'[8] The flat functionalist that his adversaries saw in him would hardly have spoken in that way.

At the Bauhaus they were hypermodern and mystical at the same time. They went on diets featuring Icelandic moss pudding and cold garlic bowls, they did breathing exercises together and engaged in ritual naked dances on the Ilm Meadows. Johannes Itten, for example, a Bauhaus master from the earliest days, a bald, monastic figure on the Tibetan model, was a devotee of Mazdaznan, a Zoroastrian-Christian-Hindu mixed religion that had many devotees in the back-to-the-land *Lebensreform* movement and had also fallen on fertile soil in Weimar. The Bauhaus people were not enemies of pleasure; their parties were legendary and were celebrated extravagantly. During the poor post-war years, if they did not have enough to eat in the Bauhaus canteen, they would often push the tables together and dance to banish their hunger. And they often lay casually on the floor together; the Bauhaus archive is full of photographs revealing an almost hippie-like abandon.

The conservative burghers of Weimar, whose pride in their beautiful city was based on its prestigious past, felt that such behaviour was a thorn in their eye. There was much mockery in the local press, and there were actual attacks on students and police operations for supposedly unseemly incidents. Far-right agitators stirred up the city's craftsmen by telling them that the Bauhaus planned to cheat them out of their meagre commissions with industrial, serial constructions. In 1925, after countless quarrels, the new right-wing regional government managed to expel the Bauhaus. The teaching body and the students moved to Dessau, which was governed by the Social Democrats. Within only 15 months they had built the new school building, world famous even today, with its neighbouring masters' houses.

There was no shortage of conflicts between the independent-minded characters. Tensions were particularly bad between the esoteric bohemian monk Itten and the rationalist Gropius. Apart from mental differences, there were also political consequences: Gropius saw his efforts to win the trust of the public as being threatened by Itten's freakish behaviour. After his dismissal, the school became more technical and marketing oriented, while the libertarian aspect remained, at least outwardly. The Bauhaus still attracted many forward-looking women in the expectation that equality was being taken seriously there. At first more women enrolled than men. That did not suit Walter Gropius at all, however; he was concerned that the high proportion of women might damage the reputation of the art school and further reinforce the widespread view that the Bauhaus was a Bolshevik madhouse. For fear of the reservations of his financiers, he passed a decree reducing the proportion of women to a maximum of a third. But it was not only pressure from outside. Many of the Bauhaus men did not think the women capable of outstanding achievements, and when those achievements were forthcoming they envied them their success all the more. Women students were relegated to photography class or the weaving mill. Oskar Schlemmer's bullying line became popular: 'Where there's wool there's a woman who weaves, if only to pass the time.'[9]

Perhaps as an act of defiance, the Bauhaus weaving mill became one of the most innovative parts of the school, or at least one of the most lucrative. Within a few years Gunta Stöll rose from being a student to the director of the mill, with her tapestries and blankets that wove geometrical planes of colour into fascinating textile landscapes, turning the Bauhaus into an economic success that assured its survival. She was never officially thanked.

Friedl Dicker developed many well-known pieces of Bauhaus furniture, and later a child-centred style of architecture for kindergartens; Katt Both designed inexpensive small apartments to ease the housing shortage; Michiko Yamawaki brought a genre-atypical severity to collage making; Grete Stern contributed significantly to the renewal of advertising graphics and advertising photography; and

Marianne Brandt posthumously received the highest price that was ever paid for a small Bauhaus object – $361,000 at Sotheby's for her 1927 metal teapot.[10] Alma Buscher developed a lot of furniture for the Haus am Horn, which would be existentially important for the school, since it was at the centre of the highly regarded first Bauhaus exhibition. Her Wurfpuppen (bendy dolls made of string) were dreamy children's toys, and her wooden building blocks for children formed arches with different radii that allowed for fantastical constructions. As the Bauhaus photographer, Lucia Moholy made a considerable contribution to the publicity for the school. Without her the memory of the Bauhaus would not be anything like as present as it is today. But her photographs were published almost entirely uncredited. She would later have bitter arguments about her copyright with Walter Gropius and his wife Ise.

Compared with normal architectural art academies the Bauhaus was a haven of free spiritedness, but when it came to hard economic interests and public recognition, many of the Bauhaus men fought unfairly for their old pre-eminence. For Bauhaus women, the birth of a child meant the end of a career; Gropius and the other leading figures lacked the social imagination for the compatibility of family and work. Even so, for the young female students and artists who had come here from all over the Republic, the Bauhaus must have been a wonderful place compared with the obstacles that ambitious women usually faced. There can have been few other institutions that left such a mountain of original photographs of confident, unconventional and happily collaborating women.[11]

These pictures can seem almost startlingly contemporary. They don't show the bobbed women that immediately let us know we are looking at women of the 1920s and apply a corresponding patina, but strong individuals who look as if they have just come down the steps of a Berlin Academy of Arts. They were original young women who had liberated themselves radically from the constricting bonds of their often provincial origins and of the age. Looking at these pictures, you sense how little separates us from them. The reason lies in their risk taking. As we flick through the Bauhaus photograph album

The weaving class in the Bauhaus in Dessau 1927–28, photographed by T. Lux Feiniger. On the left, the master and fabric designer Gunta Stölzl. The fabric class was looked down upon by male Bauhaus teachers, but was the most financially successful. (Estate of T. Lux Feininger)

a hundred years later, we actually feel as if we have burst the fetters of time – or done so again. For one unreal moment they have arrived in the here and now.

'We actually live like pigs, terribly thoughtlessly'

The Bauhaus was serious about the revolution and brought it into the sitting room. Today it's hard for us to imagine the challenge presented by the reduction of forms to a fundamental minimum. It was about much more than stylistic issues. It was about the chance to bring the atmosphere of general upheaval into the private sphere.

In many illustrated magazines, under headlines such as 'How would you like to live?', there were juxtapositions of old and new. On the left the familiar, traditional sitting room: a dense thicket in its mixture of styles, gloomy, cosy, with soft upholstery. On the right, a spartan nothing, bare steel tube furniture in a white Bauhaus cube. This was usually followed on the next few pages by the external view of the building, also as a pro and contra. On the left a playful villa with hip roof, dormer and oriel windows, and shutters. On the right a sober white box with a flat roof and large unprotected windows: the minimalist dwelling of the new age. Essentially a shell, only smoothed and whitewashed.

Reduction to the elementary forms of rectangle, triangle and circle was a declaration of war against everything that had hitherto been associated with a successful, comfortable life.

A 1927 poster for the Deutsche Werkbund – an association of artists, designers, architects and industrialists – showed an opulent historical sitting room, which still served as a model for many Germans. It was firmly crossed out in red.[12] 'Away with it!' the representatives of the New Design demanded.

They plainly had a lot of work ahead of them. It would be a mistake to imagine the interior of the houses of the Weimar Republic as all having been furnished by the Bauhaus. In most apartments, 1925 looked like 1890, like Kaiserreich (the period of the German Empire, 1871–1918), like plush and knick-knacks. Let's take the apartment of the silent film star Asta Nielsen at Kaiserallee 203 in Berlin. In 1924, anyone without the good fortune to be invited to visit could look at her apartment in some photographs in the magazine *Die Dame*.[13] It was like flicking through a kind of art museum, a wild and magnificent rollercoaster of taste. The soberest objects of all were the medieval wooden sculptures, devout figures of the saints, which loomed plaintively out from among the trinketry of later centuries. Meanwhile, Madame de Pompadour would have approved of the wildly ornamented, bulging and over-upholstered chaise-longue in the parlour.

It was an apartment from which even the owner had to take the occasional break. Asta Nielsen's summerhouse on Hiddensee was a paragon of frugality, a place where her overstretched senses were able to recover. In her Berlin home all the items of furniture were precious originals, bought at great expense at an antiques market. But most people had similar things in their sitting rooms, albeit as copies: factory-quality neo-Baroque. Whether it was cheap or expensive, for most people in the early 1920s cosiness meant being surrounded by history, living among traditional forms, however loudly the advocates of New Living shouted, 'Death to the fusty!' But it nagged away at them regardless. Was living among the opulent décor of the past really still as comfortable as people had believed it to be for decades? Doubts were growing among the residents.

People felt that they had been left behind. Revolution and the shock of inflation had changed everything. Supposedly valuable things were starting to look threadbare. What had previously looked merely velvety now looked slightly musty; what had seemed valuable now looked weird. Widespread talk of spiritual homelessness was more than a phrase; many people no longer felt that their own apartments were still welcoming, and the red X that the Werkbund had painted over their sitting room had started them thinking: perhaps this really was junk? A profound change in taste that would continue for over two generations began to take hold of people. Décor that had looked pleasing a moment ago now looked like a tumour.

Historicism had led people to decorate their apartments as a 'table of contents of their education', the architecture critic Adolf Behne wrote in the publishing company Ullstein's pioneering magazine *Uhu*.[14] Under the headline 'Carefree rooms', the author argued that everything superfluous should be banished from apartments; he himself had even removed all the artworks from the walls.

> Our apartment no longer needs to be museum, theatre and church, not even a place for display. We no longer want it to demonstrate our personality. The more rich, fantastical, romantic our lives, the more self-evident, peaceful and simple our four walls should be.[15]

Because it lacked originality, historicism had developed a curious form of greed. It had constantly piled new copies of past styles on top of each other, so that the lack of discrimination had gradually become its essence. Every gap had to be filled with trinkets that in some way looked as if they came 'from a long time ago'.

'Yes, we actually live like swine, terribly thoughtlessly,' Bertolt Brecht has one of his characters say in a satire on Bauhaus architecture as he is being led wide-eyed through one such modern dwelling.[16] Only a few years before, the character had still been lying in the mud in Arras with his fellow-soldier, and now that same comrade is hosting him in a setting without so much as a speck of dust. A few whiskies later, however, he runs rampage in the sterile Bauhaus building because 'he felt within himself a depthless desire for as many things ill-matched, illogical and natural as possible'.[17]

The advocates of the Bauhaus style had a different view. They claimed that the superabundance found in ordinary apartments took their inhabitants to the edge not only aesthetically, but practically too. In their desperate efforts to keep their cluttered surroundings clean, they had become slaves to their apartments. Very few already had one of the newly invented vacuum cleaners, but they also had huge quantities of carpets, runners, footstools and sofas. Most of the dust was only being redistributed and swept from one end of the apartment to the other.

For the 'New Person', this was not a species-appropriate setting, neither ideal nor hygienic. The modern human being cultivated a new sense of the body, trained in sports and gymnastics, that no longer matched the old-style dwellings. They had had enough of *sinking* into upholstery, *immersing* themselves in an apartment and being *wrapped* in an atmosphere. They wanted to put themselves on display – even in their apartment they wanted to be the fighter that the present demanded, to tower as a person who no longer wanted to hide in the past.

After experiments with wood slat constructions and rigid steel tubes, Marcel Breuer, born in Hungary in 1902 and only 23 years old, director of the factory workshop at the Dessau Bauhaus, invented a 'back-leg-free chair' on which one could bob up and down slightly. Traditional armchairs, soft and low, encouraged sedentary behaviour.

On the cantilever or 'Freischwinger' (free-swinging) chair, its later name, one sat as if about to spring, ready at any moment to catapult oneself back into active life. This matched the demeanor of the athletic person of 1925. Even when sitting, a certain physical tension was preserved – the sitter was springily at rest, keeping their balance and sensing their strength. It was built for people who wanted to retain some degree of movement even when seated.

The cantilever chair displayed the person in the empty space. Because one could transform one's own strength into energy while sitting on it, one felt as if one were on a kind of sitting machine, ideally suited to a space that the architects of the New Building liked to refer to as a 'machine for living'. It matched the intensely nervous mood of the era. And it also looked strikingly elegant – the epitome of modern living even today, copied and varied many times over, most recently by IKEA's Poäng chair.

But a piece of furniture like that isn't designed overnight, and not by one person. It was the result of years of work in the workshop, with many preliminary stages and the mutual influence of several designers. In the end, three designers were able to claim the cantilever for themselves: Marcel Breuer, Mies van der Rohe and Mart

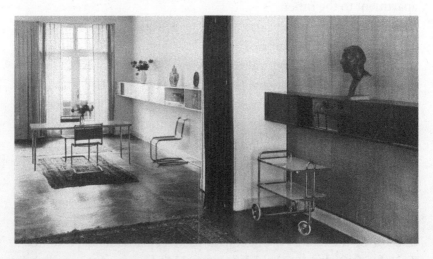

Bauhaus interior by architect and designer Marcel Breuer. With cantilever chairs, for people who wanted to be fast even when they were sitting down.

Stam. The copyright row that developed among these like-minded people is interesting even today.[18] Cooperation and competition were contradictory principles that offered the Bauhaus and its kindred spirits both solidarity and explosive material, creating a unique psychodynamic.

Apart from anything else, Gropius and his people were engineers of fame. They were geniuses at PR, masters of lobbying as well as marketing, advertising and corporate design. The Bauhaus logo, their own series of books, an unmistakeable formal language in layout and typography, and public presence in every artistic sphere, even the theatre, ensured that everything that looks ascetic and functional is called Bauhaus even today.

Door to door – new building for the urban masses

There was one sphere of society that couldn't have cared less whether a bit of stucco was stuck somewhere, or what spirit might have woven a particular chair. This sector was happy to have a roof over its head. In the poor quarters of the cities people were crammed tightly together, and viruses and bacteria had a heyday. It was damp and dirty, and strangers would often sleep in the same bed in succession. If a person left the house, in many cases a 'sleeping buddy' would come in and slip by arrangement under the still-warm blanket, before disappearing again when the first person came back. The same was true of the bathtub, if one had such a thing. The water in a tub would have to do for the whole family; the last one in would bathe in cold, dirty water.

In many apartments in rundown rental blocks there were conditions of almost indescribable squalor. Between 1901 and 1920 one Berlin medical insurance company carried out investigations into housing conditions in Berlin's working-class districts and documented them in 175 photographs that give a shattering insight into the spaces in which many people had to live. Full of junk, damp and unhealth. Because there was no money for cupboards, the contents of the households were strewn all over the place, clothes hung on nails on the walls of the rooms, washing dried on lines stretched across the rooms. Mothers sat at the only available tables, sewing sacks for money. There weren't enough chairs for the residents, so people lay about on mattresses and got on each other's nerves. In every third Berlin house there was a pub, where many people sought refuge in alcohol. But only the men – in proletarian pubs, unlike the bars in the middle-class districts, women were distinguished by their scarcity.

Everywhere there were people coughing, wheezing and sweating with fever. Sleeping sickness, tuberculosis and, above all, Spanish flu with its millions of fatalities had taught people to fear the modern varieties of pestilence. Heinrich Zille's insight that people can be killed not only with an axe but also with an apartment was doubly true. Criminality in these districts was viral; the cramped conditions did encourage a feeling of solidarity, but to an even greater extent fostered violence. In the Weimar Republic that was a source of considerable anxiety. In 1925 the liberal philosopher and author Theodor Lessing, in his semi-documentary essay about the mass murderer Fritz Haarmann, described one such place of social sickness. Haarmann, 'the cannibal', who killed and dismembered 24 boys and young men in a bestial manner, lived in a rundown part of the old city of Hanover, a 'breeding ground for lightless generations, jaundiced with poverty, breathing in decay and mildew, cursed to misery'.[19] In many larger cities parts of the medieval centres had been neglected, and now, in buildings that might from a distance have seemed picturesque, provided accommodation for the poorest of the poor:

In the evening, when the moon hung over the rotting roofs and grey chimney stacks and cast a silver light on the ghostly black river, the heavy, thin, exhausted, overworked suffering humanity emerged from their old boxes and hung and crouched over the stinking lagoon.[20]

It was not the age of these districts that was problematic, but their overpopulation. Whether the houses were four decades old or dated from the fifteenth century, the effect was the same; it was as if they were flooded with misery. Half a million people didn't even have a roof over their heads.[21] And pressure on the cities was growing. More and more people were turning their back on the country and trying their luck in the crowded metropolises. The problem couldn't be solved, but it could be eased.

Building was needed, on a scale too great for private clients. In the first years after the war, housebuilding was still stagnating, but with the introduction of the tax on inherited housing in 1925 the state created an instrument for an active construction policy. This meant that old buildings were taxed and the income used for the construction of new buildings. All over the country, charitable construction companies were set up, undertaking massive building projects. After 1924 half of all dwellings were built by charities, in Frankfurt over 90 per cent.[22] A boom began in the building of social housing and satellite towns. The authorities really had a slog ahead of them if the cities weren't to let people in the lowest-income brackets suffocate in misery. A slog meant: cheap building on a mass scale and in the shortest possible time. Lined up in rigid rows, set on green-field sites, built with serially produced prefabricated construction elements, countless thousands of apartments were produced under extremely high pressure – a huge accomplishment by the state, all the more remarkable when you consider that the German government can't get a grip on the catastrophic housing shortage we face in the present day. In Berlin alone, 146,000 dwellings were built between 1925 and 1931. By way of comparison: in the six years between 2013 and 2019, in spite of similarly high demand, 91,140 new flats were constructed.[23] In Frankfurt it was the architect and city planner Ernst May who was responsible for the construction of 12,000 new homes between 1925 and 1930. They were tiny but practical, often with a little garden in front for the purposes of self-sufficiency. Price controls made uniformity inevitable, although under certain circumstances it was possible to introduce a certain degree of originality. In Zickzackhausen on Bruchfeldstrasse in Frankfurt, two dozen three-storey cubes were built in a zigzag pattern (as the name suggests), rather than being erected in the usual dull row. The whole thing looked as if a god had not thrown some dice exactly, but sorted his building blocks – although unfortunately he only had one kind.

With the breathtaking scale and monotony of these new-build areas, the state had created an impressive face for itself, a real 'mass ornament'. The geometry of the modern age had taken hold of the little people; small house lined up next to small house as if on parade. The 'new Frankfurt' was no longer dominated by chaos; there was no charming confusion like that produced by small-scale private construction over the centuries in city centres across Germany; instead there was an almost frightening clarity. The satellite town boasted a rigid order that its residents had to fit in with. Such strict geometry was nothing new in urban architecture, of course: even in the newly built districts of the Baroque period, or in the nineteenth-century tenements, flats were stacked serially on top of one another, but living conditions had never been organised as soberly as they were under the builders of the Weimar Republic.

It can hardly come as a surprise that a lot of attention was paid in the Soviet Union to Ernst May's talent for creating affordable living spaces. In 1930 they headhunted him. May went to Russia with 20 German colleagues, and even worked there for a time as 'Engineer in Chief of the Association for the Construction of Standard Cities in the USSR'. May, now in charge of a workforce of over 800 people, saw this as 'perhaps the biggest task that an architect has ever faced'.[24] For a large-scale planner like himself, this was the fulfilment of a life's dream: to build new cities out of nothing for millions of people. Within a very short time, Ernst May was to throw up a new industrial city called Magnitogorsk, after the nearby 'magnetic mountain', in the bare steppe of the Urals. After three years, however, May fell into disfavour. Aside from the usual quarrels with civil servants, May's construction suddenly wasn't propagandistic enough for the Soviet leadership. The Stalinist need for display was unhappy with functionalist *Zeilenbau* (literally 'line construction', otherwise known as 'row-house') based on long, thin buildings. They wanted more pomposity in the décor, more closed districts and more visual axes involving grand monuments. In totalitarianism the modern age paused; May's ideas simply became too stark even for the Soviets. Equally undesirable in Nazi Germany, he later went to Kenya and ran a coffee plantation.

The Frankfurter May was only outdone in terms of productivity by his Berlin colleague Martin Wagner. Wagner was the building dir- ector of a city with an even worse housing crisis. But Wagner had more room than May did in Frankfurt; he didn't have to move his large estates outside the city, but was able to erect them among the many small towns that had come together in 1920 to form Greater Berlin. City planner Wagner found a congenial artistic partner in Bruno Taut, who was now chief architect of Berlin's non-profit con- struction company GEHAG, which was a leading player in modern large-scale housing construction. Taut almost thought on as large a scale as May, but was more concerned with loosening up serial build- ing with a variety of individual elements. He wasn't even afraid of prettifying a simple door with a wide frame adorned with a gold waffle pattern on a blue background, as if he had suffered an attack of romantic weakness or anticipated a postmodern brainstorm.

Taut built residential districts that remain exemplary for their high-level democratic construction. His Wohnstadt Carl Legien dem- onstrates that even social housing can be charming. With its preconstructed loggias, the building turns its logic outwards, curved corner balconies recall the elegance of a luxury steamer, and win- dows running around corners sweep away centuries-old building rules.

Kitchens were typical of the methods of New Building. They shrank to the size of a battery cage. Architects explained their tiny size by saying that they had measured the many unnecessary jour- neys that people had to take while cooking in a traditional kitchen. Taylorism, the optimisation of time and motion for reasons of profit- ability, had shown that housewives – the house husband was still a long way off – wasted much of their energy making these unneces- sary journeys. To shorten them, the kitchens in Reichsbahn dining cars were taken as a model and a virtue made of their tiny spaces. The 'Frankfurt kitchen' that the Viennese architect Margarete

Schütte-Lihotzky designed for the buildings of Ernst May in 1926 had an area of only 6.5 square metres. In spite of a width of just 1.87 metres, it offered what were supposedly perfect working conditions. With upper and lower cupboards, it formed the prototype of the contemporary fitted kitchen. Cooking in the kitchen was like working in the cockpit of a narrow aeroplane; if you needed a work surface, you just folded a board between the lower cupboards that faced one another. That was a practical solution, and the fact that the women in the kitchen were essentially locked away didn't trouble the designer at all. On the contrary: the separation of the sphere of food preparation (dirty) from the space of eating (clean) followed the paranoid notions of social hygiene that the reform-living movement followed at the time. The modern woman, rationalised away on democratic principles, was supposed to be invisible until the food was ready. Cooking was banished to a room that the wife only escaped when she brought in the finished food; ideally she would have changed in the meantime.

Built euphoria

Anyone who went out in the evening, to go dancing or to the cinema, left the domain of the Bauhaus aesthetic. A different architectural spirit prevailed in the glittering dance halls and entertainment palaces. A hitherto unknown glamour catapulted the guests out of the travails of the plain into artificial, glittering states of paradise.

Those who went eating and dancing in Berlin's Haus Gourmenia could consider themselves the most elegant of all. The building included a series of five very different restaurants that stretched over a total of three storeys. Diners sat in two gallery floors, one above the other, and looked down at the parquet below or at the balcony opposite. The architect Leo Nachtlicht had wanted to arrange the Haus Gourmenia – which opened in 1929 – in such a way 'that as many people as possible see each other; because people take great delight in looking'.[25] Five years after the introduction of the new Reichsmark, society had found an ideal look for itself. With the interconnected sequence of establishments – Café Berlin, Weinrestaurant Traube, the Bierstube Stadt Pilson, the American Buffet and the English Tea Room – Nachtlicht had created a complete artwork, centring on a conservatoire with branching watercourses, tall palm trees and exotic plants, with tortoises wandering about, to the sound of screeching parrots and the driving rhythm of jazz. 'Trees of light' made of milky glass tubes stretched the full height of the three storeys.[26] On the top floor was the dance hall, above that the roof garden on which there was room for 650 people among spotlit fountains and luxuriant flowers. If it rained, an electrically activated glass roof appeared above the guests. When the glass roof was removed again after the storm, 'the cleansed air is inhaled in deep breaths, and people are even more delighted with the technical development for saving a day that had begun with great pleasure' – according to the Gourmenia's brochure.[27] The owners were particularly proud of the indoor climate; with the 'Wassmuth Weather-Maker' they were 'able to make their own weather', the advertisement promised.

In every detail, the Haus Gourmenia aimed for a perfect and undisturbed artificial world. The space was an ideal 'backdrop for beautiful women and elegant men', strolling amidst a world that was there entirely for their pleasure. Waiters were supposed to dash about

like arrows fired from a bow [. . .] everything here works as if on a conveyor belt [. . .], as if by clockwork, everything is wound up, everything electrically charged – some giant must have pressed a button so that everything works, and hurries and rushes, tirelessly, without a pause for breath.[28]

To maintain the momentum, the music could never fall silent, because:

The best bands are precisely good enough to take over from one another in constant succession. Five such select orchestras play in the Gourmenia Palace. Agents of all countries are employed in New York and London, in Paris and Rome, in Vienna and Budapest, even in

Buenos Aires and Rio de Janeiro to find bands that will complete the
service to our guests.[29]

The glamorous stylistic phenomenon characteristic of buildings
like the Gourmenia were only called 'art deco' later on. In the 1920s
the concept didn't exist; at first art deco was nameless. It was only
when a subsequent generation was struck by the bravura pieces of
this ambitious decorative trend that the glamorous side of the
modern age was given its own name – in reference to a big exhibition
that had been shown in Paris in 1925, the *Exposition internationale des
arts décoratifs et industriels modernes*. The Berlin Renaissancetheater,
for example, which is now considered to be the last surviving art-
deco theatre in Europe, was seen in the 1920s as testimony to an
'Expressionist rococo'.

If art deco was only given its own name after the fact, and was
generally categorised as *Neue Sachlichkeit* at the time, this was down –
apart from a lack of eloquent theorists – to one important factor: art
deco broke just as decisively with the past as the functionalism of
New Building. Its guiding principle was not minimalism, however,
but excess. While the representatives of *Neue Sachlichkeit* concentrated on the minimum that was absolutely necessary for a good life,
the representatives of art deco saw excess as a highly necessary
matter. They too wanted to remake the world from the ground up,
but make it more glamorous. Much more glamorous. Spikes and
arches, fanned corners and aerodynamic curves gave every object a
striking appearance. And fine materials such as smooth leather, mirrors, chrome, brass, polished ivory and gleaming mahogany lent
simple forms a weighty magnificence. The domains of art deco were
fashion and jewellery, interior decoration and the temples of modern
distraction: dance halls, cinemas, boutiques, department stores,
hotels – the luxurious places that made up the euphoric elements of
the 'Roaring Twenties'. An example in Germany was the Karstadt
department store on Hermannplatz, a bit of Chicago that loomed
like an American dream from a tenement block in the Berlin district
of Neukölln. Today the senate and the district council are arguing

about the plan to rebuild the upwardly aspirational department store under the direction of the Chipperfield architecture office so that its 'Mesopotamian Metropolis' architecture can stand triumphant over the neighbourhood once again.[30] Also falling under the heading of art deco is the Universum Cinema by Erich Mendelsohn, today the Schaubühne on Lehniner Platz, which, with its elegant round bow and angular superstructures, noses its way towards Kurfürstendamm like a luxury steamer. Or the Grassi Museum in Leipzig, with its hall of pillars which looks as if it were built for Cleopatra's wedding to Albert Einstein.

Cleopatra! She was, like ancient Egypt in general, incredibly hip in the 1920s. In 1922 the discovery of the grave of Tutankhamun fired the imagination of designers, as did the Ishtar Gate, which was shown in Berlin's Pergamon Museum in 1930. Were the pharaohs not also Bauhaus artists in their way, the Pyramids a manifesto to sublime reduction? The bust of Nefertiti, shown to the public in 1924, caused a sensation and expanded people's understanding of timeless beauty. A cultural kinship was seen between Nefertiti and Greta Garbo, and turned Nefertiti and her husband Akhenaten into the faces of beer, cigarettes and coffee. Charleston dresses in the 'pharaoh style' were the last word in fashion. Stage stars such as Ida Roland and Margo Lion, forgotten today, strutted around disguised as Nefertiti. Big performances like theirs needed a suitable setting, and they found it in the grandeur of art deco. Palatial interiors like Café Uhland, with gleaming gold ceramics on the walls, ceilings that fanned out like seashells, brass and frosted glass light columns, and handrails of polished bubinga wood or palisander turned every guest into a star, a pharaoh of the twentieth century.

Art deco was an aesthetic of globalisation. It was no coincidence that its heyday coincided with the arrival of international shipping lines, passenger flights and travel agencies. Aspects of *Jugendstil* (Youth Style) – the German version of art nouveau – the pioneering utilitarian *Wiener Werkstätte* (Viennese Workshops) design movement and the Bauhaus merged with French models, but also with the American chic of skyscraper fantasies. This produced an international

Karstadt on Hermannplatz, Berlin. Half Chicago, half Babylon and yet typically Berlin.
The Art Déco department store loomed from the sea of houses. Sixteen years later it would
lie in rubble again, blown up by the SS who wanted to prevent the Soviet Army from
having access to supplies.

metropolitan style that was soon as global as the Charleston, the bob
or Coca-Cola. That brown, sweet soda appeared on the German
market in 1929, in the ribbed and bellied bottle that still exists in a very
slightly different form today. Originally designed in 1915, the Coca-
Cola bottle is the best-known and most durable product of art
deco – a coup of packaging design. It was a little piece of the world
of *The Great Gatsby* that everybody could afford.

Like the Bauhaus, art deco wanted to be radically new, but with
the stress on dynamism. It was sensual, decadent and intoxicating,
'almost orgiastic', as the architect Le Corbusier complained.[31] Art
deco flirted with the world of opium and cocaine, and presented itself
as a drug in built form. It is hardly a surprise that this intoxication

in stone should have been met with scepticism and resistance. In art deco the modern age had, for many people, been given a destructive, but also a triumphant, face; they were as uncomfortable with it as they were the severe puritanism of the Bauhaus. Furious innovation in building became the visible sign of a feeling of loss that crept upon them in their more timid moments. Bit by bit, many saw their spiritual home being lost. New morals, slender and confident young women, crazy music, cocksure bosses, rising prices in crafts and retail. And these buildings that looked distinctly un-German. The alternative had a telling name: *Heimatschutzstil* – Homeland Protection Style.

The flat roof as a matter of conscience – *Heimatschutz* architecture

In 1926, in Ullstein's spirited magazine *Uhu*, the Social Democrat-minded head of the Bauhaus Walter Gropius and the far-right architect Paul Schultze-Naumburg provided a pro and contra on the subject of contemporary architecture.[32] The 57-year-old Schultze-Naumburg built predominantly country houses for a wealthy clientele. The best known is probably the Cecilienhof Palace in Potsdam, which he built in 1917 for Crown Prince Wilhelm in the Tudor style. An illustrious collection of conservative intellectuals and artists used to meet up at Schultze-Naumburg's house in Saaleck in Naumburg, Saxony-Anhalt (a man such as Schultze liked to include his home town as a decoration in his name): these included the architect Werner March, the author Börries von Münchhausen, the painter Ludwig von Hofmann and the more liberal urban planner Werner Hegemann. From the mid-1920s, however, National Socialists such as Adolf Hitler and Joseph Goebbels were also welcome guests in Saaleck.

While in his contribution to *Uhu* Gropius insisted that people needed to move with the times and develop progressive buildings out of progressive technologies, Schultze-Naumburg argued that they should take their bearings from the rural forms of architecture of the pre-bourgeois period. In those days 'clear, extremely distinct forms' had come into being, forms which were part of the 'organic legacy' of the northern cultural circle. They had built houses 'that looked like a collection of magnificently fiery characteristic heads of rugged farers, masculine craftsmen, sensitive scholars and chivalrous aristocrats'.[33] After imitations from foreign cultures had been superimposed on the architectural identity of Germany to the point where it was no longer recognisable, there was a need to return to the traditional formal vocabulary of pointed roofs, oriel and bay windows, and shutters, to build houses once more that 'clearly declared their allegiance to the Nordic culture group'.[34]

Schultze-Naumburg was a representative of *Heimatstil* (Homeland Style), a term that had been current since the turn of the century. It meant a return to simple, traditional forms that aimed to harmonise architecture with the regional legacy. Not all representatives of *Heimatstil*, which, after intense arguments, came to be called *Heimatschutzstil* (Homeland Protection Style), were radical nationalists; many highly regarded architects such as Hermann Muthesius were also part of it. *Heimatstil*, also known as *Reformarchitektur*, often took its bearings from other geographical regions, particularly the United Kingdom. Borrowing from English garden cities, in many places it created estates of terraced houses in an undecorated, aesthetically charming rural style. Today we would call it a reinterpretation of a country-house style. Or else it reached far back into the past. The Burghof in Flensburg, a five-storey tenement with two interior courtyards, built in 1909, even contained hints of the Middle Ages.

Like *Neues Bauen* (New Building), *Heimatschutzstil* wanted to build everything from the ground up. Both trends saw their goal as lying in a movement away from 'architectural barbarism' through concentration and reduction. The Bauhaus wanted to rely entirely on the elementary, geometrical forms of building, while the Homeland Protectors aimed to return to a reduced, preindustrial architectural vocabulary. Many of them had the idea of a 'primal house' in mind. Finding the new in the archetypal was a longing that characterised both sides.

Even more interesting than the obvious differences, then, are the areas of agreement between Walter Gropius and Paul Schultze-Naumburg in the pages of *Uhu*. The far-right master builder, who would join the National Socialist Party in 1930, rejected historicism just as vehemently as the modernist Gropius, and both detested the ornamentation of the *Gründerzeit* buildings of the mid-nineteenth century. 'Inauthentic the materials, inauthentic the styles that are thrown like fancy-dress costumes over shabby, dirty undergarments'[35] – Schultze-Naumburg saw the Wilhelmine facade as nothing but a betrayal of the authentic and the true, or, in his eyes, Germanness.

If we leave the Germanness aside, we can find an almost identical argument in Gropius. He too felt that Wilhelmine decorative architecture was decadent. In the lowercase font typical of the Bauhaus, he called for more vital architecture:

> the art of building declined in past generations in a feebly sentimental vision that saw its goal as lying in the formalistic use of motifs, ornaments and profiles that covered the bodies of buildings. building became a bearer of external dead forms of decoration rather than being a living organism.[36]

'Feebly sentimental' and 'external dead forms' are not a long way from Schultze-Naumburg's 'threadbare fancy-dress costumes', which in turn sound very similar to Bruno Taut, quoted at the start of the chapter, who raged in 1920 against the 'self-importance of four-storey junk shops and bric-a-brac stalls'. Left and right met in a cult of authenticity that lies within all radicalism, as the philosopher Helmuth Plessner observed at the time.[37]

During the Weimar Republic, revulsion over 'dishonest' décor spread beyond the limits of the two camps. Even such an elegant aficionado as the author Franz Hessel felt as much aversion to the *Gründerzeit* buildings as any iconoclastic avant-gardist. The 'tumour-buildings' spoiled his strolls along the Kurfürstendamm 'where much that is hideously towering, horrifically protuberant and crept-over has been left from the worst days of private building'.[38]

It wasn't long before words turned into deeds. Precisely in the most elegant districts of the cities – on Wittenbergplatz in Berlin, for example – moves began to knock the stucco off the houses to give the *Gründerzeit* buildings the requisite sobriety.[39] The anti-ornamental taste diktat turned into an attack by the present on earlier times. The barbarism officially known as 'destuccification' was an abstruse aesthetic practice with the aim of getting rid of history. Only a new person in new surroundings seemed capable of coming to terms with the future. In the words of the historian Martin H. Geyer: 'Only someone who could forget, or who was not mentally connected with the past, seemed to be able to assert themselves in the new age.'[40]

Architects such as Le Corbusier or Theo van Doesburg dreamed of combing out cities with heavy equipment and driving out their 'romantic sins',[41] their confusion and their chaotic diversity. The socialist architect Ludwig Hilberseimer, a teacher at the Bauhaus, set out plans for the demolition of Friedrichstadt in Berlin. He wanted to tear down whole districts behind the Gendarmenmarket to make way for 18 high-rise slabs each 600 metres long – a totalitarian nightmare, which luckily remained a fantasy. Decades later Hilberseimer himself described his plans as 'inhuman in every respect'.[42]

The severity of such urban redevelopers made it easy for radical conservatives to present themselves as protectors of the homeland, even though they were the ones who were already preparing its downfall. In times of crisis increased attention is often paid to living conditions – this was particularly true of the Weimar Republic. It was no coincidence that it was the sheltering roof that sparked particularly bitter arguments. The choice of its design, whether it should be flat or pointed, became a signal and a statement. The opponents of the Bauhaus maintained that the flat roof came from North Africa and was thus deeply un-German. Others among them, such as Paul Schultze-Naumburg, felt that it was Indian.[43] Still others said there was something Jewish about it. In 1927 the conservative architect said in the *Schwäbische Merkur* that the recently completed Weissenhof-siedlung, an estate that was a showpiece of the New Building style erected under the direction of Mies van der Rohe, reminded him 'more of a suburb of Jerusalem than of housing for Stuttgart'.[44] And the National Socialist Party printed postcards with palm trees and turbaned Bedouins inserted into the estate to portray it as an 'Arab village'.

Conversely, the advocates of the flat roof were not satisfied with a sober depiction of its practical advantages, but presented it as a redeeming, healing refuge. The flat roof meant that conscience had finally awakened, Adolf Behne, a propagandist for the 'New Building', said in all honesty. It meant the end of the jagged outline of roofs which some found romantic, and which in Behne's words, 'wriggled towards the sky'.[45]

Berlin architecture critic Karl Scheffler observed irritably that it was no longer the quality of a roof that mattered, but the ideology that it expressed:

> If an architect builds a high, pointed, broadly sheltering roof, that is seen as an indication of German nationalist mentality. If he flattens the roof somewhat, something like a democratic house is produced; but if he makes the roof completely flat, he is announcing a radically communist mentality. The roof becomes an expression of a political attitude.[46]

When the Weissenhofsiedlung in Stuttgart was finally opened, it was revealed as a sensation, a constructed dream. It looked like 'a fleet of pleasure craft'.[47] If this corridor was too narrow, or that arrangement of doors impractical, overall the imagination that *Neue Sachlichkeit* had released was intoxicating: Hans Scharoun's playful villa was magically original, Le Corbusier's building meditative, Jacobus Oud's terraced houses were a sensual adventure. Nothing here was boring, and the response to the 21 houses in Stuttgart was accordingly loud and various. It ranged from extravagant praise to the aggressive threat of 'punching [its creators] in the face for hours'.[48]

The great publicity for the Weissenhofsiedlung was a thorn in the eye of the right. Only 2 kilometres away, architects of the conservative 'Stuttgart School' erected their response to the challenge from *Neue Sachlichkeit*. Under the direction of Paul Bonatz and Paul Schmitthenner, and adhering strictly to the 'gable roof rule', the Kochenhof Estate was built within a few months, and inaugurated with much ballyhoo as a triumph of traditional German architecture.[49] The houses were in fact quite unspectacular. They were pretty enough and thoroughly respectable, but why they were celebrated as a 'revival of the old urban bourgeois house',[50] and any similarities identified with Goethe's Garden House in Weimar can only be explained by the overheated culture war. Three generations later the roof has lost its ideological charge, and today the Kochenhof Estate is seen as a successful example of regional, sustainable architecture. Far removed from the spectacular originality of the Weissenhofsiedlung, it derives its charm from a pleasantly low-key realisation of traditional ideals: much more boring, admittedly, than the nearby modern buildings, but nothing like a brainless Nazi spectacle. The repellent hubris of the National Socialist monumental style was yet to come.

Today the Kochenhof Estate sits very comfortably with the ecologically minded Stuttgart middle-class families who nurture their liberal bourgeois beliefs and connect a global mindset with an interest in the preservation of regional traditions. A hip roof with eyebrow dormers is neither right wing nor left wing; beneath it, one can think beautiful cosmopolitan thoughts to one's heart's content. Even among architectural critics the estate has improved its reputation; it has largely shaken off the accusation of embodying the spirit of National Socialism. Today, the innocent houses look like mute witnesses to a historic moment when even the choice of roof design had become a hot political message, and the public debate had been hollowed out to its foundations by rigorism and self-righteousness; like a lawn by moles.

It doesn't get more modern than this. The Le Corbusier house on the Werkbund's Weissenhof estate in Stuttgart formed the ideal background for the advertisement of the Mecedes Benz Roadster.

4

'Destinies Behind Typewriters' – The Supporting Class of the New Age

'Office, home, work, love – how did she ever combine them all?'

Irmgard Keun, *Gilgi, One of Us*

At eight o'clock in the morning strange beings populate the streets

Anyone wanting to make a phone call in 1920 picked the receiver up from the cradle and dialled. Two or three turns was enough and the electricity produced made a signal flap on the switchboard in the nearest telephone office. Each line had an indicator flap next to it. The switchboard operator could tell by the drop of the flap that someone on the line wanted to speak. She (it was always a woman) put the cable of the heavy headset that hung around her neck into the corresponding socket and said, 'Hello, how may I help you?' or: 'Office here. What can I do for you?' The caller gave her the number that they wanted to speak to, whereupon the operator connected the two lines with a cable and plugged it in.[1] The 'girl from the office' could bring two people together like this up to a hundred times an hour: she was a tirelessly active synapse, a living connection cable.

Many dozens of telephone operators, often even hundreds, sat side by side at huge rows of switchboards, talking and plugging. They formed the human nodules of the telephone network, changing its connections by the second. Asking the number, plugging, asking the

number, plugging – that went on for eight hours a day. The pressure
intensified when several flaps fell at once. Then the callers would
have to wait for a few seconds, cursing under their breath and asking
to speak to a manager. Even when new operators were employed, the
rush in the telephone offices increased because the number of connections was growing unevenly. The women were supervised by men
who sat at broad desks in the middle of the vast halls, ensuring that
the operators kept their nerve.

Automatic self-dial phone calls became more commonplace throughout the 1920s: now, at first only on some local networks, one could
dial the desired number directly; this way, the electricity passed automatically through the nodal points of the network. When this
technique became more widespread, many telephone operators
were dismissed, but soon found new jobs in the booming offices that
were springing up, because the more phone calls people made, the
more work they made elsewhere. The more often and the faster
people communicated, the more administrative processes were set in
motion, the more had to be noted, recorded, invoiced, checked and
filed. The emblem of the times was no longer a smoking factory, but
the apparently emission-free palace of administration, a beehive containing honeycombs of offices and typing pools.

By day, office workers disappeared into these massive, awe-inspiring
Valhallas. These buildings told everyone where power was to be found:
at the desk. They included genuine works of art such as the Chilehaus
in Hamburg, built between 1922 and 1924, a wonderful building of
burned bricks, running together into points and peaks like a gigantic
ship's prow – the apotheosis in stone of foreign trade, bringing back its
visual ingredients from somewhere remote and unimaginably exotic.

The first high-rise building in Berlin was constructed in 1922, an
office building with an Expressionist-inspired twist: the 65-metre
Borsigturm had a jagged penthouse floor that radiated the light of
office administration far into the distance like a giant gothic lantern –
bureaucracy as a source of redemption.[2] But the claim to universal
validity embodied by the administrative office of IG Farben in Frankfurt put everything else in the shade. The enormous 250-metre-long

building looked as if it was merely the entrance to something much bigger lurking behind it. The IG Farben building may legitimately be called Kafkaesque. In the imagination it could have easily continued into an endless sequence of administrative corridors in which losing one's way seemed inevitable and any petition would be lost for ever. The Kafka-esque, as we know, is a heightened manifestation of bureaucracy, and Kafka's work, as singular as it might be, is unimaginable without that experience of administration. Franz Kafka, until 1922 chief legal secretary of the Workmen's Accident Insurance Institute for the Kingdom of Bohemia in Prague, had learned to value and fear life from the perspective of risk evaluation. As a bookkeeper of anxiety, against which his writing was inadequate insurance, and in the existentially excessive demands made upon him, he was an entirely modern character whose posthumous fame was able to grow out of an experience shared by millions. Martin Kessel, author of what is probably the most significant office novel of the 1920s,[3] called this collective experience the 'bent or seated way of life',[4] the way of life of the modern clerical worker.

Between 1914 and 1933 the number of office workers would double from 2 million to over 4 million; the rise in the number of female clerical workers was disproportionately large, and 65 per cent of the 1.2 million women employed in 1925 were under 25.[5] In absolute terms, there might not have been very many of them compared with the number of manual workers, but they were a new phenomenon on the streets, and to the surprise of many contemporaries shaped the face not only of the cities but also of the future. All of a sudden office workers seemed to have become the crowd, and had burgeoned from a manageable quantity to a barely imaginable dimension – a class full of mysteries. 'Hundreds of thousands of office workers populate the streets of Berlin every day, and yet less is known about their lives than that of the primitive tribespeople whose customs the office workers admire in films.'[6] With this oft-quoted sentence the commentator Siegfried Kracauer introduced his sociological study *Die Angestellten* (The Salaried Masses), which bore the subtitle 'From the newest Germany', and with which he wanted to shed light on the darkness of this unknown species.

Kracauer was by no means alone in his curiosity; in the Weimar Republic clerical workers, particularly the female kind, became the object of growing interest. Secretaries and shorthand typists were the sirens of the 'New Age', the object of sociological research and the protagonists of an overflowing, frivolous imagination. Film titles such as *The Department Store Princess* (1926), *The Little Shorthand Typist* (1925) and so on speak for themselves; not so *I Go Out and You Stay Here* (1931), based on the homonymous 'novel of a model' by Wilhelm Speyer, which put the confident retail employee Gaby at its centre.[7] In the James Klein revue *Laughing Berlin* in 1925, the office was put on stage. The set consisted of an enormous typewriter in which the dancers positioned themselves as keys. Wearing black letters on their heads, in their basic position they formed the German QWERTZ arrangement before their legs started swinging and they began shedding their clothes.

The idea of women pursuing professions was not a new one. There had already been Emilie Winkelmann, Germany's first architect, Marie Munk, the first judge, Lise Meitner, the first physics professor, and in 1929 Elli Blarr, the first taxi driver, but they were still exceptions even if they were typical of a now unstoppable development. Shorthand typists and office assistants were a different matter, however – they were a mass phenomenon. Their hedonism, their lust for life, their visible confidence, their tendency to appear in groups, seemed to bring fresh air to the public space. Women were no longer only men's companions, and they didn't dart home by the quickest route at night after work. They hung around, they populated the cafés, inspected the shop windows. Never had so many women had so much money of their own, made their own decisions, moved out, resigned, made their own plans. It was their taste that now helped to decide the success and failure of films and magazines, their gaze now appraised men just as men had for so long appraised women, and their intelligence helped to determine the efficiency of an office. And as customers their purchasing power was considerable. The business world had never been so dependent on women, but women were dependent on it as well. They decided which records would be bought, which cinema tickets clipped. They became a crucial target group for the booming entertainment industry. Hyperactive, 'busy at work by day, ready to dance in the evening' – the modern urban woman was redefined and reappraised: 'hard-working, beautiful legs and the necessary mixture of reliability and frivolity, blurring and contour, kindness and coolness' – this was how German *Vogue* summed up 'the woman of today'.[8]

Countless magazine articles, some films and numerous novels were devoted to the secretary: *Gilgi, One of Us* (1931) by Irmgard Keun, *The Girl at the Orga Privat* (1930) by Rudolf Braune, *Destinies Behind Typewriters* (1930) by Christa Anita Brück and *Herr Brecher's Fiasco* (1932) by Martin Kessel all revolved around secretaries. The fact that their positions were not mere trophies of emancipation, but that they were ancillary, badly paid, subordinate jobs, did nothing to diminish the interest. It was precisely that ambivalence, that oscillation between dependence and autonomy, that sparked the curiosity of the media and stirred the collective imagination. Glossy magazines such as *Das Leben* and *Uhu* sent their reporters and photographers into offices to explore the new social terrain that had formed in the smart office-block palaces. In the summer of 1929, the trendy

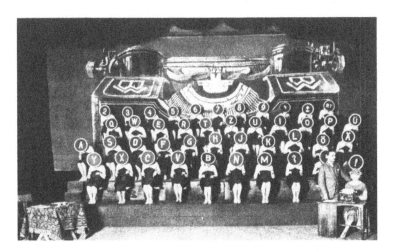

The typewriter as a stage set for the James Klein revue 'Das lachende Berlin', 1925. Each dancer represents both a secretary and a letter on the QWERTZ keyboard.

magazine *Das Leben*, published in Leipzig, published a long read, 'Zoology of the Shorthand Typist', in words and pictures.[9] This presented a whole series of female types found more or less in this form in every office: the good girl, the beginner, the factotum, the intellectual, the enamoured one, the slut, the greedy one, the oaf and finally 'the lady who for various reasons gets away with everything', but she, the magazine reminded its readers, appeared almost only in films.

Kurt Tucholsky also explored the world of office workers, and for *Uhu* he set out his thoughts about what a good secretary had to be. She was the one who made the boss what he represented in the world, by taking care of him and steering him so gently through files and corridors that he believed he was the one in charge: 'Take note,' he wrote under his pseudonym Peter Panter: 'A good secretary is invisible, inaudible and only perceptible when she isn't there.'[10]

The mutual dependencies in the system of governance in the office world were what turned the new employees into 'curious figures of social being', a class that was both difficult to define and politically unreliable.[11] Regardless of how exploited office workers might have been, they at least felt that they were superior to proletarians, since they had some role, however minimal, in directorial or at least administrative functions. Where the manual worker saw himself as the primal element in the generation of value, without whose strong arms all cogs would be brought to a standstill, office workers were the ones who assigned his work, calculated his efficiency, arranged his wages and finally paid him. However monotonous office work might have been, it was elevated above the dirt of production and played a part in the sphere of operational control. For that very reason the young women, most of whom came from proletarian backgrounds, had enjoyed an enormous boost. They were participating in the modern age, they understood its technologies and its codes, they had an understanding of fashion, even if they couldn't afford much. At home they were the ones who read out and explained official letters to their parents. They knew the manners of educated people, they picked up their turns of phrase in the office and watched how they behaved at table. They didn't wolf their soup down from a lunch bucket like their proletarian brothers, but ate with their colleagues in the big canteens or even in subscription restaurants. They lived in an exciting world, which they watched as if from outside.

Quick even when sitting down: the quiet dramas of the office

These new office buildings operated a little like merchant vessels. The lower rooms belonged to the tabulating and hole-punching machines, which marked the beginning of modern data collection and processing. Hole-punchers and sorters worked on those; little training was required for the tasks involved. The job of the hole-punchers was one of the least highly regarded and toughest of the modern administrative jobs. 'Clerks who have previously engaged in office activity find it difficult to adapt to this new work. The prestige that comes with sitting at a desk is lost, and the demands in terms of discipline become all the greater', modern organisation theory believed, and recommended that only employees who were not accustomed to anything better be taken on as 'hole-punch girls'.[12]

Upstairs, the rather better-off class of employees sat at their desks and produced the correspondence for the gentlemen whose offices were arranged around the typing rooms. This was the site of sharp-tongued conversation that would become typical, for the office was a place of social interaction. This was a particular kind of secretarial wit, balanced between detachment and intimacy, a communicative grease that was urgently required to keep the wheels of competitiveness, dependence, attraction and tedium rolling. Martin Kessel's novel *Herr Brecher's Fiasco* features a wild office argot with which the secretaries defy the boredom of the job and the demands of their bosses. Each sentence ends with an affected 'ü'; for example, in a request for a pencil – not 'Haben Sie einen Bleistift?', but 'Awa en bleie, ü – a special jargon of their own invention'[13]

Kessel's male readers will have recognised this ü-language not least because it coincided with the current prejudice that once respectable offices run by men had been overrun and deprofessionalised by hordes of chattering women who had changed the language of the office and administration. The prime cause was not the women, however, but the typewriter. It was with that instrument that slang entered the world of bookkeeping, and replaced the old specialist terms and abbreviations with which classic bookkeepers had kept things brief and precise in their handwritten documents. The typewriter granted businesspeople the possibility of delegating paperwork, and made their old, professional codes obsolete. 'With the invasion of the office by female typists, "businessmen's jargon" gradually disappeared,' the sociologist Theo Pirker observed.[14] But the perceived loss of class was usually attributed not to the women themselves, but to the boss, who often dictated distractedly:

> Abbreviations gradually disappeared. Unfortunately the blossoming, empty phrase remained. [. . .] Businessmen who were now relieved of the trouble of writing their own letters, and who no longer ran the risk of leaving blots on the page, fell into a series of bad habits, particularly the one of starting a sentence without knowing where it was going to end.[15]

The typewriter speeded up the writing process, but it did not rationalise the running of businesses. Typewriters meant that much more writing was done than before. Business letters became longer, more distracted and, more to the point, more abundant. Then, when carbon paper was invented and copies could be produced at the drop of a hat, there was no stopping the flow of paper. Sensible storage became a genuine science – to the joy of the office furniture industry and specialists in organisation.[16] This particular area grew just as swiftly as the mountains of paper in the company offices, and the armies of secretaries required to produce and control it. In the USA in 1948, when the Westinghouse company rationalised its storage system, it moved a total of 420 railway wagons full of files out of its buildings, on the safe assumption that no one would ever want to read any of them again, not least because there wasn't a hope of finding the information you were looking for in such enormous amounts of information.

In the accelerated bustle of the modern office, older clerks had few chances. Companies preferred to take on young members of staff, ideally young women who didn't plan to stay on for too long, and who could be expected to leave of their own accord by the age of 40. Older white-collar workers were 'whittled down' because they were more senior and hence more expensive. They were also thought to be less quick to adapt to new working methods than younger colleagues. 'At the age of forty many people who cheerfully imagine they have their whole lives ahead of them are already economically dead',[17] Siegfried Kracauer wrote. The cult of youth kindled by inflation attacked the older staff. Anyone who did not go willingly was bullied out by psychological terror.

> The fact that they are treated even more recklessly than might be in the interest of the companies is ultimately due to the general abandonment of old age in the present day. Not only the workforce – the entire population has turned its back on the older generation, and is glorifying youth as such to a staggering degree. It is the fetish of the illustrated magazines and their readers, older people woo it and rejuvenation tonics are sought to preserve it.[18]

Secretaries who didn't manage the leap into marriage in time risked finding themselves without a husband and without work in the middle of their lives. Many clung desperately to their jobs, even though no effort was spared to frighten them off. The independence they thought they had won with their job proved to be a temporary freedom. For ageing secretaries, working life often became a torment if they hadn't managed to win a particularly trusted position, or one that they were able to defend. On a daily basis they lost the competition with the swift fingers of the young shorthand typists, and their superiors could be brutally dismissive of them. 'Find yourself a husband', a desperate 41-year-old advises her younger colleague in the novel *Destinies Behind Typewriters*: 'If a monster came today with six

Large-space office with secretaries and 'supervisor' 1927. 'Dreaming at the type machine/ Sat the little Josephine', as a well-known popular song had it. Reality left little room for dreaming.

legs and eight arms and five mouths and wanted to have me, I wouldn't think twice, I'd take it. Marry, Fräulein Brückner, marry, [. . .] marry at all costs!'[19]

Often things weren't much better for older men. Even the most efficient bookkeeper, 'who was used to working with a pen and ink', had no chance against 'a girl fresh out of middle school, with three or four months' training on the accounting machine behind them'.[20] The old-style bookkeeper was a dying species:

an old-young man, slightly stoop-shouldered, with a sallow complexion, usually dyspeptic-looking, with black sleeves and a green eyeshade. Regardless of the kind of business, regardless of their ages, they all looked alike. He always looked tired and he was never quite happy, because [. . .] his face betrayed the strain of working toward that climax of his month's labours. He was usually a neat penman, but his real pride was in his ability to add a column of figures rapidly and accurately. In spite of this accomplishment, however, he seldom, if ever, left his ledger for a more promising position. His mind was atrophied by that destroying, hopeless influence of drudgery and routine work. He was little more than a figuring machine with an endless number of figure combinations learned by heart.[21]

When the bookkeeper's mechanical colleague became cheap enough over the course of the early twentieth century, it meant it was time to go. The production of calculators boomed, and even the Mauser arms factory got involved in the business. But the young women who were needed to feed the machines with their raw material of figures were not going to be outdone in terms of skill and speed by some old office workhorse. So the bookkeeper became a caricature: 'His fingers were like fountain pens, his ears the hooks for them, his suit sits on him like blotting paper', the novel *Die Wege des teelschen Hans* said of 'office person' Hans Lehderer.[22] These old decommissioned number-crunchers haunted the films of the Republic in the form of comical figures such as commissionaire Hasel, wages clerk Kremke or senior cashier Pichler.[23] By contrast their colleagues at the keyboards and shorthand pads – literally hundreds of thousands of them – became a cheerful, lively reserve army. Some of them are said to have used the phrase 'accumulated return account' as a pet name, or at least that was what was claimed in an article, clearly catering to male fantasies, in the magazine *Das Leben*.[24]

The Orga that provided the title for the 1930 novel *The Girl at the Orga Privat* by the communist author Rudolf Braune was a typewriter, the stiffest one available in the typing pool. It was always foisted on newcomers, specifically inexperienced ones, who had a huge amount of trouble with this monster. 'The machine, with its forty-five keys, stares coldly and wickedly, with complete disinterest, at the strong hands of this little girl.'[25] Those hands needed to be strong. 'Among the typewriters there are nimble little girls who run like weasels, busy, loyal aunts, never sullen, always helpful, and old grandmothers who are pushed onwards with a groan.'[26] To anyone familiar only with clicking computer keyboards designed to present minimum resistance, it will be hard to imagine how much strength was needed in those days to lift the type levers and strike them evenly enough against ribbon and paper to end up with a clean page of typing. And how much effort it required of the little fingers of both left and right hand to lift the kilo weight of the carriage to switch to upper case. Getting 70 error-free words a minute required a nimbleness equal to that of the greatest pianists, with the difference that here it wasn't a matter of art, but of speed.[27]

The author Martin Kessel had the finest sense for the special music of the office, for the 'busy sound of normality'. He spoke of the 'cricket whisper of typewriters':[28]

> You could hear the rustling and tickling, the ticking and creeping, the familiar sound of office activity, and the fact that people were also present intensified the impression of busy-ness. It often sounded like the gnawing of mice.[29]

'I want to stay pretty for as long as I can'

It is a truism to observe that the office world had its erotic side, and the truism is borne out by statistics. In the course of the 1920s up to 25 per cent of young women office workers in retail married their boss – a startling figure that shows how constricted living conditions were in comparison with the present day, how small the radius from which partners could be chosen.[30] Offices were places where matchmaking took place, but to an even greater extent they were places of harassment and unwanted advances. It was almost impossible for a female employee to rise through a company except by marrying her superior.[31] Office life was enlivened by attraction and dreams of rising up the company ladder, but also poisoned by cynical exploitation, calculation and tragedy.

'Herr Mahrenholz? A particularly sticky man' – with these words the secretary Gilgi in *Gilgi, One of Us*, the first novel by Irmgard Keun

from 1931, describes her boss: he is sticky, she says, but 'not dangerous. I can deal with him easily. [. . .] I don't think men are nearly as
bad as people always say. [. . .] The important thing is to have the
knack of dodging them.'[32] But that didn't always work. Things usually became more difficult when the women didn't want to dodge
these men, but instead fell for their assurances of serious intent.
Rudolf Braune's novel *The Girl at the Orga Privat* concerns a shorthand typist who is expecting the child of one of her bosses. She is
forced to have an abortion, dismissed from her job and dies from the
consequences of the operation. Christa Anita Brück's novel *Destinies
Behind Typewriters* describes the odyssey of a secretary who has to
keep taking on new office jobs.[33] She endures an ordeal of sadistic
harassment, sexual attacks and unpleasantness of all kinds: 'Trem-
bling forty times over at what comes next, what kind of misery, what
variation of torment, because I can't count the few good employers
that I've had.'[34]

The gloomy representation of the world of work in *Destinies
Behind Typewriters* did not go uncontradicted, however. In the book
by Irmgard Keun, who herself worked as a shorthand typist for four
years, before trying her luck as an actress in 1927, and who started
writing shortly afterwards, Anita Brück's novel is explicitly mentioned in front of the main character Gilgi and dismissed as a trivial
jeremiad. This kind of 'tragedy of insult' could not halt her desire for
advancement:

> I take pleasure in getting ahead by my own efforts. [. . .] I have no tal-
> ents, [. . .] I can't paint pictures or write books, I'm completely average
> and can't bring myself to despair over the fact. But I want to make as
> much of myself as I can. I will go on working and learning new things,
> and stay healthy and pretty for as long as I can.[35]

This is the sound of *Neue Sachlichkeit*, coupled with the pursuit of
advancement and the paradox of an almost dramatic modesty. Gilgi
wants to be free and independent; her idea of freedom includes
unconditional realism, because she doesn't want her ambition to be

dimmed by unrealistic expectations: 'My claims are never higher than the possibilities of achieving them, and that makes me free.'[36]

Even though life brings her plans to nothing in the end, the author does not repudiate her heroine's modern determination for self-advancement, any more than she denounces her thirst for life or the little tricks with which she helps her career along, 'little upward-from-below glances', by influencing her boss.[37] She guides him by making herself small. Gilgi, the average girl, 'one of us', imagines an existence that brings her upwards step by step as long as she is skilful and ambitious enough. 'I have to achieve everything step by step. Now I'm learning my languages – I'm saving money. [. . .] I may even end up with my own business.' Her plan for life is thwarted – how could it be otherwise? – by love, which takes her out of the office to coddle a struggling author.

The office world produced its own promises, which painted reality in rose-tinted colours, particularly in the dynamic years of economic growth. The days of the work–life balance were plainly still a long way off, but the idea that employees needed to feel good about themselves was still very much in vogue. In August 1929 Ullstein's *Uhu* published a picture story about an office outing. The head of a Berlin company had a special idea for the annual excursion: he chartered a Lufthansa Junkers plane to fly to the nearby state of Mecklenburg. His 11-strong team, from the apprentice to the senior bookkeeper, landed in a green meadow. They got out with their picnic baskets and laid out the white blankets for lunch right beside the plane – with the photographer from *Uhu* always present. They had even brought a gramophone along. There was food and drink, there was flirting and teasing – the company mood was splendid. The story ended with a rousing cheer for the boss – but not without a reference to the power relationship, which could have gone in a very different direction:

And there is a genuine-sounding cheer at the end of the speech by the little secretary when she asks him on the part of everyone never to let them go flying [i.e., be fired] otherwise than in an aeroplane. With a boss like that, who would want to go flying in any other way![38]

The reportage was plainly faked, or at least the story was adapted to the punchline. It's entirely possible that the magazine contributed to the chartering of the plane. But readers will have seen the report as entirely plausible, because in fact many companies did a great deal to keep their staff in good spirits. Worker satisfaction was identified as an important resource by business management. Exhaustive 'staff regulation' included measures to intensify a sense of belonging and 'events that engrossed the mind', such as joint parties and vacations in holiday homes belonging to the company.[39] Many businesses set up company sports clubs, 'football, light athletics, boxing, handball, rowing, gymnastics, hockey, swimming, tennis, cycling, jiu-jitsu – nothing has been forgotten.'[40]

Anyone who worked in small shops with three or four colleagues, or in modest offices in the provinces, could only dream of such a work atmosphere. Most office employees worked in small-scale, cramped conditions. But the urban department stores and large-scale offices were at the focus of sociology, the press and culture. It was here that the future was getting under way, and here that the contradictions clashed most clearly. While most of the young office workers lived in modest rented rooms, or at home in miserable circumstances, every morning they crossed the threshold into a more tasteful life, particularly when their workplace was in one of the spectacular palatial office blocks or one of the glittering department-store temples. Everything about this life was concerned as much with appearance as it was with reality. Office workers had to be well dressed; if not actually elegant, then at least in the latest fashion. No one who saw these women at work would ever have dreamed of the miserable conditions in the poorer districts to which they streamed at the end of the working day. Cramped courtyards, damp walls, shabby furniture and dim light – the antithesis of the bright, modern office environment that filled the popular imagination during the latter half of the 1920s, in which everything seemed to be on the up.

In the morning they would apply their rouge and adjust the locks of their bobbed hair into kiss curls in the style of the American silent film star Louise Brooks, and put on an expensive-looking dress in which they could have stylishly gone dancing. When these young women prepared for their job, they had already half emerged from their woebegone existence, which they escaped entirely as soon as they had pulled the apartment closed behind them to hurry to the office. A warped situation that the drama of this secretarial class staged again every morning.

Much the same was true of the young male office workers or salespeople: the clerk would look in the mirror and see someone that wasn't quite him, but rather the person he promised to be. Visually he represented a status that he hadn't yet reached and perhaps never would. The desire for advancement was inherent in his job, however small his real chances might have been. He worked on the threshold of something better, on the interface with a higher social class that he studiously tried to imitate. The more successful he was at that, the more secure his job seemed.

This 'will to happiness'[41] particular to the status of the clerical worker encouraged his loyalty to his superiors and towards the world of work as a whole. Politically speaking, then, the clerk was diametrically opposed to the revolutionary; dismissal was not a reason to revolt, but a tragedy to live through.

The warped economy of happiness associated with the office life meant even more to women than it did to their male colleagues, because they embodied the novelty of the age to a much greater degree. With their pointedly fashionable appearance, their bobs, their short, swinging dresses, their bold lipstick and their quickwittedness, honed in countless plots and wisecracks, they were the spitting image of the feminine type which they knew from the glossy magazines, and which in real life was more at home in the upper class. That was where the 'New Woman', the darling of the culture industry of the Weimar Republic, was able to flourish. These were women who could afford their ostentatious independence, and often didn't need to earn anything to do so. These were women who rode expensive motorcycles and drove expensive cars, like Erika Mann or Maria Therese von Hammerstein, who travelled the world at their own expense, like Clärenore Stinnes, who played tennis, learned to fly or at least studied chemistry, who idolised their own sex and who calmly and publicly defined the terms of their own sexual identity.

Many young office girls closely resembled this ideal of libertarian bohemia that was propagated in the media, but they were not remotely close to being a part of it. It only appeared as if the cultural avant-garde were sitting at typewriters, as if woman like the young author Ruth Landshoff-Yorck, the photographer Annemarie Schwarzenbach or the artist Renée Sintenis had become a mass phenomenon, as if the 'Roaring Twenties' had been so turbulent, volatile and lascivious that the excitement had spilled into the machine-rooms of bureau-cracy, leaving the typewriters coated with gold dust from a night of frenzied dancing that had to be blown away each morning. That was the fantasy of the decade, and that was how many of the young typ-ists imagined it as well.

'Fashion and eroticism painted over the lack of satisfaction intrin-sic to the job', wrote the historian Ute Frevert, summing up the fact that the often dreary work at the keyboards was warmed by a fire that fed on the illusions inherent in the world of the office.[42]

Intellectuals in the office – cameos from the upper class

With their ultramodern bearing, many female office workers yearned for a lifestyle that far exceeded their traditional attitudes to life. They weren't nearly as permissive as they seemed to be. 'One need only hear,' Siegfried Kracauer wrote in 1930,

> Trude, a salesgirl in Moabit, moving away from her made-up col-leagues, who are, we might add in passing, equally ill-disposed towards the workers whom they serve; how judgmentally she speaks of the flighty girls who dine at Kempinski in the evening, in the company of gentlemen. [. . .] Inherited concepts of morality, religious ideas, suspi-cion and traditional wisdom from meagre lodgings – that is all part of it, in untimely opposition to the prevailing practices of life. One

should not forget these undercurrents. Where they are present, they lead to difficult conflicts between individuals and the environment.[43]

Many young secretaries who had come from small towns to Berlin, Munich or Cologne oscillated between the moral ideas they had brought with them and their experience of the astonishingly loose morals of the city. Some suppressed their concerns, while others fought internal struggles with their consciences. Kracauer, here every inch the alert reporter, spent a lot of time among office workers, kept his ears open and was even given access to the correspondence of a young couple thinking about the future. He quoted the female partner – Käthe – who, in a comical mixture of business German and intimacy, enquired of her 'beloved youthful colleague' what he thought about the following question:

What in fact is our position on sexual intercourse? Should young people engage in such intercourse prior to marriage? I answer in the affirmative, on the condition that the persons in question are sufficiently mature and mentally in accord.[44]

What is striking is that Kracauer describes the predominating permissiveness as a thoughtlessness that has been forced on people.

The sexual permissiveness that predominates today is a concern for many young people in the lower secretarial circles. They would like to express their own feelings; they resist the system that tries to define their existence, and are overpowered [*übermannt*] by the system.[45]

'*Übermannt*' – the term is a telling one. Kracauer saw the inexperienced young women he met, who had often escaped rural or working-class backgrounds, as victims of a libertinism from which men in particular tended to profit. The 'typewriter girls' presented themselves as emancipated urban flappers, with short hair and skirts and smart backchat, but they didn't have the inner independence and intellectualism to defy the coldness of the modern world. The drama of social immaturity also plays a part in Irmgard Keun's novels, in which women present to the world a kind of freedom for which they lack both the self-confidence and the material conditions. So, for example, the 'artificial silk girl' Doris, newly arrived in Berlin, wants to become 'a glamour', a living light of the kind that haunted the worlds of fashion, nightlife and the imagination. Since it was an imitation, lacking the real social conditions that made such a life possible, that 'glamour' only created additional conflicts.

At times of economic and personal setbacks, the eagerness with which modern lifestyles from Berlin's trendsetting scene were imitated by girls in shops and offices could easily flip into the feeling of being patronised by remote elites. From 1930 onwards, androgynous play with gender roles and ostentatious permissiveness were perceived more and more as decadent, false and destructive. These ambivalences could be studied precisely in the microcosm of the office. The workforce was by no means homogeneous; it included those who had risen from the working class, alongside fallen daughters from the educated middle class who had been deprived by inflation of their financial safety net.

Office literature was full of intellectual secretaries who turned the heads of their co-workers with their ideas as well as their boldness.[46] But they could equally easily be dismissed as snooty and ignored accordingly. In the novel *Herr Brecher's Fiasco* this role is played by the privy councillor's daughter Mucki Schöps, who is forced to work in an office after the death of her husband. Many women (and men too, although it was easier for them to advance) were obliged to work full-time 'below their skill-level', even if they were above their superiors in terms of education and intellect. Others only made brief cameo appearances to finance temporary phases of experimental independence. They swept like comets through the secretarial world as admired role models, who gnawed away still further at the value systems of the simpler girls.[47] Dora Benjamin, the wife of the philosopher Walter, worked as a secretary for a time. Presumably she unsettled her colleagues just as much as her husband unsettled the traditional practice of philosophy.

The Berlin secretary Albertine Gimpel became the icon of 'secretarial bohemia',[48] if not of the 1920s as a whole. She is known worldwide by the name of Sonja.[49] In 1928 the artist Christian Schad painted her in the Romanische Café and called the painting simply *Sonja*. In her little black dress, invented only three years before by Coco Chanel, and hence ultra-modern at the time, Sonja is sitting alone at a table in the legendary literary meeting place. She is smoking Camels and using a long cigarette holder to keep her fingers from turning yellow. On a table behind her is a bottle of sparkling wine in a cooling bucket. Also sitting behind her are two men; the painter has moved them so far to the edge that only a shoulder of each is visible. The ear of one is, however, known to everyone in Berlin; it belongs to the famous poet Max Herrmann-Neisse, who was in the café every day. But the poet is a side issue, a marginal figure in the literal sense, since Sonja sweeps everything else aside.

The world-famous painting hangs in the National Gallery in Berlin. Sonja is a silent majesty, not a frivolously chattering Gilgi, misunderstood perhaps, but still unmistakeably an authority. Her seriousness and her loneliness don't quite fit with the sparkling wine; there is something gloomy about her, a darkness that emanates not from her black dress, but from her gaze, before which the viewer shrinks. This woman has already seen a lot, but at the moment nothing and no one has anything to offer her. The day has been stressful, and the night may be too, but this moment belongs only to her.

The fact that Sonja, in spite of her enormous individuality, represents a type is confirmed by the comparison with a secretary at Westdeutscher Rundfunk, photographed by August Sander, the great physiognomist of the Weimar Republic, in 1931. It's one of 60 portraits that form the *Face of Our Time*, one of his famous volumes of photographs. We don't know the name of this secretary, either real or fake. She too sits smoking, she too penetrates the viewer with that gloomily indifferent gaze that is ready for anything, that thinks everything is possible. Presumably her boss's communications crossed her desk day after day, for her to pour them into letters; every day she was witness to his power, and its instrument. Her hair severely parted,

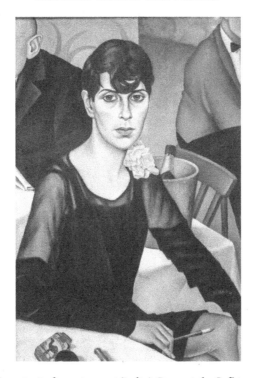

Christian Schad's portrait of a customer at Berlin's Romanische Café in 1928 became one of the most famous works of Neue Sachlichkeit. It shows Albertine Gimpel, a secretary with the oil company Olex, after work. It became well known under the title Sonja. *At the top left, the ear of the poet Max Herrmann-Neisse.*

androgynous in line with the times, and at the same time very modern, she looks into the camera, which captures her for ever, before going back into the anteroom – one of 250 employees making radio broadcasts in Cologne.

Unlike manual workers, secretaries did not have easily identifiable identities. They stood with one foot in the world of the bourgeoisie, if not in the corridors of power, with the other still – or back – in the reality of the proletariat. They spent the least on food, much less than the proletariat, but the most on leisure, sport, cinema, cabaret and radio, much more than the bourgeoisie.[50] They were the most effective target group of the new entertainment culture. Threatened with social decline and oscillating between appearance and reality, somewhat incapable of solidarity because of the internal structures of competition, the rough wind of economic crisis blew particularly cruelly through their ranks. They embodied the dynamic of the Weimar Republic most convincingly, and were at the same time most strongly exposed to it. Unlike workers, they would have trouble finding a scapegoat if things started to go downhill.

Precarious Balance: The Death of Ebert, the Arrival of Hindenburg

Politics and the many ideas that are proclaimed these days. Everyone is allowed to speak his mind, and it is bad to stand so far apart as I do.

Siegfried Kracauer, *Georg*

The president sits a posthumous test – and so does the Republic

At the end of February 1925, Friedrich Ebert died at the age of only 54. The medical diagnosis cited protracted appendicitis leading to peritonitis. The protraction, in turn, was the consequence of a deep insult that the president had experienced at the hands of a Magdeburg court, which had been processing a libel action that Ebert had brought against a journalist from the *Mitteldeutsche Presse*. As so often, it concerned an accusation of treason, frequently brought by the political right. The journalist was found guilty, but in its summing up the court established that as a member of the January strike in 1917, Ebert had himself committed treason, because the strike had weakened the defensive power of the German Reich. The strikes in the munitions industry, called by the Spartacist alliance, had been directed above all against the poor food situation and the continuation of the war. At the urging of the workers, Ebert and his chancellor Philipp Scheidemann had led the strike but had then called for moderation – in line with the views of the SPD, which had not supported the strike.

Ebert was enraged by the court's ruling. It placed an extraordinary amount of responsibility on his shoulders, wholehearted statist that he was. A more frivolous character would have dismissed the judge as a far-right lunatic, but Ebert had a nagging sense of dishonour. Depressed and bitter, he neglected the treatment of his inflamed appendix and ultimately failed to survive it. As soon as the news of his death had reached the outside world, something strange happened. The Republic held its breath. Ebert, who had been granted only emergency rations of recognition while in office, received it in abundance after his death. All of a sudden he struck those left behind as a mighty father without whom the future would have been even more uncertain. Even conservative newspapers saw their country as orphaned. Now that he was gone, the former working-class pub landlord, the stocky little saddler, mocked as a miscast, undistinguished president impersonator, was seen as a stabilising anchor who had held the Republic together with superhuman powers. The newspapers wove him page-long obituary wreaths, stressing the 'uncommonly fortunate worthiness, a worthiness that was not exaggerated' that he had added to 'his natural tact, his innate calm'.[1] Knowing that 'a task lay in his hands' had always provided a 'feeling of complete reassurance', the *Vossische Zeitung* wrote.[2]

The writer Gerhart Hauptmann called for a lying-in-state in the Neue Kirche in Berlin in order to underline the venerability of the deceased. However, the *Kunstwart* ('Art Guardian') of the Republic, Edwin Redslob, who was responsible for the memorial service, had other ideas. On 4 March the coffin was carried in solemn procession from Ebert's house via the Reichstag to Potsdamer Platz, with several stops, celebrations and addresses along the way. It then carried on to Heidelberg, his place of birth. Unexpectedly large crowds lined the streets to bid farewell to Ebert and file past his coffin. At each stop Redslob had organised speeches 'of extreme simplicity and at the same time of extreme size and weight': 'a worthy celebration of the Republic for its late saviour and defender', the *Berliner Tageblatt* wrote.[3] For this moment, in which such huge crowds participated, the Republic appeared to have much more support among the population than one might have imagined from normal everyday life.

The impressive, moving funeral, which added an effective closing touch to the less than brilliant office of the late president, was a quiet triumph for a man who provided the aesthetic accoutrements of the short-lived Weimar Republic from start to finish. Not many people had survived all the confusions and changes of government as intact as Edwin Redslob, *Reich Kunstwart* and trained art historian. The curious-sounding office of 'art guardian' chiefly served the look of the Republic, from the design of the Reich eagle and the stamps via flags and orders to the organisation of the annual celebrations of the constitution and state funerals. We might mock this today, but for the young Republic the aesthetic of the state was not to be underestimated, because it had to provide something that would come even close to gripping the minds of the nation in the way that the pageantry of the German Empire, impelled by Kaiser Wilhelm's hunger for prestige, had done. This was a nearly impossible task; unlike the German Empire, the sober Republic lacked the transcendent component 'of God's mercy', the inner logic of which had justified the ceremonial grandeur. But in the case of Ebert's funeral, as with the previous memorial service for the murdered foreign minister Rathenau, it was successful. Here Redslob was able to achieve a gravity that stood comparison with imperial spectacles without sharing their often ludicrous tackiness.

The appraisal of the *Spandauer Zeitung* shows how important it was for the Republic to radiate dignity as well:

For the first time, and surprisingly quickly, the German Republic has had to elaborate a ceremony for the burial of the imperial head of state. The task of preserving the dignity of the Reich and the Republic, while at the same time avoiding excessive pomp, was solved with taste and joy. Anyone who witnessed the preparation of the funeral route, the Reichstag forestage, the decoration of the house of mourning and Potsdam Station, must admit that the uniform direction by the Reich Kunstwart Dr Redslob was a great success. The row of large laurel trees all the way down Wilhelmstrasse, the dull black obelisks in front of the house of mourning and in Pariser Platz, the green-swathed advertising pillars, the black-draped candelabras, the forest of black banners by the entrance to the Tiergarten – it all looked serious and solemn, without seeming overdone.[4]

At the death of its first president, almost the whole Republic seemed unusually to be at peace. Thanks to its master of ceremony Redslob, the young Republic had passed a test of dignity. At the stroke of 11 on the morning of the funeral, public and private traffic was halted for five minutes. The workforces of the big companies also gathered in the streets for a brief reflection. Only Munich University did not comply with the ministerial decree to close for the day, justifying this with reference to the negative response from the student body, which was even less well-disposed towards the Republic than was usual among scholarly young people.

The hero of Tannenberg in blackredmustard

How would things continue now? The extensive unanimity of those days did not last for long. The greatest concern was to be found abroad. The German newspapers were surprised to quote the obituaries by their British, French and American colleagues. The Americans in particular were concerned that the Hohenzollerns might try to return to power, and Crown Prince Wilhelm might stand for election as Ebert's successor before going on to reintroduce the monarchy.

What happened next could easily have been mistaken for this horrific vision. Seventy-seven-year-old Field Marshal Paul von Hindenburg, close victor in the second round of presidential elections on 26 April 1925, actually looked like a substitute kaiser. Hindenburg, the 'hero of Tannenberg', liked to appear in a spiked helmet (*Pickelhaube*) and with rows of medals on his chest. His wavy moustache stuck out powerfully over his wide cheeks and gave him the appearance of the perfect Wilhelmine edition of the president. Grizzled Hindenburg's career extended deep into Prussia's glorious past. In 1866 he had taken part in the battle of Königgrätz, and in 1888 he had sat vigil by

Wilhelm I's body. The grotesque claim of having lost the war 'undefeated in the field' sounded best coming from him. Now he had been democratically elected president, beating the decent lawyer Wilhelm Marx, member of the Catholic Centre Party and candidate of the republican-inclined *Volksblock* (People's Block).[5]

The fact that a small, relative majority of citizens had decided in favour of the former head of the Supreme Military Command and inventor of the 'stab-in-the-back' legend dismayed the republicans, who had just interpreted the broad sympathy over Ebert's death as an indication of trust in democracy. 'Now more than ever: long live the Republic!' was the defiant headline on the front of the liberal *Berliner Volkszeitung* after the vote count; they tried to console their readers with the calculation that the victor Hindenburg still only represented a minority, since the Communists had split the anti-nationalist front with a candidate of their own, Ernst Thälmann.[6] Conversely, the right-wing *Berliner Börsen-Zeitung* was triumphant: 'The national idea is on the march: Hindenburg is Reich President!', stressing that the campaign, 'the battle for our nation's soul', had by no means been won. And in passing, the *Börsen-Zeitung* made it clear what it thought of democracy. It was not about majorities, but about unity: 'The important thing is to win back not only the majority, not only the two-thirds majority for the nationalist idea, but the unity behind the fatherland that made our nation a giant in 1914.'[7] How nationalists implemented the struggle for the soul of the nation if their powers of persuasion were not sufficient was made apparent on the election day: with cudgels, iron bars and pistols, their thugs outside voting stations left many people injured and several dead.

For his friends on the far right, however, Paul von Hindenburg proved at first to be a disappointment. He did obstruct a number of laws aimed at the partial expropriation of the princely houses, but by and large the new president was loyal to the democracy that had brought him to power. Hindenburg enjoyed playing the role of president of the entire nation, and to that degree did not act according to his reactionary convictions, as the favourites around him had hoped. The monarchy seemed clearly to be a thing of the past, even for the

Even visually, Ebert's successor Paul von Hindenburg was a step backward. With his spiked helmet he signalled his attachment to the past. In practice, the helmet was something of a curse. The gleaming tip poked out of the trench and gave away the location of its wearer. Many soldiers screwed them off or wrapped them in dark cloth.

monarchist Hindenburg. Many contemporaries even associated him with the hope that right-wing conservatives might in due course come to terms with democracy and integrate with the Republic.[8] Was it not a good sign that in his swearing-in ceremony Hindenburg was wedged in among the black, red and gold flags of the Republic, 'blackredmustard', as the opponents of the Republic mocked? A representative of the good old days at the head of the modern Republic – Germans in search of harmony interpreted this as a big step in the direction of inner peace and unity.

★

With the 1928 Reichstag elections, the mood in the country swung back towards the left. The Social Democrats became the strongest party in government again, and under Chancellor Hermann Müller formed a four-party coalition government. From left to right on the political spectrum, these parties were: the Social Democratic Party (SPD), German Democratic Party (*Deutsche Demokratische Partei*, DDP), Centre/Bavarian People's Party (*Bayerische Volkspartei*, BVP) and German People's Party (*Deutsche Volkspartei*, DVP) – almost a new edition of the big coalitions of the earliest years. Overall, those parties that were loyal to the Republic were strengthened, and the German Communist Party, the KPD, had been too. But the most important thing was: the anti-Semitic, nationalist German National People's Party, the DNVP, had sustained heavy losses, and the still tiny National Socialist German Workers' Party, the NSDAP, regis-tered losses as well. Democracy emerged from the elections confirmed and re-established. Gustav Stresemann remained foreign minister and visibly continued to ensure continuity. The right-wing menace seemed to have been banished, but the bourgeois *Vossische Zeitung*, under the headline 'The leftward march of the voters', summed up the situation with only partial relief:

> Everywhere in the Reich voters have opted against the former right-wing government. In the zeal of conflict they shot beyond the target. They marched leftwards to the cry 'Never again German nationalist!' and overleapt the centre.[9]

Things would become difficult in the longer term, the *Vossische Zei-tung* continued, if the centre was missing. The *Berliner Tageblatt* was more optimistic.

> The significance of the election for domestic politics lies in the German people's thorough rejection of German nationalist dema-goguery and ambivalence in a strong new affirmation of the German Republic, whose opponents have been roundly defeated.[10]

The struggles to form a government, however, revealed the almost unbridgeable differences between the SPD and its bourgeois coalition partners. While ministers got their act together quite quickly, their parties persistently thwarted their desire for compromise. The SPD was particularly adept at doing harm to the members of its government. In the dispute over the construction of an armoured cruiser in November 1928, SPD MPs required their ministers to vote against a cabinet ruling that they had approved two months previously. The whip made it possible to force ministers to toe the party line and thus sacrifice their credibility and dependability.[11] A similar game developed in the centre which, out of concern for its Catholic profile, shifted further to the right than was bearable for the viability of the coalition. Stresemann also had his work cut out moderating the industrial magnates in his DVP and moving them away from their most worker-unfriendly demands. The fragile balance of power in the Reichstag held as long as things were looking economically rosy. But the mood was growing more irritable, the tone more vitriolic, and attempts to find common ground were abandoned. For far too many players in the Republic, the following applied: 'Principles were upheld and compromise scorned.'[12]

Flag dispute on a Baltic beach

The blockades between the government and the parties that constituted it provided welcome arguments for the opponents of democracy.[13] These disagreements illustrated their assertion that the state was the prey of a feuding political caste that was fighting over it like a pack of wild dogs. Prime examples of this are the words that the sculptor Karl Donndorf wrote for the illustrated volume *Germany's Heads of the Present Day on Germany's Future*:

It is not quality but the majority of votes that decides things in Germany. The feud runs deep through parties and hence the parasitical red-tape bureaucracy that has settled upon party forces out of

excessive caution. The rise of Germany, which lacks a reckless dictator, is suffering from this fruitless overload.[14]

A telling picture of the political mood was played out on the
beaches of the Baltic. City-dwellers travelled there in the summer,
entrenched themselves beside their sandcastles and demonstrated
their political attitudes. They hoisted flags: the adherents of democracy flew the black, red and gold banner. The black, white and red
flag, in the colours of the old Kaiserreich, was planted by the German
nationalists. The two groups viewed each other suspiciously from
sandcastle to sandcastle. All it took was a spark for hatred to explode.
Many locals found this awkward. The 'Reich war flag' was too much
of a defining presence on the beach, the spa administration of the
resort of Ahrenshoop complained in the summer of 1928. Everywhere one looked, black, white and red flapped in the wind. There
was clearly a greater need for affirmation on the far-right than on the
Republican side, which also flew flags in neutral colours for the sake
of a peaceful holiday. The right-wing vacationers were also inclined
to steal the black, red and gold flags of the Republic to keep the beach
'clean'. An exasperated Ahrenshoop spa administration complained
to one newspaper about the 'charge of lunatics' who fell upon the
village with their 'political petulance' in the summer, while for the
rest of the year one would find a Social Democrat sitting next to a
German nationalist in the local card-game club, 'and neither could
understand why on earth they shouldn't be the best of friends'.[15]

There were opportunities for political feuds everywhere, but there
was little dialogue. People limited themselves to flag waving, to the
use of symbols and styles. Hair, clothes, musical preferences and the
choice of daily newspaper were outstanding ways of demonstrating
political attitudes. Conflicts shifted from solid political issues to culture, fashion, lifestyle, all of which also betrayed political attitudes,
but which had less obvious connotations and stopped short of making
an overt statement. This aspiration to artistic distinction was among
the things that made the 1920s into one of the most creative decades
of history. The cultural life of the time could be considered as a

'communicative laboratory of togetherness and opposition', a
'laboratory of multiplicity', which prompted a heyday of diversity,
but also one of separation and division.[16] While on the one hand Germans were communicating to an unfamiliar degree, via phone calls,
newspapers and the radio, at the same time the different camps were
gruff and silent in their treatment of one another, and only eloquent
within their own bubbles, cut off like the holidaymakers behind their
sandcastles. 'The left, in so far as it was aware that there were intellectuals outside its own camp,' the American historian Walter Laqueur
wrote, 'regarded their [the right's] outpourings as mere gibberish on
which no sensible man would waste much time.'[17] Conversely, 'the
German right regarded the left-wing intelligentsia as a noxious element [. . .] more dangerous than gangsters', because they were 'helping
to bring about the spiritual murder of an entire nation'.[18]

There were, however, countless people who did not want to be
assigned to either of the camps into which the Republic, if they interpreted the signs correctly, had divided itself. They went dancing,
strolled around in the crowd and felt lonely. The helpless, thoughtful
person who could find no place for himself in the excitable collectives
was one of the most common figures in the literature of the time.
'Not knowing where one belongs', 'simply going on living', became a
burden in view of the many people inspired by the flourishing visions
of salvation. 'Politics and the many ideas that are proclaimed these
days. Everyone is allowed to speak his mind, and it is bad to stand so
far apart as I do,' Siegfried Kracauer's dithering hero Georg complains
in the novel of the same name, and can still find no refuge for his
troubled mind.[19] And in Erich Kästner's novel *Fabian*, published in
1931, Fabian's friend Labude writes in his farewell letter: 'We are
standing at a historical turning point, where a new vision of the world
must be constituted, everything else is pointless.'[20] As a melancholic
he was armed against everything, he claimed, but now he felt like a
ridiculous figure, small in a great age that was becoming greater by
the day.[21]

Since debates around hard political themes were becoming increasingly fruitless, the desire for discussion found release in less clearly

occupied territories. There were certainly people who read both the right-winger Ernst Jünger and the communist Bertolt Brecht, the reactionary elitist Stefan George and the left-wing commentator Kurt Tucholsky. The variety of Weimar culture was enormous, and there were many omnivorous consumers among the public. Many people were preoccupied with the question of what could bind together a great variety of conflicting attitudes to life. Only recently liberated from the authoritarian order of the Kaiserreich, they became mystified by the issue of what it is that actually holds free individuals together, what reliably regulates their coexistence and keeps them from constant clashes and collisions. The city in particular, with its coordinated modes of transport, its opportunities for individualistic self-development on the one hand and the crowd's patterns of motion on the other, became a test case for the future viability of the modern age. Traffic, the most important medium of this newly accelerated life, became the focus for people's anxieties and high-flying expectations. With its whirling spirit of cooperation, its written and unwritten rules, and its wordless, intuitive accommodations, it became the training ground of modern society – and also its symbol.

6

Traffic as the Art of Citizenship

It was as if the earth suddenly lost its gravity and liberated me. I held tightly on to the steering wheel, but my feet were far away and found no purchase, and I myself was light and empty and could fly safely through space and my breath was also very light and almost superfluous.

Annemarie Schwarzenbach

This air of freedom, brazenness and petrol.

Gabrielle Tergit

'Never too near or too far': the city and the sense of touch

Where there are people there is also traffic. Traffic is the fluid of their coexistence, their motion in space, the transportation of their goods. The purpose of traffic is both to produce and to avoid contact. People want not only to reach one another, but to pass by one another unharmed.

People need each other, and they are afraid of each other – both of these facts are proved daily in traffic. It is a mirror of desire, of unrest and vitality. In the Weimar Republic it assumed such density and such magnitude that it became frightening.

Immediately after the war, private cars were still an absolute luxury. Those who owned them also had chauffeurs to ferry them around. But within a few years cars became everyday objects. Between 1924 and 1932 ownership of privately owned vehicles in the German Reich multiplied fourfold, from around 132,000 to 497,000. In the same period the number of lorries multiplied by five, from 30,000 to over 150,000. And within ten years the number of motorcycles increased by a factor of 30 to 800,000. While horse-drawn carts still rattled along country lanes, the rural calm seldom interrupted by automobiles, in the cities the roar of combustion engines drove anyone with sensitive hearing to distraction:

> Four-hundred-pound power units belch their way coarsely along with a deep, complacent roar. Shrill whistles ring out intermittently. Huge automobiles, 'record-breaking' eight-hundred-pounders, groan, grunt, squeak, beep and honk. Motorbikes hiss and snort through the silent night.[1]

These are the words of the philosopher Theodor Lessing, who had brought out a pamphlet urging caution: *Noise: A broadside against the loud sounds of our life*, published as early as 1908.

No end to growth was in sight. Since motorbikes and cars were made increasingly cheap by assembly-line manufacture and the cities were attracting more and more people, fantasies of the future made way for a dystopian density of traffic. It seemed only logical that cities would soon look as Fritz Lang had prophesied in the 1927 silent science-fiction film *Metropolis*: they would grow steeply upwards and downwards, and aeroplanes would float along the gorges between the buildings and under bridges that connected the residential towers at dizzying heights.

The most vital German city novel so far, Alfred Döblin's *Berlin Alexanderplatz*, was published in 1929 and begins with gridlock on an existential scale. The novel's main character, Franz Biberkopf, is already unaccustomed to traffic after a long stay in prison. On the day of his release into life as if from a protective womb, when he is cata-pulted from the tram into the condensed tumult of Berlin, he experiences a kind of birth trauma. The raging traffic comes charging

Traffic on Leipziger Strasse, Berlin, around 1925: 'The cars raged and jangled on ceaselessly, house-front by house-front' at the end of the decade in Alfred Döblin's novel Berlin Alexanderplatz.

at him, nothing seems to want to stay in its place, even the roofs look as if they are slipping and about to plunge down upon him – Biberkopf flees terrified into a house doorway.

From now on the trauma of the traffic won't leave him. About 60 passages in the novel are devoted to Biberkopf's insecurity. Again and again he fears being thrown off by the city; he anxiously checks the roofs as he walks through Berlin to make sure that they aren't starting to slide. He is never allowed a relaxed stroll; he marches, he fights his way through, he runs against a city that its creator Döblin has organised as a hyperactive surface, a space that can rebel, that develops its own hubbub of voices and constantly addresses the protagonist. Here the surroundings do not group themselves obediently around the main character as they might in a classic novel, they move according to their own laws, they can rise up and literally shake off a person. This is the modern city as man's antagonist – much more than a mere dwelling place, it is a social space that can achieve autonomy and turn the movement of a human being into its opposite. And at the same time it is a place of longing, full of promises and gripping density of experience.

In the 30 years between 1875 and 1905 the number of inhabitants in Berlin had more than doubled from 1 million to 2. In the ten years from 1920 until 1930 an additional 500,000 people had arrived, bringing the total to over 4.3 million. No one could have guessed that the peak had been reached. Instead they were sure that the city would become more and more cramped, and that it would happen increasingly quickly. For many Berliners the imagined future of their city existed alongside the present, as if in time lapse; they lived with one foot in what was yet to come. Berlin presented itself as the 'fastest metropolis' in the world. The symphony of the big city played constantly in the background, and the experience of the capital, which was in fact very quiet in some places, was overlaid by anticipated turbulence. Every traffic jam, every hint of a crowd, prompted the anxious certainty that worse was on the way – Babylon and Gomorrah, the sci-fi version. Multiplied with the threatened dangers from criminality and vice, the city was also perceived as a flourishing thicket and a devouring jungle, technology as hostile nature, as a Moloch – a devouring monster – that threatened to consume its inhabitants.

*

The architect and city planner Martin Wagner, Berlin's municipal building surveyor since 1926, had been brought in to keep gridlock at bay. In a series of lectures and essays that coincided with the publication of Döblin's novel, the passionate Social Democrat, inspired by the possibility of planning the future and by the immensity of the tasks that it involved, set out how he imagined the reconstruction of the city in accordance with the needs of the future.

Wagner saw himself as the 'director of the global city', and the city itself as the 'constructive housing of a machine for work and comfortable living'.[2] Using the example of Alexanderplatz, he wanted to show what modern city planning was capable of doing: 'The square of a global city is a sluice for traffic, almost constantly full, the "clearing"-point of a network of veins of the first order,' he explained. 'Traffic must be guided across the square with as much speed and clarity and as little interruption as possible.'³ But Wagner, one of the first prophets of the car-friendly city, had more in mind than merely cutting his way through the confusion of the streets and airing cramped neighbourhoods with wide avenues. He suggested a 'differentiation of thoroughfares'. Pedestrians, trams, cars, horse-drawn hackney carriages, handcarts and cyclists would no longer have to fight against one another, but would instead be guided in a circle, at different levels. This multi-storey 'roundabout' might have come to nothing, but in Alexanderplatz Wagner did introduce a roundabout, although here it assumed an elliptical form.

Once it had been completed, the result was sobering: the cars now curved spaciously around on the large ellipse, while the tramlines crossed in the empty middle of the square. Two office blocks, unadorned in the *Neue Sachlichkeit* style but very elegant, with impressive cubic light towers on their frontages, lined the square to the west. The eastern edge was worse. It didn't actually exist. A generous space had been created here with the wrecking ball, but there was no money left to build on the vacant lots. In 1929, because of the looming global economic crisis, the investors pulled out, so the huge empty spaces simply continued to yawn there. Later, the anti-urban void would conform to National Socialist taste, and the urban planners of the GDR were also happy with it – its rough lack of welcome remains unique to the square even today.⁴

Until Martin Wagner's rebuilding measures, Alexanderplatz had been an intoxicatingly beautiful but also a chaotic place. The many department stores and shops, including the Hermann Tietz store with supposedly the longest shop facade in Europe, the huge Central Market Hall, where the horse carts of the farmers from the surrounding countryside regularly caused traffic jams in the morning, the short- and long-distance railway lines, the grand hotel, huge numbers of office blocks, and restaurants such as the famous Aschinger – all meant large crowds. At the middle of the whole thing stood 'Berolina', a colossal 14-metre figure in a chain-mail vest, who was supposed to embody the proud city of Berlin. And she embodied it fairly well, with her surprisingly charming features.

But after the reconstruction, stout Berolina no longer matched her roadworthy 'clearing point'. She was too eighteenth-century for the Berlin magistrate, and Urban Surveyor Wagner had always imagined the spirit of the new age as being 'fat-free'. 'The modern mass,' he wrote, 'wishes to appear fat-free, like an aeroplane, a diesel locomotive, an engine, etc.'[5] So buxom Berolina ended up in storage. She would only be reinstalled, to the applause of an emotional Berlin populace, by the Nazi magistrate. But that was a deceptive triumph typical of the Nazis: in 1942 Berolina was finally melted down for munitions production.

When they saw the new plan for the square, the horrified managers of Tietz department store declared themselves willing to give its wonderful Wilhelmine facade, with its opulent curves and the proud Atlas figure on the gable, a functionalist redesign – so great was the fear of being swept away by Berlin's dynamic planning project.

Martin Wagner dreamed of a city that could rebuild itself generation after generation – a constant spirit of renewal. But the costs of demolition and reconstruction had to be covered at top speed. For that reason, he defined the ideal plan for a global city not only as having the smoothest possible crossing traffic, but as producing a profit:

> The *flowing* traffic in the square must be set against a *standing* traffic that holds tightly on to the purchasing power of the crowds of people crossing the square (shops, bars, department stores, offices etc.). In that way one arrives at a concentration of buildings whose 'alignments' must be adjacent to the lines of motion of the pedestrians, which is to say the purchasing power.[6]

In Wagner's plans consumption had almost exactly as great a part to play as traffic, since in the end someone had to pay for this permanent progress. Every 25 years urban construction investments were to bring in a profit so that the next generation was able to engage in a redesign. 'In our time there is no longer any place for petrified eternal values,' he said.[7] If every generation could rebuild

Alexanderplatz, 1935. By the 1930s, the lively, busy square of the immediate post-war years had become a 'speedy cosmopolitan square', car-friendly, but also quite bleak.

the city as they saw fit, the 'aesthetic problem of urban development' would solve itself.

Wagner believed that happiness could be built, rationalised and fairly distributed by planning measures. For conservatives, this was a hideous idea, a gratuitous destruction of natural order and inequality. For most of them, the cities, with Berlin at their head, were irrevocably lost, breeding grounds of cosmopolitanism and cultural Bolshevism, women's emancipation and liberalism. In 1918 and 1922 the philosopher Oswald Spengler, the supplier of culturally pessimistic slogans directed at the city, had claimed in his two-volume doorstopper *The Decline of the West* that the emergence of global cities had throughout history been a sure indication of a culture's decline. The development of the global city had regularly meant the beginning of the end of a mature civilisation. It replaced homeland with cosmopolitanism, it robbed people of their respect for tradition and organic growth, it transformed the people into a crowd, it despised the provinces and farmers and hence the foundations of its own existence, and, not least, it was damned by its innate intellectual arrogance to steer itself towards its own end.[8]

If the right declared its devotion to the countryside and its folk traditions, the left praised the city and its free spaces. Joseph Roth professed himself in favour of traffic. The author and journalist, who was born in 1894 in the Galician shtetl of Brody, and who had come in 1920 from Vienna to Berlin, wrote a hymnic declaration of love to the *Gleisdreieck* (the word means 'track triangle'), an unadorned Berlin junction of two underground train tracks close to Anhalter Station and to the strange place where an elevated railway ran through the middle of the second floor of a rental block: 'I declare my admiration for the *Gleisdreieck*. It is a symbol and the initial focus of a circle of life, fantastical product of a force that promises the future.' After this beginning, Roth got into his flow:

This is what the heart of a world looks like whose life is wheel belt swing and clock-strike, the cruel beat of the lever and the wail of sirens. This is what the heart of the earth looks like, which rotates a thousand times faster on its axis than it wants to teach us by day and night shift; whose incessant rotation looks like madness and is the product of mathematical prescience; whose furious speed presents itself to sentimental backward-lookers as the brutal annihilation of internal forces and healing balance, but in reality produces life-giving warmth and the blessing of movement.[9]

Amazing what hope of the future traffic could inspire in such a profoundly melancholy man. Roth, who worked for the *Börsen-Courier* and the *Frankfurter Zeitung* among others, was filled with sadness at the decline of the Austrian monarchy, but celebrated the beauty of soot and iron all the more defiantly: 'The landscape is given an iron mask', he cheered, and saw along the tracks iron 'guards sprouting upwards and signals blossoming in bright green'.[10]

'Asphalt literati' was the term the National Socialists used for convinced urban authors such as Joseph Roth, Alfred Döblin, Erich

Käsnter, Lion Feuchtwanger, Gabriele Tergit and Vicki Baum. In 1929, when the *Vossische Zeitung* asked him to take part in the survey 'Does Berlin inhibit or encourage artistic creativity', Alfred Döblin replied as enthusiastically as one might have expected of one of the asphalt literati:

> Over all it has a powerfully, inspiringly enlivening force, that excitement of streets, shops and cars is the heat into which I must allow myself to be beaten if I'm working, which is to say always. That is the petrol on which my car runs.[11]

★

The Cologne-based scholar Helmuth Plessner wrote a philosophical celebration of traffic in a higher, communicative sense. In his 1924 book *Grenzen der Gemeinschaft* (Limits of Community), a 'Critique of Social Radicalism', he developed a theory of coexistence in which he advocated the virtues of good traffic, using 'traffic' to refer to all levels of social interaction, not only in the street. Plessner's 'relationship theories of coldness'[12] were a plea for an anonymous society, striving to strip the phenomenon of alienation of its horrors and stress its positive sides. He advised making social traffic as pleasant as possible, with people coming 'never too close nor too far' from one another, so that to some degree they could get along with one another without accident. Tact, in particular, was necessary, Plessner said, a thoughtful response to the truth, a willingness to maintain a balance between honesty and consideration: 'Sparing the other for my own sake, sparing myself for the sake of the other.'[13] In order to get on in society, one had to know how to disguise oneself, keep one's opinions to one's chest and wear masks. 'Tenderness' was important, 'obligingness that does not oblige', a 'culture of restraint'.

For Plessner, the modern age required a cheery face; 'tact', 'respect for the other soul', was the magic formula that preserves an anonymous society from collisions, makes it loveable, smooth and ultimately exhilarating. The second-last chapter, about the 'hygiene of tact', practically swings, it has rhythm and energy, and here too the symphony of the big city rings out, in philosophical application.

In fact, the ability to negotiate a roundabout, to synchronise oneself, to communicate quickly with swift gestures and glances, to switch lanes gently, was in many respects like being at a party where one is constantly switching conversational partners and, amidst convivial small talk, keeping people pleasantly close and at a distance at the same time. 'Where does cordiality begin, where does it stop?' Plessner asks.

> Where does it cross over into sociability? Where does the familiarity of community circles begin, where are we allowed to relax and build on kindness, love, understanding and insight? If tact doesn't tell us, we are betrayed and sold. Feeling, checking, saving face, but never with too heavy a gun, without superiority – a sure sign of weakness – without insistence, open, but never without reserve, determined, but also flexible, lovable, but never creeping – everyone knows these oscillations whose amplitude decides man's dignity, standing and value in society.[14]

The analogies between social traffic and street traffic are obvious; for that reason traffic also became a central topic of the Weimar Republic, because the most contrary individuals had to learn to rub shoulders fluently. The extent to which they seemed to have achieved this, and at such pace, could be seen as the secret code for a future society based on intuitive conflict resolution, while in reality the debates were becoming increasingly hurtful, political positions increasingly irreconcilable. Siegfried Kracauer was fascinated to watch police offers and experienced taxi drivers greeting one another and communicating fleetingly with inconspicuous gestures, how the officers ceased to be holders of high office and instead became 'functionaries of traffic'. Traffic sent very new instructions to the brain; new hybrid forms of concentration and intuition were used, new capacities for spatial and dynamic vision, a sixth sense for the coexistence of an unfamiliar quantity of variables. It was impossible not to be spellbound at the effect that new systems of rules had on people. For example, traffic lights: the fact that amber appeared between red and green gave rise to extensive observations that attempted to trace what traffic was doing to people. Kracauer reflected on the meaning of the three-phase traffic light:

> This amber marks the transition from one resolute state into another. It cautions pedestrians and automobile drivers to pay attention and liberates them from all reflections that the compulsion to consideration commanded when signals changed suddenly. By introducing an intermediate light, caution is to a certain extent objectivised and initiative displaced from people.[15]

In other words: amber allows people to doze peacefully during the red phase. Something that has passed wordlessly into our DNA today had to be analysed at length.

Plessner's reflections became explosive against the background of the debate around society versus community. These slogans concealed different visions of the essence of social cohesion; in community, cohesion is defined by descent and by common values that are passed down; in society, by rules governing the coexistence of people who are potentially alien to one another. Their forms of traffic require an ability to compromise, and tact.[16] *Völkisch* theorists stressed community, democratic ones society. (The term *völkisch*, essential to the National Socialist vision, refers to members of a national community, relates to the promotion of German purity and greatness, and carries strong racist connotations.) For the far right the case was quite clear: community is German, society is alien to us. The cultural critic Helmut Lethen came up with a fine phrase: 'When traffic becomes the central topic, creatures that wish to put down roots will suffer.'[17]

Democrats, on the other hand, had pace on their side. The worship of speed, the aesthetic presentation of traffic in a global city, the profound connection between fashion and cars – this was the bearing of a democracy connected by fate to growing affluence and the certainty that things would keep going forward in the long term. Of course, there were also some among them who did not join in with the application of political significance to the phenomena of city and traffic. Under his pseudonym Ignaz Wrobel, Kurt Tucholsky described Berlin's traffic as pure invention, a media phantom that matched the deep urge of the 'new German' to feel the way he imagined Americans felt: 'Living in a city that has a "Ssitti" and a "Brodweh" lifts their spirits.'[18] That was why the Berlin press was busy

> drumming a new fixed idea into the Berliner: traffic. The police support them splendidly in this. The attempts currently put in place to organise traffic, to grasp it statistically, to describe, to regulate, to drain and feed it are practically ridiculous. [. . .] Is there really so much of it? No. if you come to Berlin, a lot of people will ask you with an almost pleading expression: 'Berlin traffic is colossal, isn't it?'[19]

It wasn't, Tucholsky replied, Berliners just imagined a bleak spectacle like the one in Paris: 'Berlin does not have this traffic, but it imagines it does, and the police regulate this imaginary traffic as no one in Paris has ever regulated it, nor ever would.'[20] This notional 'traffic plague' spread to the rest of the country: 'What Berlin has, Bückeburg deserves. No car far and wide, but two traffic policemen; a car on the horizon: and wild waving, honking and whistling begins.'[21]

It was true: the familiar mixture of inferiority complex and boastfulness was lived out in Berlin's description of itself as the fastest city in the world. But even Tucholsky's dismissiveness wasn't free of pose. The marketplace of opinions was not dissimilar to what we have today: it's always tempting for a well-known op-ed journalist such as Tucholsky – 'Tucho', as he was known – to sign off calmly on a debate that has become too heated. Then the only option is the discipline of skilful deflation, of which Tucholsky was a master. But there will have been a reason why, in 1924, the traffic police that he so disdained set up Germany's first traffic light, housed in an 8-metre-high tower. Twenty-six tramlines and five bus lines crossed Potsdamer Platz; contemporary films show a considerable swarm of cars, horse-drawn

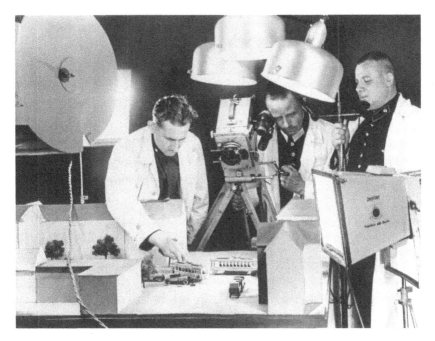

Traffic scientists. Experts simulate a possible traffic accident in the film studio of the Berlin police in 1932.

carriages, handcarts, motorbikes and pedestrians. At peak times that would have made even a car driver of today break out in pearls of sweat.

Potsdamer Platz assumed mythical status at a speed entirely in line with the velocity-driven times. Even today no tour guide will neglect to mention that it was once the most traffic-filled square in Europe.[22] For many visitors from the provinces who travelled to their capital, following the motto 'Once to Berlin', the experience of turmoil at Potsdamer Platz was a must. Baedeker recommended comfortable vantage points: 'The lively bustle may be comfortably observed from the Bellevue patisserie (N.), the café of the Fürstenhof Hotel (S), and the Josty patisserie and the Pschorrhaus restaurant (W). In the evening bright neon signs.'[23]

A city without people

The city was particularly challenging to painters. On the one hand there were the lovers of traffic: Lesser Ury painted magical representations of night-time urban traffic using impressionistic lighting effects; Ernst Ludwig Kirchner turned Potsdamer Platz into a circular rotating stage on which two elegant passersby with feathers in their hats turned into shrill sensations, their proportions dramatically distorted: the square is small, the two graces enormous. But what might be more surprising is the counter current: some painters whom we now see as strong proponents of *Neue Sachlichkeit* created a very quiet picture of the city. Their melancholy urban still-lifes look like a protest against the cult of speed that dominated their time. So Gustav Wunderwald's Berlin street landscapes are usually deserted. At most a lonely couple, deliberately drawn far too small, wanders around the mountainous buildings. These are images of almost ghostlike peace that draw much of their power from the absence of traffic.

Wunderwald's paintings look like sets – until 1918 he earned most of his money working as a set painter in the theatre – for a life that has yet to be performed or accessories for a play that has been cancelled. What a contrast with the stage sets for the plays of Erwin Piscator, which kaleidoscopically depict the bustle of the city via the use of photomontage. Wunderwald's streets, on the other hand, are stripped of all excitement. But this is done in such a radical way as to intensify the sense that in reality these streets are different. Standing before their painted silence, the noise returns for a moment in the mind of the viewer. The charm of this magical realism lies in the aesthetic opposition to the turbulent reality; what remains uncertain is whether this emptiness is oppressive or beautiful. Similarly mixed feelings are created by the Dresden street paintings of Wilhelm Lachnit,[24] influenced by Giorgio de Chirico's 'metaphysical realism', or the deserted streets and industrial paintings of Carl Grossberg, who even managed to paint Berlin's AVUS race track without showing a single car.

Other *Neue Sachlichkeit* artists such as Reinhold Nägele[25] or Wilhelm Heise[26] painted dense scenes of traffic, but they look strangely paused, as if frozen solid. That is partly to do with the diktats of the concise outline, a central stylistic feature of *Neue Sachlichkeit*. The almost hyperreal precision even of distant objects makes every passerby, every dog, every automobile stand out clearly. In this way, they produced extremely precise images swarming with detail, through which you can walk in your imagination like a child through a picture book. In contrast to Impressionism or Expressionism, where details blur in the flow of colour and the dominance of emotions, and everything is united in the stream of the crowd, in the urban themes of *Neue Sachlichkeit* each person remains self-contained, even when there are hundreds of them. Every individual is as identifiable as a pinned insect. There are no blurs of motion. The city squares, seen under a microscope, thus look at once idyllic and alienating. In them, the individual is frozen and alone, captured with the finest of brushes and separated from the others; each on his own, alone in the crowd.

The Cologne painter Anton Räderscheidt simply left out the other participants in the traffic. His chosen subject was himself, always portrayed as a dark figure in a tight-fitting black coat and wearing a bowler hat. Almost redundantly, he stands in front of the modern grid facades of large office buildings, in empty, abandoned city streets. Räderscheidt painted fantasy and horror paintings at the same time, pursuing the idea that our loneliness increases along with the number of people surrounding us. In their spiritual poverty they are so far away that the painter simply erases them from the cityscape.

In 1914, in his poem 'Cities', the poet and dramatist Alfred Wolfenstein describes loneliness in the crowd like this:

> Our walls are thin as skin,
> So that everyone joins in when I weep,
> Whispering forces its way across like bawling;
> And how mute in a remote cave
> Untouched and unlooked-at
> Everyone stands far away and feels: alone.[27]

Flaneurs and car drivers

It is an unavoidable fact that melancholy is also a part of urban happiness; city traffic is a tireless sequence of meetings and farewells. 'In the human funnel, a million faces,' Kurt Tucholsky wrote of passing encounters in the big city: 'Two strange eyes, a brief glance, / the brows, pupils, eyelids – / What was that? Perhaps your life's happiness . . . / Gone, vanished, for ever.'[28]

In the 1920s the city stroll was a literary genre of its own, nurtured above all in the arts section of the more serious newspapers. The 1920s saw an intense engagement with the theme of movement in cities. Back then, authors such as Franz Hessel insisted on slowness; they saw themselves not as participants in traffic, but as its observer, as dissidents of the general hubbub and also as educationalists. They effectively coached their readers in traffic, always maintaining the balance between the lonely observer and the pedestrians' immersion in the flow.

Franz Hessel delivered the finest example of ambitious strolling in his 1929 book *Walking in Berlin: A Flaneur in the Capital*. The intelligent loafer had plenty of time. The son of a banker had inherited so much money that he was able to study Orientalism without any great urgency in Munich around the turn of the century, without finishing the course, preferring to write here and there, and enjoying the extensive entourage of the wonderfully unconventional Fanny Gräfin zu Reventlow in the elegant Munich district of Schwabing. Incidentally, the beautiful countess died – we are still on the topic of traffic – in 1918 from the results of a bicycle accident. In 1906, Hessel moved to Paris, where he stayed until shortly before the First World War. Post-war inflation wiped out Hessel's inheritance, so the polyglot bon viveur, whose first novel in 1913 was tellingly entitled *The Junk-Shop of Happiness*, suddenly had to get to work. 'Get to work' is meant literally here. The book *Walking in Berlin* begins with the author's description of himself as a troublemaker. He strolled through the streets so slowly, Hessel wrote, that he was constantly in the way of busier people. To

those who rushed hastily by he appeared as an outsider, even as someone shady. 'In these parts one has to *must*, otherwise one *may* not.
Here one does not go somewhere, but *to* somewhere. It is not easy for
our kind.'[29] In fact, the 1929 Street Traffic Act permitted stopping only
'when pedestrians are not disturbed or obstructed by it'.[30]

Franz Hessel didn't have to *must*. In his mind he was still a gentleman of leisure. His wife Helen worked as a fashion journalist for the
Frankfurter Zeitung, and her income helped. In every respect the two
were a remarkable pair and more than that: with Franz's best friend,
the French author Henri-Pierre Roché, they had a *ménage à trois* that
lasted over 13 years – they even kept a shared diary together. In 1962
François Truffaut filmed the story of their cohabitation in *Jules et Jim*,
which would build a kind of spiritual bridge between the libertinism
of the 1920s and that of the late 1960s.

Hessel took up the profession of flaneur with the same enthusiasm
with which he followed the twisted path of his heart; he was not
afraid of instructing his readers in the proper ways of strolling. The
most important thing was not to have a fixed destination in mind
when promenading, but rather to allow oneself to drift through the
city.

> Flaneuring is a kind of reading of the street, in which human faces,
> stalls, shop windows, pavement cafés, tram tracks, cars and trees
> become letters of the alphabet with equal status, which assemble into
> words, sentences and pages of a book constantly renewed.[31]

The city as text – that was a central image of newspaper arts pages
in the 1920s. Siegfried Kracauer, who had been Berlin correspondent
of the *Frankfurter Zeitung* since 1930, wrote a little city column with the
title 'The view from the window'.[32] From his apartment in Sybel-
strasse in Berlin he looked westwards over a somewhat chaotic
cityscape: the exhibition centre could be seen, a tangle of train tracks,
allotments and the radio tower, on which a sphere of light rotated at
the time, pointing the way for aircraft to Tempelhof Airport. The
blinking light looked like a lighthouse, 'and when the storm wails, it

flies over the high sea whose waves wash the field of train tracks'. This urban landscape had not been intentionally shaped by planners, but by random events and the needs of an increased volume of traffic on land and in the air. Kracauer ended his painfully beautiful text with a sentence which, on closer inspection, is nonsensical in several ways at once, and which can still cast light if not necessarily illuminate. 'Understanding of cities is tied up with the decipherment of their dreamily uttered images.' One should not spend too much time reflecting on this sentence; but if one does, one might wonder: can images be 'uttered', and dreamily, at that? Can they be 'deciphered? And what might an 'understanding of cities' be? Hard to imagine finding such a sentence in a newspaper today. But special times require special measures. The excessive demand on logic in Kracauer's closing sentence corresponded to the excessive demand that cities made on the senses and on reason. To that extent, the sentence was extremely precise.

And somewhat habit forming. It is because of such wayward stylistic escapades that the melancholic flaneurs of the arts pages remain popular even today. Benjamin, Kracauer and Hessel posthumously became the sweet poison of a generation of students of German; at the peak of his fame in the 1980s the figure of the flaneur practically enjoyed cult status. But one other species of traffic pioneer in the 1920s lives out a shadow existence in the cultural memory, although one that has proved much more crucial for the problems of the contemporary world: motor-car drivers.

'Thinking ore' and singing cars

In the 1920s the motor car assumed a high status from which it still benefits in the present. That decade saw its potential to influence the social psyche unfolding, along with the problematic promise of individual freedom that makes it so difficult to bid it farewell.

At the beginning of the century the motor car was still the exclusive province of the wealthy, for businessmen, ministers and senior officials. It was quite natural that a paid chauffeur should be sitting at the wheel; passengers allowed themselves to be driven about, usually with the roof up. But soon the self-drivers began to arrive; they had passed their driving tests and enjoyed the intoxication of speed, at least until a speed limit of 65 kilometres an hour was imposed.

The playwright and poet Bertolt Brecht dreamed of owning a car, although he could also be scathing about the Weimar culture industry's credulous devotion to technology ('God has returned in the form of an oil tank', he wrote in his poem '700 intellectuals pray to an oil tank'), but he was equally happy to pen a hymn to the elegant automobiles of the Steyr company. The fact that Steyr also manufactured weapons, including the Mannlicher Stutzen, a hunting rifle, only made Brecht's heart beat all the faster:

> We come
> From a gun factory
> Our little brother is
> The Manlicherstutzen.
> Our mother, though, a Styrian oar-mine.
> We have:
> Six cylinders and thirty horsepower.
> We cling to the bend like adhesive tape.
> Our engine is
> A thinking ore.
> We drive you so smoothly
> That you imagine you're in bed
> That you imagine you're driving
> Your car's shadow.

Steyr was so touched that it gave the poet a four-cylinder vehicle as a fee for his advertising verse, and a second when Brecht immediately crashed the car into a tree. But the accident had not happened out of sheer clumsiness, and, according to Brecht at least, it was only pure presence of mind that it hadn't been much worse. The business-minded Brecht was smart enough to report the accident, in which he sustained slight injuries, to the illustrated magazine *Uhu* and supply them with material for a story that was several pages long. According to this narrative, the poet had found himself driving straight towards another overtaking vehicle that was unable to re-enter its own lane in time. In order to avoid a collision Brecht had needed to steer his car to the side. *Uhu* reported:

> Brecht's car was thus forced to dodge, and by pulling powerfully on the brake and immediately releasing it again he managed to drive into the nearest available tree. He succeeded in hitting the tree with the middle of the radiator and thus stopping the car. The radiator was crushed, and the belching front side of the chassis bent around the tree, but it also held the car firmly in place. The accident resulted in insignificant injuries.[33]

The magazine illustrated the report with several impressive photographs. Steyr was grateful for the extra advertising. After all, Brecht had done everything correctly, the use of the snub brake was exemplary, and the poet had demonstrated that even a serious accident with such a valuable car, with truly 'thinking ore', could have a happy outcome.

There was one prominent voice on the left who had already discovered the threat from the motor car that many people see in it today. In his 1929 novel *10 HP* the Soviet author Ilya Ehrenburg, also widely read in Germany, saw the car not as a source of all evil – that was capitalism – but as a symptom of it. For Ehrenburg the motor car 'tears flesh apart, it blinds the eye, devours the lungs, strips reason away. [. . .] The motor car laconically drives over pedestrians. [. . .] It is only fulfilling its purpose: its vocation is to eradicate human beings.'[34]

Storm of Steel author Ernst Jünger, still eager for the experience of battle, saw some form of compensation in traffic. He experienced the honking in commuter traffic as 'whistling, wailing notes in which an imperious threat of death finds direct expression'.[35] He saw the many victims of traffic as a kind of collateral damage of the modern age and of *Neue Sachlichkeit*:

Traffic has really developed into a kind of Moloch which, year in, year out, devours a quota of victims comparable only to that of war. These victims fall in a morally neutral zone; the way in which they are perceived is statistical in nature.[36]

The number of deaths from traffic accidents in Germany was 5,867 in 1929 – a high price to pay for the fact that the car connected city and country, beach and mountain, bringing the country closer together. Many people lost their lives in twisting villages that suddenly saw themselves having to cope with overland traffic for which they had not been built. New roads were needed, and in 1926 planning began for the first autobahns. One of these, the HaFraBa between Hamburg, Frankfurt and Basel, did not make much progress, but the first 'cars-only road' between Cologne and Bonn was inaugurated as Germany's first autobahn on 6 August 1932 – by Konrad Adenauer, mayor of Cologne from 1917 until 1933 and a resolute anti-Nazi in the ranks of the Centre Party. The notion that Hitler had brought autobahns to the Germans is pure propaganda. To lay claim to the idea, the Nazis later demoted the Cologne–Bonn stretch to a mere country road. For the other stretches of autobahn, in most cases they used the already existing plans from the Weimar Republic. Even the idea of building autobahns as a way of creating labour came from Konrad Adenauer: in order to give work to as many unemployed people as possible he had forbidden the use of bulldozers.

The improvement in overland traffic made it easier to escape the city for a moment. 'Blissful hours in nature, hours of freedom, far from the bonds of the everyday', an Opel advertisement promised in 1930. The car was a symbol of modernity and at the same time a means of escaping it – twin aspects of its seductive force. People could drive into the countryside, to the beach and into the mountains with a picnic basket and a gramophone in the boot. Often the journey was the destination and movement the chief purpose of the outing.

One incorrigible traffic hooligan was Erika Mann. The daughter of Thomas the Nobel laureate was a passionate devotee of speed.

She loved hurtling through the villages and getting chickens between
her wheels in such a way that they then reappeared unharmed in the
rear-view mirror. She gave readers of the illustrated magazine *Tempo*
her recipe for driving away the blues: dashing out of the city and scar-
ing the villagers:

> It is only when you are roaring through the sullen, rainy cow towns,
> so that the puddles spray around the ears of the passersby and only
> sheer chance protects you against disaster on the bends, that you start
> feeling better. On the open country road, the chickens, spirited crea-
> tures that they are, shamble towards you as you hurtle along at 70.
> Now you can even ensure that they pass directly under the car,
> unharmed by the wheels. Exactly as if the sun were shining.[37]

In the press she talks coquettishly about her many fines. It was only
when she was driving her father about that Erika Mann had to watch
her speed. The Nobel prize-winner owned two large automobiles, a
Horch and an open-topped Buick, but couldn't drive himself. Instead
he loved waving graciously from the back seat as the Buick glided
through Munich.

In Berlin it was possible to indulge in an addiction to speed without
endangering the lives of chickens. On the AVUS you could really put
your foot down. The first racetrack in Germany had been opened in 1921
as an 'Automobile Traffic and Training Road' (Automobil-Verkehrs-und
Übungs-Strasse). You couldn't get very far on it – 9 kilometres in a
straight line and 9 back again, with two elevated bends in between.
The private road was not connected to the public traffic network
until 1940. Anyone who wanted to dash along the AVUS, 'amidst
swarms of other cars dashing by like planetoids or gunshots', as the
Swiss author Jakob Schaffner exulted, had to pay ten marks.[38] A three-
month ticket cost a thousand marks – a sum that must have seemed
obscene to most Berliners.

Part of this price was down to the fact that it was the 'inflation
king' Hugo Stinnes whose investment had made the construction of

the AVUS possible in the first place. Stinnes's villa on Douglasstrasse to the west of Berlin, where his daughter Clärenore grew up, was within hearing distance of the AVUS. The roar of engines may have contributed to the fact that Clärenore had a lifelong addiction to cars. When the AVUS was opened she was 20, at 24 she won the 'all-Russian test run' and a year later, in 1926, the German Grand Prix – on the AVUS, a stone's throw from her house. A year later, at the age of 26, she set off on a round-the-world trip by automobile, much of it through regions that had never seen a car before.

As her family objected to the journey, she had to seek sponsors. The Adler company gave her a three-speed 50hp Standard 6, which she called 'the little one'. She had reclining seats put in for sleeping. She set off with 148 eggs as an emergency store, three pistols for self-defence and three evening dresses for diplomatic purposes, accompanied by the Swedish photographer Carl-Axel Söderström and a technical team in a lorry. Foreign Minister Stresemann had issued her a diplomatic passport and had oil and petrol stored at German embassies as a precautionary measure. The support team gave up in Moscow; Clärenore Stinnes and Söderström continued on the journey alone: over the frozen Lake Baikal, through the Gobi Desert, via Beijing to Japan. Here they loaded 'the little one' on to a ship and made the crossing to Lima, from where they travelled over the Andes. Back in Berlin, after almost 47,000 kilometres, Clärenore Stinnes married her Swedish companion. She had been required to persuade him several times not to interrupt the hellish journey, and in the end he was hardened enough to marry her. They had drunk water from the radiator to keep from dying of thirst, they had escaped tribal princes and warlords by the skin of their teeth, and had nearly frozen to death on several occasions.[39] Clärenore Stinnes was one of the incredible number of strong women of this decade who dared to travel out into unknown continents, into the air, into science and art. And in spite of that sensational journey, she was not even the most prominent in the circle of popular women drivers. Some of them were real virtuosos at dealing with the media.

Up and away – women at the wheel

In the trendsetting glossy magazines, cars and women were a magical combination that kept reappearing in different forms. It was *the* sign of changing times. The new age was dashing onwards with a woman at the wheel. Eight cylinders controlled with no apparent effort, and the 'gentleman racer' had been overtaken once and for all.

There are countless front pages and advertisements in which beautiful women sat in beautiful cars, often accompanied by a beautiful, slender greyhound that looked as if it obeyed every word. Like their cars, however, these women had to be able to present themselves well. They had to look elegant and majestic – or else athletic, boyish and unattached.

Erika Mann knew how to give outings in her beloved Ford a new twist, and keep her *Tempo* readers engaged with spirited travel columns. She and her brother Klaus published a travel guide to the Riviera. For the series *What You Won't Find in Baedeker* they proposed an early form of individual tourism, now recommending a grand hotel, now a small pension, often accompanied by tips for cheap parking. Soon, however, the driving became much more important for Erika Mann than the places she visited. Happiness came in the form of a journey, while the landscape became mere shadows and Europe 'merely a place to drive through', as she put it. On a 10,000-kilometre rally, launched by the German Automobile Club, from Munich through Switzerland via France, Spain, Portugal, Italy, Yugoslavia and Hungary and back to Berlin, she zoomed 1,200 kilometres over land every day, and in the short breaks she even found time to dictate her racing reports to the *Tempo* editorial team.[40] Once, she herself summed up this rather questionable way of experiencing space: 'Rome? Just a washing opportunity.'[41]

For women such as Erika Mann, driving at speed was intoxicating. The automobile gave the sexes equal opportunities; it allowed the modern woman to leave her classical role in the dust. Small wonder that the liaison between women and cars almost assumed cult status.

The self-portrait of Tamara de Lempicka in a green Bugatti was practically ubiquitous. The jet-setting painter, of Russian-Polish origins, had painted the image for the cover of the July 1929 edition of the women's magazine *Die Dame*. She sat grandly at the wheel, her hand gloved in soft leather, a scarf wrapped opulently around the neck of the Madonna of the motor car, while her eyes beneath her leather cap were narrowed to sceptical slits and her red lips in a frivolous moue.

One long scarf was the undoing of an equally elegant woman. In Nice, in September 1927, the dancer Isadora Duncan was throttled by her loose red silk scarf after it got caught in the spokes of the wheel of her sports car.

Another reputation inseparably identified with cars is that of Ruth Landshoff, one of the most glittering figures of Berlin's party and culture scene. 'Girl driver Ruth', as she called herself, loved cars with all her heart. The niece of the publisher Samuel Fischer and daughter of the opera singer Else Landshoff-Levy was one of a kind in Berlin high society. Even as a young girl she hurled herself with insatiable curiosity into the cultural scene, drifting through its parties, gallery openings and premieres. She tried everything: modelling, dancing, acting, writing, dog breeding, the sexes. There was hardly anyone that she couldn't bewitch. Ruth Landshoff was a real it-girl and more than that. The painter Oskar Kokoschka broke into her boyfriend's apartment to paint her portrait. She played croquet with Thomas Mann and was disappointed at his stiff performance. When she had read the thousand pages and more of the diaries of Harry Graf Kessler, probably the busiest socialite of the decade, she noted proudly: 'Of the people listed in the index I knew 315' – personally, of course.[42] She even played a minor role in F.W. Murnau's 1922 film *Nosferatu*.

At the age of 18, Ruth Landshoff moved out of the parental home and lived for a few years with Karl Vollmoeller, 26 years her senior and no less illustrious. Vollmoeller was truly multitalented; he had already proved himself as an archaeologist, poet, dramatist, theatrical entrepreneur, racing driver and aeroplane engineer by the time Landshoff moved in with him. His play *The Miracle* was such an international success that he made a fortune from it alone. Later, he would work on the screenplay of Josef von Sternberg's *Blue Angel* (1930) and secure Marlene Dietrich for the main role.

The fact that young Ruth was living with Vollmoeller did not mean that she had abandoned her desire for experimentation. Outwardly it even appeared as if he subsidised her erotic escapades, or at least she appeared even more in love with life by his side than she had before. She lived an openly bisexual life – like many women of that decade she liked to dress in men's suits and ties, and did everything she could think of to escape the narrow limits of her gender role. She had an intimate friendship with the wealthy Swiss industrialist's daughter, photographer and author Annemarie Schwarzenbach, whose attractive masculine features also made her an icon of the 1920s, and who was also, of course, wild about cars – her own took her as far as Persia and Afghanistan.

Karl Vollmoeller loved girls, and so did Ruth Landshoff. In the 'Vollmoeller system' she had assumed the 'dubious role of constantly bringing new and younger women to this man in his mid-forties', the author Jan Bürger writes.[43] One must imagine the Vollmoeller house as a 'casting studio for some of the most important film and theatre productions of the Weimar Republic'.[44] In his memoirs the director Géza von Cziffra describes Landshoff's role for Vollmoeller in these terms:

> She always gathered young girls around her, she sorted them, and those selected ended up in the bed of Vollmoeller, who passed them on to his friends after a time, like a used car. [. . .] Whenever Vollmoeller and Landshoff turned up with two or three pretty girls for afternoon tea in the Eden Bar, people whispered to each other, using car language: 'The Vollmoellers are having a test drive!'[45]

Harry Graf Kessler spoke of Vollmoeller's 'harem on Pariser Platz'. There is one often quoted passage from his diaries in which he gives an account of a Vollmoeller party with the famous dancer and actress Josephine Baker:

I drove to Vollmoeller's harem on Pariser Platz and found there, apart from Reinhardt and Hulschinsky, among half a dozen naked girls, Miss Baker, also completely naked apart from a pink muslin apron, and little Landshoff [. . .] as a boy in a tuxedo. Baker danced with extreme grotesque artfulness and stylistic purity, like an Egyptian or archaic figure performing acrobatics without ever falling out of her style. The dancers of Solomon and Tutankhamen must have danced like that. [. . .] The naked girls lay or danced around among the four or five tuxedo-clad gentlemen, and little Landshoff, who really looks like a handsome boy, danced modern jazz dances to the gramophone with Baker. [. . .] Between Reinhardt, Vollmoeller and me, all of whom were standing around, Baker and Landshoff lay in an embrace like a pair of young and beautiful lovers.[46]

Quite a scene – three men appraising a group of naked women, and trying to imagine ways in which they could be used in the culture industry. Karl Vollmoeller wanted to write a ballet for Josephine Baker, a 'courtesan's tale', of course. Kessler wanted to contribute a mime based on images from the Song of Solomon, with 'Baker in costume (or non-costume)',[47] and 'little Landshoff' as Solomon in a tuxedo.

The 'Vollmoeller system' demonstrates the complete ambivalence towards sexual liberation in the Weimar Republic. No one can rule out with any certainty the possibility that Vollmoeller's salon was as repellent in its way as the office of the film producer Harvey Weinstein. However, Ruth Landshoff stood by Vollmoeller after she had split from him and become a promising author, and in 1930 she married the young and extremely handsome businessman David Yorck von Wartenburg. Even later on, after Vollmoeller's death in 1948, she took care of his literary estate. She doesn't seem to have felt exploited.

Ruth Landshoff knew very well that she was living outside the rules. 'I don't refer back. I anticipate', she wrote, but she still felt like a typical representative of her generation, and even sometimes considered herself its voice.[48] From 1927 onwards she began to work as an author for Ullstein. The publishing house placed big hopes in her, and her provocatively cheeky fresh tone was intended to lift writing out of the stiff and tortuous prose that had become commonplace among many Ullstein authors. Things began brilliantly: with her first article, 'The low-hp girl', she was introduced in the magazine *Die Dame* as the coming thing. What was crucial was her visual appearance. She posed twice for the article with her white six-cylinder Adler convertible – a dazzlingly beautiful car with a light-blue leather top. In one photograph she sat at the wheel, in the second she was sitting on the kickboard, her hair ruffled by the wind, a cigarette in her mouth, absently stroking her dog. Even down to the pied coat, whose pattern repeats the fur of the pretty animal, the picture is a perfect image of wealth, youth, beauty and female independence.

Within the circle of car-driving women writers, Ruth Landshoff concentrated on the lifestyle aspects of the subject. Unlike Erika

The author and actress Ruth Landshoff with her six-cylinder Adler convertible. She has chosen her coat to match her dog. She wrote motoring columns for and about 'girl drivers' for various newspapers. 'We stopped being sweet little darlings a long time ago,' she wrote, 'now we are brave, independent lads.'

Mann she was less interested in speed than in what one looked like. But no leather trimmings: if 'you imagine having to repair break-downs yourself, bring an overall with you and a leather blanket to put on the ground,' she recommended to her women readers.[49] She kept them constantly up to date with new tips on equipment. Opportunities for spending money were inexhaustible:

> Of course you already have a practical cigarette lighter in your car. But wouldn't it also be nice to have a nice silver case on the dashboard of your car that spits out cigarettes when you press a button?[50]

Such a thing was a must-have. Ruth Landshoff promoted and marketed, wrote spontaneously and very youthfully, in a skilful teenager style that was particularly striking in the context of the often fussy mode of her milieu. She didn't even balk at the idea of a love story in which a car could feel and suffer, and serve as a faithful, pastel-coloured boyfriend to its owner. She reminded her 'girl drivers' to give their sensitive cars grateful kisses on their shiny radiator noses, before leaving them alone in the garage.[51]

The erotic charge of the relationship between woman and car became a fixed idea in the fashion-conscious circles of the Republic. In 1932, in the magazine *Querschnitt*, also published by Ullstein, Karl Vollmoeller claimed: 'The telephone and the car are currently secondary sexual characteristics of the young girl.'[52] He reported from America that at student dances 'two thousand cars belonging to young girls stood outside the club houses or hotels'. After the dance the young people would regularly make their way to the cars for erotic purposes. 'Strict morals from Boston to San Francisco raise no objections to this. It's the universal fashion. And it's quite seemly. The car hides everything.' At the end of the article he asked himself and his readers: 'Where would today's young girl be without her light-blue, dove-grey or white cabriolet?'

This article was written at a time of high unemployment following on from the economic boom, when even a tram journey was too expensive for millions of young women. The freedom embodied by

Ruth Landshoff was light years away and yet quite close, proclaimed as it was from every newspaper kiosk. In the eyes of the unemployed, this kind of freedom must have looked like either an invention by the wealthy or simple mockery. When emancipation comes from above, and is so closely related to wealth, at a moment of crisis it cannot be perceived as anything but humiliating and insulting. The majority of Germans went on foot, sat crammed together on the commuter train or took the standing carriage in the Reich railway.

In the famous 1927 silent film *Berlin – Symphony of a Great City* by Walter Ruttmann – a swift filmic cross-section through 24 hours of urban life – traffic was defined not only by car tyres but by train wheels and coupling rods, by tramlines and horses' hooves, cartwheels and handcarts. But above all by shoes. People ran, dawdled, strutted, sauntered and marched. Berlin was above all still a city of pedestrians, whose paths were constantly being crossed by the flow of vehicles. Like Franz Biberkopf in *Berlin Alexanderplatz*, many struggled to make their way through the city, anxious less they lose the thread of their fragile life story in the tumult of an increasingly uncertain metropolis.

Marieluise Fleisser presented a less glamorous picture of women drivers in her novel *Mehlreisende Frieda Geier* (Flour Saleswoman Frieda Geier), published in 1931.[53] Frieda Geier is a travelling saleswoman in southern Germany. In her Opel Laubfrosch ('tree frog'), the little 4hp model, she drives around the country and tries to sell flour to wholesalers – flour that poor people always find overpriced. For Frieda, a 'free-acting agent',[54] a woman under stress, the Laubfrosch is not a boyfriend but a work tool, and a reluctant one at that.

> The Laubfrosch makes a spectacle like a little green demon and rattles and shakes her bones to the marrow [. . .]. She knows every bend in the road by heart. She knows where the Laubfrosch makes an involuntary jump into the air. Today she's a bit late, she lets the frog have its leap. It looks ridiculous when she cranks the light vehicle to the brink of its peak performance.[55]

It wouldn't have occurred to Frieda Geier to write a 'hymn to traffic', as the writer Martin Kessel had put it in 1925 in far-off Berlin: 'Bare cobblestones, from you I draw triumph and victory', he wrote, and continued: 'Now, carousel, forget all thought of danger!'[56]

Seven years later, in Kessler's office novel *Herr Brecher's Fiasco* there is a wonderfully melancholy sketch of traffic in rainy Berlin. Not a trace now of triumph and victory. Frau Perdelwitz, an elderly, unhappy secretary, unsuited to life's daily struggle, 'snuggled up into the falling damp' and hurried home along Friedrichstrasse. Behind her

> loomed the rugged massif of Friedrichstadt, a big, rocky, mist-swathed shadow above which, mirrored in the ether, an eternal dust trickled, a million-fold reflection of the energy that is light, and is repeatedly coaxed forth by machines and human hands. The trams rang out, crowded, illuminated coffins; they were clearing out for Sunday, they were depopulating the office buildings and of the countless passengers each one who had reached his house number paused, gripped the handle and disappeared.[57]

For now, traffic had done its duty. They were home.

7

The Charleston Years

Here and there two young girls dance together, sometimes even two young men; it's all the same to them.

Thomas Mann, 1925

'They pay, and you must dance'

Before Billy Wilder had any idea that he would one day live in Hollywood and be considered one of the world's greatest film directors, he worked as a gigolo in Berlin. The young journalist, paid by the line to write commentaries and reports for Ullstein newspapers, was strapped for cash. Since he, like hundreds of others at the time, was passionate about dancing, it seemed an obvious way of making some money. A dream that had a dark side. For two months in 1926 he went to the Eden Hotel every day to dance. From 5.30 to 7.00 in the evening in a dark suit, from 9.30 in a tuxedo. A wave of the hand was enough, and Wilder had to hurry over. He would bow politely and say, 'Will you allow me a little dance, miss?'

Gigolos – also known in German as *Eintänzer* (dancing partners, or 'dancers in') – were there to be hired. The waiter was informed, and he would discreetly instruct the dancer to visit the customer's table so that he could politely invite her to dance. If single women lacked the courage to ask for a dancer, the gigolos were required to issue the invitation themselves. Less attractive women were always asked first.

'Between two women, thou shalt always choose the fatter one' was one of the ten gigolo commandments that the journal *Revue des Monats* recorded in 1926. Another read: 'Beware of love, for it makes the legs go limp.'[1] The hotels and large dance halls hoped that their range of gigolos would ensure large numbers of women visitors, who wanted to get their money's worth without having to sit around waiting for too long. The head of dancing at the Eden, one Herr Isin, told Wilder what was required: 'You are not here for your pleasure, bear that in mind. You have to dance. In fact, the less you like them, the more honestly and conscientiously you will perform your service. The dancer's first commandment is: there shall be no wallflowers. He has to pluck them, because that's what he gets paid for.'[2] That was how Wilder told the story a few weeks after the end of his period of engagement in late 1926, in a report for the newspaper *B.Z. am Mittag* in which he enterprisingly wrote about his job as a gigolo.

It was not only single women who relied on gigolos. Sometimes a whole family would turn up for a tea dance and Wilder would dance with the older daughters as well as the mother, and at the end the father would press a tip into his hand, discreetly enough not to be noticed by the rest of the family. Saturday, when the dance hall was packed and 50 couples were frantically doing the Charleston on the parquet while the band urged them ruthlessly on, was the toughest for the gigolos. It was hard to keep track of people in the throng and make out the customers most in need; it was hard to communicate with them and be heard shouting against the noise.

It was easier on weekdays. Wilder didn't dance quite as well as his colleagues, but he 'was better at dialogue', as he confessed to his biographer Hellmuth Karasek much later.[3] Wilder, who would enjoy fame decades and a war later with such fabulous films as *Irma la Douce*, *Sunset Boulevard*, *The Apartment* and *Some Like it Hot*, improvised romantic dialogue in real time: 'May I ask you a personal question?' he would murmur during a slow foxtrot. 'But of course!' – 'Do you know what you remind me of?' – 'No.' – 'I don't dare say it.' – 'Have a go!' – 'A wonderful soufflé' – 'A soufflé?' – 'Prepared by angels. On a terrace by the Mediterranean. Delicate as a breath, with

'When your heart is breaking, show a smiling face! – They pay, and you must dance.' A gigolo takes a break at the bar of the Eden hotel, 1930.

a splodge of divine jam in the middle.'[4] As often as not, such flim-flam would end in a romantic stroll or a trip home together.

Wilder's long article in the *B.Z. am Mittag* was published in several instalments. It was so good that from now on he made his living from the newspapers, and no longer had to rely on his gruelling job in the Eden Hotel. Upon leaving, on the advice of the poet Klabund, a reluctant dancer with whose wife he had also danced in the Eden, he asked his boss for a reference:

> Mr Billy Wilder worked in our establishment between 15 October 1926 and the present. Mr Wilder was able to adapt to the most spoilt clientele in every respect. He proved himself well in his post and always acted within the best interests of the hotel.[5]

The gigolo stood between the new age and the old. He combined the chivalrous manners of former times with the altered power relations of the present. The modern woman had only to go out and immediately she had a dance partner; she just had to order him from the waiter, who added him to the bill. If he knew how to keep a smart and amusing conversation going, a successful evening was guaranteed. Young mothers also attended afternoon *thés dansant*. Aside from the palm room in the Haus Vaterland pleasure palace there was even a professional crèche. The children were kept busy there while their mothers danced the afternoon away.

The gigolo system combined a radicalised democratic market economy with traditional courtship rituals. The man asked the lady to dance, but only in return for a direct transfer of money. The cavalier as marionette – the gigolo embodied a radical variation of the tact and masquerade praised by the poet Helmuth Plessner as the essential qualities of a modern society.

'Handsome Gigolo, Poor Gigolo' is one of the most famous songs of the Weimar Republic, a tango composed in 1928 by Leonello Casucci to lyrics by Julius Brammer from 1924. There are countless recordings of it, the best-known sung by Richard Tauber with his soft and elegiac tenor voice, which charmed its way into the ear and lingered there. His melancholy sweetness let the subject matter seep almost unnoticed into the consciousness. The song deals with the battlefields of France and the end of the war, when the world 'unravelled'. One war veteran scrapes a living as a dancer. He is sad, and yet he must laugh because he is paid to.

> Handsome gigolo, poor gigolo
> Think no more of the times when you
> Could ride through the streets,
> Gold-braided, a hussar.
>
> Your uniform gone, your darling bids adieu –
> Beautiful world, you unravelled!
> Even when your heart is breaking
> Show a smiling face –
> They pay, and you must dance!

One could dance wonderfully well to the tune of this handsome, poor gigolo, or relax to the sounds it made, even though the song referred to the social dramas of the time. Many of the people working as dancing partners were officers and impoverished aristocrats, because they had reliably good manners. For many women there was something especially piquant about being invited to dance by a former hero. A dashing presence on the dancefloor was all that remained of former glory. At the same time the song was a kind of shoulder-clapping offer of integration to the uprooted former troops. Sharing their misery, they swayed their way into the new age, into the rhythm of the unloved Republic. The song was a sentimental declaration of consent, a lively, sweet and painful reconciliation with defeat. It is amazing how much political controversy was being crooned in there. One of the successful recipes of Weimar entertainment culture lay in not simply repressing its dramas but standing up to them and in a sense dancing around with them.

'Shimmy shake!'

Any account of the Weimar Republic without mention of the dance phenomenon would be hollow. No cultural history could fail to mention it, and the period has often been summed up as 'dancing on the volcano'. Plainly people were also aware of the significance of dancing through a crisis, even as they hit the dancefloor. There has probably never been a time in which dance was so frantically revered as the 1920s, or in which so much thought has been devoted to it. From artistic expressive dance via revue dancing to bopping on the dancefloor – dancing pulled people along, it changed them, it invented ever wilder forms of excitement. Soon people were dancing everywhere, in elegant cafés and corner pubs, even in the water; on hot days couples rocked one another from side to side while up to their knees in the Wannsee, to music from a gramophone or even a band. Thomas Mann irritably observed his children's generation:

Here and there two young girls dance together, sometimes even two young men; it's all the same to them. They do it to the exotic sounds of the gramophone, which is fitted with robust needles to make it as loud as possible, and it rings out its shimmies, foxtrots and one-steps, its double foxtrots, African shimmies, java dances and polka creolas – wild, perfumed things, sometimes yearning, sometimes exacting, with their strange rhythms.[6]

With the end of the war, a dance style had emerged from the USA which fascinated the European continent and revolutionised the world of dancing, particularly in Germany. Where previously couples had drifted across the dancefloor in skilful spinning motions, struggling not to stand on each other's feet and perform their practised steps with as few mistakes as possible, the shimmy brought an unimagined freedom to the parquet. Now people danced almost on the spot to whipped-up rhythms without touching one another. It saved on both space and embarrassment: if the hall was full enough, no one even noticed if someone didn't have a dance partner. The ballroom was conquered by a spirit of individualism, along with a desire to try new things out. Where in the old days it would have been unthinkable to step on a dancefloor without having first taken dancing classes, the new dances could only be learned by imitation. People no longer had to practise fixed sequences of steps, constantly harried by strict dance teachers – they just threw themselves into the mêlée and got dancing. In 1922 dance teachers formed an association to wage a campaign against the 'misuse of dancing freedom', and to 'standardise' newly emerging dances. Young people had completely lost the 'dread of seeming unprepared', they lamented.[7] In fact, the association managed to shape the equally new foxtrot, which had originally left a great deal of room for breaks, jumps, knee-bends, straddle steps and solos, into the slow and sedate version most commonly practised today.[8]

The shimmy consisted essentially of a shake of the shoulders combined with a slight back-and-forth movement of the torso. In terms of physical sensation, it's much closer to dancing in today's clubs than the social dancing that had previously prevailed. The explanations

with which people tried to make sense, after the war, of the new patterns of movement of African-American origin, seem touchingly
naive today. In the brochure *Jazz and Shimmy*, published in 1921, it was
claimed that 'shimmy shake!' meant 'shake your nightshirt!' 'One
needs only to try out the movement with which a night-shirt is shaken
from the shoulders in order to have the characteristic shimmying
motion.'[9]

The shimmy is supposed to have originated somewhere in the
region of the present-day Congo, as it was thought that people
danced on the spot with great brio and energy. 'Every part of the
body can be activated independently. That immediately excludes
the diametrically opposite capacity for "isolation" typical of the unified European ideal of movement,' the dance historians Astrid
Eichstedt and Bernd Polster explain.[10] Once you had more or less
mastered the shaking of the shoulders you could start moving the
pelvis, and already you had your shimmying down to a T.

Many Germans enjoyed this liberating shake, but they also held it
in considerable suspicion. From a historical distance, and with the
benefit of hindsight, the dances of the disaster-threatened Weimar
Republic look like grotesque dances of death, in which mask-like
caricatures wave their fake limbs around; the ecstatic scenes on the
dancefloor look like a kind of infernal spectacle in which a deeply
divided society tried to forget its differences. Socially critical contemporaries such as Otto Dix, George Grosz and many others dubious
about carnal pleasures portrayed the bustle of the dance halls as a
repellent form of indulgence that contrasted provocatively with
other people's misery. In one much-cited passage, Klaus Mann added
his bit to the debate in 1942, looking back at the 'hopping addiction':

A beaten, impoverished, demoralised people seeks oblivion in dance.
[. . .] Dance becomes a mania, an idée fixe, a cult. The stock market
humps, the ministers wobble, the Reichstag turns cartwheels. War disabled and war profiteers, film stars and prostitutes [. . .] – everyone
hurls their limbs about in gruesome euphoria. [. . .] People dance
away their hunger and hysteria, fear and greed, panic and horror.[11]

Looking back, this vision is quite understandable; the First World War and inflation were already enough to make the dance craze look perplexing. 'The homeland is dancing on the skulls of its dead. Away with such undignified festivities!' the Reich veteran association demanded in the Catholic journal *Volkswart* in 1920.[12] Revulsion at the new hedonism on the part of dancers made it impossible to paint them as anything but ugly, impertinent, greedy and lustful. But the dancers themselves felt free and enchanted in a historically new way. A hitherto unknown feeling of exuberance took hold of them. The draftsman and advertising designer Robert L. Leonard, a passionate dancer and ladies' man of the Wilhelmine style, had become incurably addicted to jazz after the war – even his dog drank to a shimmy beat, he claimed. 'Madness has won,' Leonard crowed:

> the revolution, the expressionism, the Bolshevism in the ballroom. [. . .] A deafening din, a wild dance and everyone is hypnotised. The oldest people succumb to the furious atmosphere, an unimagined *joie de vivre* skips through the hall. A waiter falls over with a full tray, and no one notices – it's part of the music. Two gentlemen slap one another – part of the music.[13]

The author Hans Siemsen was a fan of the shimmy because it put people in a state of euphoria and allowed them to get out of themselves. It loosened them up and took away what in a hierarchical state might wrongly have been called their dignity. Writing in the *Weltbühne* in 1921 he dreamed about what might have happened if Kaiser Wilhelm had danced the shimmy:

> And jazz has another fine quality. It is so completely undignified. It sweeps away any notion of dignity, of correct posture, of dash, of starched collars. Anyone who is afraid of making himself ridiculous can't do the shimmy. The German schoolmaster can't dance it. The Prussian reserve officer can't dance it. If only all ministers and privy counsellors and professors and politicians were obliged to dance to

jazz in public! How cheerfully they would all be stripped of their dignity! How human, how nice, how comical they would become! [. . .] If the Kaiser had jazz danced, none of it would ever have happened! But oh! he never learned it. Being the German Kaiser is easier than jazz dancing.[14]

Knee-bends, windscreen-wiper feet, rowing arms – in the Charleston the whole body was ecstatic and mechanical motion. It was felt to be wonderfully undignified. Dance teachers complained: 'Never have people been so unabashed at being imperfect.' Photomontage by the photographer Yva, 1927.

Kurt Tucholsky made an interesting observation, also in the intellectual journal *Weltbühne*. When he listened to an African-American jazz band in a Berlin dance club, he noticed that the musicians were 'completely matter-of-fact', which is why it wasn't right that they dress in silly, brightly coloured suits. Tucholsky was of the opinion that the musicians should work in ordinary clothes. They're working: what they do is the very opposite of romanticism. They emphasise the everyday. They want the listening cattle commissioner, the postal official, the haberdasher – they don't want to elevate them to the bright realm of dreams, where things are at their bluest, but they have a deep understanding of the salary of the woman in the street and the financial difficulties of the motor-car manufacturer. Their music clatters to the same beat as the typewriters that the audience left behind two hours before, their song is the cry of the stockholder, set to a rhythm, their dance is the dance around the Golden Calf. The jazz band is a continuation of business by other means.[15]

If we follow Tucholsky, jazz did not seduce people out of reality, but pushed them even more deeply into it, dancing their bodies and their minds into a state of euphoria, and synchronising them with the forced tempo of the new age.

*

The rapturous experience of community in the ballroom grew even more intense in 1925 when the Charleston conquered the dancefloors. From a sociological point of view, we might interpret it as an early form of 'industrial' music, in that it imitated the mechanical aspect of the modern age. The Charleston turned dancers into acrobatic marionettes.

Even the hands are active, they touch all parts of the body as if in a state of ecstasy. Then there the X- and O-shapes of the legs, as knees and feet turned alternately in and out. The dancer can bend his back or even go into a crouching position.[16]

Knee-bends, windscreen-wiper feet, rowing arms – the whole body is involved in a movement that is both mechanical and ecstatic. Most characteristic are the hands, which cross over the bending knees, giving the Charleston its angular appearance and prompting the optical illusion that it is the knees and not the hands that are crossing.

The complicated interweaving of so many isolated movements made the body into the copy of a machine in which the individual limbs smoothly intertwine. If coordination was successful, a kind of floating state arose as if of its own accord. In this respect the Charleston resembled the daily acrobatics of life.[17]

Musically, the Charleston was inclined towards the wide-screen format. The big dance cafés had bands 'that send everything crashing down and bring vim and verve to the most boring people', in the words of the 1928 Berlin travel guide *What You Won't Find in Baedeker*. Fanfare-like brass sections, strumming banjos, hard, clattering drums and wailing saxophones that gently smoothed the piston-like beat – that was the basic sound. Sentimental passages on the violin consoled the heart, assisted by the accordion, while a jubilant clarinet occasionally rose out of the stamping rhythm and cheekily encouraged the thrashing dancers to keep going.

The gramophone allowed people to dance at home and in the countryside. Between 1925 and 1929 record sales had risen tenfold, to 30 million discs a year. Illustrated magazines recommended practising in front of the mirror. So what Friedrich Hollaender had prophesied in his 1926 song 'I Dance the Charleston' came to pass: everyone danced the Charleston.

> If you can, you can
> and if you can you dance
> till morn.
> Papa does it, Mama does it
> Aunty does it
> even in the kitchen
> Marie does it.
> I dance the Charleston,
> you dance the Charleston,
> he dances the Charleston
> we all dance the Charleston.
> And what about you?

The Charleston was an uplifting dance. It fired up the ego and inspired people to express their own emotions through dance. Expressive dance was very fashionable on stage, and now everyone could do a bit of it on the dancefloor. Most importantly, the Charleston didn't require partners. Whether they were flat-footed or danced like an angel, it was up to the individual. No one needed to pay attention to anyone else or worry about getting somehow tangled with one another. Dancers just enjoyed being caught up in the dancing crowd. It was the dance of an unbridled love of life, a self-empowerment of the individual within the cheerful multitude.

The Charleston was particularly enjoyable for women. They didn't have to be led, and were usually the more active, exuberant participants. It was much easier and less complicated to dance the Charleston than the tango, for example, in which the gender roles were strictly assigned. The Charleston was athletic and action-packed. The woman was no longer pushed across the dancefloor like a dolled-up chess piece, no longer swung and bent about in suggestive gestures of conquest. She was no longer a diva whom the man proudly manoeuvred. Man and woman suddenly enjoyed absolute equality on the dancefloor, and the same effort was required of both. Dancers did, it's true, benefit from being slim and athletic, as wiry and agile as possible. Here, the dignified matron had as little chance as the stiff-hipped cavalier of the old school. Bosoms and generous hips were frowned upon, and fashion designs favoured the pencil line. The Charleston dress was cut straight at the top and the skirt started low on the hips in an attempt to suppress, as far as possible, any feminine lines.

While most women complied with the requirement of the boyish look, and the less slim among them had to come to terms with being out of fashion, men stuck rigidly with the tuxedo or the suit, which tended to be worn oversized during the 1920s. The dancing jacket, on the other hand, which was supposed to encourage more sporting activity on the dancefloor, was a fashion failure. At its boldest it was cut like a kimono – a step too far for all but the most extrovert of men.

Out of Africa

For most Germans the shimmy and the Charleston were their first encounters with African-American culture. Many hotels engaged Black musicians or Black waiters. African-American bands toured the country under names that would today be recognised as being racist, such as 'Sam Wooding and his Chocolate Kiddies'. Sidney Bechet, who would soon become one of the most internationally famous representatives of New Orleans-style jazz, was regularly to be heard in the Haus Vaterland. Josephine Baker, born in St Louis, Missouri, came to Berlin in 1926 at the age of 19. Karl Vollmoeller, the boyfriend and patron of Ruth Landshoff, had met the dancer in New York and arranged for her to be given engagements in Paris and Berlin. She was a greatly admired sensation in both cities, and everyone was desperate to meet her, to spend at least a few minutes in the company of the famously wild dancer. She was 'an idol of bronze, tanned steel, irony and gold', the author Jean Cocteau raved.[18] Pablo Picasso saw her as a 'present-day Nefertiti'.[19] Such projections were brought down to earth when one saw the insatiable appetite with which she devoured her favourite food: frankfurters and potato salad.

Josephine Baker's speciality was exoticism, a style that was known as 'la danse sauvage' – 'savage dancing'. With a short skirt made of bananas and a curious habit of crossing her eyes during her dramatic breaks, she skilfully parodied dusty ideas of 'savages'. She could stretch her belly and hips forward like a kangaroo, the Berliner Börsen-Zeitung wrote.[20] Josephine Baker was 'the most authentic of women', the newspaper went on: 'She is the purest expression of the Negro spirit.'[21] It was meant appreciatively, and yet the praise was tainted with racism. The worldly Josephine Baker, a dancer originally from St Louis, had grown up in Philadelphia and New York and was celebrated in Paris, but the paper's comment was an attempt to reduce her to the animality of her supposedly primitive heritage. Other papers tried psychology: Josephine Baker revealed 'the unconscious that throws our whole philosophy into disarray'.[22] Or misguided frivolity: 'Her bottom, with the greatest respect, is a chocolate pudding of agility, and she is rightly proud of this gift of nature.'[23]

Nature? Baker was a complex, artificial figure with a parodic sense of the most modern cultural trends. Not only was she a great singer of cabaret-style chansons, but if she switched to hot jazz a moment later, she tended to stress the mechanical, Chaplinesque attributes of the Charleston, in contrast with her bark-and-banana skirts, particularly since she wore an ultra-modern, artificially prepared bob: as a dancer she was an avant-garde piece of multi-media performance art. Max Reinhardt was fascinated by her and tried to lure her from the world of light entertainment and turn her into a serious actress in his Berlin theatrical empire. She felt honoured, thought about it briefly and then returned to the Folies Bergère, one of the great and radiant cabarets of Paris.

In the 1920s Black people were no longer unknown in Germany. That was partly as a result the humiliating human zoos that had put 'the life and activity of foreign peoples and human races' on display in many European countries. But even aside from those racist spectacles there were people of African heritage in Germany who had arrived in the country in a great variety of ways. Some were left behind as 'presents', whether as servants or curiosities, after official state visits, others because they had been sent to Europe for an education by their affluent parents, still others out of a spirit of adventure and because they wanted to experience the world. Some members of this small minority of Black Germans had served as members of the African auxiliary troops of the German colonial ruling forces and now lived in Berlin and other cities. They had carried weapons and heavy equipment, but had also fought as soldiers against the British and sometimes even against their own people. They were witness to the atrocities that German troops perpetrated against indigenous peoples, as occurred in German South West Africa, and were sometimes forced to take part in the massacres themselves. With the defeat of 1918 the colonial territories were also lost. Some of the conscripted Black soldiers came to Germany with their returning white 'comrades'. Here they were valued as living witnesses of a proud colonial past, albeit in a suspect and condescending way. Revered as 'loyal askaris' (*askari* means soldier in Swahili), their existence served to furnish the distorted picture of supposedly benevolent German rule in Africa, which was painted on trading cards and pulp magazines. Some of these 'loyal askaris' were happily married to German women and presented themselves in the usual family photographs as proud leaders among their white relatives.

One of these was Bayume Mohamed Hussein from Dar es Salaam, who called himself Husen. He was the son of an askari, and from 1914, as a ten-year-old child soldier, he had fought for Germany before being seriously wounded in 1917. After holding a position on various ships, Bayume Husen came to Berlin to claim some outstanding pay, but he lacked the necessary papers. Instead, he took a job as a waiter and a piece of living window-dressing in the pleasure palace of Haus Vaterland, where he was deployed alternately as a 'Turk' or an 'African'. Husen was plainly very popular with the public. In 1933 he married a seamstress who was pregnant by him, had two children with her, and also adopted another child that he had with another woman. On the side, he taught Kiswahili at the Seminar for Eastern Languages of Berlin University.[24]

The colonial pride directed towards Black people in Germany was suppressed soon after the end of the war by a hate campaign started by soldiers: this was based on talk of 'black shame'. This was the slogan applied to the deployment of North African soldiers by the French Army within the occupied Rhineland who had supposedly abused German women.[25] In an article about the appearance of a jazz band, Kurt Tucholsky mentioned the widespread talk of 'black shame': 'It is very difficult to say the word Negro in German today, without people interrupting you with a cry of "black shame". But black shame seems to me to be more of a French shame, and raped Abyssiniers do not disavow the rhythm of N***** songs for that reason.'[26] What is startling is that Tucholsky uses the offensive term in an article that expressly seeks to defend the music.

When the French finally withdrew in 1930, the author Carl Zuckmayer wrote in a newspaper article that rather than speak of 'black shame', one should instead speak of the shameful behaviour of whites:

> Shame in the treatment of Black people, because there is no sensible reason to describe their military deployment with any word other than slavery. The poor fellows coughed themselves to death in huge numbers in our foggy, damp, wet, cold winter climate; cemeteries in Mainz and Koblenz bear terrible witness to what these Africans owe our civilisation.[27]

Black Germans were depicted as 'beasts' in countless caricatures and inflammatory flyers. This led in time to attacks on the askaris who had been accepted, and indeed valued, only a short time before. In May 1921 the Black entertainer and actor Louis Brody, from Cameroon, turned for help to the *B.Z. vom Mittag* with a letter in the name of the 'African Aid Union':

> We are not the immoral and uncivilised race that we are now generally claimed to be in Germany. We must remind the Germans that Lettow-Vorbeck [Commander of the *Schutztruppe* – colonial German troops – in German East Africa] did not wage the war in Africa alone, but that the indigenous people took part, and that they proudly laid down their lives for the German flag. The Black people who live in Berlin and the non-occupied territories of Germany are from the former German colonies, and are not yellow or Black people from the occupied territory. For that reason we ask the Germans to be careful, and not constantly to inflame public opinion against them with reports about the black shame.[28]

In many respects Black people living in Germany were often treated with respect and curiosity, particularly since many of them showed little inclination after 1918 to become citizens of the mandatory powers of France or Britain, as the Versailles Treaty allowed them to do. One tragic example of integration is Gustav Sabac el Cher, the son of August Sabac el Cher, a Nubian boy given as a gift to

Prince Albert of Prussia from the government in Cairo in the 1840s and later employed as a 'Court Moor'. Gustav became senior music master of the Royal Grenadier Regiment, and played several times before the kaiser and his entourage. He and his band now performed military marches in Berlin's Tiergarten, while his sons Horst and Herbert Sabac el Cher played dance music with their own band in elegant bars in the capital.[29]

As a military veteran loyal to the kaiser, Gustav Sabac el Cher had even become a convinced devotee of the *Stahlhelm* ('steel helmet') association of frontline soldiers. Many affluent Berliners saw him as a credit to their salons, famed as he was for his charisma and charming conversation. In 1930 he and his wife Gertrud opened the Café Sabac el Cher in the town of Königs Wusterhausen in the east of the country, which was also intended as a meeting place for his old *Stahlhelm* comrades. But when racism became an increasing feature of everyday life and public discourse towards the end of the Weimar Republic, the veterans came to see their Black comrade as an embarrassment, and they avoided his café. The Prussian-minded conductor, now retired, refused to accept the betrayal. On 30 January 1933, a year and a half before his death, he wrote in the family chronicle of the Sabac el Chers: 'Führer: Adolf Hitler. The Reich is unified and as one. Germany's ascendancy is beginning.'[30]

Gustav Sabac el Cher thought, felt and played music in a more Prussian way than most of his white fellow citizens. It was the modern culture industry that required Black people to act in a certain way: in cabarets and music clubs throughout Germany Black people were often reduced to a representation of 'the Other'. They were engaged as exceptions, as non-whites, as the opposite of normal life – viewed as the 'savage' that civilised man had left behind and now wanted to enjoy as art.

As in the case of '*Negerkunst*' (Negro art), as it was called at the time, which had enchanted Expressionism and now enlivened many cool Bauhaus settings with a dash of 'primitive' vitality in the form of artefacts stolen from the colonies, Black music was also credited with superior qualities in some respects while at the same time being despised in others; at any rate, it was seen as unsuited to modern life, except on dancefloors after the working day. There, people were described as dancing 'like savages', opening themselves up to a repertoire of movements that gave the notoriously stiff Germans the opportunity to experience their bodies in new ways, and took them to ecstatic heights in which the ego seemed to become weightless.

Famously, 'primitivism' and 'primitive' art assumed an important place in the artistic discourse of the Weimar Republic. Germans saw themselves as being entirely rational, and mature enough to turn to the primitive and the archaic and recognise in it a kind of prehistory of themselves. The pioneering abstract painter Wassily Kandinsky saw a 'profound kinship with the primitive', with regard to his effort to 'depict the deeply essential' without spending too much time on correspondences with real-life phenomena.[31] Even before the First World War, the art theorist Wilhelm Worringer saw modern people as being inevitably open to archaic images of the world, since all progress in thought and research had made the world bigger and more complex, while human beings were made smaller: 'Cast down by the arrogance of knowledge, man sees himself as being once again just as lost and helpless in the face of the image of the world as primitive man.'[32]

So-called 'primitive' energies from the depths of the unconscious, a source of great fascination and the object of psychological study, were released in a socially acceptable way in dance. Many people enjoyed the feeling of being able to shake off all conventions through dance, and to discover an existential freedom in which the political promise of the Republic seemed to be fulfilled for one precious and entire moment.

The Charleston and the shimmy were equally hated by philistines on the right. The right-wing former lieutenant commander Manfred Freiherr von Killinger, who commissioned the assassination of the centrist politician Matthias Erzberger in the summer of 1921, raged against both 'racketeering Jews' and 'snot-nosed brats with waisted jackets and shimmy shoes'. 'Do you believe,' he rhetorically asked the hated, smartly dressed dancer, we would envy him? No, certainly not, above all not for the beating that he will sometimes get from us. [. . .] Money is your god. It gives you what you need for your life: jazz band, dances, Jewish theatre, drinking sparkling wine, draping your women with jewellery and fur. World divide us from you.[33]

Killinger's threats drip with the loser's thirst for revenge. For him the origin of the shimmy was one thing above all: American.

The relationship of most Germans to the Black musicians to whose music they danced so ecstatically was filled with anxieties, longings, projections, prejudices and awkwardness. Appreciation and defamation fed almost seamlessly into one another. So, for example, the trendsetting magazine *Tempo*[34] illustrated a story about the success of Black music in Germany with peaceful pictures of a band playing music but gave the article the alarming headline: 'Negroes invade Europe'.[35] In the article, the 'acknowledgement of Black people as fully valid human beings' is condescendingly welcomed on the one hand, while on the other the paper has no compunction in describing the appearance of a very small number of musicians and dancers as 'the advance of Negroism [*Negertum*]'.[36]

At the same time, conservative observers were less troubled by the relatively large numbers of Black musicians than by their popularity with the enthusiastic public. The feared 'advance' was not spatial but cultural – an advance into the soul of the West, which in its decadence thoughtlessly yielded to foreignness in a shameful act of self-betrayal. The well-known ballet critic Werner Suhr blustered about African dance music in the same special edition of *Tempo*, under the headline 'Why do people dance?' In his article Suhr borrows from the author Oswald Spengler's cultural pessimism concerning the internal depletion and weakening of white culture, which he claimed was wearied by war and conventions:

The European wants to have the stronger forces and unbroken excitement of intellectually backward races. He is weary. [. . .] No longer a match for sophistication and cultural music, the educated man wishes

to anaesthetise unease and despair with the harsh disharmonies of
naive melodies.[37]

And for that reason, 'at the most crucial moments, and with dangerous consistency, he assumes the gestures of a formerly oppressed,
blacker race'.[38]

Meanwhile, the at least partly agrarian origins of jazz, the Charleston and its many stylistic variations had long been overlaid by the
ultra-modern influences that it had received in the great cities of
America and Europe. Jazz sounded less like the plantation than it did
the stamping and whistling of railway trains, the thump of punching
machines and steam hammers, the rhythm of conveyor belts and the
hum of city traffic. It was the accompaniment to the growing
demands that people made of life, the private risks that they took on
the way to greater independence from the judgement of their contemporaries, on the way to individual autonomy. It was also the
accompaniment to growing consumerism. Jazz was a source of
movement, the acoustic engine behind more carefree years before
the 1929 economic crisis, impelling people on to ever greater achievements, whatever their style of dress, whether they danced enraptured
or in a spirit of self-irony.

Appearances by Weintraub's Syncopators, led by the Breslau jazz
musician Stefan Weintraub, were highlights of the art of musical collage, thrilling their enthusiastic audiences with their mixture of
passion, sentimentality and sobriety, melancholy and optimism. Weintraub's Syncopators combined elements of classical music, tango,
waltzes and chansons, and amalgamated them into a cheerful jazz texture that drew people from their seats. Very different, quieter, but
similarly ambiguous was the self-satire of the Comedian Harmonists,
an a cappella group that had internalised jazz and performed it without instruments. A wonderfully tender male-voice-choir sound for a
world that was not perhaps quite as carefree as it pretended to be.

In fact, at the peak of the 1920s, American-influenced music represented only a small part of the sound to which people danced so
enthusiastically. The sound-world in the big dance palaces was in fact

tantalisingly multicultural. In Haus Vaterland in Berlin, within an hour wandering from hall to hall, one could dance to sounds from New York, Budapest, Vienna, Rome, Buenos Aires and Munich. Incidentally, whether at the Hofbräuhaus or Paulaner beer halls, it was in Munich and Bavaria generally that American music made the least headway; rustic dance music thoroughly rejected the jagged notes issuing from the Prussian capital. One exception to this was the Deutches Theater in Munich, where the restaurateur Hans Gruss put on modern revues. In 1929, however, a planned appearance in the city by Josephine Baker was forbidden by the authorities. In the Free State of Bavaria oompah tunes – the 'Alpine Polka', for example – had the upper hand even during the Charleston years.

Shisha pipes in Haus Vaterland, an office in Moka Efti

Dancers in the big cities had no trouble finding the venue of their choice, most easily in Berlin. People went to the Alkazar, the Dorett, the Groschenkeller, the Tabasco, the Ewige Lampe, the Faun des Westens or the Sing Sing – to give a few particularly euphonious names at random. There were about 140 dance halls to choose from, apart from countless bars where the tables were pushed aside so that people could trip the light fantastic if they felt like it. Many pub landlords, even in the countryside, felt obliged to invest in a piano to keep up with the desire for fun.

People with more worldly tastes would visit one of the massive dance palaces. There, hundreds of employees busied themselves to provide an intoxicating evening for crowds of pleasure seekers in several different dance halls. If you wanted to disappear into the masses, this was the place to be. The crowd enjoyed its own company, Siegfried Kracauer wrote. He saw the big dance halls as 'pleasure barracks' that regulated 'the pleasure of the armies of clerks' just as the offices regulated their labour.[39] That was a subtle piece of thinking, but it ignored the pleasure that the ranks of office workers felt when they went out for the evening. The denial of any kind of individuality to these dance-hall denizens, their characterisation as a barrack-based army, reveals the over-sensitive reflexes of a piqued left-wing elite rather than the actual states of mind of those in the crowd. Many people could afford the Moka Efti or the Haus Vaterland – the senior white-collar workers, admittedly, but there were still enough of them to fill the dancefloors.

One of the first and most elegant venues for dancing and eating was the Haus Gourmenia, mentioned earlier, which was inimitably designed by the architect Leo Nachtlicht and opened in 1929. In spite of all its refined and extravagant technological accoutrements, it lacked table telephones, which represented the latest fashion in the dance-hall trade. Dance-palace connoisseur Knud Wolffram has an illuminating explanation for this: 'Clearly they thought such a petty-bourgeois-looking means of communication for shy people could not be imposed upon the Gourmenia clientele.'[40] In West Berlin people were worldly enough to conduct small talk. Or else they said nothing and watched.

The first Berlin venue to introduce table telephones was the Resi in the east of the city. This 'technological dance hall' was also the most traditional Berlin dance palace. The manager of the Resi, Paul Baatz, inventor of the disco ball, was an obsessive tinkerer who was constantly coming up with new gimmicks for his venue, from the 'confetti light' to a pneumatic tube mail system. Table telephones were praised as a 'social invention' and as 'interpreters for the timid'. Each table had a number, which was visible from a distance, and a light signal. If the light was blue, it meant that calls were undesirable, while a red light indicated a willingness to receive them. Using the pneumatic mail system running between the tables one could also send written messages or chocolates. But practical objects could be dispatched as well: a sewing case in a fake tortoiseshell box for 1.50 marks, for example, or a gift-wrapped vial of lilac-scented perfume for the same price.

When Doris, the titular 'artificial silk girl' from Irmgard Keun's novel *Das kunstseidene Mädchen* pays a visit to the Resi in the book, she is even sent a whole bottle of cognac by pneumatic mail,

Dating 1930, in the 'laboratory of the modern age'. Initial contact was made from a safe distance by table telephone in the Femina Bar. One dialled the glowing number of a particular table and carefully sounded out whether an approach was likely to be successful.

'accompanied by a stylish note', as Doris triumphs, from a suitor who is 'small and fidgety and has eyes like burned plush'.[41] The Resi is entirely to her taste, 'it's nothing but colour and a rotating light, it's a drunken illuminated belly that's illuminated, it's a huge work of art'.[42] And when her companion Franz has to go outside for a moment her telephone immediately rings to give him some competition.

Moka Efti on Friedrichstrasse, according to its own advertising 'a piece of the Orient in Berlin', was entered via escalator – an ultra-modern accessory. The second unique feature of this venue was the Middle Eastern look of the 'Mohammedan rooms'; the third, the fabulously good coffee with which Giovanni Eftimiades, the owner of the Moka Efti, had first made his name. His establishment set out to be a self-contained world: there was a hairdressing salon and an office where secretaries waited obligingly to serve customers by fin-ishing off the correspondence that they had forgotten to do during the day. Sixteen billiard tables stood at the ready, as well as a chess room and two dancefloors. The most regular performer here was the band leader James Kok, the very definition of a ladies' man. On his posters Eftimiades claimed that dance afternoons in the Moka Efti had, thanks to Kok, become 'the meeting place for Berlin housewives'; 'the select band of artistes unleashes storms of applause every day'.

The biggest and most spectacular dance hall, and the one most magnificently uncertain of its own taste, was Haus Vaterland on Potsdamer Platz. A giant. This pleasure palace, which belonged to the Jewish Kempinski family business, deliberately played with national and international characteristics. This 'fatherland' was global and intimate at the same time, or so its lyrical publicity material claimed: 'Over its four storeys, you can lose yourself in the university of the world, whose most beloved and enticing beauties are on offer to the guest in unparalleled quality.' Visitors stepped from one backdrop to the next, choosing between the Japanese Bar, the Grinzing district of Vienna, the Löwenbräu brewery in old Bavaria, the Wild West Bar, the Hungarian Czarda, the Italian Taverna, the Turkish Coffee-House, equipped with real shisha pipes, and the Bremen Galley – a mock-up of a ship's kitchen. In each room one looked at artfully arranged panoramas that showed the foreign landscapes in as true-to-life a form as possible. Various bands strummed music more or less appropriate to the themed rooms. The Haus Vaterland was a glorious travesty of a world which had suddenly become smaller thanks to aeroplanes and Zeppelins. But because that world was beyond most people's reach, the easiest thing to do was to turn it into a series of gastronomic opportunities.

The centrepiece of this noisy building, which accommodated 10,000 people and was attended by over a million in the first year after it reopened in 1928, was formed by the Bacchic 'Rhine terraces'. While the river lay on the far western edge of the country, for many Germans Father Rhein represented the mythical centre of the homeland, particularly since the French had only recently occupied its territory. The river that flowed through Haus Vaterland was the Rhine at its most beautiful: the panorama behind the 'Rhine terrace' restaurants captured the view of the Loreley rock overlooking the river. Model boats sailed on the waterway, and model aeroplanes flew overhead. Every hour there was even a storm with thunder and lightning, produced by Mephistophelian *son et lumière* technology. Rain fell from sprinklers on the 6-metre panorama, which filled the whole width of the room. There were flashes and crashes, but the sun always rose radiantly again. 'The earth of our homeland enchants us with its magical grandeur', as the Kempinski publicity department loftily put it.

Heading off after an opulent meal by the national papier-mâché river for an unsteady gastronomic exploration of the world, served by geishas, cowboys and vineyard girls, and carrying on drinking before finally 'being served coffee by a courteous Moor' – for Berliners and their provincial visitors this was a patriotic evening of the first degree.

Haus Vaterland on Potsdamer Platz, Berlin. Eight restaurants and cafés under one roof, as well as a dancefloor and big cinema. Panormas represented landscapes from far and near, and there was also an artificial thunderstorm every hour at dinner on the 'Rhine terraces'. The Vaterland was Berlin's number one tourist magnet.

Sixteen Vaterland girls also high-kicked in time, polonaise-ing through the rooms and fighting off the advances of inebriated guests.

The young student Inge von Wangenheim, a rising actress and passionate communist, spent a few months earning some extra money in the Haus Vaterland, where her mother was a cloakroom attendant. She sewed costumes, 'fripperies', for the Vaterland girls and often had the chance to watch them rehearse. For Inge von Wangenheim the revue was 'the backside of the muse' that she pursued, the 'rear end of art'. She was filled with revulsion as she saw the hopping of the half-naked girls, whose 'horrific lives' she could only imagine, the 'whimpering saxophones', the raging director. 'In the wings everything was as naked, as shameless, as cynical, as direct and straight-talking as the direct connection with schnapps, boasting and speculation required,' she wrote in her autobiography, *Mein Haus Vaterland*.[43] For Inge von Wangenheim, the nightspot was a sardonically chuckling capitalist inferno of amusements that was kept going by conscience-free, corrupt pseudo-artists:

> The song lyrics, the dirty jokes, the political references in the dialogue, the music, the costumes – it was all deliberately tailored – by people who should have known better – towards corrupt taste, towards stupidity, towards the barbarism of the reactionary gang of philistines on the 'Tegernsee', on the 'Rhine terraces' and in 'Grinzing', all quite shamelessly . . . 'Eat or die', said great Kempinski, said great Krupp, said great Flick, great Thyssen – said all the other great ones – and one ate![44]

In these words we hear the voice of a raging idealist who would two years later join Truppe 1931, an agitprop theatre of the 'Communist Cell of Berlin Artist's Colony'. But one also heard similar revulsion from the right: 'Everywhere the addiction to pleasure raises its head' was a phrase that one heard repeatedly, as if a demon had crept across the land, swallowing up everything that was true and good and beautiful – a huge devouring snake that was alternately identified as Americanism or 'cultural Bolshevism'.

One thing is certain: the many Berlin dance palaces could never have survived if they had been frequented only by Berliners. 'Berlin, you bar of the planet', Yvan Goll wrote.[45] Karl Vetter, director of the press and publicity department in the Berlin tourist office, put it more prosaically. He saw the big revue theatres and dance halls as 'a necessity for the city's transport policy'. If each Berlin resident visiting a revue was given a white mark, and every incomer to the city a green one, 'you would soon have a sea of green in front of your eyes', he wrote.[46] Not much has changed in that respect, by the way. In Berghain and the other famous Berlin clubs of the present day, the city's residents form a vanishing minority. According to the motto 'Everyone has to come once to Berlin', the willing visitor to the capital in the 1920s was given a little dose of intoxication that was supposed to last him half a lifetime. His hangover the next morning taught him just how finite pleasure was.

The elective Berliner Joseph Roth took his cynicism to the big dance palaces: 'Sometimes, in an attack of cheerful melancholy, I step inside one of the usual Berlin night spots, not to cheer myself up, but to enjoy the schadenfreude that the sight of industrialised frivolity gives me.'[47] One night when his sadness grew so great that it 'forced him to experience the pain of pleasure-seeking city-dwellers of all classes', he set off on an odyssey from the smart venues of West Berlin to the rather démodé establishments of Friedrichstrasse, and last of all to the dives of North Berlin, 'which are populated by the so-called lumpenproletariat'. Along this route the schnapps got stronger, the beer lighter, but in spite of his increasing tipsiness he was aware: standards steadily decreased as he progressed. Listening to a weary saxophone player by someone's pavement table, he had an idea how the 'entertainment industry' got through its staff: first, the saxophonists in the luxury bars lost 'their wind', he wrote in the detailed account of his bar crawl, then in the medium-range clubs they lost their hearing, and finally they ended up stone-deaf in the 'proletarian bars'. Much the same was true of the dancers. They would go north, where the money was scarcer, and gradually put on weight.

The intellectuals sat grumpily in the midst of the merriment and studied their more superficial compatriots. Joseph Roth would not even allow the other guests a melancholy like his own. He believed that the 'fops' on the café terraces, with 'fake world-weariness in their glazed eyes',[48] were merely imitating the blasé indifference attributed to them in magazine articles. He denied them any genuine emotions: their thin-lipped mouths were 'retouched by nature itself, borrowing the artificial devices of photography'.[49] Their mechanical smiles, which they put on day in, day out, consisted only of 'baring their perfect teeth'.

Nothing but lies, nothing but a facade, and one 'which is not wrested from the depth, but is only an imitation of it', Siegfried Kracauer wrote of Haus Vaterland.[50] He was troubled by the fact that the world of beautiful surfaces – 'not the world as it is, but as it appears in popular songs' – actually worked, that people were clearly taken in by it.[51] The editor of the Berlin arts section of the *Frankfurter Zeitung* seems to have been unwilling to accept that office workers also enjoyed a complex and ironic relationship with reality, and didn't fall for stage sets like wide-eyed dreamers. At the same time, inauthenticity was almost a beacon, or at least a sign of the time. In 1928 the French fashion designer Coco Chanel had declared diamanté and costume jewellery to be respectable. It was a liberation: now it was possible 'to wear a fortune that isn't worth anything'.[52] Even though the masses had been virtuosos at playing with illusions, Kracauer plainly believed they were stupid enough to fall for them. Where the artistic dreamworld and reality coincided, it was down to a desire for imitation on the part of the immature: 'Cinematic sensationalism and life normally correspond when the typist mademoiselles model themselves on the examples they have seen on screen; but perhaps the most deceitful models are stolen from life', he wrote in 1927 in the famous article 'Little Shop Girls Go to the Cinema'.[53]

Information Manipulation Theory was well and truly born. The dreamworld of the entertainment industry distracted from the real-life situation to suppress criticism of its conditions and alienate people from their actual existence. It served as an escape from the reality of offices, it was a 'counter-attack against the office machine'.[54] At the same time the James Klein Revue was showing *Berlin Laughs* at the Apollo Theatre, set in the office itself. The Berlin dance teacher Hanna Kurzer, who taught young office workers expressive dance, usually for the purposes of relaxation and leisure, referred to everyday office life in her teaching methods, as in the living typewriter mentioned earlier. The magazine *Das Leben* reported:

> For example the word 'Not' is represented. At the moment when the teacher utters the word the letters N, O and T jump up from the keyboard and form a group that expresses the meaning of the word in dance.[55]

The entertainment culture of the Weimar Republic was brazen enough not simply to run away from realities. It picked them up, processed them and then faced them head on. That might sometimes have led to a sickly sweet affirmation of existing conditions, but it wasn't a mere flight from the everyday. Popular songs addressed poverty ('Both You and I'), sub-standard housing ('When I Go to My Cinema on Sunday'), the intoxication of consumerism ('No Time to Be Happy'), the pressure to perform and self-exploitation ('Six-day Race') and the misery of veterans ('Handsome Gigolo, Poor Gigolo'). The light-entertainment muse of 1920s Germany, like popular culture today, did not skirt around suffering, but helped to process and endure it. That's precisely what the people who wanted radical change, and needed rebellious foot soldiers to impose it, found so aggravating about it.

8

Self-optimisation:
Perfecting Leisure and the Body

If you go to the theatre as if going to church or the courtroom or school, that's a mistake. You should go to the theatre as if going into a sporting event.

Bertolt Brecht

Lunapark

A week after the November Revolution, on 15 November 1918, industrialist Hugo Stinnes and trade union leader Carl Rudolf Legien reached an agreement on the division of the working day into three. From now on days would be divided into eight hours of work, eight hours of leisure, eight hours of sleep – a demand that the labour movement had been making for decades became a reality, and office workers were included from 1919. Sunday was the only work-free day, Saturday for now remaining a working day like any other. Six years later, when the magazine *Uhu* carried out a survey among trade unionists and business managers asking what they thought of a 40-hour week, the employers' representative Alexander Fläsch replied brusquely: 'The five-day week is out of the question for Germany, and does not even merit discussion.'[1]

There was no point mentioning that free weekends were also on the agenda. Soon, it said in *Uhu*, the 'weekend' would be imported from America: 'We chew gum, and box and spit when we need to, but we're only just starting to find out what a weekend is, and have to translate it from Long Islandish to Wannseatic.'[2] The trade unionist Theodor Leipart campaigned for a work-free weekend, but faced a widespread sense that people wouldn't know what to do with all their leisure time, and would only come up with foolish ideas. Leipart assured his listeners that workers would use their leisure sensibly, for the purpose of getting fit through sport and continuing their education. An increase in leisure time was urgently needed so that performance could be continuously restored and even increased. For that reason, it would also indirectly be of benefit to capital.[3]

In the middle-class press there was widespread concern for people's moral constitution, although unsurprisingly enough this concern extended less towards the morals of the middle class itself and more towards the masses; most middle-class people were content to see the lower classes exhausted. 'The art of saving the strength of the nerves and building up reserves of energy for the next day during the leisure hours' was sadly not yet as well developed in Germany as it was in England – this was the concerned opinion of the cultural journal *Querschnitt* ('Cross-Section').[4] There was much talk of a progressive 'enervation' caused by a fidgety urban culture of entertainment. For this reason, in 1930 the German Hygiene Museum in Dresden devoted an exhibition to the 'healthy organisation' of leisure time and called for more of a 'will to health'.

At the same time, we cannot really say that people in the 1920s did not want to make more of themselves. On the contrary: this was a decade of self-perfection in the most comprehensive sense. Many people attended classes in painting, photography and expressive dance, they learned foreign languages or 'played a bit of sport'. And if we agree with the historian Johanna Niedbalski, even pure pleasure had a deeper, encyclopaedic quality. Thus, the Lunapark in Berlin offered a whole universe of entertainments, customarily advertised as a 'World Exposition of enjoyment'.[5]

For the author Joseph Roth, 'the God of sensations' had placed the Lunapark right at the end of the already entertainment-packed Kurfürstendamm in Berlin, effectively as its punchline.[6] In this most famous amusement park of the 1920s, one could start with the shooting range and move all the way to an up-to-date merry-go-round, either dining out at a smart restaurant or eating sausages from a stand, sipping champagne or guzzling beer. The Lunapark presented itself as extremely modern – the rollercoaster, for example, was at first called 'Cubist' before being redesigned as 'Expressionist' by the painter and graphic designer Josef Fenneker, and finally ending up as a 'scenic alpine ride'. The Lunapark's nearest rival Ulap (Universe-Regional Exhibition Park) had its own painter in residence – Hans Baluschek, still famous today for his penetrating, realistic depictions of working-class life. Here, just up the road from the Lunapark, in the district of Moabit, he had cobbled together a nostalgic 'old Berlin' out of cardboard, plaster and glue, to the fury of the Communist Party journal *Rote Fahne* (Red Flag).

The Lunapark had an 'iron lake', a wobbly set of stairs with a fan at the end that blew the ladies' skirts up, a spinning 'Villa Madhaus', a large wave pool, a hippodrome, a boxing ring in which the prize-fighter Max Schmeling won his first title in 1926, a revue stage, fireworks every night and much else besides. The restaurants are said to have offered 16,000 seats in all, with 1,500 staff serving at its peak.

But when was that peak? The 1920s might have been Lunapark's historic zenith, but they were also its end. The park, which opened in 1909 with a universalistic concept, essentially belonged to the Belle Époque with its optimistic World Expositions, suggesting a comprehensive totality that now, two decades later, already appeared naive.[7] In addition, more and more stress was now placed on social distinction. As the decade advanced, the different classes began to keep to themselves and remain cleanly separate according to lifestyle and assets. Only a short walk from Kurfürstendamm to Kaiserdamm, for example, there was a chic ski slope where high society skiers could gather exclusively to practise their slaloms and downward runs. The artificial slope was roofed, but perhaps more important than that it was 'high-class', which meant that the skiers could display their new expensive equipment untroubled by the presence of the lower orders. In the Lunapark, however, one met the whole of Berlin, and that wasn't always an unalloyed delight. Anyone wanting to be successfully entertained here in the long term had to invest huge sums of money, since the appeal of the attractions soon wore off and Berliners, brought together in large numbers, grew bored.

The businessmen who kept Lunapark, Ulap and similar large projects afloat were a strange collection of characters. Insatiable gamblers, born entertainers, magicians – mostly with a background in light theatre or film. One of them, Siegbert Goldschmidt, was a cinema owner, actor, theatre director, musician, jazz-band leader, journalist and association official rolled into one – a multitalented individual, albeit one whose career came to an abrupt conclusion when bailiffs and a cohort of police arrived at his home to collect his unpaid debts.

This field required a lot of money to keep going; over time the big amusement parks were transformed into limited companies. Leo Kronau, who managed Lunapark from 1926 before becoming director of Haus Vaterland in 1927, had previously made a name for himself as an impresario in Vienna and the United States. In the Luna Park on Coney Island – which gave the Berlin park its name – he is believed to have been involved in the Trip to the Moon ride. Here, after a bumpy journey in the *Luna* spaceship, in the course of which they were shown pictures of the Earth as seen from space, visitors landed on a papier-mâché mock-up of the moon. The doors of the vehicle opened and passengers were served green moon-cheese by costumed Selenites.[8]

In America, Kronau had learned how to rustle up huge sums of investment for such spectacles. Initially his business model was also profitable in Berlin, but over time it became extremely risky. Anyone who didn't keep coming up with new ideas was unable to bring in big money over a long period of time. The pressure to innovate ate away at the budget and at the nerves of those involved. Part of the economic tragedy of the big entertainment spectacle lay in its innate richness. The promising world of glitter made way for disappointment as the participants grew weary. As a result, any number of amusement-park managers retired exhausted, ultimately defeated by the struggle against habit and overfamiliarity. Lunapark survived the ending of the Weimar Republic in 1933 by just over a year, while Ulap closed its gates for ever as early as 1925. In August of the same year, the *Reichsbanner Schwarz-Rot-Gold* (Black-Red-Gold banner of the Reich), an organisation of the centre-left Social Democratic Party, the centre-right Centre Party and the centrist German Democratic Party dedicated to democratic republicanism, had held its party there to celebrate the constitution, filling the park with a sea of republican flags and thus making it twice as fashionable for the 'sensation and pleasure-seeking bourgeoisie' that the Communist *Rote Fahne* had identified as the park's target group.[9] It did no good in the end, however, and Ulap went under. The organisers had run out of ideas, and the desire for ever new entertainments was ruthless. Pleasureseekers are easily bored, as the organisers of the amusement parks discovered to their cost.

In the cinema: visible voices

While one group of young people escaped the cities as *Wandervögel* and hiked through hills and dales in search of a unified and meaningful life in nature, another group sat in stuffy cinemas to be enthralled by stars such as Charlie Chaplin, Willy Fritsch, Lilian Harvey and Marlene Dietrich. Cinema was the paid-for leisure activity number one – a sector that was growing powerfully. During the 1920s an evening at the cinema became much like the experience we know today – no longer a fairground booth, but a temple to the moving image. The decade experienced the birth of talking pictures and a visit to the cinema became almost as much of a treat as a visit to the theatre.

In the early 1920s most people didn't go to see a particular film, they just went to the cinema. For that reason, many cinema owners didn't think it necessary to set a particular time for the screening to start. Films were just shown one after the other, in any order. People came and went, they pushed their way along the rows of seats in the middle of the film and watched for as long as they felt like it. If the projectionist wanted to go home early he just played the film speeded up; silent films can take that. More importantly, there was no need for the audience to listen, so they made any amount of noise, chatted, applauded or commented bawdily on the action.

To heighten its impact, the silent film relied on a musical accompaniment, with scores usually supplied by the distributors. The better the cinema, the bigger the orchestra – in unambitious cinemas they were happy enough if there was at least one musician present, working away at his out-of-tune piano. Largo when loving eyes met on the screen, crescendo when doom approached, presto when expressions turned fearful. That was how Friedrich Hollaender, the popular revue and chanson composer, had started: as a schoolboy he had tried to keep up with the pictures, with one eye on the score and the other on the screen.

Over time cinemas became grander, particularly in the cities. The real movie palaces stood comparison with the finest hotels. Elegant foyers allowed a gentle transition from the real world into the projected one. As time went on, a visit to the cinema slowly became a precisely scheduled event, and the film had to start at a given time. Before the feature there was a newsreel, showing contemporary pictures from all over the world: 'native dances, floods, races, military arms displays, babies and elephant seals – the usual uninformed chaos that doesn't ease an understanding of the world, but rather obstructs it.'[10] With these words the newspaperman Kracauer described the new competition from the film industry. *Deuligs-Wochenschau*, the popular newsreel, would have been torturously slow given our present-day viewing habits. After the caption 'Hindenburg visits the regional government of Braunschweig', which stayed on screen for an eternity, viewers saw the old president of the Reich for several minutes, travelling by coach, shaking hands and delivering an address. About what, the audience was not told, since everything was silent. But contemporaries still watched enthralled.

To enhance the cinemagoing experience, the big picture palaces experimented with additional gimmicks. For example, a pompous orchestral overture might be played at the beginning of the evening, perhaps accompanied by a ballet or a mime. A mistake, it turned out, because three-dimensional dancing reduced the potential impact of the two-dimensional film image that followed. The film was a disappointment after the real bodies on stage.[11] In the end the movie-house managers trusted their audiences to respond to film alone, and to do without third-class add-ons from high culture.

The entertainment industry quickly understood that things didn't have to be so stiff and polite, because as soon as the lights went down the audience forgot themselves anyway. The darkness of the cinema auditorium merged the audience into an anonymous crowd, unlike the theatre, where members of the better sort of society could appraise one another in the semi-darkness. The cinema was the first real mass medium that produced the same passions in everyone, from managing director to shop assistant, from diva to shorthand typist, and turned them into an anonymous urban audience.

Everyone was equally enthralled by the moving pictures. Its magic was enough to get something out of a dull President Hindenburg on walkabout, but as soon as the massive Zeppelin appeared, hearts beat faster. That behemoth was the great pride of almost all Germans. And then when the terrible vampire Count Orlok, alias Nosferatu, stretched his long claws out towards the lovely Ellen, his victim, all composure vanished. Audience members would frequently clutch their neighbour in horror, regardless of who was in the next seat. In 1920, the art historian Konrad von Lange of Tübingen University had warned of the darkening of cinema auditoria on moral grounds.

In many respects film refocused the senses. Because there was no sound, gestures and facial expressions acquired greater significance; in the silent film, more attention was paid to the repertoire of human gesture than in normal everyday life with its attendant sounds. Viewers began to *see* language. The actors helped with extravagant gesticulations and dramatic movements of the lips. Consequently cinemagoers learned a kind of lip reading. The silent film viewer sees differently, and the silent film star speaks differently; Edvard Munch's famous painting *The Scream* looks almost as if it has been copied from a silent film.

In 1924 the Hungarian film theorist Béla Balázs, who lived first in

Vienna and later in Berlin, published his ground-breaking work *Visible Man*, in which he celebrated silent film as a liberation of expression from the tyranny of the voice. Until then the body had been seen as subservient to the word, the true bearer of meaning; silent film, on the other hand, made it the soul's chief means of expression.[12] At any rate, it helped to bring the body still further into the centre of attention, where it had been since the war. There was a desire to show skin and bones, and many people wanted the clothes to be stripped from the body entirely in emulation of the expressive dancer Anita Berber. Part of the reason the bob hairstyle was so popular was that it revealed more of the face. An angular chin, a prominent cheekbone, were now to be put unequivocally on display and no longer draped in wavy curls.

The emotion that a silent narrative can generate is apparent even today in the films of Charlie Chaplin, which easily hold their own in the colourful, noisy world of television. Chaplin knew how to make gestural language speak in a way that reduced the spoken word to shame.[13] And in fact people had become so used to the peculiar intensity of the silent film that the prospect of seeing the first talking pictures, which arrived in 1927, did not seem enticing in the least. In surveys by film distributors as to whether audiences would prefer to see film silently or with sound in future, the silent film almost always came on out top. The first talkies were failures, not only with critics but with audiences as well.

One of the first, in 1929, was *The Land without Women* by Carmine Gallone, filmed silently and with music, sound and dialogue added later. The sound quality must have been lamentable; the critic Rudolf Arnheim heaped scorn on the film. Things went well at first, but then the moment came when the director thought it was time to have the characters speak:

So it was that Conrad Veidt's old mother opened her mouth and, with the trumpeting voice of a boozed-up elephant, whispered comforting words to which her son replied no less sonorously, but chewing all the S sounds. Now that the ice was broken, the speech took the upper hand, but it didn't really work for anyone. [. . .] The S seemed to have been deleted by the censor. 'Don't forfake me!' the lady pleaded, tearing up an important letter, which made a crackling noise.[14]

The avant-garde of the country saw sound film as cultural decline. The dancer Valeska Gert and her companion, the actor Aribert Wäscher, caused such a disturbance at a screening of The Land Without Women that the police removed them from the cinema.[15]

All of a sudden cinema audiences had to be quiet, because otherwise no one could hear anything. This imposition of discipline was very unwelcome; if a sound film was a success with the public, that wasn't good either, because one could not applaud wildly without drowning out what happened next.

There were also material concerns behind the protests: the cinema musicians feared for their jobs, spoken theatre sensed competition and some of the big silent film stars were completely unsuited to sound film. Harry Liedtke (The Love of a Queen) had been an effective heartbreaker hitherto, but he had an unsuitably squeaky voice that cancelled the effect of his smooth and handsome face. His singing role in the film I Kiss Your Hand, Madame (1929) had to be redubbed by the singer Richard Tauber. For the beau Bruno Kastner, whose picture hung in countless girls' rooms, the talking picture was a disaster. His speech impediment meant that the roles dried up. Kastner, who had acted in over a hundred films, hanged himself in his hotel room in 1932 at the age of 42.

By the time of the celebrated Josef von Sternberg film Der blaue Engel (The Blue Angel) in 1930, the talking film had arrived, even though Emil Jannings played the stiff, conservative Professor Rath, who falls in love with a cabaret singer, with a theatricality that was still stuck in the aesthetic of the silent film. But Marlene Dietrich, still unknown at the time, who played the role of Lola and earned 25 Reichsmarks, only a tenth of the wages of the famous Jannings, exploited the advantages of sound film to the hilt. Not only in the song 'Falling in Love Again', written by Friedrich Hollaender and still famous today, but also because of her reticence as an actress. Dietrich had immediately recognised that the sound film allows actors to present themselves sparingly and all the more intensely as a result.

But the finest German film of 1930 was silent. Like *The Blue Angel* it concerned a leisure activity. *People on Sunday* was a real independent auteur film (although the term hadn't yet been coined). Four people, unknowns at the time, wrote or directed. They would later have international careers in Hollywood, quite independent of one another: Billy Wilder (*Some Like it Hot*), whom we met in the last chapter as a gigolo; Curt and Robert Siodmak (*The Devil Strikes at Night*) and Edgar G. Ulmer (*Detour*). The man behind the camera was Fred Zinnemann, who would establish his fame as a director in 1952 with the western *High Noon*. *People on Sunday* was the first film almost all of them had worked on. It only came about because Robert Siodmak had been given 5,000 Reichsmarks by his uncle and was able to cover most of the costs with that. The actors were appearing in front of the camera for the first time too, mostly playing themselves. Five young Berliners who have only just met spend a Sunday together on the shore of the Wannsee: a model, a record seller, a film extra, a taxi driver and a wine dealer. Out of the city, which lies there on a Sunday as if abandoned, deserted and enjoying a rest from its inhabitants. A picnic on the beach, various dalliances, a walk, a boating party, the tram home. The camera follows the protagonists with virtuoso agility, observes them tenderly as if it too were benefiting from the Sunday leisure time it is allowed to participate in – and from the curiosity with which the five protagonists appraise, approach and repel one another. A photographer on the beach offers to take souvenir photographs of the mass of excursionists, which gives the film the opportunity to look at the summer holidaymakers individually and provide a sociologically interesting cross section. It ends with the caption: 'Four million people wait for next Sunday'.

The film is early *cinéma-verité*, the opposite of the Expressionistic, highly artificial horror dramas with which German cinema enjoyed holding its audiences spellbound and terrified. No spinechilling chiaroscuro lighting, no reliance on threatening papier-mâché mountains, no bat ears or somnambulant staggering as in *Nosferatu* or *Dr*

Caligari, just a loving look at the simple life and what people hope to get from their free time: a bit of joy. Little expense, few costs, no sensations and yet a huge success. Refined camerawork that calmly observes the characters' quick movements, a quiet film that derives its material from normal life, based on an undramatic approach to drama – *People on Sunday* is, for all the highfalutin radicalism of the decade, a miracle of sensible pragmatism, floating just above solid ground, and ultimately one of the great films of the twentieth century.

'Poets should box'

Five years previously, another film had attracted attention, one that also led out into the fresh air and was populated by non-professional actors: *Ways to Strength and Beauty*, a UFA Kulturfilm by Wilhelm Prager, showed fitness training from classical antiquity until the present day. With many warning undertones and even more naked, athletically taut skin, it is about 'hygienic gymnastics', 'rhythmic gymnastics', expressive dance and choreographed mass sport. Both audiences and critics were enthusiastic. The *Film-Kurier* saw the gymnastic displays of two young women not only as 'examples of an almost unearthly physical harmony, but also true poets in their unclothed bodies'.[16] The pair were devotees of the American trainer Bess Mensendieck, whose sculptural fitness exercises were practised by many people. She was a predecessor of aerobics advocates such as Jane Fonda, so popular, in fact, that the word 'Mensendiecken' was used for practising gymnastics. The two bodies, arched and rotating towards one another, became an iconic image of the Weimar Republic.

It is probably no coincidence that one of the performers in *Ways to Strength and Beauty* was the unknown Leni Riefenstahl, and in fact the film does look aesthetically like a predecessor of her 1938 Nazi propaganda film *Olympia* about the 1936 Berlin Olympics. But this heroic aesthetic of the body did not have National Socialist connotations.

Even Siegfried Kracauer, otherwise so ideologically critical, enjoyed the 'play, dexterity and rhythm' and expressly recommended the work for young people.[17] The conviction that exercise was something owed to the body was widespread in all political camps, particularly since neither the 'sitting, bent way of life of the office worker' nor the smoky, dirty cities encouraged a healthy lifestyle.[18] Even if it was not the highest good, 'physical fitness was still a significant part of a proper human being', Kracauer said in his review of the film.[19]

But what was 'a proper human being'? A whole one, perhaps? That was how one critic from LichtBildBühne saw it at any rate: 'Here the cinemagoer is shown in the most insistent and effective way what he must do to be a whole person,' it said in the announcement for the film.[20] It was not a long journey from the 'whole person' to the 'New Man', that promise of salvation that had been roaming around in the most varied political contexts since 1918, which had almost become common property, and which had also crept into the most apparently harmless areas of life: 'In contrast to a cohort of young people wasting away, we are witnessing the appearance of a new generation for whom fitness means life', the Illustrierte Filmkurier wrote of Ways to Strength and Beauty.[21]

Apart from the athletic moments in classical antiquity, there can scarcely have been two decades in history as body-obsessed as the brief span between the world wars. It adopts such a prominent place in historical memory because the media of the time focused on the physical existence of human beings with extraordinary intensity. Two controversial tendencies were involved in this: injury to the body and physical fitness. The world war had left 700,000 invalids, who reminded people of its horrors by hobbling and begging in the streets. The 'war wounded' shocked the uninjured as 'living monuments to horror', the journalist Erich Kuttner wrote in his 1920 article 'Forgetting' in Vorwärts, the journal of the Social Democratic Party. Missing noses, half-destroyed faces, figures dragging themselves along on roller boards, shocked passersby and reminded them of the injury done to the national body, which overshadowed even the better years. It was better not to think about it, the affluent economy advised, so the spirit of the age did everything it could to repress these living monuments as quickly as possible and instead to erect stone ones. There was not a village without a symbolic monument for those left in the field.

The mass mutilation of the body had hugely increased awareness of its vulnerability. Appreciation of the inviolate body had risen accordingly, and even more so for the strong body that was capable of defending itself. Both the injured and the toughened body were perceived with hyperreal intensity. It is no coincidence that Otto Dix, who had so impressively painted the ravaged, ragged bodies in the trenches and battlefields, also attributes a shocking and disturbing physicality to his sitters in the portraits of his fellow men in peacetime. Dix exaggerated: bulges protruded to excess, red skin glowed, bushy eyebrows bristled, blue eyes were piercing or watery. The people portrayed by Dix assumed a fearsome impact. This also applies to artists such as Karl Hubbuch, Otto Griebel or Hainz Hamisch, even if they did not go quite as far as Dix in monstrosity. And hyperrealism was not limited to ugliness. The magic realist Christian Schad painted naked skin with its fine veins, shadings, irregularities and coverings of hair with a concision that went beyond reality. His *Semi-Nude* of 1929 shows a skin so transparent that the organism beneath delicately surfaces – an illusionism with something obsessive about it that corresponds to the preoccupations of the age.

Each in their own way, war and silent film taught new ways of seeing the body, with indirect consequences in all areas of culture. The silent film released an explosion of body language that carried other genres along with it. In the exotic dances of Veleska Gert and the naked dances of Anita Berber, which she presented as 'dances of vice, horror and ecstasy', in the androgynous raptures of her husband Sebastian Droste, who offered his sinewy body to the touch in convulsive twitches, and finally in the choreographies of the big revues, which had up to 300 women dancers march on stage to display beauty provocatively to the masses and the parade ground – in all these spectacles the body was simultaneously glorified and manoeuvred. Philosophy also kept pace: Martin Heidegger and Ludwig Klages placed physical being and the body at the centre of their anti-idealistic thinking; Heidegger by ecstatically extending physicality.[22] And in the ideas of eugenic reform the body became the source material for disastrous breeding strategies and racist delusions of selection. The 'New Man', an old acquaintance by now, was to be won by forcing excellent human material to reproduce and preventing by force the weaker material from doing so.[23] The 'cultural philosopher' Ernst Günther Gründel, for example, in his 1929 book *The Humanity of the Future: The West Between Summit and Abyss*, demanded a

> planned *Ausfartung* of our race, the first formation of our future, in terms of both culture and the biology of our population in line with our own will to humanity: the creation of a new man, the supreme man of the future.[24]

The body was also presented in a new way in modern photography. The 35mm camera meant that sports photographs could be captured with a new level of drama. Worm's-eye-view pictures deified their subjects; the photographs of the Bauhaus master Moholy-Nagy, striving skyward, set the tone: they showed a balancing act of bodies apparently freed from the force of gravity, shot from a dramatically low point of view. Camera pans created motion blurs and conveyed a dynamic that had never been seen before. Hundreds of thousands of postcards circulated in the Reich showing naked athletes, 'tanned, shaven and lit in such a way that their muscles stood out in relief'.[25] They set standards for everyone. The body must be supple, fat-free and swift to react. In order to keep up with the pace of the new age, it was put on a diet and trained. The concept of self-optimisation, without which the repertoire of contemporary lifestyles is hard to imagine, was born on a mass scale.

*

Sport enjoyed an unparalleled boom in the Weimar Republic. That applied both to active participants and to spectators. Over 6 million people took part in organised sport, and in 1931 the German Gymnastics Association alone, just one of many such groups, had 1.5 million members. Gymnastics, meaning naked gymnastics, had already been mythologised even before the war, but now it shed some of its historic mustiness. Millions of manual and office workers were organised in company sports associations, paddling canoes, playing volleyball or hockey, or other imported kinds of sport. This included football, which only became the German national sport that we know today in the 1920s.

The desire for a well-trained body and playful communal experiences yielded collective displays that have sunk deeply into the national pictorial memory, such as sports-wheel gymnastics. Here, pieces of sports equipment consisting of two tyres the size of Leonardo da Vinci's *Vitruvian Man* were set spinning by an athlete wedged inside them. It was not entirely clear whether the person was squeezed into the device or heroically set himself rolling, but the elegance of the sports wheel was seductive if somewhat grotesque. It was invented in 1921 by the railwayman and trade unionist Otto Feick in the military prison in Mainz. He had been put there for two years by the French occupying forces for sabotaging trains as part of his patriotic resistance. Six years later the sports wheel was so widespread that participants moved in groups and formations, rolling about in synchrony. It looked as if huge hamster wheels had come adrift from their moorings – a strange image in which freedom and imprisonment merged. The sports-wheel song was sung: 'One only finds true joy in sport when one has a sports wheel to practise on.' Pilots used the wheel for training, because it also improved a sense of balance and orientation, and German sports colleges officially elevated it to the status of a teaching aid.

One American import that became an iconic sporting event of the 1920s was the six-day race. Here, in a celebration with a carnival atmosphere, 13 racing cyclists spent six days and six nights monotonously cycling round and round an oval track in a smoky hall. Similar staying power was demonstrated by some visitors who weren't seen at home for six nights, but who did leave the sports hall during the day to go joylessly about their work. 'Would Herr Wilhelm Hanke, 139 Schönhauser Allee, please go home,' the loudspeaker announced on the third day of the Berlin race, 'as his wife has died.'[26]

The noise in the halls was deafening. Sometimes several bands were playing at the same time, and the spectators were constantly subjected to the rather sluggish *Sport Palace Waltz*, whipped up at certain moments by the shrill whistles of the public. Beer flowed, mustard dripped, people met and yelled at one another. The expert proletariat sat far out in the cheap seats, the smart set inside the arena, reached by a bridge over the track. It was here that the better demi-monde sat, the bigger and smaller moguls of showbusiness and film, high-class prostitutes, authors, newspaper men, gangsters and local politicians. Sparkling wine flowed, jazz bands kept the mood going, and young dancers did a passable impression of the Tiller Girls. In the middle was a man with a megaphone who commented on the state of the race and called out the names of the sponsors, who kept offering special prizes: a hundred marks for whoever wins the next five rounds! One furniture company donated bedroom furnishings for the winner of the next sprint, and the prospect of a roast duck made many of the racers speed up for a round.[27] On the edge of the 'internal stage' were the 13 boxes in which the cyclists took a break, had a massage and slept, under the eyes of all the spectators.

This curious hybrid of sport and variety entertainment was a popular social event, a noisy, ecstatic, agonising real-life metaphor for the six-day week. The communist singer Ernst Busch sang of the six-day race as a capitalist treadmill that defied rational explanation:

> Hey, keep those pedals going,
> Round and round the wooden oval.
> Hey! Hey! Hey! Hey! Hey!
> Planks splinter, tyres explode,
> Three jazz bands play at once,
> Hey! Hey! Hey! Hey! Hey!
> Six days in a row, round and round –
> No mortal knows: why? What's it for?

Everyone's fascinated, everyone's involved!
Everyone's excited, everyone's cheering! Hey!
Six days in a circle, round and round –
And not a soul knows why!

The severest criticism of the six-day race – although it might be more accurately described as a racist attack – came from the far right, from the Nazis. As they saw it, this mixture of show and professional sport, which they already viewed with suspicion, was mostly controlled by the Jews. In 1933 the Nazi organ *Der Angriff* (The Attack) wrote retrospectively: 'Anyone who was allowed to look behind the scenes knows that the events were organised by Jews. It was when Jews held their greatest power that the six-day races were at their most popular.'[28] The Nazis took a dim view of the hedonistic chaos that prevailed in the Sportpalast, seeing it as a prime example of 'cultural Bolshevism'. On the other hand, the sport and culture journalist of the liberal left Berlin newspaper *12 Uhr Blatt* (Twelve O'clock Paper), Curt Riess, 'naturally' a Jew in Nazi eyes, was fascinated by the spectacle. He saw a public that was eager and hungry for pleasure being circled by the riders like a star by its planets:

Their faces were masks of excitement, determination, exhaustion, pain – because time and again the fallen were carried off and yet a few minutes later they were racing around the track again with bandaged knees and arms. That was what I couldn't take my eyes off.[29]

That was what life was like, many felt, seeing the six-day race as a condensed version of their lives.

*

There can hardly have been a period in recent cultural history that brought art and sport as close together as the Weimar Republic. The avant-garde painted racing cyclists, tennis players, high divers, swimmers, pole vaulters, discus throwers and, again and again, boxers.

Boxing was the favourite sport of the cultural scene. George Grosz, Rudolf Belling, Renée Sintenis, Rudolf Schlichter, Conrad Felixmüller and many others painted or sculpted boxers. The author Vicki Baum had a punching ball next to her desk, which she would thump when her work wasn't going well. In her work breaks she went to the Kurfürstendamm boxing studio of Sabri Mahir, who trained some high-profile figures. Bertolt Brecht also had a punching ball; he would have liked to have been a boxer but was too delicate and had a heart condition. As a consequence, he held the reigning heavyweight champion, Paul Samson-Körner, in high esteem. He made friends with him and wrote a biography of the boxer as a serial for the sport magazine *Die Arena*:

> If you go to the theatre as if to church or the courtroom or school, that's a mistake. You should go to the theatre as if into a sporting competition. This isn't about fights in the ring with your biceps. These are more delicate scraps, fought with words.[30]

In 1926 the author Frank Thiess even recommended in the pages of *Uhu*: 'Poets should box, literature would be in better shape.'[31] He wrote for pages, with sideswipes against coffee-house literati and scribbling drunkards, about how he had transformed his 'war-weary body, weakened by illness and overwork', into a toughened one. His shoulder circumference had increased by 14 centimetres, and his body was now protected by a slight muscular armour that delighted him 'like a great discovery or a new truth'.[32] The article was illustrated with naked photographs of the poet. Clad only in an extremely brief loincloth, Thiess presented his well-defined body, turned and bent and showed the astonished reader what a hunk one can turn oneself into. Thiess's exhibitionism and his missionary teetotalism must have been a huge thorn in the side of the delicate Brecht, an industrious boozer: 'Sport for the sake of hygiene is repellent', he wrote in a reply to the conservative author that was unfortunately never published.[33] He too had bought a punching ball, he said, but only dealt it a few angry blows when the mood took him. Compulsory fitness

Vicki Baum was, like many artists and writers, fascinated by boxing. She trained regularly in the Sabri Mahir sport studio on Kurfürstendamm.

according to a timetable was an atrocity as far as he was concerned: 'I'm in favour of sport because and for as long as it is unhealthy (risky), uncultivated (so not socially acceptable) and an end in itself.'[34]

The boxer seemed to his contemporaries to be *the* athlete of the modern age. He stood for the speed of response that one needed to keep up with unbridled capitalism. He was combative, self-reliant and lonely. His models, his rules of battle and his style came from America, the source of almost everything that became popular in Germany in the 1920s.

Probably the biggest boxing fan in the culture industry was the gallery-owner and journalist Alfred Flechtheim, who was a passionate dealer and collector of the avant-garde, and an intermediary between the German and French scenes. The rich 'art Jew', as the anti-Semites called him, represented Pablo Picasso, Georges Braque, Paul Klee, Max Beckmann, Max Ernst and many others. And he loved boxers and the sport as a whole. As founder and publisher of the cultural journal Der Querschnitt, he wrote in the first issue in 1921: 'Der Querschnitt sees it as its duty to introduce boxing to German cultural circles. In Paris, Braque, Derain, Dufy, Matisse, Picasso and Vlaminck are enthusiastic devotees, and Rodin barely misses a fight.'[35] Within a few years, Flechtheim had achieved something that would probably have happened even without him: boxing became a matter for high culture. In 1925, when Flechtheim described a fight by his idol Hans Breitensträter, the association between boxing and culture had already been established:

That this battle, in which strength, spirit and experience combine to win, was an artistic matter, more artistic than all Berlin theatrical performances, is known to all those who had the great good fortune to witness this unique drama. I congratulate Breitensträter on this fight. The experiment was Kokoschka-esque [referring to Oskar Kokoschka, the dramatic Austrian painter].[36]

At Alfred Flechtheim's parties, the wealthy and powerful bathed in the glow of the people being talked about – 'all outsiders in their way', as Max Schmeling enthusiastically wrote in his memoirs. Athletes were well-respected guests there. But when high culture opened itself up to the athletes it wasn't always without a certain condescension. If one listens carefully, one can hear it alongside the admiration. In 1925 the art critic and journalist Hans von Wedderkop, whom Flechtheim appointed his successor as publisher of Der Querschnitt, described the first appearance of the boxer Breitensträter in Flechtheim's salon – in Querschnitt itself, of course, which had in the meantime developed into a somewhat snobbish trendsetting magazine for the cultural elite. Wedderkop studied the heavyweight like a work of art, identified the stylistic influences that could be seen in him, drew out their provenance and allowed the reader to participate in the way in which, by weighing up contradictions, he had very gradually reached his judgement of aesthetic taste. He was startled above all by the fact that Breitensträter had 'neither a figure from classical antiquity, nor one corresponding to any known ideal of artistic beauty'.[37]

> Nor is it Greek. Not a trace. No Greek from Saxony. The memories of our brains, poisoned as they are by classical cliché, must be destroyed. Fixed images must make way so that a new image may form. [. . .] What is more: he has nothing of Myron, of his sharp heaviness, or of oily Praxiteles. Not a mixture, either. He is from Magdeburg. It would be easier to assimilate him to a fundamental American concept.[38]

One of Flechtheim's favourite artists was the wonderful photographer Frieda Riess. She was famous for her refined, flattering

The photographer Frieda Riess photographed the young boxer Erich Brandl in 1925, not in a defensive fighting pose, but as a vulnerable, immaculate body. The half-length nude appeared in Alfred Flechtheim's cultural magazine Der Querschnitt.

portraits of members of the 'highest circles', which she made in her studio on the Kurfürstendamm in Berlin, including many actors, writers and painters: Gerhart Hauptmann, Emil Jannings, Lil Dagover, Max Herrmann-Neisse, Anna Pavlova, Alexander Archipenko and of course Ruth Landshoff-Yorck. She shared Flechtheim's weakness for boxers. She was the one who photographed the young prize-fighter Erich Brandl completely naked, as mentioned in the Preface. But rather than flooding him with the unerotic sunlight of nudist 'free-body' culture, whose stereotypical heroism had become a commonplace, her spotlights lovingly and entirely erotically modelled the impeccable body. The photographic session is a milestone on the long journey of women's emancipation, as it turns the male body quite naturally into the object of a sexualised female gaze. These intimate pictures also ended up in Flechtheim's gallery – and in the pages of *Querschnitt*.

The Blue Light – Leni Riefenstahl emancipates herself as well

In 1931, the 29-year-old dancer and film actress Leni Riefenstahl, tired of being typecast and told what to do, decided to make a film of her own. She wanted to write scripts, establish her own company, and decide for herself where and how she could do things. She could only do that as the main actress in a film that was entirely her own. Many people knew Riefenstahl from the mountain films *The Holy Mountain* (1926), *The Big Jump* (1927) and *The White Hell of Piz Palü* (1929) – dramas set in the thin air of the highest altitudes, with glittering, snowy wastes and icy cold, which had opened up new dimensions in the cinematic conquest of space. Leni Riefenstahl herself was always centre stage, as a bold conqueror of the mountain peaks, filmed from breathtaking perspectives. She was the only woman on set, among wild cragsmen such as Arnold Fanck, Luis Trenker and Sepp Allgeier, who competed bitterly for her. Riefenstahl's speciality lay in almost freezing to death and still looking good. 'Probably the most likeable and usable alpinist in German film', was the view of *B.Z. am Mittag*. Usable? In the long term her position in the male world of the mountain film was oppressive, and, for an egomaniac like Leni Riefenstahl, even untenable.

In 1931, heedless of the financial crisis, she borrowed 50,000 marks from a producer who was besotted with her and joined forces with the left-wing intellectual film theorist Béla Balázs, a man well versed in the world of evocative gestures. Together they wrote a film story about a young outsider, denounced as a witch, in the archaic alpine world of the Dolomites. Expelled from the valley, and now living at a dizzying altitude, both desired and persecuted, the mountain girl Junta embodies a kind of feral beauty. She alone knows and has mastered the difficult route to a cursed vein of crystal high in the mountain peaks. On nights when the moon is full and the crystal glows blue, it exerts a magical attraction on young men. They climb towards the peak and, being less skilled than she is, fall to their deaths. The villagers' hatred for Junta, nimble as a mountain goat and guardian of the blue glow, becomes even more intense.

With Béla Balázs, three cameramen and a small cast, Leni Riefenstahl first set up in Sarntal in South Tyrol, recently incorporated into Northern Italy, before venturing further up into the Brenta Dolomites. Balázs and Riefenstahl masterfully choreographed the mountain farmers and the valley-dwellers, who cluck together like chickens. They stretch their heads up in synchrony and, still in synchrony, they turn their weathered, bitter faces towards the camera. How Balázs and Riefenstahl shared the direction of the film is unknown, and they were both cinematic novices. Leni Riefenstahl also played the part of wild Junta, her mythical alter ego, and physically gave it her all. She stands between waterfalls with spray flying around her, drenched to the skin. Barefoot, in a threadbare dress, she climbs a monumental rockface. When the camera zooms out, she can be seen right at the top, tiny as a fly, crawling almost weightlessly up the rock.

Oh, if only she didn't open her mouth! In the few scenes of dialogue, half in Italian, half in broken German, she fails completely.

The supposed 'child of nature' suddenly becomes a working-class but upwardly mobile Berliner, and everything built up by her physical grace comes crashing to the ground. In the end, Junta veils her face and, in incongruous soft focus, turns herself into a saint revered by the villagers' descendants. Riefenstahl's self-portrait as the Madonna hung in her apartment until her death.

Leni Riefenstahl's ambition knew no bounds. Even as an actress she wasn't the kind who wasted breaks in shooting on rest and recreation. She had studied what went on behind the camera very precisely, noting how directors worked. She had observed all their tricks and was convinced that she could do an even better job. The list of names that she ruthlessly swept out of the way for her career was a long one, and even Béla Balázs's name appears only briefly in the opening credits for *The Blue Light*. She expected a great deal of her crew, making them adopt the riskiest camera positions, and she herself had no qualms about shooting hazardous scenes. To make it as a director, she had to be better than anyone else. She experimented with new film stock, sprayed water on the lens and filmed fog against the light. The mountains became characters in their own right, just as they had been in the daredevil mountain films that Riefenstahl had made with Arnold Fanck, and the physiognomies of the non-professional actors had a gripping, documentary intensity: angular, pinched, suspicious peasant faces that looked impossibly inhospitable in the harsh side light. Surly, primeval faces that had become fashionable to put on film because they formed a strong counterpoint to the alert faces of the big city.

The Blue Light came second at the 1932 Venice Film Festival. The *Film-Kurier* went wild, writing of the premiere: Riefenstahl, 'a courageous woman with full faith in her work and her obsession', had 'collapsed the pallid sky of heaven, and the moon and the dubious nights of mysterious mountain nature gleamed above us'.[39] And the best thing was: the prophetess counted for something in the Fatherland; visitors would stream to cinemas to find a film that was 'German in style and art'. The author did not elaborate further on what that might mean. The director had as yet shown no far-right inclinations.

When everything was still open and the future a blank page: the actresses Marlene Dietrich, Anna May Wong and Leni Riefenstahl in 1928 at a ball in Berlin.

On the contrary: her film criticised a collective witch-hunt of an out-sider; the peasants seemed more like gruesome backwoodsmen than the mythical 'food-producers' who would be celebrated by the Nazis. It was not yet clear what Riefenstahl would become, who she would woo and who she would encourage. Only one thing was clear: she had higher peaks to climb.

'I'm only really cheerful in my association'

The vast power of urban entertainment culture sometimes leads us to overlook a form of leisure activity from which many Germans drew warmth and sustenance: meetings of their associations. Some

10 per cent of Germans were active in an association, whether a rifle club, veterans' association, volunteer fire service, money-saving association, homeland association or singing club. As television, which would later keep people in their sitting rooms, was yet to be invented, and radio was only making its way slowly into German houses, people had to make do with each other if they didn't want to get bored or stay at home and read. For that reason alone the Weimar Republic was considerably more sociable than the present day.

People came together for a particular purpose set out in the association's statutes, such as the nurture of German song, and added a social component. Membership of such an organisation involved a great many obligations. While the culture of consumption and distraction was constantly spreading, and atomising individuals from one another, the association brought people together again. Its significance for social cohesion was enormous. The association – within the context of a certain like-mindedness – allowed encounters between people who would otherwise rarely have mixed. In the countryside, large families were gradually dissolving, and more and more housemaids and farm labourers preferred to live away from the farm. Villages were also becoming increasingly different from one another. But agricultural workers, farmers, shop owners and dignitaries came together and found a forum for dispute and reconciliation.

Associations held a particular charm for many members because of their hierarchical component. Chairmen, honorary chairmen, advisory committees and their representatives, treasurers, bookkeepers and youth officers were elected, criticised, dismissed, confirmed or voted out – an intriguing organisation of leisure time that amounted to a game played with real pieces. Every association was a happy combination of common purpose and mischief. Here one was somebody. 'My association is the place where I'm cheerful. I look down on those who are not members', Kurt Tucholsky wrote in 1926. 'High above us the statutes float. The evening hours fly by like minutes.'[40]

People felt at ease, they chatted and gossiped, swore and drank, and made spectacles of themselves. They practised their skills. Some sang, others fired rifles. They helped each other and looked after one another. In many villages there were 'patient support associations' or 'cash loan associations', which helped when banks refused to. Let us take the little village of Korschenbroich in the Lower Rhine as an example. Two thousand people lived there, or 5,000 if we include the surrounding area. They were organised into at least 35 associations, as the list below indicates, even though the largest, the veterans' association, is absent – its existence was so obvious in every village that it doesn't even get a mention.

- 'Wreath of Song' Male Voice Choir Association
- 'North Star' Drummers' Corps
- 'Myrtle Wreath' Society
- 'Cecilia' Male Voice Choir Association
- 'Thalia' Theatre Association
- Korschenbroich Gymnastics Association
- 'Recovery' Society
- 'Arion' Male Voice Choir Association
- Neersbroich Sports Club
- Korschenbroich Football Club
- 'Cecilia' Church Choir
- Marian Young Men's Congregation
- Marian Young Women's Congregation
- Catholic Mothers' Union
- Catholic People's Union
- Catholic Vestments Union
- Saint Sebastian Shooting Fraternity
- Bachelors' Shooting Society
- Catholic Labour Union
- St Donatus Fraternity
- 'Airmail' Messenger Pigeon Association
- Korschenbroich Volunteer Fire Service
- Herrenshoff Volunteer Fire Service
- Korschenbroich-Pesch Beekeeping Association
- 'Black' and 'Blauloh'

- Rabbit Breeding Association
- Korschenbroich Beekeeping Association
- Korschenbroich Craftsmen's Association
- Korschenbroich Bakers' Association
- Agricultural Subscription and Sales Cooperative
- Agricultural Mess Pesch
- Horse Insurance Association
- Fatherland Women's Association
- 'Swallow' Messenger Pigeon Association
- 'Homeland Love' Messenger Pigeon Association[41]

There was sociability in abundance. At the same time, the trans-regional party-political associations and youth organisations that would also have existed in Catholic Korschenbroich are no more listed than the veterans' association. The associations were containers of trad-ition and ensured the maintenance of regional qualities. Liturgical wall hangings and fabrics for Holy Mass were embroidered in the Catholic Vestments Union. In the Rabbit Breeding Association they competed to see who could breed the biggest long-eared buck, and they would also have discussed the political matters of the day. The modern age had arrived in the village just as it had in the nearest small town: agricultural workers had grown more confident and argued furiously for higher wages; the workers in the surrounding factories voted left or far left and hated the farmers for their reaction-ary views; and young people were flocking to the city, where the women in particular hoped for more independence. Associations in the provinces had a lot of wounds to heal.

As rapid as cultural changes were, life here still followed a different pace, even if one had to move with the times when it came to win-ning souls. The leaders of the Marian Young Men's Congregation, for example, reckoned: 'Only through gymnastics, sport and hiking can large circles of young people be weaned off the enervating and demoralising modern bustle of amusement'.[42] So with gritted teeth the pastoral caregivers introduced sport as a way of doing battle with the modern age. As a general rule, however, moods in the provinces changed more slowly than the cloud formations that drifted above them in high summer, and for many of the residents of Korschenbroich even Kaiser Wilhelm had been an arrogant Protestant modernist without whom they would have been spared the whole mess that had taken place since 1914.

There was politics at play in every association: it was the kiln in which latent emotions were baked into hard convictions. What went on in the associations was consequently of interest to politicians. The SPD (Social Democrats), KPD (Communists) and NSDAP (National Socialists) launched countless associations themselves, infiltrated others or took them over. Regional investigations show how persistent the NSDAP was in its attempts to seep into associations and make a show of itself in local festivities. Whoever gained the upper hand in the organisation of 700th or 800th anniversary celebrations, always prepared by local associations, had taken an important step in the battle for people's minds. And the political parties were themselves social groups that provided diversion and friendship for many at the end of the working day. You could go camping in a right-wing or a left-wing way, you could go for a far-right or a far-left hike.

Outwardly, most German associations were apolitical, and set great store by party-political independence, but their views of the world were entirely fixed. Many so-called 'citizens' associations' – rifle clubs, fire services and singing fraternities – had emerged from the Citizens' Defence Groups (Einwohnerwehren) that had formed during the November Revolution of 1918 to defend property against marauders and had then stayed together for the sake of the camaraderie. Apart from their official purpose – saving money, putting out fires or commemorating heroes – they were for the most part rigidly anti-republican or at least anti-socialist in spirit.[43] The rifle clubs were able to connect with the good old days not only through their curious pomp but above all through shooting. Since the Versailles Treaty had left the German Reich with only a rump army, militarism lived on only in competitive shooting. Here, in this 'militant conviviality',[44] even in the relatively good-humoured and prosperous years of the Republic, there was a constant reservoir of political reaction.

In accordance with their statutes, the veterans' associations in the villages looked after monuments and the welfare of those left behind. But mostly they just sat together and drank. There were 29,000 associations with a total of 2 million members in the Kyffhäuser League alone, established in honour of the Emperor Barbarossa who, legend had it, was sleeping in a cave in the Thuringian mountains. The veterans' associations were a convivial echo of defeat. They tried to overcome the trauma and reinstate a sense of honour with big speeches. Women were even active in some veterans' associations. Their duties were to sew the countless lines of bunting that the associations exchanged with one another, and the weaving of wreaths.[45] If that was not enough for these women, and they wanted to have their own say, they could join the 'Fatherland Women's Union', which was in turn involved with 52 other women's associations in the 'German Women's Committee for the Struggle Against the War-Guilt Lie', in opposition to the Versailles Treaty and its War Guilt clause.

Naturally enough, Jewish war veterans also wanted to keep the sentimental memory of the war alive. The rise in anti-Semitism reinforced their desire to preserve the recognition of their courage and the memory of their fallen comrades. Excluded from many veterans' associations, they came together in the Reich League of Jewish Frontline Soldiers, of which around half of all surviving Jewish soldiers were members. For a time the Reich League had more than 50,000 members, making it the strongest Jewish organisation in the Weimar Republic. It fought for something that was actually quite obvious: the recognition of Jews as part of German society. In their statutes it says:

> The Reich League of Jewish Frontline Soldiers sees the basis of its work as lying in total commitment to the German homeland. It has no goal and no aspiration outside of this German homeland, and most strongly resists any efforts to estrange us German Jews from this German homeland.

Struggle, against whomever

In the combat units of the political parties, determined characters found an activity that went beyond the harmless understanding of the term 'leisure'. After work, they engaged in civil war, or at least in preparations for it. They were trained in both attack and defence. As well as the radical parties, those loyal to the Republic – the SPD, the DDP (German Democratic Party) and the Centre – had their own *Reichsbanner Schwarz-Rot-Gold* (Black-Red-Gold banner of the Reich) organisation, which combined bibulous conviviality with a distinctly combative approach. Given the growing militancy on both left and right, it was clear that the Republic could consider itself lucky to have these 1.5 million members on its side.

The brutality of the extremist combat units, however, meant that the Republican *Reichsbanner Schwarz-Rot-Gold* was pushed very much to the edge, even though after 1932 it had three times as many members as *Stahlhelm* (Steel Helmet), the SA (*Sturmabteilung*, Storm Troopers) and *Rotfrontkämpferbund* (Red Front Combat League) combined.[46] The Republic, even though it finally succumbed, was better equipped to defend itself than it might have seemed in retrospect. Flag consecrations, torch processions and strictly graded march pasts were the favourite pastimes of the Reich Banner, but above all they enjoyed holding celebrations at which it was repeatedly emphasised that they were willing to defend the Republic 'to the last drop of blood'. In fact, more than 100 members of the Reich Banner would lose their lives in the last five years of the Republic – mostly fighting a militant youth who outdid their fathers, defeated in 1918, in fighting power and determination, and who wanted to undo the ignominy that in their eyes afflicted the whole nation.

It was here, on the extreme right, that the seeds of the frontline-soldier novels that had become the favourite reading matter among young men sprang into life. Along with the expectations of salvation that had inspired the rhetoric of the youth movement, this produced an explosive mixture. Four and a half million young people had joined forces in an Association of Youth Groups, whether scouts,

Wandervögel (the hikers' associations) or the 'Quickborn' Youth Movement of Catholic students. Their youth-obsessed leaders pumped
them up with such a sense of self and mission that they felt they were
a match for anyone. The new saviour was bound to come from their
ranks, on that much they could agree. Many saw themselves as the
White Knights predicted in the youth movement's pamphlets. They
were celebrated there as

> noble bodies and souls loyal to death – illuminating the filthiest cran-
> nies with beauty and well enough bred to occupy any role; merged in
> comradeship with the people while at the same time captivating
> leader figures; proud in the handsome steel helmet, and humble with
> the helmet doffed in prayer.[47]

A pederastic cult of youth mingled with saviour fantasies into one
more phantasmagorical variation on the 'New Man', which would
supposedly leave an 'insanely torn cultural life' far behind.[48]

In the late 1920s this supposedly redemptive youth cult became
even more militant. Inspired by the heated mood on the political
fringes, the time seemed slowly to be arriving for the young heroes,
who had been preparing for struggle for so long, against whomever.
Paramilitarism existed in almost every milieu, inspired by a great variety of convictions. The Catholics had their 'Windhorst League', the
National Liberals the 'Young German Order', the Communists their
'Red Front Combat League' and the NSDAP their SA, the repellent
culmination of political violence.

For the historian Sven Reichardt the martial battle formation is a
non-partisan phenomenon of the Weimar Republic:

> The fascination of homogenised physical movements expressed in the
> discipline of the close-formation march rubbed off on demonstration
> styles of every political colour. The new style of assembly with march-
> ing and ceremony, uniform and flag, symbol and ritualised greeting
> was articulated in a great variety of milieus as a stylised drama of
> unity and struggle.[49]

In the geometrical order of the combat troops the power that the young men felt within them multiplied into a collective body whose violence could be unleashed on command. The SA were infinitely pleased with themselves; the National Socialist propaganda illustrations always show them as clean-shaven, chiselled, broad-shouldered in impeccably fitting uniforms, and their opponents as unshaven, bent-backed and with brutal, thuggish features. Similar clichés, although in reverse, appeared in left-wing propaganda, but the right-wing version was visually more well-established. In the National Socialist self-image, three stereotypes came together in the combat leagues: the vigorous frontline fighter of the world war, the wheat-blond settler of agrarian romanticism, and the 'physically consecrated "Aryan"'.[50]

From 1930, when the storm clouds once again appeared on the horizon, many radicals from the young generation of soldiers who had made their fragile peace with the Republic in the years of slow economic growth felt that that period had only been a break in the fighting. They saw themselves as 'warriors camped in bourgeois sitting rooms', ready at any moment to line up once more in the ranks of the elect.[51] And even younger ones who were mad enough to regret that they had not been able to take part in the world war saw the civil war-like tensions during the economic crisis as a chance to prove themselves. They were determined to make a better go of it than their fathers had done.

In fact, the cold militancy of the young had hardly anything in common with the sentimental war games of their elders. Most of the young men who were organised into combat units had nothing but mockery for the largely ritualised commemoration of the fallen and the ponderous parades on the feast days of the fatherland.

No rifle club party, no firemen's ball, no city jubilee to which the fattest old codger doesn't cram his belly into his uniform before the eyes of his astonished wife. You can get bawled out there, domestic duties are forgotten and off it goes like in the olden days.[52]

1932 leisure activities in the combat unit: the SA marches through Berlin. There were combat units of every political colour. The groups of the pro-Republic Reichsbanner Schwarz-Rot-Gold *were superior in numbers to the others. The SA, however, outdid everyone else in brutality.*

For years, young people had fled to the woods to avoid just such stuffy bourgeois scenes, escaped to the countryside with the agrarian Artaman League, a back-to-the-land movement eventually absorbed by the Nazi Party, to help with the harvest, and sought communal experiences by the campfire that dispelled the domestic fug. But the insults grew as the crisis worsened, and the hiking became more defiant. 'In hiking and wandering you should carry and feel the space that encloses you, and thank it with your breath,' the old spirit of the *Wandervögel* recommended.[53] Hiking, with its aspiration to harmony with nature, made way for the aggressive conquest of space associated with marching. Consequently, even the dreamy, idealistic *Wandervögel* were caught up in the maelstrom of a warrior cult to which many different political trends adhered, however antagonistic they might have been to one another.

For the cult of the body in the 1920s, choreographed mass experience turned into a more intense form of self-intoxication. Just as the troupes of girl dancers amalgamated themselves into a single leg-twirling millipede, combat units also synchronised their members into a formation that was more than the sum of its individual parts. These young men were apparently invulnerable when, assembled into a single body, a many-legged fighting machine, they marched on the cobbles with their boots. Many were enticed by organisations that had made hatred their political programme. The most devastatingly unbridled violence was unleashed by anti-Semitism. *Der Angriff* (The Attack) was the name given to the newspaper of the Berlin NSDAP. The editor was one Joseph Goebbels.

Between Woman and Man – Gender Doubts

What may be described as male, what as female? We can say nothing
or little about it. It is probably not a fixed quantity, but something
transformed by evolution exactly like everything else that we
easily turn into something absolute.

Trude Wiechert, 1931

'The fashionable, skinny half-boy'

In the early years of the twentieth century, could there have anything
more drastic than the pitched battles of the First World War? Yes, in
fact – the change in the status of women. That at least was the view
of Stefan Zweig, one of the best-known authors of his time. Zweig
was quite certain that 'a future cultural history of this complete
revaluation and transformation of European women' would ultimately be more disruptive than the war.[1] He was convinced that women
had radically changed, and the rest of the country with them, and
that this shift ran deeper than all the changes in architecture, traffic,
technology or even politics. Not only had women's appearance
undergone a radical change between 1905 and 1925, their behaviour,
their speech and their thought had changed as well.

And what about men? They seemed to have stayed more or less the
same; at least that was how it seemed to men themselves, since most
of them, pragmatic by nature and habit, thought comparatively little

about themselves. However, many men shared the feeling of standing on the edge of a great upheaval, with women at its centre. According to their characters and political viewpoints, they viewed the emancipation of women with concern, anxiety, pity, acquiescence, joy or loathing. In the 49-year-old Stefan Zweig pure joy predominated. He remembered with disquiet the visual appearance of women in his youth and was gladdened by the natural way in which they now came towards him in the street:

> Those corseted creatures, wrapped to the throat in folded fabric, constrained in skirts and petticoats, legless, artificially wasp-waisted, artificial in all directions and in every movement – that historical woman from only the day before yesterday has within only a generation become the woman of today, with her bright, open body, a light dress flows flowing clearly over it like a wave, this woman who – please do not be alarmed! – is as open to the wind and the air and to the eyes of men as was once only true of ladies who should really go unmentioned, in *maisons closes*.[2]

These are the words, we would say today, of a gleeful old hedonist, his views on women's emancipation prompted chiefly by voyeuristic desire and the hope of sexual adventure. The pleasure of Zweig, known for his erotic obsessions, reveals the ambivalences of an emancipation that many men applauded with enthusiasm – enthusiasm that we can of course now see as suspect. The fact that women now came towards them 'half naked', as was repeatedly stated, satisfied their lascivious glances. Men of an older and more conservative stripe, on the other hand, saw the new fashion as meaning a loss of what they understood as femininity, something, in fact, that should both be hidden and emphasised. In their eyes, the fact that women's bodies were now as straightforwardly delineated as men's, that nothing was billowed, ruched, upholstered or tightly laced, seemed like an inversion of the natural order of the sexes.

It was not only the ideal of the female body that was changing – the same was true of the male. The male body was supposed to be trained, slender and able to defend itself, but also smooth. Beards suddenly looked old-fashioned, only suited to old men who still had one foot in the Kaiserreich, such as President Hindenburg, with his bushy moustache. The modern man was beardless, or at best neatly clipped like Corporal Hitler from Braunau, who had managed to trim the growth on his upper lip into a square shape, thus finding a middle position between Kaiserreich and the modern age. Traditionalists saw younger men as 'effeminising' in their exalted urge to achieve slender lines and smoothness. The magazines were full of grooming products for men, and even the *embonpoint*, the term proudly used for prominent bellies, had become a cause for embarrassment. It was kept flat with a tight belly-band, which could be ordered discreetly by post. Unthinkable for men of the old school.

Softness had become distasteful. Where rounded curves had previously been the ideal of womanhood, edges and angles were now the rule. Figures in fashion magazines grew gaunt, tall and smooth. Breasts and waists had gone; flowing locks had made way for smooth, short styles, often protruding very slightly from tightly fitting caps. The absence of extravagant hats and decorative wavy hair exposed more of the face, leaving room for pert and disdainful expressions. This led to the appearance of a certain haughtiness, because the less clothing a woman wore, the more she had to armour herself with the cast of her face. Women's facial expressions now became in a way more manly, with heroic and defiant features, in Robert Musil's words, 'boyish, comradely, athletically brittle and childlike'.[3]

While initially during this period tight-fitting dresses reached to the ankles, in the course of the 1920s skirts became increasingly short, in line with the requirements of athleticism and pace. Skirts must be 'not exaggerated, not overdone, but suitable for the rapid steps of the contemporary woman', wrote the tennis player Paula von Reznicek. They should be suited 'to her eighty-kilometre-an-hour speed, her boyish face'.[4] The author and feminist Ilse Reicke saw athletic clothing as a 'liberation of the body from the restricted motion imposed on it by a tittivated, straight-laced fashion or a philistinism that is quite alien to the body'.[5] The arrogant vamp-like creature that

dominated fashion designs during the inflationary period soon made
way for a carefree delight in motion. But what remained, and consoli-
dated itself throughout the decade, was the androgyny of the
feminine fashion ideal; in 1931 the author Elsa Maria Bud spoke of the
'fashionable, skinny half-boy'.[6]

Politics with hair-scissors: the bob

If the zone between the sexes had until now largely been a no-man's
land, explored only in exceptional situations and in subcultural niches,
it now became a public space, populated by deliberately dubious,
ambiguous beings who had no wish to identify fully as either female
or male. In the Weimar Republic, oversensitive as it was to issues of
the body, changes in clothing and hairstyles were more than mere
manifestations of fashion that came and went as the mood took
them. The ideal appearance of women visually assimilating to the
silhouette of men was reflected in other processes that were shaking
political and social life. Androgyny was part of that revolution, and
accordingly highly politicised.

'That's enough now!' the *Berliner Illustrirte Zeitung* raged in an article against the 'masculinisation of women'.[7] The bob had long been
seen as a joke, the article argued, but now that even the curls of the
pageboy cut were disappearing and many women were opting for the
masculine Eton cut 'with the hair brushed firmly backwards', it was
time for 'healthy male taste to turn against such foul fashions, whose
excesses had been transplanted from America'. It was 'repellent for
any proper man' if a woman looked like 'an effeminate boy'. The bob
was seen as a look suited to prostitutes or prison warders, only fitting
for an 'impudent Jewish face', according to the far-right anti-Semitic
Völkische Frauenbund (Völkisch Women's League), founded in 1924.[8]
'The braid is Aryan, the bob is Jewish', this organisation insisted – a
ridiculous opinion, given that short hair was equally disapproved of
by Jewish conservatives. As late as 1928, two nurses in Cologne's
Jewish Hospital were dismissed for having their hair bobbed.[9]

Cutting off long hair was a political statement that girls in many families, particularly in the countryside, paid for with shame and insults, sometimes even with beatings. The bob, even though it was soon standard in the cities, was seen as a badge of individuality since, like the accompanying cloche hat, it revealed the lines of the face more clearly, and emphasised the nose. 'Clothes and hats today look as if they could be worn only by this particular woman, as if they had been designed for her alone,' noted the fashion journalist Stephanie Kaul.[10] The politicisation of hairstyles was expressed in the proud sense that with the pageboy cut one offered one's forehead to the world, one showed character and intelligence: 'The forehead really seems to be the seat of thoughts that can be "worn" freely and openly,' she rejoiced in the fashion journal *Die Dame*, at the same time

Louise Brooks wore the bob with the famous 'kiss curls'. The film star came to Germany in 1929 to make two films, Pandora's Box *and* Diary of a Lost Girl, *both directed by Georg Wilhelm Pabst.*

setting out what the bob really meant: it was a self-empowerment, the hairstyle of democracy.[11]

Self-confidence did change with styles in clothing. Clothes did make the person, as the proverb has it, by giving people a particular outward-facing sense of themselves that reflected the one within. A certain attitude was expressed through fashion, but it was also defined by it. Fabric and spirit engaged in a dynamic reciprocal relationship. The tone of young women changed accordingly. The new lack of self-consciousness was often perceived as impertinence. A mocking note, a confident stubbornness, a new matter-of-factness, but above all a new emphasis on the question: what do *I* really want from life?

The radical variation of the bob was the Eton cut mentioned above. A real boy's hairstyle, brushed fiercely back, with a shaved nape or a severe parting. There was nothing teasing about the Eton cut, no kiss curls, those provocatively styled locks that pointed forward at cheek level, as worn by the American film actress Louise Brooks (*Pandora's Box*). Of course, the Eton cut was popular with some lesbian women, who used it to announce their sexual orientation. But it was also fashionable among heterosexual women, charmed by the idea of playing with traditional sexual insignias and experimenting with their identity – laboratory workers of the modern age, experimenting on themselves. The Eton cut, also known as the gentleman's cut, captured in breathtakingly beautiful images by photographers such as Yva or Marianne Breslauer, captured severe women's faces that caught the nerve of the time.

In her memoirs, Marianne Breslauer later wrote that she 'fell instantly' at the sight of her androgynous favourite model, Annemarie Schwarzenbach. For Breslauer, Schwarzenbach, a wealthy industrialist's daughter from the circle around Erika and Klaus Mann, was

the most beautiful creature I have ever met. [. . .] Annemarie was a person of whom it was impossible to tell whether she was a man or a woman; she looked to me like the Archangel Gabriel standing by the gates of Paradise.[12]

Erika Mann and Annemarie Schwarzenbach (with cigarette). The pair combined writing, driving fast cars, a desire to travel and love for one another. The latter was unequally distributed, however. Erika Mann loved the actress Therese Giehse even more. They got up to all kinds of things as a threesome.

As a young man the poet Peter Huchel, would later become the editor of *Sinn und Form* (Meaning and Form) in the GDR, wrote an enthusiastic hymn of praise to the new androgynous creature, 'Die Knabin' ('The Boyess'), which revealed some difficulties in summing up the phenomenon in verse while steering clear of old-fashioned notes.

> Braided girl of the forest years.
> Boyess of the city today, you have cut your hair,
> wide-eyed doe of the underground railway.
> feline and velvet in your furs.

Silky moon, nacreous under stockings.
short-skirted nymphs climb into the car.
Twitching stars advertisements in their hair,
Go gypsy-like to cinema and bar.

Far from your braids and maternal years
the plane will carry you more swiftly.
Boyess of the cities, your hair sacrificed.
doe-hipped, slender creature of the boulevards![13]

Rittmasters with bosoms – the cultural appropriation of the monocle

In 1930, the author Emil Lucka rightly observed that women were becoming more similar not to men but to boys, although they didn't always stop there.[14] Some particularly extravagant women also borrowed the symbols of mature men: the top hat, the walking stick and finally the monocle. They liked wearing men's shirts and baggy trousers, and gave themselves delicate fluffy moustaches on their upper lips with kohl pencils.

The most provocative attack on male identity was probably the ironic appropriation of the monocle. Towards the end of the nineteenth century, the eyeglass had become a status symbol of the upper classes, of officers above all. It was considered a sign of a special kind of masculinity. The monocle only stayed in place if the man held it there with his facial muscles. He would then strut around with one half of his face distorted, and with his shoulder tensed. It was the clear-eyed Joseph Roth who discovered why the monocle suited clenched and neurotic men so well. It acted as an emotional brake. The monocle served as a reminder to avoid spontaneous reactions; sudden laughter, for example, would unfailingly make the glass fall to the floor. The wearer was condemned to a stiff body posture, and became accustomed to reacting as slowly as possible to spontaneous things and events. 'That is the reason why his face is so empty and so nobly discreet,' Roth observed.[15]

Some men considered the monocle sacred. In his novel *Half Way*, Edwin Erich Dwinger fantasises a hideous feminist attack on this fragile symbol of masculinity. He relates how his hero, the Freikorps volunteer fighter Rittmaster Count Truchs, falls into the hands of a proletarian Spartacist troop during revolutionary unrest in 1919 and is grossly abused. A young female factory worker subjects the aristocrat to the worst of torments. After all kinds of torture, she shoots him in the belly: 'deep in his abdomen he felt as if he were being sliced with knives.'[16] Finally the woman shoots him dead. Then the corpse is desecrated: 'The woman jumped onto his face, grinding his monocle, that accursed symbol, over and over again into his eyes with the heels of her rough shoes.'[17] You don't need to be a psychologist to recognise these grotesque fantasies of violence as primitive castration anxieties with which a panicking, insecure man reacted to the stronger position of women in the Republic.

A curious couple were shown strolling on the front page of the *Berliner Illustrirte Zeitung* in November 1927. A man and a woman in elegant suits, each with tie, pocket handkerchief and cigarette holder, the woman's short hair parted even more severely than the man's. The only things that distinguish the woman from her companion are her skirt and shoes, but she also wears a monocle in her severe face. Behind them is a pair of people whispering, whom the newspaper has saying, 'What do you make of Fräulein Mia?' The reader was challenged to give an answer; they were to complete the caricature with as witty and appropriate a retort as possible. They reached with notorious Berlin wit to the elegant, stick-thin man-woman Mia: 'That girl looks like a man, and he looks like a girl.'[18] Another jokes, 'Now they've fused the sexes on top of everything.' A third thinks that God hadn't quite finished when he made the two sexes, and says, 'When God sees these two, he laughs: Did I make three back then?' Yes, clearly: Fräulein Mia proved that the idea that human beings only came in two sexes often didn't tell the whole story, and that people were well aware of this.

Berlin's Third Sex was the title of a book by the sexologist Magnus Hirschfeld, which was originally published in 1904 and which read like a guidebook to the queer places of Berlin. The gender debates about LGBT+ are by no means an original development of the early twenty-first century; they had a massive prelude a hundred years ago. Even the idea of gender polarity was already current in the 1920s. In 1928 the author Franz Blei welcomed the coming end of 'a bipolar erotica, which placed a terrible burden on both men and women'.[19] The writer Emil Lucka was convinced that the gender model was due to break away from a polar organisation and lead to a new 'confusion':

> The ideal is, although this is perhaps unspoken: sexlessness, and I think I have noticed that even faces are losing their focus, and that an inter-mediate cast of face is forming, not quite male and not quite female.[20]

Magnus Hirschfeld tried to classify a whole palette of 'intermediate steps' between man and woman. His institute in the elegant Tiergarten district became a much-visited salon of the Berlin intellectual world – and the whole of Berlin the epicentre of the international gay scene. The British music critic and author Edward Sackville-West wrote enthusiastically to E.M. Forster:

> There are even large dance spaces for inverts. And some of the people one sees, huge men with breasts like women & faces like Ottoline [Morrell, the eccentric British aristocrat], dressed as female Spanish dancers, are really quite unintelligible.[21]

His British author colleagues W.H. Auden, Stephen Spender and Christopher Isherwood, who were also gay, made queer Berlin known around the world and created a myth that still lingers in the city today.

There were about 100 venues for gay men in the city, and about 30 for lesbian women. Not all were exclusive – what was much more typical of the mood in the city was that some gay bars were also frequented by straight people and served as general meeting places for the social scene, such as Toppkeller in Schwerinstrasse. And it was notable that many straight men and women campaigned for a strengthening of the rights of gay people.

*

It was not only in the wealth of sexual identities, but also in normal everyday life that the men and women of the Republic came closer together than had been customary in imperial Germany. They worked in the same offices, they shared benches at universities, and sat unselfconsciously together in dance halls and at the beach. At the weekend they went on outings into the country together, in big groups of friends. This was less normal than it sounds. Even in Germany around the turn of the century, it would have been unthinkable for girls and boys to go hiking together unsupervised, as was the custom among many *Wandervögel* bodies. This closer coexistence produced a largely unfamiliar sobriety in relations between the sexes.

Where men and women were no longer able to avoid one another in everyday life, new ways of mingling developed. It had to become quite natural for men and women to live side by side. The author Franz Blei felt that this was a great liberation:

> Freedom from that sexual overstress whose falsity no one could endure any longer. Young men recognised that there were more important things than constantly falling head over heels in love, girls that there were more valuable things than making oneself 'desirable'. First they wanted once again to exist in the world for their own sake.[22]

Emil Lucka also sensed a strong resistance to the 'polarity of the sexes' in the younger generation. They weren't keen on the idea of being forced into the emotional exclusivity that love had traditionally called for. In particular, it was in the *Wandervogel* movement that Lucka saw the classical ideal of love being replaced by a kind of tender comradeship: 'This generation's eroticism is called *amitié amoureuse* [amorous friendship]'. In place of 'love as a primal force', they had access to 'a hundred shades and sub-shades of a spiritual and

intellectual world of the emotions that oscillated between camaraderie and erotic attachment'.[23] 'There should be no difference between
friend and girlfriend, the aspiration is towards a close and very spiritual relationship, which is often achieved. The ideal is, although this is
perhaps unspoken: sexlessness.'[24] Against this unisex backdrop, erotic
attractions of all kinds were possible, both gay and straight. And
according to Lucka, in the fashion ideal of the boyish woman, men
were not yearning for their own kind, but for 'a more delicate, more
charming, younger brother', a better version of themselves.

Strong women, insecure men

In this uncertain emotional terrain it was easier for women to satisfy
their need for independence. There have been strong autonomous
women in every era, of course, but now, at least in the progressive
part of society, it almost became the norm. The year 1925 saw the publication of *Das Junge Mädchen* (The Young Girl), a 'design for living' by
the women's rights activist Ilse Reicke, which encouraged her readers
to find their own way in life. This guide was aimed less at future
mothers and caring wives than at responsible female citizens who
were urged – for example – to start reading newspapers at a younger
age and to form opinions about everything. The cover showed a
narrow girl's face with a strikingly high forehead, the head supported
between index finger and thumb in classic thinker pose, looking the
viewer seriously and resolutely in the eye.[25] The image, a self-portrait
by the 27-year-old illustrator Lieselotte Friedlaender, showed a young
woman as well equipped for the vicissitudes of life as it was possible to
be. This 'girl' would stride alertly through life and neither mistake a
skirt-chaser for a hero nor a loudmouth for an intellectual giant.

The ideal of female independence could only flourish because
such women were urgently needed by the economy. They needed to
be educated (or at least able to type), critical and pragmatic, hard
working and ambitious. The wages might have been small, but they
allowed these women to free themselves from their families.

After the war, it was no longer rare for women to take an approach to life that involved self-realisation and not just caring for others. These women's careers were no longer rigidly set out for them. Existing social relations had been shaken up by war and inflation. Disruption and new opportunities went hand in hand. Anyone who had achieved a good education and had any degree of intellectual independence could see life as an adventure whose possibilities had to be grabbed with both hands. Such careers were rare, and far from easy, but the freedom to leave what had once been a well-worn path was now also more available to women. They interrupted their careers when they no longer felt fulfilled in them, they ended marriages that had become unsatisfactory, they moved house when their place of residence became too stale and constricting. The 'patchwork biography', according to the theorist Ulrich Beck a phenomenon of postmodernism, had its predecessors in the Weimar Republic, and not only as a result of economic hardship.

In 1923, one former senior employee of a scientific company wrote to her correspondent about the course of her career:

> When I no longer found my work in the service of science satisfying, I chose to spend a year in Tegernsee, staying with a friend whose children I tutored; when being dependent on a millionaire's wallet began to grate, I became an apprentice potter, then journeywoman and director in a rural pottery, lived in a log cabin and enjoyed the healthy mountain air. For a year now I have been employed as artistic director of quite a large majolica factory, and enjoying every kind of happiness and success.[26]

This progression, with its many twists and turns, its emphasis on the pleasure principle as a decision-making criterion and preference for creative artistic craft over the academic profession, is an entirely modern biography that would not be out of place in the present day.

A letter that a young woman wrote to a psychotherapist in 1930 has more of a 1970s ring to it. She insisted on a sexual freedom that worried her fiancé:

His jealousy makes me furious and his moral reproaches annoy me, even though they should really be laughed at. [. . .] He is unhappy when I go dancing without him. I read a lot [. . .] but that doesn't fill the day. So one ends up going for walks, making acquaintances and having adventures. I am certainly not a bad person, but I also want to get something out of life. [. . .] I can't bear the fact that my fiancé doesn't understand me. Sometimes I think we should part company. He should give me my freedom and go his own way. But then I feel sorry, because he means very well, and if he were a bit more generous we would be a good match for each other.[27]

The example may not be representative, but it shows that erotic buccaneering was no longer exclusively a masculine preserve. The literature of the 1920s was full of women taking charge of their sex lives. They no longer needed to be wild and tragically excessive, instinctive creatures like Lulu in Frank Wedekind's plays *Earth Spirit* (1895) and *Pandora's Box* (1904), but could be quite undramatic, down-to-earth, spirited women like Lina Gade in the wonderful 1933 novel *Frau ohne Reue* (The Unrepentant Woman) by Max Mohr, who flees her wealthy husband. It could be a cheerfully chatty reporter called Louis Lou in *Die Vielen und der Eine* (The Many and the One) (1930) by Ruth Landshoff-Yorck, one of the first examples of German pop literature, or the model Gaby in the novel *Ich geh aus und du bleibst da* (I Go Out and You Stay Here, 1931) by Wilhelm Speyer, who brightly expects her boyfriend to grant her unlimited self-determination. The titles alone are telling enough; these are light novels that don't skirt around the moments of loneliness and despair that these women can sometimes experience when they insist on their independence, but their good-humoured affirmation of life doubtless gave insecure male readers the feeling of standing downwind from history.

'Men's insecurity with regard to women has become practically unbearable,' the journalist Axel Eggebrecht complained.[28] No one these days had any idea what one might expect when one began a conversation with a woman. Every flirtation was like a suicide mission with an unforeseeable outcome, because 'so-called emancipation' had made women unpredictable.

Greater self-confidence among women prompted anxieties even among progressive-minded authors. The most wonderful phobias are found in Erich Kästner's novel *Fabian* from 1931. The titular hero's girlfriend leaves him because she wants to enter a more profitable relationship with a producer, one which will benefit her film career. That may seem tough enough, but poor Fabian goes on to find himself in the clutches of ever more monstrous women. Women who 'snack on little young men as if from of a bag of bonbons', as the book accusingly puts it, women like Irene Moll whose husband, a lawyer, pays men large sums of money to sleep with his wife.[29] She then humiliates them horrifically, and he is allowed to watch. Of course, Fabian is one of them. On the taxi ride to the Moll apartment he is almost raped, and matters continue in a similar vein once the door closes behind him. 'So, now the little boy comes to the slaughter,' Irene Moll says, and hurls the delicate, melancholy young man to the floor.[30] In the end, after an odyssey through the Gomorrah of Berlin, where imperious women like Ruth Reiter, known as 'the baron', keep things under tight control, Fabian decides to leave Berlin for the Ore Mountains on the Czech border – with one particular hope in mind: 'Perhaps up there he might become something like a man.'[31] Up there in the provinces, there was still hope.

Erich Kästner's grotesque, nightmarish fantasies testify to an insecurity that would have found appreciative resonance among male readers. More determined characters refused to settle for insecurity, and instead sabre-rattlingly called for an end to Weimar democracy. For right-wing thinkers, the Weimar Republic was 'effeminate'. 'The state [*der Staat*] is male in gender', the writer Friedrich Georg Jünger stated flatly, implying that the supposedly feminine republic (*die Republik*) was not a state, but rather an anomalous mutation that needed to be overcome as quickly as possible.[32] In 1930 the privy counsellor Georg Fritz wrote in an essay that the 'temporary predominance of female degeneracy' in the Republic had only been made possible by the 'suppression of purely masculine and purely

feminine natures' in favour of a ubiquitous culture of 'inauthenticity': 'It is an insult to nature and cannot last. A male leader's energy,
a soul-shaking event can and will bring it down.'[33] In reactionary caricatures the Republic was often represented as a woman, a plump
matron, devouring her sons. 'Not only are we disarmed, we are
unmanned,' the *Deutsche Wehrverein* (German Defence Union, a right-
wing nationalist association) complained as early as 1918.[34] In
right-wing thinking, the Republic would never shed the stigma of
emasculation. The fact that military defeat coincided with the introduction of equal rights for women was always seen as more than a
coincidence. The stigma of Versailles had to be expunged on all
fronts.

In fact, it was not revolution but the war that had provided the
impulse for emancipation. Divided from their husbands, who were
fighting in the battlefields, many women had taken over men's work,
and learned that a city could be run even without men. On what
grounds, then, could they be denied equal rights?

The author Arnolt Bronnen, a former iconoclast and *enfant terrible*,
who had over time moved from the left to the far right, saw the war
as one of the causes of emancipation but gave the connection a characteristic twist. In his essay 'The Female War Generation', he claimed
that the war had a lasting impact not only on men, but above all on
women, alienating them from their true nature. While men had
found a new meaning in war, he argued, it had deprived 6 million
women of the bond on which their balance depended: the one with
their beloved partner. Men found 'a new balance: in the enemy',
while the world of women had taken an unsteady turn.[35] With catastrophic results, in fact: in Bronnen's eyes, women had become
lecherous, impertinent, unpredictable and insane – lustful figures of
the kind that Kästner's Fabian had been forced to endure, 'contemptible' creatures such as the American silent film actress Barbara La
Marr, or the Berlin naked dancer Anita Berber, who had sacrificed her
beauty on the altar of drugs and the art of entertainment. 'They
threw their lives away, in every sense, and they lost them, in every
sense. There is nothing more wretched than the lives of these women,

and nothing more salacious.'[36] Greatly preferable were the hard-working women who aspired to their own income and made themselves useful to achieve it. There was a good side to that, Bronnen went on, because men had more interesting things to do than attend to mundane tasks. In all 'natural and stabilised times [. . .] men had had more important concerns than the mere acquisition of daily bread', by which he meant devoting themselves to war, philosophy and art. 'But women were emancipated, they took care of the fields, they ran textile mills, they were the economy.'[37] If we bear in mind the work that had been taken from men, emancipation wasn't so bad in the end: 'perfected slavery'.[38] He, Bronnen, was at least man, and rogue, enough to declare this situation almost ideal. The world had bigger plans for men; the tasks 'will once more have to be addressed once more with greater seriousness, with more acute severity'.[39]

Given such disparagement, it must have been easy for Bronnen to part company with his wife. His male friends were more important

Women in men's jobs. The first woman to pass her apprenticeship exam as a butcher, 1925.

to him than anything. He later voluntarily shared his new bride Olga with Joseph Goebbels.

Bull necks, archangels, character studies and pea-brains – on the physiognomy of the Weimar Republic

Judging by the stock of images from the 1920s that have lodged in the collective memory, the decade must have been populated by willowy young people who enthusiastically put their beauty on display. The *Revue des Monats*, *Das Magazin*, *Uhu*, *Tempo*, *Die neue linie*, *Die Dame*, *Der Querschnitt* – in issue after issue, all of these magazines showed pictures of perfect bodies, chiselled like classical heroes by the harsh shadows thrown by spotlights, in swimming costumes or summer dresses. It was as if each sex envied the attractions of the other, as if they were vying with one another in an urge to achieve perfection. If the world was about to go up in flames, what did it matter as long as one looked good – or at least that's what the stories about dancing on the edge of the volcano suggest. The reality looked very different.

The image of the age presented by most of the leading media had little to do with most people's reality. Outside of the country's fashionable, people were remarkably unimpressed by the diktats of the fashion world – apart from the bob hairstyle, which had reached the remotest corners of the provinces, where it incited girls to rebel. Men, however, remained largely resistant to the demands made on them by fashion. Many of them even seemed to oppose the spirit of the age and distinguished themselves by emphasising their uncouth ugliness. The American author Thomas Wolfe loved Germany, although his passionate devotion was mitigated by the many bull-necked and obese people that he saw there. In his travel articles he often calls the stout figures with the shaved napes 'Huns', a nickname that had become popular during the First World War. He visited the country six times between 1926 and 1936, and each time he was depressed by the many 'thick creases (. . .) and 'fleshy neck(s)' that shocked and fascinated him with their rawness carelessly on show. He often recorded them in his diaries, he was so struck by them, the 'young gentlemen with duelling scars on their faces and older ones with shaved spherical heads, little piggy eyes and three bulges above their shirt collars at the back'.[40]

The 'Huns' really did put their ugliness on display. They clearly considered it a privilege not to pay any attention to their appearance, as a visible badge of their intellectual autonomy within a Republic in which a stylish appearance was supposedly part of the recipe for success. Without them! These corpulent characters, who later became a Nazi cliché, amply embodied the alternative to the 'glittering smartness' of the Weimar elites, 'that whole flea-hopping wit-dandy-crowd' from Berlin, in the words of one such stately Bavarian character in Lion Feuchtwanger's novel *Erfolg* (Success).[41] Things had come to a pretty pass if one was supposed to be ashamed of one's cosy paunch. On the contrary, it was something to be carried proudly around, especially as the rest of the Republic succumbed to hunger.

Becoming the object of the sort of appraising gaze with which men traditionally observed women as if it were the most natural thing in the world – this kind of man would have found such an idea laughably presumptuous. And for good measure, it was precisely such repellent men who had the gall to attribute unattractive facial and physical features to Jews, and obsessively paint them with hooked noses.

The ugly Nazi and the city slicker dancing to the edge of destruction – two stereotypes that form extreme and telling antitheses in the broad panorama of physiognomies that made up the face of the Weimar Republic. In its very extremes it seems contemporary to us today.

*

The trendy face of the decade was created on Kurfürstendamm, in the photographic studios of Frieda Riess, to take one example. Riess was born in 1890 in Czarnikau in Prussia, present-day Czarnków, and actors, composers, authors, painters, film stars and diplomats flocked to her studio to be photographed. Riess was extremely skilled at capturing her models in a gesturally vivid, expressive and painterly style, which used shadows and blurring to give depth and texture to her portraits. She was able to bring the complicated inner lives of her sitters to the surface and fix them on paper to magnificent effect.

A few hundred metres from the studio of the famous society photographer was the studio of her colleague Yva, ten years her junior. Her clientele was less prominent, but her studio no less successful. Born in 1900 as Else Neuländer-Simon, Yva shaped the pictorial language of many of the illustrated magazines published by the Ullstein company. By the age of 28 she had more than ten female colleagues working for her, helping her keep the media machine supplied with pictorial material. Thanks to new printing techniques, the pictorial content of the magazines had increased many times over, and the public's hunger for images remained insatiable. The photograph was *the* mass medium of the 1920s. Yva specialised in photo-stories. She staged risqué photo-novels that were both highly entertaining and of excellent visual quality. At the same time, she experimented with multiple exposure, and became famous for her 'synoptic style', which made her objects appear to dance. For this reason she was often mentioned in the same breath as Man Ray, the American Surrealist, living in Paris at the time, who was one of the great pioneers of modern photography.

Yva's fashion photographs pursued the hedonistic ideals of the leading Berlin scene. Around the beginning of the 1930s her protagonists, originally happy to put their own beauty on display, became more and more statuesque. In the end, they looked like monuments to a perfection that was put almost arrogantly on view. One 16-year-old who spent two years as an apprentice to Yva after leaving school in 1936 was deeply influenced by this quiet heroism: Helmut Newton.

Some of Yva's pictures would have fitted in well with the idealising style of later Nazi fashion photography. But Yva, like Frieda Riess, was Jewish. That alone made her an enemy of the Nazis, however neatly her pictorial language might have sat aesthetically with the new classicism in fashion photography.

Riess and Yva's portraits were highly artificial. Anyone wishing to form an idea of what the real physiognomy of Weimar Germans might have looked like should flick through the work of August Sander. It too was artificial, but in the opposite direction. He wanted not beauty, but reality. His book *Face of Our Time* was published in 1929. The portraits provided a photographic cross-section of the whole Republic, from the farmer in the Westerwald to the modern Berlin architect. The 'Hun' type was just as much a presence as the 'young tango dancer', but both, even though they remain prominently represented in the collective memory of the Weimar period, were an absolute minority in *Face of Our Time*. Instead Sander devoted himself to the amazing range of the 'normal'.

From the mid-1920s onwards, August Sander, born in 1876, set himself the ambitious goal of recording the 'people of the twentieth century' on his photographic plates. Shown frontally in the picture, in poses they had chosen themselves, and in their typical clothing, the sitters were intended to represent both themselves and their class, their origins, their region, their convictions. They were individuals who stood for something collective, people honed and stylised by life into types, as Alfred Döblin wrote in his preface to *Face of Our Time*. In Döblin's eyes Sander was practising sociology 'without writing', 'comparative photography' devoted to the 'cultural, class and economic history of the last thirty years'.[42] *Face of Our Time* would be the foundation of a comprehensive portfolio of 600 photographs, organised by class and profession, but also by city and region, political activity, degree of integration and marginality. The project was not concluded when Sander died in Cologne in 1964, but the work as it stands is enormously impressive: a unique collection of people, magnificent in their diversity, sad in their identifiability as types.

Most of the pictures were produced in the Weimar Republic and constitute a comprehensive bestiary of its population. There they stand and sit, like a butterfly collection: the authorised signatory holding his umbrella stiffly in the air like an exclamation mark; the pinched notary with his black Dobermann; the banker whose figures appear to have added up, he looks so pleased with himself; the three smart young farmers on their way to a dance, determined to make a conquest; the unemployed beggar-woman, unconsciously adopting an S-shaped posture, the formula for humility in medieval sculptures; the Archduke of Hessen-Nassau, in the statesmanlike pose of the president of the Reich on the 20-pfennig stamp.

Face of Our Time is a kind of field guide, a 'training manual', as Walter Benjamin called it, for the classification of Weimar society.[43] Portrait volumes showing a cross-section of society were highly thought of at this time. In an age that had fallen deeply into chaos, people wanted to be sure of their physiognomy. At the same time, *Face of Our Time* is a document of the photographer's persistence. We can also see how many traditions extended into the modern world – centuries-old traditions that were about be swept away for ever by the tumults of the twentieth century. 'It was a time in which many people preserved intact and decorous traditions in their souls, but those traditions no longer found fulfilment in any shared public life', Golo Mann wrote in his preface to a selection of Sander's *People of the 20th Century*, published in 1971 under the title *Menschen ohne Maske* (People without Masks).

Many of his sitters have a way of presenting themselves that seems appropriate to them – they wear clothes that are supposed to express their social class, their standing, their place in a world that no longer exists in such an orderly form. Three-piece suits appear with startling frequency among the men. Regardless of their class, they have to have a suit. The jacket was taken for granted in everyday life, but the waistcoat had to be there too. Even Erich Mühsam, the revolutionary, wears one, and his two comrades back up his Bertolt Brecht leftist look. The four students, grouped close together deep in thought, also wear waistcoats. Among the farmers of the Westerwald it is considered only fitting, the grocer wears one under his aprons and another one stretches comfortably over the belly of the retired civil servant, decorated by a gold watch chain. Even some workers wear waistcoats of a coarse fabric. The coal man, in fact, carries his filthy load through the city, wearing a white shirt under his waistcoat. Only where work clothing, traditional costumes or overalls are required does the waistcoat disappear, in the pictures of the customs officer and the postman, the vicar and the soldier, the corps student and the master pâtissier. The rest wear the clothing of bourgeois equality – bankers, burghers and farm labourers. While their faces, their physical posture and their hands might betray the sometimes extreme differences in their social positions, the largely identical suits of Sander's protagonists, where they are well-worn or fresh from the tailor, reveal a sense of democratic belonging. They introduce a breath of civic dignity into the 'face of our time'.[44]

The variety of the faces is fascinating, of course, but so are their archaic appearance and their conformity to type. Most of the faces 'fit'; they correspond to what one might expect of their profession. Manual work, often practised for generations, has marked and

A farmer going to church, 1925. The photographs of August Sander show the persistence of traditions in physiognomy and mentality in the Weimar Republic; faces and attitudes, shaped by work and experience.

identified these people; the landscape has shaped them. But within the narrow bounds of social moulding, the person shines through, and truly charracterful faces appear. Such individuality requires as a counterbalance the fetters of origin, of region, of class if it is to flourish. Personality matured in the conflicted interplay of social roles into which people had been forced by the fixed traditional social order.

In Sander's collection, the faces of the women are less determined by their environment. While among men the division of labour has often shaped the physiognomy over generations, and the various crafts of tailoring, sowing, bookkeeping, teaching, healing and trading have been etched on the features, the women seem freer from such social conditioning. Whether rich or poor, city-dweller or villager, women's activities were more similar to one another's than men's. The skills required for housekeeping, child rearing and providing emotional support for the family were more universal than those that men nurtured for their specialised professional lives. It is probably for this reason that Sander's women appear less specific; it's easy to imagine many of them in a great variety of settings and in different social classes. Less informed by bonds to particular professional environments, they are more open to the modern age. They also experiment more with themselves than the men do, as we might conclude from their more audacious fashions and the ubiquitous bob.

Sander's men are more energetically drawn according to position, craft and class; they appear more determined by external forces, moulded more extremely, to the point that they look quite odd. As a result they constitute a physiognomic panorama that lets many aspects of the imperial age carry over into the cold freedom of the Weimar Republic. Truly modern faces had a different look, often ravaged by the effects of war and inflation.

The country had largely recovered, but the shock of that fatal levelling was still deep in people's bones. The faceless mass became the sign of the age. The highly differentiated social structure that was still apparent in the smaller towns had broken down in favour of a freedom of nominally equal chances in the cities. The aesthetic search for the 'human being as such' corresponded to this abstract equality. A prime example of this is the work of the photographer Helmar Lerski, who brought out the highly regarded volume *Köpfe des Alltags* (Faces from Everyday Life) in 1931. In extreme close-up he stripped his models – whom he brought to his studio from the labour exchange – of all the attributes that might have given away their social origins, such as fashion choices and occupations, and used harsh lighting to sculpt their faces into dramatic physiognomies of naked existence. These often raw faces have lost everything cosily familiar and demonstrate in unsettling directness something like 'creaturely dignity' – existential philosophy with the camera lens, with more than a hint of supercilious light-sculpture.[45] 'People no one knows, people who don't know themselves, are the best bearers of this new and special kind of light-art', the foreword to the book tellingly puts it.[46] And later: 'This is a street-sweeper who never dared to raise his head throughout his life. The camera straightens him up, and a dictator might envy him his imperious profile.'[47]

Individual – type – people. Even portrait photography revolved around the relationship between the individual and the mass. In 1933 the artist Werner Heldt identified the dominance of the mass as an oppressive collection of faceless airheads, a 'march of nothings': an urban square filled with empty circles, with the occasional banner or a flag. It can be read as a counter-image to Sander's *Face of Our Time*. Instead of characterful faces, empty eggs. Sander's documentary photograph showed individuality as being produced by work. If that work disappeared, what would remain of the people who did it?

10

The Work Runs Out

And sometimes I think it would be a good thing if I lost my job, because then I wouldn't have to worry about what it's like and how people bear it.

Hans Fallada, *Little Man, What Now?*

New York miscalculates, and the stone starts rolling

The foundations of the Weimar Republic started to shake one Friday, except that no one noticed. The 'Black Friday' that has gone down in history was a retrospective coinage. For contemporaries, 25 October 1929 was a perfectly normal day. The mood was still relaxed the following day. Of course, people in Germany had noticed the plunge in values on the New York stock exchange (it was 'Black Thursday' there), but in America the situation settled down very quickly, to some extent at least. The *Berliner Börsen-Zeitung*, an anti-Republic newspaper that enjoyed bearing bad news, was sure that the 'upset' was only temporary. The collapse of the New York stock exchange didn't make it to the front page of any of the German papers; it featured right at the back, in the financial section. And didn't the German press have cause for optimism? After all, the American crash was the consequence of an unheard-of boom in shares, which had affected small savers and led to wild overvaluations of securities. 'How is that going to affect anyone here?' German investors said to themselves. In the view of the Commerzbank, the New York crash could even have advantages for Germany. The American money market would quickly recover, and until then there would probably be an increase in US investment, because the American market had become too uncertain.

Over the weeks that followed, that confidence still prevailed. Eight days after 'Black Friday' the stocks and shares section of the *Vossische Zeitung* summed up the situation on the trading floor: 'Solid all along the line.'

Behind the backs of the protagonists, however, trouble was brewing and slowly making its way towards Europe. America withdrew its money. The stock market crash had liquidated many private assets and left the US banks with any number of bursting credit bubbles. Their customers had allowed themselves to be sucked into foolish adventures: to profit from the stock market boom, a lot of people had borrowed money and put it in shares. When the illusion of continuous growth went up in smoke, they were left with nothing but debts. The 'Great Depression' began, and three years later a quarter of Americans capable of work were unemployed. To remain halfway solvent, the afflicted American banks withdrew from European businesses whenever they could. As a result, the American crisis became a global economic crisis, which hit Germany worst of all. The losers of the world war were at the centre of a bizarre carousel of debt that the war had left in the global economy.

The German state had constantly received credits so that they could pay the reparations set out in the Young Plan. With this money the European victorious powers paid the debts that they had accrued in America to finance the war. The cycle had remained remarkably stable for years but now turned into a downward spiral that affected victors and losers alike.[1]

In spite of this crushing war-debt burden, in the years leading up to this Germany had experienced an intoxicating boom. This had been financed by additional debts, although these seemed to be covered by solid growth. With the boom, illusions also grew. And with affluence came the appetite for more – a spirit of optimistic expectation took hold, of the kind that fires up any healthy economy.

The thermometer of the economy and the general mood: quotation boards at the Berlin stock exchange in 1930.

The characteristic trait from the beginnings of the Weimar Republic, of living cheerfully beyond one's means, knew no bounds in the boom time. The Charleston years tended to dance in one direction only: steeply upwards. The department stores had overtaken the churches in visual power, constantly redesigning themselves as temples to consumerism. Their foyers looked like dreamy operatic backdrops, and Karstadt in Berlin-Neukölln felt like New York – a superstore with a huge roof garden and a direct U-Bahn connection.

The cities competed, too, and tried to trump one another. They rivalled one another with magnificent cultural buildings, as princely states did in former times. Late in 1927, a worried Foreign Minister Stresemann asked the mayor of the city of Duisburg how he could persuade the victorious powers to drop their reparation demands when Germany was spending as much money as if it had won the war:

> The fact that the Prussian state has spent 14 million on the rebuilding of the Berlin Opera House, and may end up paying over 20 million in

total, is leading the whole world to the conclusion that we are obviously swimming in gold. No victorious state has done anything like this. The fact that Herr Adenauer [Konrad Adenauer, mayor of Cologne] is building a wonderful exhibition hall and boasting that he has installed the biggest organ in the world in it has the same effect. The press exhibition in Cologne is described as the most luxurious that has ever been achieved in this field. Frankfurt am Main had a deficit of 2.5 million marks in its musical exhibition. Dresden is building a Hygiene Museum with government funds. [. . .] Please be so good as to tell me what I am supposed to say to the representatives of foreign powers when they say to me that all these things look as if Germany hadn't lost the war but won it. I no longer know how to respond to these accusations.[2]

The credits with which the blossoming cities financed their new swimming pools, theatres, concert halls and housing estates were, like the government and business credits, largely raised in America, although via the German banks. This went reasonably well for a time, but dependence on the dollar dragged Germany into the maelstrom of the American depression. In 1929, when the American speculation bubble burst, the Americans cancelled the credits that the German banks had planned, then did the same with their customers; the state, businesses and private individuals lost their liquid assets.[3] Money became scarce and expensive. At last, the German government took on even more debts. Ivar Kreuger, the world-famous 'Match King', gave the government a credit of over a 125 million dollars in October 1929, on 'Black Friday', as it happened. In the 1920s the Swede Kreuger was the man that cash-strapped states approached for funds, which he supplied in huge quantities. In return, he demanded a monopoly for the sale of matches, which made him creditworthy in the eyes of banks that operated internationally. But even that carousel ran out of power: on 12 March 1932, Ivar Kreuger, the star of the international finance world, killed himself in his Paris apartment. Even he had run out of money, and his empire was on the brink of collapse.[4]

Almost the whole world had succumbed to the financial illness. America and Germany were hit worst. Building projects were halted, planned investments cancelled, production closed down. One example, which has already been touched upon and can still be seen today: the emptiness of Alexanderplatz in Berlin. The wonderful buildings along its edge – the 'House with 99 Sheep Heads' (a private four-storey house with 99 stucco sheep heads on its facade), Jung's Pharmacy, the Hahn department store, the Aschinger beer hall – had already been demolished when building projects in the eastern part of the square were halted and postponed indefinitely. The American investors had pulled out. The vision of the city planner Martin Wagner for the 'cosmopolitan square' could only be half completed with the two *Neue Sachlichkeit* buildings by the architect Paul Behrens, while to the east the square simply remained undeveloped. Even today it has a stubborn inhospitality that plainly cannot be healed by any kind of makeover. It opens out into a huge void left by the global economic crisis.

Black zero: budgetary consolidation at any price

A lack of investment means less work. The first dismissals followed. The number of unemployed grew, while the state's finances shrunk. Unemployment wasn't only oppressive for those affected, it also put pressure on the state, which mounted exponentially. Unemployment insurance was designed to cover a maximum of 800,000 people and could be extended if necessary to 1.4 million at the most. The Social Democrat-led cabinet under Chancellor Hermann Müller collapsed in March 1930 in a dispute about how these people were to be cared for. In Müller's Great Coalition the conservative parties, as ever, had argued for a reduction of social benefits, the Social Democrats for higher taxes and welfare contributions. Three days after Müller's resignation, President Hindenburg decided to go with the conservatives. He appointed as chancellor the centrist politician Heinrich Brüning, a pious, ascetic, modest man who until his appointment had lodged in two furnished rooms in the working-class Berlin district of Alt-Moabit. Brüning moved into the chancellor's palace to take up his business with only a suitcase. He had plans for a severe economy drive, which he wanted to push through even against the wishes of the Reichstag. His government had no parliamentary majority behind it, but the SPD ministers of the old cabinet were replaced by conservatives simply by the president's mandate.

This was the first so-called 'presidential cabinet' of the Republic – a government that wasn't elected by the Reichstag but appointed by the president. This break with parliamentarism was made legally possible by the instrument of an emergency decree, included in the constitution to keep the state capable of working in an emergency. The circumvention of majority rule in the formation of the government would have consequences for future developments, since it meant that the already bruised reputation of parliament deteriorated still further. With the displacement of the strongest faction by far, and the installation of a minority government in favour of conservative elites, Hindenburg and Brüning took a clear step towards an authoritarian state. To see it as necessary, as many did at the time, meant reducing democracy to a fair-weather form of state, incapable of putting together workable majorities.

Hindenburg considered Brüning to be the right man for the job, because as a backward-looking Catholic trade unionist he promised to appeal both to parts of the workforce and the employers behind him. And in this he would initially be right. The duped SPD repeatedly supported him through gritted teeth in the Reichstag at the last minute, because in their eyes he was initially preventing even worse things from happening. So in spite of his painful economy drive, Brüning was able to stay in power for two years and two months, in the course of which prices, wages and social welfare payments shrank and the number of unemployed increased, until on 1 June 1932 he was replaced by the arch-reactionary Franz von Papen – again at the instigation of the elderly Hindenburg, who was on increasingly bad terms with the 'Hunger Chancellor', as he had come to be known. Not because Brüning was slashing welfare for the poorest, for example, but because he wanted to cut grants to East Prussian Junkers (large landowners), and Hindenburg himself was one of those. Brüning and his interior and defence minister Wilhelm Groener had also made themselves unpopular with Hindenburg's friends by outlawing the SA, whose behaviour had assumed terrorist features. But the group around Hindenburg and the leadership of the armed forces (the Reichswehr) saw the combat group as a reserve army ready to fulfil any future rearmament policy, and as an important instrument for putting down workers' uprisings. For that reason Brüning had to go. The hardline conservatives had assumed power in the background.

How was Brüning able to hold on for so long? His catastrophic austerity had made the social situation worse and worse. There was only one reason he was able to find enough agreement for his economy drive during two years of depression: the trauma of inflation still lay deep within German bones. Under no circumstances did anyone want to inflate the amount of money in circulation again and ease the crisis with increased welfare-state payments. Instead, the state had gone in the opposite direction, on the downward trajectory into deflation. For anyone who still had a job under the old conditions, falling prices at first looked attractive, since standards of living even seemed to be rising. As a result, the crisis was delayed and not equally felt by everyone – unlike inflation, whose poison had an equal effect on both large fortunes and small purses. Deflation had more potential for division. The fact that incomes also fell with falling prices, inevitably leading to job losses, was a different matter altogether and was for many who looked down their noses at blue-collar workers an almost unimaginable outcome. It was only over time that fear for jobs became universal.

★

For the nationalists and their agitators in magnate Alfred Hugenberg's right-wing media empire it was clear where the cause of the predicament lay: in the 'enslavement of the German people' by the reparation demands of the victorious powers and the 'treasonable politics of appeasement' of the democratic parties. They demanded an immediate refusal to pay. Such requests had been customary for some time but received further impetus as a result of the desperate state of the public coffers. The majority of Germans weren't yet willing to join in; a referendum against the Young Plan, called in late 1929 with a huge propaganda campaign by the Hugenberg press, failed, as the plan was rejected by only 13.9 per cent of voters – a last sign, triumphantly celebrated by the democrats, of the loyalty of the wider majority towards the Republic.

Admittedly almost everyone saw the reparation burden as being wildly excessive, but most people still had faith in civilised negotiation. Brüning was convinced that it would have to be proven in practical terms to the victorious powers that the level of reparations demanded could not be mobilised even by the severest austerity measures. Germany would have visibly to starve, and then the Allies would finally see sense and offer more moderate conditions. He deliberately factored in a growing degree of social unrest to move the victors to relent. The pious hardliner called this 'making a weapon out of sickness'.[5]

A risky path, paid for with the hunger and discontent of a growing army of people without work or bread. Sheer misery, familiar from the years of inflation, returned on a mass scale. More and more desperate people could be seen standing on street corners, first individually, but then becoming a more familiar picture: men and women in their fine office suits from better days, with a sign around their necks: 'Any work accepted.' They barely had any other options, since unemployment benefit was only granted for six weeks. Entitlement to support, paid for by contributions, soon turned into charity generously bestowed. Day labourers received nothing at all and were left with only the options of begging or stealing if they hadn't managed to find a short-term job.[6] In the morning they stood in crowds outside the market halls, tussling over the best places in case a trader showed up and wanted a dogsbody for a few hours.

A yarn manufacturer from Delmenhorst is the final straw – the plunge is unstoppable

While hunger gnawed at the bottom of society, in the upper echelons the problem was the embarrassment of bankruptcy. On 12 May 1931, Jakob Goldschmidt, director of the Darmstädter und Nationalbank, Danatbank for short, lost his composure. In some accounts of the event the director of the second biggest bank in Germany is said to have thrown an office chair at the head of his best customer, in others he is only supposed to have thrown it. Either way: Georg Carl Lahusen, the victim in the first account, survived. A short time before, he had declared himself utterly bankrupt to his banker, to whom he was 48 million Reichsmarks in debt. Lahusen owned the 'North German Wool-Combing and Worsted Spinning Mill', Nordwolle for short, in Delmenhorst. There, over 4,500 workers, most of them women, manufactured worsted wool in the second biggest mill in the world – it was like a city of its own, with city walls, a fortress tower, kindergartens, its own hospital, lending library, dormitories, and houses for office and manual workers that varied in size and quality according to the ranks of their residents, all in north German clinker brick, dark red and richly structured – a jewel of industrial architecture.

Crammed together in the simplest houses were immigrant workers from Silesia and Poland, locally known as 'wool-mice'. They first cleaned the wool that came from the big farms and flocks that the Lahusens had owned in Argentina for two generations. The wool arrived in great bales, half of them still consisting of grease, sand and excrement, in Bremerhaven and was delivered directly by railway to Lahusen's factory. There they first went to the Leviathans, the name for the huge washing machines that liberated the wool from the dirt of the Argentinian pampas and the long journey. After that, they were prepared for the actual spinning process – amidst the deafening noise of the chains, transmission belts, rollers and conveyor systems of the carding and combing machines. The work was not without its dangers, and the factory's own hospital could not complain of a shortage of patients. The factory buildings stretched out over a vast expanse, shed roof pressed against shed roof, with gothic brick decorations. Overall, Nordwolle made a quarter of the world's yarn.

The Lahusens lived on the factory site, in a magnificent villa built by their father, shielded from the eyes of the workers by a high hedge, a wide front garden and the extensive park that the family had all to itself. However, the house soon became too cramped and dingy for the dashing heir to the wool fortune; in the idyllic nearby hills of Bremen, Switzerland, Georg Carl Lahusen had the family's old summer residence torn down and built the palacial 'Hohehorst Mansion' with 107 rooms. It was ready to move into by 1928, and at last Georg Carl was living in line with his station. The 'prince of wool' was seen as a respectable, because generous, member of Bremen's business community – even though his ostentation put him at odds with the modest north German mercantile tradition. To make a stir in the centre of Bremen, Lahusen moved the administration of his business empire from Delmenhorst to the city, where, shortly before his bankruptcy, he opened an office building in the style of giant corporate headquarters – even today, it is home to Bremen's regional finance directorate. By now Nordwolle owned 11 manufacturing plants throughout Germany, as well as several subsidiary companies and 22 sales outlets. Lahusen even had representatives in China and Japan.

Because of the poor economic situation, Danatbank had taken a closer look at the balances of its debtors. The bank was especially concerned about its biggest customer, the long-pampered Lahusen. In May 1931, the worried banker invited the factory owner to an inquisitorial dinner in his private Berlin apartment. The dessert course was accompanied by a revelation. Lahusen had to admit that for years he had embellished and falsified his bank balances. He had moved some of the debts into the accounts of a firm called Ultramare, which he had founded for this purpose in the Netherlands. When Lahusen finally admitted this, the chair went flying. Goldschmidt summed the situation up succinctly: 'Nordwolle is done for, Danatbank is done for, Dresdner Bank is done for, I'm done for.'[7]

That was an understatement. Many others were done for, people and banks; 22,300 office and manual workers were under contract to Nordwolle and its subsidiaries alone, and they feared for their jobs. Danatbank was insolvent. But that was by no means everything. In mid-June, when Goldschmidt found himself obliged to go public about the debacle, the worries of all German savers and investors intensified. Anxiety moved to the whole credit system. Many banks had failed in the past, but the case of Danat was a special one. Trust in the economy was completely abandoned. Nowhere seemed safe enough to keep one's money. Feverish rescue attempts held the Reichsbank and the Foreign Office on tenterhooks. Weeks before, President Herbert Hoover of the United States had announced a moratorium on German debts, and the issue of reparations was finally addressed. France was going to object, but had second thoughts when Hoover announced that he was also going to allow deferral of payment on French debts.

Too late. On 13 July 1931, Danatbank, the Dresdner Bank and the Rheinische Landsbank all closed their counters. This time the banking crisis – unlike the 'Black Friday' of 1929, which had barely registered – was on the front pages of all the big newspapers for days. Hindenburg and Brüning tried to calm the situation and issued guarantees for the deposits of savers – a recipe that Angela Merkel and Peer Steinbrück would follow 75 years later in the 2008 banking crisis. The president of the Reich gave his word that the state would prevent Danatbank from going bankrupt and ensure its accounts were safe. That helped to some extent, but it wasn't enough. In response to news of the failure of Danat, people across the Reich streamed to their banks to withdraw their savings. To wait out the worst of the panic and keep accounts from being emptied, Brüning and Hindenburg responded by ordering two days of bank closures.

On Wednesday 16 July, when the counters opened again, the leader writer of the *Vossische Zeitung* summed the matter up. In spite of the oppressive situation, he was pleased to note that the city of Berlin, which was accustomed to unrest and street battles, had remained quite peaceful. Two days of bank closures had gone by and nothing had gone up in smoke. It seemed almost like a miracle. The journalist expressed his hope that Berliners would remain as serene as this in future and appealed with teacherly cunning to their manliness:

> Everyone has something to lose, if only illusions. But manliness means not being defeated by the threat of loss. Observing that a whole city, a whole country, has become manly – that is the beautiful thing, that is the uplifting Berlin experience, in the midst of a fateful emergency that has so suddenly afflicted us all.[8]

Hidden in this emotional response to a state of peace, however gloomy, was anxiety about the uproar that had for so long gripped the country. 'A people that has become manly,' the author went on, 'must also overcome the feminine liking for argument, scolding and fruitless mistrust. [. . .] Self-confidence must always be a part of manliness.'[9] A pious wish.

*

This pedagogical desire to appeal to the macho honour of the turbulent men who were engaging in brawls on a daily basis shows how uncomfortable Germany's cities and villages had become. The potentially violent far right had been the second-strongest faction in the Reichstag for over a year. If the NSDAP had still been correctly seen as an insignificant splinter party in 1928, with 2.6 per cent of the vote, in the Reichstag election of 1930 it had received 18.3 per cent, while the SPD had lost 5 per cent. With 24.6 per cent, the Social Democrats were still the strongest faction, but because of Hindenburg's emergency decree they were still in the opposition. The *Vossische Zeitung* called Brüning's minority cabinet by Hindenburg's favour 'a silent dictatorship'. Meanwhile, on the political margins the potential for violence was becoming increasingly likely and anything but silent.

In Braunschweig, in October 1931, the NSDAP demonstrated that it was seeking power outside of parliament. The party bussed in tens of thousands of uniformed men from across the whole of the country for an SA torchlit procession through the little town. After that they ran rampage through the medieval working-class district to intimidate its residents, two of whom were fatally injured in the street battles. If the claimed number of 100,000 participants had not quite been reached, the result was intimidating enough: the press saw the spectacle as a 'dress rehearsal for civil war'. Quite rightly: in his journal *Angriff*, Goebbels interpreted the Braunschweig march as 'the announcement of the unalterable end goal'. He also referred to the alliance formed a few days before under the name 'Harzburger Front', with the *Stahlhelm* and other competing forces of the National Opposition, which he and Hitler secretly despised, as a 'tactical partial goal'.[10] They could hardly have been clearer about what they were after: all the power, undivided and ruthless.

Unemployed, and not on benefits

By now the number of unemployed had climbed to 4.5 million, having trebled within the three years since 1928. In 1932 these unfortunate people were joined by an additional 1.5 million – mass unemployment on an almost unimaginable scale. Almost 30 per cent of the workforce was now unemployed, and among trade union members this rose to 43.7 per cent. Actual unemployment was somewhat higher, as many people abstained from registering their joblessness. They went to the countryside in the hope of being able to get by more easily there, while others had their benefits stopped and were thrown back on charity hand-outs[11] or gave up standing in queues outside the offices and looking for work, and instead resorted to underhand means of making money.

Alongside the army of the unemployed, the numbers of homeless were also growing. Here and there, the first ragged tents were seen on Berlin streets and vacant lots before they were quickly cleared by the police. Countless thousands moved into allotments and lived there illegally in draughty shacks that they had cobbled together themselves. These colonies, which had turned from hobby garden plots into actual slums, were known as *Stempel-lido* – the 'stamp lido'. A luxury, of course, in comparison with the situation of others who loitered about in the grim 'warm rooms' set up for homeless people to survive the icy winter days. A miserable crowd crammed on to the benches of the former tram depot in Ackerstrasse in Berlin, which was constantly overheated by glowing stoves and a complicated system of pipes: 'So hot that it stinks hellishly. The emanations of hundreds of unwashed bodies, worn and dirty clothes and the clouds of bad tobacco seethe and boil in the heat.'[12] Even though the corridors were so packed that it took both hands to push one's way through, deals were being struck everywhere, 'a rag shop, a junk bazaar [. . .], even human bodies were on sale'.[13]

Anyone who had a little money and liked things quieter could sit around for hours over a beer in one of the crowded pubs, where a huge variety of subcultures blossomed, including bizarre forms of poverty-driven prostitution, spurred on by deafening bands in which frustrated musicians played their hearts out for a shrinking pot of money. Every now and again, well-to-do citizens from the better districts would come to such infernos for the purposes of poverty tourism. Even without the nefarious deals, the outlandish music and the exhibitionist displays of the sex workers, however, they were hardly less oppressive. The American Berlin correspondent Hubert Renfro Knickerbocker observed in 1932 that in one Berlin pub, Zum Ollen Fritz in the Wedding district, there were 40 people but none with a drink in front of them apart from two old men who had settled for a malt beer. They all sat there brooding.[14] 'When a German is so poor that he can't afford to buy himself a glass of beer, he has reached the bottom,' he concluded in the *New York Evening Post*.[15]

Anyone with 50 pfennigs to spare spent the night in a shelter. Seasoned homeless people refused to have their clothes disinfected, even though it was part of the service there. Disinfection destroyed people's clothes, they told Joseph Roth: 'They would rather live with undamaged lice than with even more ragged clothes.'[16] It was 10 pfennigs cheaper at the institution run by Schlummermutter

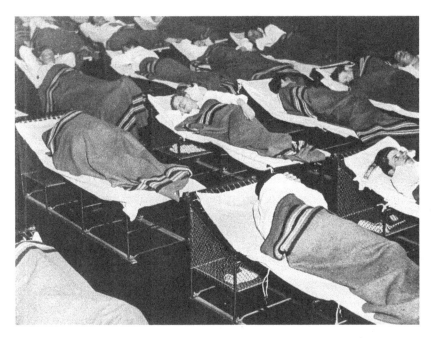

Homeless shelter for young people in Berlin Charlottenburg, 1932. It would have been almost impossible to fall asleep sober. Private tenants also offered mass places to sleep for forty pfennigs a night.

('Sleep-mother') Olga, about whom Ernst Haffner wrote in his social-reportage novel *Blutsbrüder* (Blood Brothers), the portrait of a clique of jobless young people. 'Silesian Olga' ran a night shelter in a basement apartment in East Berlin, one of many privately run shelters in the run-down 'Hinterhof' buildings. On the floors of two rooms she had laid out straw sacks on which a horde of people thrown together by fate slept every night. If someone couldn't afford the 40 pfennigs and was good-looking enough, he could spend the night for free, in her bed.

> But Olga is just a pile of rattling bones. Her generosity with regard to the overnight fee is feared by the young men. Hardly anyone goes to the hostel without money, because he knows what awaits him.[17]

Then the only remaining option of a place to stay was one of the many sandboxes that stood on some of the street corners. One would lie down on the grit that was stored there for use against black ice. If there wasn't any, one would have to *tippeln* ('foot it'), the term applied to roaming the night streets, battling against fatal sleep, which one hoped one could catch up on in the pub the next day.

Two of the young people whose fate Ernst Haffner was researching had found a trick for getting hold of the most valuable asset of all: work. Chance put a bit of money in their hands, and they invested it cleverly. They went from apartment door to apartment door selling old shoes. They repaired them as well as they could and sold them for a small profit. For a few weeks they had managed to be independent citizens who were able to make money by using their own wits.

Work and home: the land of timeless industry

In 1930 a volume of photographs published by Ullstein crashed into these early years of misery. It was called *Deutsche Arbeit* – 'German Work' – with the subtitle 'Pictures of Germany's resurgence'. It contained 92 photographs by Emil Otto Hoppé, one of the best-known photographers of his time, who worked all over Europe, above all in the United Kingdom. Ullstein turned Hoppé's industrial pictures into a concise document of Promethean power: gigantic turbine plants, smoking coke furnaces, electric motors the size of two-storey houses. Under the heading 'Space overcome' there were pictures of train tracks, bridges, radio towers, factory cable cars, floating wheat cranes, a Zeppelin under construction, all photographed as monuments of growth and design, captured in all their sober power. The images showed landscapes of steel, wire and concrete; iron giants among which tiny-looking men moved, feeding them with coal and oil. Most of the pictures were free of people; it was as if these huge plants were autonomous and had made their creators superfluous. They looked like the protagonists of a ghostly, fully rationalised world, a landscape turned factory, so perfectly automated that it had excluded almost all human beings from its production process.

A sentence from the foreword to the volume written by the author Bruno H. Bürgel must have seemed strange in context: 'Only work gives one a right to joy in life!' he wrote under the title 'The song of labour'. Bürgel, a convinced Social Democrat, cited the widespread idea that there was only one 'true nobility', which was that of the sweaty brow. Membership was acquired by hard work. He drew idyllic pictures of a busy country with a division of labour, which could only become a home through the hard graft of all:

The German Fatherland is the land of tireless labour, the land of mines and kilns, of rolling mills and millions of spindles. It is the land in which the farmer does battle with a long winter and frugal mother earth, the land in the middle of a continent through which the kilometre-long queues of goods trains travel in all directions of the compass, the wide rivers bear golden burdens, the cranes rattle day and night by full storage containers. [. . .] Infinitely complicated, infinitely diverse is German labour in the twentieth century, a century that needs both the blacksmith and the precision engineer, the man in the control room of an electricity plant that supplies a whole province with light and power, the little worker humming her little song at the spinning machine.[18]

By 1930, when the volume was published, and even more so in the two years that followed, that must have seemed like sheer mockery to its readers. When Ullstein had planned the book many months before and Bürgel had written his hymn to labour, they could have had no sense that it was coming out at the beginning of the most violent economic crisis, and that 6 million people would soon be clamouring for the right to a bit of joy in life. Poor timing, but it does show all the more clearly just how far things had fallen, because so soon before the economic crisis Bürgel was still able to express the connection between labour and happiness without the slightest apology.

According to German tradition, social status was strongly bound up with work, which meant that job loss was particularly devastating. 'He who does not work shall not eat' – the quotation from the Apostle Paul was used by both Adolf Hitler and the Communist leader Ernst Thälmann, and ranked quite high in the canon of German folk wisdom. A jobless person was thus inevitably breaking a universal commandment; he lost a sense of belonging; he felt like a freeloader at the expense of those who constituted the busy engine that kept modern life going. He felt homeless.

The jobless don't dream of revolution

In their misery, the unemployed quickly became targets of political agitation. Communist and Nazi provocateurs mingled among the queues outside the labour exchanges and tried to make an impression. Ernst Jünger, pioneer of the far right, saw the unemployed as a 'reserve army' with which the authoritarian state of the near future could be established: 'Hidden here is another form of wealth that bourgeois thought is incapable of revealing. Millions of men without occupation – that very fact is power, is fundamental capital.'[19] Psychological capital for the construction of the new, anti-bourgeois state that he joyfully saw on the rise. However, the jobless were not as easy to agitate as Jünger thought.

Unemployment was a collective destiny that was endured individually. Even though there were millions who were suddenly without work, they saw themselves as being entirely thrown back on their own devices. They had lost their colleagues and most of the social milieu in which they had spent their daily lives for so long. No sooner had a jobless person received his dismissal papers, along with best wishes for the future, and stepped into the street through the company gates for the last time, he saw the world differently; he saw it from outside. So he found himself alone, even though there were 6 million who shared his fate and hundreds with whom he crammed into the 'warm room'. It was part of the misfortune of the unemployed that they didn't form a social class, that their fate was only connected with that of other people by something negative and non-existent. It was only the lack of something, 'joblessness', that defined their existence; that was why the bond that connected them with the others was so weak. When they sat together, they often stared gloomily ahead of them, moved away from one another, and avoided meeting each other's eyes – at least that was how the Expressionist Karl Hofer saw things in his famous painting *Unemployed* from 1932. He painted the trees in the background as if they, rather than the apathetic men, were stretching their arms into the sky.

Because of their isolation from one another, the unemployed remained relatively unorganised. Groups of jobless within the trade union movement, of which there were several thousand, were limited to the former workers from the factories of heavy industry. Every now and again the Communist Party managed to organise hunger demonstrations and protests against unemployment. For example, 6 March 1930 was named International Day of the Unemployed, when large-scale demonstrations were held in European cities – with no discernible effect, as even *Die Rote Fahne*, the Communist Party journal, admitted.[20] More often there were anarchic disturbances and fights in labour exchanges and welfare offices. Nerves there were on edge, and arguments quickly escalated, becoming noisy and violent until the spark passed to the people who had been standing in line for hours. Furious crowds forced their way into the offices, threw files and furniture out of the windows, and chased the officials out of the building. Then they set about trashing the place, until two massive cohorts of police arrived and the truncheons flew.[21] To bring more order and discipline to the conflict, the Communist Party organised self-defence corps for the jobless, who stood guard in the offices, organised orderly retreats when riots broke out and marched in the evening against the SA, where they exchanged blows with their opponents on the other side.

Overall, however, the results of their attempts at mobilisation were disappointing, as they themselves repeatedly confessed. The KPD lacked the motivation for detailed socio-political demands, because they didn't want to stir the reformist illusion 'that significant improvements could still be achieved in any area'.[22] Good socio-politics meant 'clearly showing the necessity of winning power'.[23] Since 1929 the KPD had relied once again on revolution; like the NSDAP, it wanted the overthrow of the whole system or nothing. The once middle-class jobless, however, felt little inclination to embrace a dictatorship of the proletariat. And to everyone else, the KPD's unchanging recipes for full employment sounded like so many clichés: in 1930 the central committee of the KPD announced a 'pro-gramme declaration for the national and social liberation of the German people': 'By introducing the seven-hour day and the four-day working week, through a strong economic alliance with the Soviet Union and by raising the purchasing power of the masses, we will expunge unemployment from the world.'[24] Labour would become a duty: 'With Bolshevist ruthlessness we will enforce the principle to all bourgeois idlers: he who does not work shall not eat.'[25] That must have seemed fairly remote from reality to the unemployed outside the labour exchanges and in the 'warm rooms'.

Unemployment led not to demonstrative acts of social disobedi-ence, but to resignation and apathy. Anyone who didn't stubbornly fight against this aimlessness threatened to lose their internal bal-ance. Most unemployed people gradually lost their sense of time, the habit of doing nothing meant that even the simplest tasks required a massive effort, and homes and hygiene were neglected. The socio-graphic study *The Unemployed of Marienthal*, carried out by three young social psychologists in 1932 in an Austrian factory village that had lost all of its employment, spoke of a 'shrinking of the expres-sions of life'.[26] Even though the inhabitants now had a lot more time, for example, the number of loans from the village library declined sharply – even though it was free. One villager said: 'In the old days I learned the workers' newspaper off by heart, now I just take a look at it and throw it away, even though I have more time.'[27] Politics was for people in work; the unemployed saw the world as outsiders who had lost even the right to get involved in the civil war that was brewing on the edges of society. Only the young tried to make contact with others, and doing so via the combat units on right and left, or the many gangs of children and teenagers whose leaders were known as 'bull' or 'cow' according to their sex.[28]

The fact that the electoral successes of the NSDAP rose in proportion to the unemployment figures does not mean that that it was primarily the unemployed who voted for Hitler. On the contrary: they mostly remained loyal to the parties they had always voted for.[29] More important for the success of the Nazis was fear of unemployment among those still in work. The fear of falling radicalised the middle class and drove them towards the National Socialists. 'I think constantly about the unemployed,' says Hans Fallada's Pinneberg, in the novel *Little Man, What Now?*. Careworn and anxious, the husband and father is still clinging on to his job as a salesman in the menswear section of the Mandel department store, but worries about the future. 'And sometimes I think it would be a good thing if I lost my job, because then I wouldn't have to worry about what it's like and how people bear it. This way, you're always under pressure.'[30] When you've reached the bottom, you don't need to worry about freefall.

Intellectuals and artists came under particular pressure from the global economic crisis – only in a few rare cases did they enjoy permanent employment, and they were either indirectly or directly dependent on the public's ability to pay. Journalists who were paid by the line were the first to be affected by declining reader numbers. Freelance writers with an idea to pitch, or waiting for an assignment, sat for hours in the waiting room of the *Berliner Tageblatt*.[31] In their youth, many intellectuals had assumed that they were going to able to rely on inherited money or trust funds later in life (the German term was *Rentenkünstler* – 'pension artists'). Inflation had shattered their plans and forced them into what we would now call the 'precariat'. The historian Jörg Später wrote about the situation of the intelligentsia:

Intellectuals like [Walter] Benjamin and [Ernst] Bloch were free-floating above all in the sense that they had been thrown into the market without a fixed position, without social or pension insurance, without financial support, more than any generation before.[32]

That applied to both left-wing and right-wing intellectuals, and to freelance academics in general; the fact that so many members of the NSDAP came from university and student circles has to do not only with their conceited arrogance but with their unsuitably bad professional prospects. By 1932 the NSDAP had achieved dominance in student organisations.[33]

'Productive and parasitic capital' – wounded honour among workers and anti-Semitism

The Nazis countered the fear of social decline by exalting the 'Aryan race' as superior to all others. Now, though, it was in deep trouble. The trouble, as the NSDAP defined it, was 'the yoke of slavery to interest rates'. They found the economic crisis easy to understand. They didn't linger over the minutiae of economic analysis but interpreted the economic crisis as a chapter in a global historical struggle in which the Germans would either win or be destroyed for ever. In their bombastic narrative, the 'little man in the street' rediscovered a role with which he could identify. All of a sudden his fate had given him a meaning far beyond his private life; he was involved in a drama which, according to Hitler, had begun millennia ago in the deserts of Egypt and the icy wastes of the north, when the different attitudes of 'Israelites' and 'Aryans' towards economy and workers had been shaped.

In the grand opera of Nazi economic theory the German was characterised by work in the emphatic sense, as someone who saw employment as duty and a job well done as a token of his honour. This mythical worker stood right next to the soldier and the farmer, the so-called 'food-producing class', at the centre of Nazi ideology. This did not mean worker in the narrower sense of someone who worked for wages, but a 'type', as discussed in the writings of the similarly minded Ernst Jünger, a supremely modern type who would sweep away the sated bourgeois and build a completely new state, dominated by united will to increase the affluence of all. The *völkisch*

National Socialist students after a fight with Communist fellow-students. Friedrich Wilhelm University, 1932.

worker identified by the Nazis as typically German could be embodied equally well by the honest craftsman, the farmer behind his plough or the doctor at the operating table – it was the creative attitude, the work ethic, the conception of service that defined this mythical German worker. In the concept of fulfilment of duty, the 'workers of the brow' could feel an affinity with the 'workers of the hand' without feeling that their class privileges had been seriously threatened.

By putting work centre stage and emphasising its anthropological universality, they managed to address people's fear of unemployment across the social classes. Nothing rankled so much with the middle classes as being lumped together with the proletariat, let alone falling under its rule. But feeling as one with the working class in an emphatically inflated concept of the *Volk* was a different matter altogether. In the vision of labour as one of service and the fulfilment of duty, here

presented as 'typically Aryan', leading clerical and manual workers
found the offer of an identity that flattered them both: equality for
which neither side had to pay. The upheaval of society tugged at people's nerves, and they longed for unity and community. A joint
frontline deployment for a better world, everyone in his place – such
an idea was balm for the soul of people who were tormented by anxiety about their livelihoods and feared nothing more than the feeling
of becoming outcasts by losing their jobs.

The economic crisis dealt a deep wound to the German work
ethic. The idea that hard work was no longer worth it, because the
'achievement principle' had been annulled by a mysterious depletion
of the economy, touched a fundamental principle of the middle class:
the conviction that everyone was a master of his own happiness.
Instead of the equality of opportunity promised by this idea, bankruptcies followed in quick succession, while at the same time cars
were getting bigger and bigger, neon lights brighter, clothes more
elegant, department stores more luxurious. What was happening
was incomprehensible. How was it possible that no one could halt
the decline, and that no one seemed to understand its causes? In the
general bafflement, the narrative of the Jewish global conspiracy, at
first almost universally mocked, spread its evil and seductive poison.

Why the economy continued to plunge in spite of all manner of
efforts and measures was in fact not easy to understand. Even today
economists fail to agree as to the most important trigger. Was it a dis-
proportionate dependence on America? A structural excess of debt?
Brüning's excessive deflation policy? The mania for rationalisation in
large-scale industry? Over-production? Protective tariffs in the economy and industry? The overstretched social welfare system? The
interconnections of heavy industry that made a controlled drop in
production impossible? Business leaders, who had already shown
themselves to be the epitome of a curious kind of naivety, were
'flying blind', as we might say today. Economic historian Harold
James came up with a particularly fine description, referring to the
pricing policies of the major companies: industry had 'become so
highly organised that it was not prepared to face the reality of the

market'.[34] No one had the faintest idea what to do. The extent to which this was true is revealed by the radio address of the new chancellor, Kurt von Schleicher. Ideally, he would have sent his citizens back to the land: 'The deeper reason for the hardship of Germany and the world,' he told his listeners on 15 December 1932, 'lies in the fact that too many people have lost their connection with the soil, lived crammed together in cities, and are hit more severely by any change in the economy than the man on his own clump of earth.'[35]

In this atmosphere of bewilderment and helplessness hatred found a great opportunity. 'The Jew' was drawn as the opposite of the *völkisch* worker, a person who did not work, but made his money by doing dubious deals, whether in the antique trade or as a major banker. He too was a figure shaped by myth. In Nazi economic theory he represented the 'parasitic' capital that went for the throat of 'productive capital'. 'Parasitic' capital lived on the work of other people, enriching itself with interest and interest on interest, effortless and bloodsucking. While the German found his fulfilment in honest toil in the service of the community, the Jew found satisfaction only in 'mammonism and materialism'.[36]

These clichés were hardly fresh-minted; they belonged to the repertoire of traditional attributions of characteristics, since many Jews in medieval times, excluded from the craft guilds and forbidden to acquire land, had needed to move into trade and moneylending. Their money was more than welcome, but when it came to paying it back, hatred would regularly break out. The good-humoured, honest German who is taken in by the devious Jew and ruined by burgeoning interest rates was part of the standard narrative in which failure was turned into victimhood. Over the centuries, this core narrative grew into a whole system of mental attributions that were characterised as typically German or Jewish – the former good-hearted, cordial and honest, the latter cunning, unfeeling and coldly intellectual. The fact that this was all too obviously constructed as a source of comfort for stupid people and losers did nothing to diminish its attractiveness in times of trouble and worry.

'The Jew', according to Hitler, lacked any creative ambition; he was condemned to live as a parasite on the body of the creative races.[37] Any attempt to counter the idea was met with trite commonplaces of this kind. There was no point listing the examples of hard-working, skilled Jews. Freeloading was a 'racial destiny' that no Jew could escape: 'He can't help it, whether he wants to or not', Hitler had explained in his programmatic speech on the subject 'Why are we Anti-Semites?' in the Munich Hofbräuhaus in 1920.[38] A Jew who did not correspond to this construction was, in this account, only a piece of mimicry, a tricky deceit. In this way anti-Semitism protected itself against any reality check – a conspiracy theory that could not be rationally invalidated or empirically contradicted.

Hitler blew the racist stereotype of the parasitic Jew into a global conspiracy: Jewish high finance was sucking the strength from the German economy, its 'Social Democratic henchmen' drove its victims to it, Jewish department stores were ruining German retail, Jewish-made junk was depriving German craftspeople of the foundation of their existence. Even factually, talk of Jewish high finance was nonsense: yes, half of all private major banks were in Jewish ownership, but in the economically more important major equity banks the proportion of Jewish owners was at only 1 per cent, equivalent to their proportion within the population.[39] It was true that Jews were on average more successful. Centuries of life as a minority in an environment that repeatedly turned hostile or suspicious had made them more adaptable than the well-established Germans, so that a greater-than-average share of the 564,000 German Jews occupied top positions in culture and business.[40] Of the Republic's 40 German Nobel Prize-winners, 11 had a Jewish background – for example Albert Einstein, James Franck, Gustav Hertz, Otto Meyerhof and Otto Heinrich Warburg. Instead of pride, their fame merely prompted envy.

Hate-filled Nazi propaganda grew in parallel with misery; the Jewish-run department stores, supposedly 'oriental bazaars' in spite of all their gleaming modernity, were identified as arch-enemies alongside the banks. Eighty per cent of department stores belonged to Jewish owners, although the biggest one, Karstadt on Hermannplatz in Berlin, the cathedral to Americanism, was not one of them. The department stores, strikingly visible though they were, made up only a small part of retail as a whole. But the discount battles in which the department stores engaged during the years of crisis, and the massive deployment of advertising, made life hard for small traders, many of whom were of course Jewish. 'For ten years we have been experiencing a planned annihilation of the middle class,' Hitler claimed in Munich in 1929. 'If a new department store is built on Dachauer Strasse, that means the ruin of a thousand shops.'[41] There was plainly something in that, although there were not even a hundred shops to be ruined in the area around Dachauer Strasse. But what was 'planned' about the annihilation, and why the whole middle class? And why would it have been in the interest of the department stores to ruin the purchasing power of their customers? In 1930, the Nazi paper *Der Stürmer* explained: 'If a Jew has built a department store, he has no concern, no thanks for kind Christians. Only one thing concerns him: competition to the death, to the ruin of the Christian.'[42] At a mass rally, one Fräulein Zander of the German Women's Order informed her audience that 'the weapons with which your sons will be stabbed in the back' were being forged with the profits from the 'Jewish palaces'.[43] And the *Völkische Beobachter* contrasted the dazzling chic of the stores with the supposedly desperate fate of the salesgirls: 'Apart from bad pay and humiliating treatment, in the department stores the girls are often victims of Jewish lechers.'[44] Every promotion, every pay rise had to be paid for by having sex with the head of department. *Der Stürmer* fantasised in all seriousness of a planned 'violation of non-Jewish virginity', because the Jews knew 'that the only peoples who can be incorporated within the plan for Jewish global domination are the ones whose women yielded to the Jewish race'.[45]

At New Year's Eve 1929, on the threshold of the 1930s, it was still unimaginable that almost half of Germans would one day follow this kind of nonsense. In the Reichstag elections of 1928 the NSDAP had received only 2.6 per cent of the vote. The Germans had just been through a 'year of misfortune', the *Vossische Zeitung* wrote at the turn of the century, but seen from close by it had been much better than people thought.[46] The trade associations deliberately talked things down to get more out of it for their clientele. 'Is an economy so ill if it has 7 to 9 billion marks left over for building after covering its daily requirements?' the paper asked, giving a painstaking account of how things were better than they seemed.

Still, the 1920s came to an anxious end. In Hamburg, the parrot-related disease of psittacosis had broken out, electricity and gas were going up in price, and the New Year's Eve 1929 issue of the *Vossische Zeitung* contained only seven job adverts, including an office messenger job for someone seriously wounded, a job selling subscriptions door to door, and a homeworking job making bootlegs.

In the same New Year's Eve issue, the Hermann Tietz department store announced special prices to cheer up their customers. A million pairs of socks at 28 pfennigs each! Wertheim had a sale on too, crêpe de Chine, pure silk, 3.25 marks a metre. And the *Berliner Börsen-Zeitung* could still report that the joke trade had come up with all kinds of new ideas for a successful New Year's party: chocolate made of plaster, creaking hats, and 'all kinds of devices for making a racket'.[47] In the 'New Year's Eve decoration for the ladies' world', the cabaret top hat still featured, even if it was in decline, while the tiara was on the way up. The unknown reporter had spotted a tiny but telling fashion detail in the tiara. Plainly women were no longer interested in irony and dressing up, not even on New Year's Eve. The journalist quite naturally expressed the view that this was 'in line with the times'. He probably had no idea just how right he was.

II

The Mood Plummets, Taste Adapts – Cultural Conflicts in a Time of Depression

But now I seriously advise you to think about the mass, so that you can establish who and what it is.

Alfred Döblin, 1931

'It Only Happens Once, It'll Never Come Again': peak performances in spite of the crisis

The economic crisis was experienced with mixed feelings. It did not consist of a grim, grey uniformity that put everything that happened into a depressive minor key. It did not erase contradictions but intensified them. People laughed and danced through the crisis, they happily spent their money, made plans, started their studies, flourished.

In spite of diminishing economic power, in 1930 many of the great achievements for which the Weimar Republic would be famous were yet to come. The crossing of the North Pole in an airship, for example. The *Graf Zeppelin*, beloved of many Germans, returned from a successful scientific expedition to the Arctic on 31 July 1931. It brought with it a wealth of spectacular photographs and valuable measurements of the nature of the far north. The Soviet–German research team had made a precisely timed contact with the Russian ice breaker *Malygin*. For days, the rendezvous between the airship and the ice breaker was the focus of conversation, particularly since the famous Italian polar researcher Umberto Nobile was on board the *Malygin*.

Then, in 1932, Werner Heisenberg received the Nobel Prize in Physics for his definition of the uncertainty principle. Germany thus once again became known as the place for atomic research, the key to the most powerful new technology of the future. There were also innovations in the field of education: in May 1931 Hanover city library opened as the first tower-block library in Europe.

Over a number of months, many Germans felt pride in the flight of the Do X around the earth. The biggest passenger aeroplane in the world at the time, built by Dornier on Lake Constance, could transport 160 passengers and land and launch on water. Its spectacular appearance was partly down to the 12 propellers that were arranged over the wings and the body of the plane. Equally exciting were the pictures taken from the passenger liner *Bremen*, which worked the transatlantic sea route to New York. Two thousand kilometres before its destination, an aircraft equipped with launching sleds was catapulted from its deck into the air. It dashed ahead, carrying the mail transported on the vessel the rest of the journey to New York. In this way it reached its destination 22 hours early.

New discoveries in aerodynamics made cars and trains faster, and changed the face of technology. The Bauhaus principle that the function of an item should be made outwardly visible was revised; cars were covered in a flow-optimised shell to reduce air resistance. The rocket set new standards for the accelerating pace of life and filled the imagination with ideas of conquering space. The prototypes fired into the air from Berlin did not travel further than 200 metres, but the cinema had already anticipated the future: in Fritz Lang's 1929 science fiction silent film *Woman on the Moon*, a rocket launch was shown with the first countdown in history, and viewers experienced breaking the sound barrier and the magic of weightlessness. Rockets also influenced train design: the railway zeppelin, also known as the propeller train, thrilled technologically minded young people. In 1931 it reached a maximum speed of 231 kilometres an hour, powered by a propeller in the rear of the railcar.

The opening of the Cologne–Bonn autobahn in August 1932 was also forward-looking in terms of economic policy, because its

investment commitments were dependent on labour-intensive construction methods. Bulldozers and conveyor belts were forbidden, to
employ as many people as possible and reduce unemployment – an
anti-cyclical investment measure that revealed the far-sightedness of
the young mayor of Cologne, Konrad Adenauer. (As noted earlier,
the NSDAP did not come up with the idea of the autobahn as a
method of work-creation – later an oft-cited propaganda myth.)

In 1930 the Kant garage palace opened in Berlin, a four-storey car
park with room for 300 cars. The 'two lane spiral ramp' and the functionalist glass facade once again fed into the dream of a dynamic
urban machine. Many other architectural jewels that would later be
seen as symbolising the elegance of the 1920s did not open until
the 1930s. Berlin's Shell building by Emil Fahrenkamp, for example,
with its undulating limestone facade that made it look as if stone
could be bent. Or the Schocken department store in Chemnitz, built
by Erich Mendelsohn, also elegantly curved and nonetheless severely
structured – a building that was in 'floating balance', as the architecture critic Julius Posener said, a building 'that moves in peace'.[1]

The trademark of a completely new form of mass democracy was
the house of the Reich Radio Company in Berlin, directly opposite the
radio tower, also known as 'Haus des Rundfunks'. The massive building, 150 metres long, five storeys high, with two internal courtyards,
built in 1931 from plans by Hans Poelzig, was not only a national broadcasting institution as it is today, but also the headquarters of a
vast Reich-wide organisation, the Reichsrundfunkgesellschaft, which
incorporated nine regional broadcasters (much like the ARD organisation in the present day). These were partly privately owned, partly
publicly – newspaper publishers and record producers were involved,
but the state always had to be the majority owner.[2] It was a colourful
mosaic of businesses from the early days of radio, brought together
into a rapidly growing broadcasting company – soon a quarter of all
Germans would have a connection to it. To supervise the new media
power, a complicated network of supervisory committees consisting
of institutional influencers, watchdogs and advisers was established,
because even the people who ran the company were not entirely

comfortable with the huge power potentially enjoyed by this new medium.[3]

The 1930s began promisingly in literary terms as well: it saw the publication of Robert Musil's *The Man Without Qualities*, Hermann Broch's *Sleepwalker* trilogy, Lion Feuchtwanger's *Success* – novels about society, which in their different ways dealt with the whole of life and forced their divergent protagonists into a unified picture. Contrasting with these were the aforementioned Irmgard Keun's *The Artificial Silk Girl* and Erich Kästner's *Fabian*, two books that drew a subjective, very relaxed tone from the crisis, of boundless *joie de vivre* on the one hand and flouncy bitterness on the other. Theatre, which had been doing extremely well, weakened during the crisis after Erwin Piscator and Max Reinhardt gave up, while the cinema went from strength to strength. From an artistic point of view, in 1931 *M* (the German title translates as *M – A City Searches for a Murderer*) stood head and shoulders above the crowd. Fritz Lang's thriller tested the governability of the modern city. It explored how an individual could be tracked down using two competing surveillance systems: the police and organised crime spread their very different nets to hunt down a child-murdering serial killer.

Sound cinema had overcome its teething problems and enjoyed great success with its thrilling revue films. In 1930, in the feelgood romantic movie *The Three from the Filling Station*, the protagonists take over a petrol station with some success, and the film moves with them through expensive dance halls that the viewers could no longer afford. In *Congress Dances*, the most expensive film of the Weimar years, Lilian Harvey sings the comforting showstopper, 'It Only Happens Once, It'll Never Come Again', without which public life was for a time unimaginable. Under the direction of the revue manager Erik Charell, hundreds of extras surged and danced, while the camera appeared, by the standards of the time, to have 'gone wild'. 'Everything moves, everything turns,' the *Neue Berliner Zeitung* wrote admiringly.[4] People recognised themselves in the good old days, and for a moment felt the whole force of history.

The year 1932 saw the release of the crisis comedy *A Blonde Dream*,

The zeppelin over the Berlin radio tower, both promising big changes. The radio tower sent a light circling at night like a lighthouse. This picture by the photographer Alfred Gross appeared in 1928 in the Berliner Morgenpost.

again with Lilian Harvey in the leading role, along with Willy Fritsch. Two window cleaners and a homeless aspiring starlet live in a wild allotment colony and don't know who's supposed to be in love with whom, if at all. The sweetly sad crooner 'Somewhere in the World There's a Little Bit of Happiness' became an indelible part of the German collective memory, sung generations later by performers including Nina Hagen, Udo Lindenberg and Die Prinzen, and Jonas Kaufmann. For the unemployed there were reduced-rate tickets for 30 pfennigs. Seldom had misery looked as good as it did here, so unctuous, so sugary, so thrilling.

Then, in 1930, Max Schmeling brought the heavyweight boxing title to Germany and kept it a year later, in a fight against the

American Young Stribling. But all of this was not enough. The mood was plummeting, unstoppably.

Rule of the inferior: nothing but trash?

A deep pessimism spread through the country, and not just that. Germans were increasingly getting on each other's nerves. People could no longer hear one another. The dawn of the 1930s in Café Deutschland was like the morning after a wild party, when the light exposes grim corners, empty bottles and weary faces. The sparkling wine was flat, the guests were hollow-cheeked and gaunt, the band were packing their instruments away. A carefully nurtured revulsion with the world, the preserve of elitist young conservatives, was de rigueur in many circles. The year 1930 saw the republication of Edgar J. Jung's book *The Rule of the Inferior*; the title soon became a catch-phrase, used daily as a derogatory characterisation of the Republic, whose art was increasingly dismissed as so many daubs, its excitements as overinflated, its hopes as illusionary. The cheerful parties had run out of steam, and not even arguing was fun any more. It became chic to drift bleakly through the streets, which could be done with superior melancholy, as in Erich Kästner's novel *Fabian*, or with genuine hatred, as in the national revolutionary writer Franz Schauwecker. 'This age is worthy of nothing but destruction,' he grumbled, longing for the raining steel of the First World War.[5]

Degradation, levelling, decay – words like these, the ill-tempered vocabulary of cultural pessimism that had been permanently part of the background noise of the 1920s, now found their way into the liberal press and darkened the atmosphere.

By 1930 the cultural landscape had visibly taken shape, between the twin poles of an optimistic belief in progress on the one hand and a critique of modernisation on the other. The liberal bourgeoisie gazed serenely on the world. Problems accumulated, but they seemed to be solvable, progress would sort everything out. Even such an elegant fellow as Heinrich Mann felt on top of the world, because he was still convinced about the civilising power of the city. In 1930, he read before a random audience in the newly opened Karstadt department store on Hermannplatz in Berlin, 'in the corridor between food and confectionery'.[6] Here of all places, in this vast cathedral to consumption, which looked as if a fantasy from *Metropolis* had come to life, the president of the Literature Section of the Academy of Arts read to an audience shoving past him with full shopping bags. Later he admitted: 'This anonymous appearance of mine in a flowing crowd that made no concessions on my account, is among my purest memories of public life in the Weimar Republic.'[7]

But culturally optimistic voices such as his gradually went on the defensive. For more and more people, the modern age was losing its sheen. Reinforced by the economic crisis, doubts were growing about whether the modern way of life, with its remoteness from nature, its addiction to novelty and its constant time pressure, was really the right way.

Doubts about the circulation of commodities also increased. Cultural criticism and a concern for health combined to form a romantic anti-capitalism. Contemptible Mammon ruled, it was said, when one had to count every pfennig once again. The dance around the Golden Calf was frequently mentioned, as if people were already distancing themselves from a moneymaking society to which they might soon no longer belong. On the left, the critique of commodity fetishism was already part of the traditional anti-capitalist attitude, while on the right it joined forces with anti-Semitism to form a plausible mixture of resentment and a critique of civilisation. Suddenly a lot of people had a sense that it wasn't just wrong to succumb to the enticements of the world of commodities, but 'un-German' and 'degenerate', to use a favourite term of the 1930s. Many people felt as if they were in a branch of America, remote controlled by the victorious power that held Germany in the stranglehold of the Young Plan and secured its superior economic power with cultural power.

'American film is the new global militarism', wrote the film critic Herbert Ihering. 'It is advancing. It is more dangerous than the Prussian one. It does not swallow up individuals. It swallows up whole peoples.'[8] The doctor and author Curt Thomalla, film expert at the Reich Committee for Hygienic National Education, claimed: 'Germany will sooner or later be Americanised. So: bluff, kitsch, noise about nothing, loud extravagance, enticing facades, in a word: American!'[9]

The teacher Luise Solmitz noted in her diary in 1931: 'clutch bags come from American lack of culture [. . .] No bigger than a small handbag, with make-up powder tins, lipstick and nail files. The content reveals the level of culture.'[10] The teacher was particularly appalled by Mickey Mouse, an animal figure with

> the kind of sickly, grotesque and tasteless manner that only an American brain could dream up, not a German animal-lover or person of taste, who would be able to find something droll, characterful or animal-like in it. But we are Germans, and Mickey Mouse is running rampant in a way that would make one feel ill. On coats and caps, as a bookmark, in sweets, in rubber, wherever you look, this dreadful monster that has sprung from an American brain is accepted without criticism by stupid Germans. Not just by children.[11]

The idea that Germans would go along with any old nonsense that came from the United States troubled the grouches who notoriously felt foreign in their own country. The crowning glory of imported flim-flam was the yo-yo, the rosary of the global economic crisis. Admittedly even Goethe had played with the toy in Venice, but by 1932 the Filipino immigrant Pedro Flores had developed the spinning wooden disc still further. Professionally marketed by the Detroit investor Donald Duncan, and given a new legend and all kinds of new tips, the yo-yo became a fashion that spanned the globe – a pandemic, many people thought, an addiction.[12] This 'chewing-gum for the hand', as Siegfried Kracauer called it,[13] held people in its thrall – people played with it in offices, on street corners, in the playground. Pubs held yo-yo competitions; hotels held yo-yo dances. The world record for endurance yo-yoing was won in 1932 by a 14-year-old from the Ore Mountains on the Czech border. His yo-yo went up and down 4,000 times; he broke the previous record, held by a girl from Budapest, of 2,946 up-and-downs. There were countless yo-yo popular songs and even a now forgotten yo-yo film by Fritz Kortner, *Fräulein Yo-Yo*. The yo-yo fad vanished again after only a few months, as quickly as it had come. In the middle of the economic crisis, it had briefly provided distraction, competition and small victories. For a short time it even brought the miracle of full employment to the toymaking town of Fürth in Bavaria.[14]

The viral yo-yo wave was a phenomenon of the still young mass society, and as such it provided an opportunity for countless diagnostic speculations about escapism, leisure, the dumbing down of society, and the ups and downs of different eras. A feast for the newspaper arts sections. With his dexterity, the player conjured the day when 'everything will go spinning nicely again', the *Vossische Zeitung* felt.[15]

That day did not come, however. The yo-yo was not about to solve the problem of the lack of meaning that many people felt in their straitened circumstances. Perhaps they saw the yo-yo above all as a distraction, typical of Weimar's entertainment culture, from the oppressive problems that everyone faced, a flight into pointless virtuosity in which any street urchin could become a regional master. People were caught up in a frenzy of activity so that they didn't have to think about the meaning of life, Albert Schweitzer claimed. That sounded good at first, but who was manipulating people, who was pulling the strings? Where there are victims, must there not also be perpetrators?

Critics sought for the cause of the depression, and homed in on a central feeling of emptiness and fragmentation. The falsity, the superficiality that was seen or imagined in public life, was interpreted as a consequence of the denial of the national character. On the left there were polemics about the shallowness of modern society, the compulsion to keep smiling, the nurture of tact, the solicitous 'esprit' that was held to be derived from Western cultures, as if the bourgeoisie were as foreign as the term that they used to define their class. Elegance in a crisis looked like decadence; blunt, plain speaking seemed more authentic than well-constructed phrase making. People, it was argued, had lost their honesty, the pithy Lutheran form of Germanness, the craftsmanlike creativity and the peasant qualities that the Nazis had elevated to the model of the people.

Even George Grosz, the harsh caricaturist of Weimar society, who mockingly exposed the supports on which society rested, came out in favour of the traditional in German art, the old-master aspect that was supposedly deeply rooted in the people. In 1931 the convinced anti-militarist and resolute opponent of the Nazis argued for Germanness in art, for 'simplicity, temperament and feeling'. In 1916, he had anglicised his name in protest against the war (his name was originally Georg Ehrenfried Groß), and now, in the journal *Kunstblatt*, he raged against anglicisms and foreign fashions. He appealed to his artist colleagues not to make their pilgrimages to the 'philistine French Mecca' on the Riviera, but to Farther Pomerania, where the air was hard, uncomfortable and draughtsmanlike. That was a challenge, in contrast with the 'burned-out, calm ground of the South'. Artists, he argued, should re-establish their connections with 'Multscher, Bosch, Brueghel and Mäleßkircher, Huber and Altdorfer'.[16] Grosz reassured his readers that he was not thinking in *völkisch* terms, not stressing national characteristics in the racist manner of the Nazis, but rather linked his demands with an awareness of tradition and a closeness to the people with a such a scornful vision of capitalist city life that his stance was barely distinguishable from the anti-Republican revulsion with civilisation on the part of the right. The text is quoted at length because it shows how intense disgust with the Republic could be, even in an intelligent man who hated the Nazis and who had left the KPD because he had personal experience of the brutality of the Soviet system. But it also shows how close many elements of that fundamental criticism are to us. Ecological concerns are combined with theories of manipulation; the need for consumption was encouraged, Grosz said, to keep the economic machine in motion:

For it would be the death of production and prosperity. Impossible to imagine that tomorrow no forests are being transformed into paper, impossible to imagine a civilisation with fake silk stockings and ties. No. Needs must be encouraged. Always keeping on at the masses. Comfort in the name of progress. The raising of standards above all else. It is drummed into us daily. Living without vacuum cleaners and cars is not really living. We need only look at American magazines. True documents of uninhibited civilisation. Three quarters advertisements, more and more needs. [. . .] Ready made such and such. It won't rest until the North Pole has been artificially thawed and the Eskimo chained to a conveyor belt. The city, a true example of hydrocephaly, office town, a place of profits and fairs. After the working day dubious entertainments, hasty, noisy, fake and glittery, to pep up the tired businessman for a few hours. But not to make him think. Money, women, sparkling wine. Cheap theatre. So that they have no time for anything serious apart from their exhausting business. Revues and the endless stupidly pre-digested pictures of the cinema. Their wives, made-up, manicured, hollow accoutrements, neglected, with gigolos in hotel rooms and at tea dances. What sort of life is that?[17]

Is life nothing just because an artist doesn't like the way it is lived? Make-up bad, factory products bad, sparkling wine bad, women who take men for themselves, very bad. Craft, on the other hand, good, tradition good, sense of seriousness particularly good. 'Let us pull down the stack of manufactured objects, and all the factory trash and show the ghostly nothing behind them,' Grosz said, appealing to his artist colleagues. But oh, artists like him were only 'crumbled, fallen ruins of a past time', he went on, and knew: a change was coming.[18] He would rather be seen as second rate, Grosz said, than give up using his pictures to say something about 'our national community', and he didn't mean it ironically.[19]

In the same year, Grosz lost his contract with the gallery-owner Alfred Flechtheim, who found himself in increasing financial difficulties, and even demanded that the artist return advances he had given him. It was America, in fact, and its tired businessmen, who helped

Grosz out of the mire. In 1932 he was given a teaching post in New York. On 12 January 1933 he moved to the United States and brought his children out after him. A few hours after he left, the SA feverishly came searching for the 'cultural Bolshevik', broke down the door to his studio and wrecked everything they found there.

It's all the more troubling, reading Grosz's essay in *Kunstblatt*, to sense the extent to which both right and left, even though they were deadly enemies, had come together in their hatred of the establishment. George Grosz had always portrayed Germany as whorish, greedy, reckless and repellent, as a horrible, low dive, but it is still startling to see how little support the Republic received from someone like him when it came most heavily under fire.

Grosz set valuable German work against junk, authenticity against 'factory rubbish', honesty against commerciality, Gretchen, the traditional image of the German maiden, against the whores of civilisation. He bounced merrily back and forth between criticism of consumerism and moral preaching. Turning a critique of capitalism into cultural criticism made the attack complete: capitalism appeared as a single demoralising institution that drove love out of sex, quality out of commodities, respectability out of work and meaning out of art. As in the years of inflation, the brothel became a fixed idea, a poisonous metaphor for a Republic that was supposedly starving to death. Until then, though, the place needed to be radically cleansed from top to bottom.

*

The aversion among cultural critics to the bustle of Weimar was, of course, not entirely unjustified; much of society went on acting as if all that glittered were gold. It was no coincidence that the cabaret would later become a metaphor for the Republic as a whole. Things that had once been merely frivolous in the context of poverty came to look obscene. Modernity revealed its shortcomings, pragmatism its lack of heart, constant irony its blasé indifference. There was much to complain about, and quite rightly. But the fatal inclination to overdramatise things that had been present in the Weimar Republic from the beginning meant that keen-eyed cultural criticism automatically led to hysterical cultural pessimism. What prevailed 'spiritually, culturally and artistically [was] formlessness, fragmentation, mishmash, the most godforsaken hopelessness that there had ever been' – this, and similar, was the tone of the articles that worried 'intellectuals' wrote when commenting on the times.[20] All of a sudden the style was hysterical; there was barely a question that wasn't a crucial one, no trend that couldn't be psyched up as a historical turning point. Once again, at every available moment people saw themselves at the 'portal to a new age'. Even demands for more inward reflection were formulated as an unequivocal call for a radical change of direction: 'Today the topic is: the mass, the cries. The goal: a document. Tomorrow the topic will be: inwardness, the self, silence. The goal: structure!' was one of the many inflationary sounding diagnoses of the age.[21]

The fatal tendency towards radicalism and dramatisation did not stop with the economic crisis. The overheated hopes of salvation that had been attached to New Living, the New Woman, the New Cosmopolitan City or the New Life were followed by new worries and boundless disappointment. The crisis was huge and the poverty great, but neither was it as hopeless as it was held to be by wide circles of people. It was not the really starving who painted it in the worst light, but the middle classes who were tormented by anxiety and whose confidence had fled. The National Socialists had just the ticket for such fears. They were skilled at turning an economic depression into a mental crisis, and describing it in such a way that even people who were reasonably well off grew maudlin and felt profoundly in need of salvation. It was seldom material poverty that the far right targeted, but psychological pain – the 'heart-breaking fragmentation' – that Hitler diagnosed in his people.[22]

The 'New Human Being' dissolved in self-pity. Enthusiastically awaited at the beginning of the Republic, he or she strode grimly over 'those invisible battlefields on which the intellectual structures of the west have been ground to dust' – that was the partisan

description given by the chronicler of the Conservative Revolution,
Armin Mohler.[23] While some people played yo-yo, others felt revulsion and rage, and imagined a national liberation like nothing seen
since the battle of the Teutoburger Wald, when the Teutonic warriors defeated their Roman invaders.

The political right were not short of inflammatory rhetoric. Their
writings are full of plausible paradoxes, like the 'melancholy enthusiasm' with which people were to go into battle, or the promise of a
miraculous resilience. 'The German enjoys his defeats, because they
are rejuvenating', the far right author Franz Schauwecker claimed:
'He walks calmly through his disasters, as they merely contain his
future victories, indeed they make them possible, they are their preconditions.'[24] In the heat of such rhetoric, facts meant as good as
nothing. Contradictions weren't troubling – they were merely the
cherry on the cake. That was how the wealthy Alfred Hugenberg was
able to declare war on the ruling class to which he himself belonged.
In 1931 the financial and media entrepreneur roared at the founding
assembly of the Harzburger Front: 'Here is the majority of the
German people. It calls to the leaseholders of the offices, the holders
of power and the political leaders, the owners and exploiters of dying
organisations, it calls to the ruling parties. A new world is on the
rise – we don't want you any more!'[25]

Campaigns of optimism for the climate of consumption

The bourgeois forces who had an interest in the social order continuing as it was had little effective to say in response to these brutal
declarations of war. Trust in the young Republic, which was now
living through its second violent economic crisis, was flagging from
month to month. How was one to counter the growing disturbances?
Liberals looked on helplessly at the anxiety and hysteria, hatred and
blood-lust that were growing. In 1931 the Leipzig librarian Hans
Praesent brought out a book of pictures under the title *The Way*

Forward! A Picture Show of German Peak Performances.[26] The volume of photographs, which was published by the otherwise very right-wing publishing company Breitkopf & Härtel in Leipzig, wanted 'to hold up before the German people, at the time of its greatest need, a mirror of its capabilities' and presented miraculous technical accomplishments, from the Zugspitzbahn cable car to the Mittelland Canal that crossed the River Elbe on a bridge.[27] Readers gazed in wonder at the Voith spiral turbines, mammoth projects such as the 'giant boat lift', as well as portraits of thinkers from Heidegger to Einstein with brief and cheering commentaries. What was needed now, according to the preface by the head of the Zeppelin works, Hugo Eckener, was only 'faith – faith in the mission of our own people'.[28] Confidence was the fuel that would carry the engine of the economy over the mountain.

Ullstein, threatened by a drop in circulation and advertising revenue like all newspaper publishers, relied on optimism. In that field, the insight that much economic power relied on a healthy atmosphere turned into a conviction that one only had to believe hard enough in an upswing and it would come about all by itself. In its customer magazine *Ullstein Bericht* the company never tired of asserting that things were about to get better. Ullstein's popular newspaper *Tempo*, founded in 1928, by its own conviction the most modern daily newspaper in Germany and without a doubt *the* newspaper of modern consumerism, bravely kept the crisis out of its pages. Anyone reading *Tempo* would have had a sense of living in a better future, in a world full of cars, telephones, fridges, electric drills and holidays abroad. Even if many of these objects were still far too expensive for the German market, the optimistic editorial direction worked well as long as the economic figures were pointing upwards and wages were rising. Readers were content to be fed on the hope that eventually they themselves would belong to the world of modern consumerism as it was portrayed here. That confidence had now gone. Hans Fallada, not without reason, makes a shop window the site of his hero's greatest humiliation in the novel *Little Man, What Now?* But in February 1931, while motor-car producers were going bankrupt one after another, *Tempo* wanted in all seriousness to tell its readers that the introduction of a 'people's car' was on the verge of happening. They even gave away the psychological method that allowed them to make such outrageous promises: 'We urgently need to create a different fashion, a better mood-fashion. [. . .] It is wrong to assume that the economy consists of figures, or emerges from figures. [. . .] The impulse always comes from mood.'[29]

In principle, it was not so wrong to believe that transfiguring the conditions represented a practicable way of hindering the downturn. This valiant attempt on the part of a newspaper to buck the economic trend by sheer effort of will inevitably came to grief in the absence of state investments and an austerity policy of zero growth. The *Ullstein Reports* of 1932 contained sheets of paper that the companies who advertised with Ullstein were supposed to distribute to their customers: 'He who buys makes work! Work makes earnings, with which your goods are sold. Therefore fight with us for healthy purchasing optimism and start, in your own interest, in your own backyard.'[30]

We can hardly assume that such desperate actions 'against the fear of buying' boosted confidence in the future of the republic. On the *Tempo* team, at least, the mood was plummeting. Suddenly even *Tempo* was warning against the pace of modern life: technology was 'rushing so far ahead of our souls that we hobble along helplessly behind it'.[31] The newspaper of the dashing reporters that had pretended for four years that it was reporting in real time ('every line a novelty') was now arguing for slowness: more neighbourhood, less city.

The uprising of the provinces: agrarian romanticism and ecology

The halo of the city faded with the economic depression. The crisis had also spread to the countryside, but very few people were going hungry. There was always something to eat, even if you had to steal it from the field. Nonetheless, the situation was pitiful here too. Prices had dropped, taxes had risen. Many farmers could no longer pay back their debts and fell behind on their tax payments. Bailiffs became regular guests in villages, usually accompanied by two police officers, because the furious farmers would often reach for axes and pitchforks to chase the officials off their land. In 1929 the Republic learned that farmers could go on strike as well. After a demonstration by farmers in Neumünster, close to the Danish border, for months farmers refused to supply the city with meat, grain and milk. The whole of the German north, particularly the area of Dithmarschen, saw unrest, riots and bomb attacks. In the east, too, where there were hardly any smaller or middle-sized farms, but where barracked agricultural workers worked for the landowner and his administrator, conflicts escalated.

Farmers had not warmed to the Republic from the outset. At the time of its proclamation in 1918, the war was still going on as far as they were concerned. During the war, farmers had to give a considerable share of their harvest to the state – at prices far below market value. State control had been intended to keep the cities supplied with meat, milk, potatoes and grain throughout the conflict. As hardship had not come to an end all of a sudden after it ended, the government had simply stuck to the system of forced contributions; it was not until 1923 that grain production had been returned entirely to the free market. In the eyes of the farmers, that was only typical: as far as they were concerned, the SPD had a reputation of serving only their urban clientele and giving city-dwellers the best possible prices at the farmers' expense. But in the eyes of the rural population the other parties, as soon as they were in government in Berlin, also only considered the wellbeing of the city-dwellers and exploited the farmers to the best of their ability. In fact, their tax burden had risen hugely in comparison with pre-war times, even though the productivity of agriculture had dropped during the war. Very few had tractors, and many small farmers didn't even have a horse to put before their plough or cart; cows were used as draught animals.

However, German agriculture was far from uniform; it altered drastically when one travelled from east to west or north to south. It's hard to imagine a country more diverse than that of Germany, where farms operated according to completely different principles and traditions from region to region: in the east were the large landowners with their agricultural and seasonal workers; in the northwest and Bavaria, many medium-sized farms with farm hands and maids; in the southwest countless part-time farmers who worked in nearby factories during the day.

As great as the complicated differences in interests might have been between large landowners, large and small farmers, teams of farmhands, reapers, and owners of smallholdings, there was one point on which they almost all agreed: the Republic did nothing for them. The SPD had never succeeded in establishing a long-term bond with agricultural workers, and the principle of collective bargaining in an industrial factory is not easily transferable to a farm; it soon became apparent that everyday life and work in the countryside could not be divided so easily into the three parts of work, leisure and sleep that now formed the working day in the city. Time worked differently in the rural world. Agricultural life was very much at odds with the principles of the SPD, and the KPD was perceived as inhabiting a completely different world.

Part-time farmers could have formed a bridge with the modern age, since in southwest Germany in particular they were responsible for a large proportion of agricultural production. Here the male members of a family went to the factory during the day; they took care of the farm in the evening and at the weekend. But it was the agricultural part of their lives that brought them all the pride of their divided existence. Their patches of earth turned them into something better, or at least more secure, with more 'confidence and self-respect' compared with the purely industrial workers who went hungry every time there was a crisis.[32]

So in many respects the countryside was at odds with modernity. Its inhabitants suspected the city-dwellers and felt short-changed, undervalued, underestimated. The fact that people had streamed to the city from the countryside for years had nagged away at the

confidence of the villagers. The best had moved away, people complained, as if it were a sign of stupidity to stay. That so many young
women had fled to seek their fortune in the city was also seen as a
serious blow to rural men. Bruno Tanzmann, one of the most eloquent spokesmen on behalf of farmworkers, saw the women who
left as facing a terrible fate, seduced by 'greed, pleasure seeking, by
hollow noise in every area of life, by noisy oriental Jewish nonsense
in state politics, department stores, theatres'.[33] The women there
were 'vamps', alienated from motherhood – they replaced washing
with make-up and work with roulette and tennis. For Tanzmann and
his companions the city was 'the mass grave of the German people'.
They were destroying the nation's legacy, wrecking people spiritually
and physically. A people that was too good to work the soil of the
homeland would write itself out of history.[34]

Along with a group of like-minded people, Tanzmann founded the
German Agricultural College and the 'Artaman League', which
attracted 30,000 mostly very young members with its euphoric
approach to farming in general and its organised 'settlement trips' to
the east. Tanzmann, from Oberlausitz on the Polish border, was one
of the few real farmers among the many propagandists for plough
and soil, a stubborn character who provided the Nazis with arguments and devotees but was equally likely to pick a fight with them.
Most representatives of an agrarian romantic critique of modern life
didn't come from the countryside at all but from the cities. The farmers were flattered by the songs of praise that these *völkisch* radicals
sang to rural life. The countryside was a big blank field in which –
alongside the economic suspicion of actual farmers – very different
plants of ideological resistance to modern life were able to flourish.
Anyone who opposed the Republic from the right could find any
amount of potential for protest here. One conveyor-belt conformist
Nazi was Walther Darré, a polyglot businessman's son and horse-
breeder taken on by Hitler in 1930 as an agricultural affairs adviser.
That same year, Darré wrote the book *A New Aristocracy of Blood and
Soil*, which combined theories on animal husbandry, anti-Semitic

racial nonsense and peasant romanticism into an apotheosis of the Nordic human being. The Nordic racial aristocracy which, according to Darré, slumbered in the genes of the rural population, had little to do with the struggles and anxieties of real rural life, but was all the more flattering to the humiliated rural soul.

Darré, Tanzmann, Rosenberg and some others gave the NSDAP the propaganda ammunition they needed to beguile the rural population – loudmouthed and uncouth enough to appeal to the farmers as much as their farmhands, the Junkers as much as their reapers. And they expressed their hatred of the city in such a way that the city-dwellers could share it, since they saw themselves as victims of an alienation that supposedly made them ill in the longer term. Darré and Tanzmann identified the city as something essentially alien to German nature, an originally oriental invention. In their eyes cities were places of nomadic thinking and a rootless culture, places of globalisation that could never replace a real home.[35]

One creature similar in essence to the German, however, was the pig. In 1933, Darré devoted a racist pamphlet to the innocent animal, with the lovely title: 'The Pig as Criterion for Nordic Peoples and Semites', in which he made the relatively immobile domestic pig a distinguishing feature between the sedentary Germans and rootless foreigners.

The most stubborn agrarian romanticism was to be found not in the countryside but in the city. Urban young people went to the countryside weekend after weekend as *Wandervögel*. Many of them dreamed of being settlers – 'East-land travellers' – for at least a year as part of the settler movement in east Germany. Here they could join the 'army of ploughmen' to free the countryside of Polish seasonal workers, but above all to improve their own fitness by sowing and harvesting. In the years of growing unemployment the urge to travel to the thinly populated northeast became so strong that the local residents felt threatened by the hordes of reckless, immoral people coming there from the city in search of work.

City-dwellers who stayed at home could satisfy their longing for the land by looking at picture books. *Die von der Scholle* (The Ones

Pastoral scene with guitar-toting Wandervögel. Forest, field and heath were dream locations for stressed city-dwellers, and for many the home of the 'real' Germany.

from the Land), for example, published in 1931, showed 'fifty-six portraits of down-to-earth people', as the subtitle had it. The pictures showed earthy types who, as the preface claimed, formed the foundation on which the rest of the nation was constantly renewed. 'Everything else passes. The peasant remains. He is *Volk*, as it was, German *Volk* as it will be.'[36]

Those who could only dream of settling the land at least paid attention to healthy diets. The vegetarian, health-food promoting *Reformhausbewegung* (Reform House Movement) boomed, along with the holistic, mystical teachings of anthroposophy, an educational and creative system established by the Austrian teacher and architect Rudolf Steiner. The year 1928 saw the foundation of the biodynamic Demeter League, and in 1932 the Demeter Seal was introduced to guarantee the production and processing of biodynamic foodstuffs. The book market was also dominated by a yearning for the land. The Weimar Republic was typified not only by city novels, but by their opposite, peasant novels, which painted a picture of an unalienated, manageable, archaic life. Here a man was still a man, the earth was fertile, and the reward for labour was tangible and tasted as pure as only a fruit can taste that one has planted oneself.

The day ended peacefully at evening, and love, modest and rich, didn't cause the usual annoyance that it did in the city.

If we seek a counterpart in literary history to Heinrich Mann, the academician who stood amidst the crowds of Karstadt department store lovingly reading out loud, we will find him in the village school-master Karl Heinrich Waggerl from the region around Salzburg. This 33-year-old, too ill from tuberculosis to practise his profession, published his debut novel with Insel Verlag in 1930. The book was a raging success: *Bread* sold 90,000 copies. The book's subject matter was as sparse as the title was short. A man who appears as if from nowhere, finds a piece of land in the wilderness and makes it blossom.[37] He cultivates, sows and harvests – a life reduced to its most elementary components. A few planks, stones, a stream that he has to divert, a goat and the skill of his fast-learning hands – for the reader from the city, *Bread* was a healing treatment for the senses, particularly for someone who feared the loss of his job in the economic crisis. *Bread* tasted like the glorious sweat of primal drudgery – an apotheosis of labour, like many successful books of those workless years. For Waggerl, the modern age began in the next village; as a reader one is always happy when the hero is able to turn his back on the little town, with its seething intrigues, and get back to his plot of land.

With the economic crisis, *völkisch* authors received enough of a boost to go on the attack. In 1930 the Hamburg author Wilhelm Stapel, a fanatical anti-Semite, openly called for an 'uprising by the countryside against the city':[38]

> Just as the peasant from the German countryside begins to feel rebel-lious against what is being played out in Berlin, the educated German will resist what the intellectuals of Berlin are propagating. The spirit of the German people is rising up against the intellect of Berlin.[39]

Stapel became the self-appointed spokesman for the silent major-ity that felt duped by the Berlin cultural scene, which supposedly shaped the culture of the Republic. Rather than edifying aestheti-cism, what one saw in the city was nothing but libertinism, women's emancipation, coarse language and disrespectful irony. Until the beginning of the depression these ingredients had constituted the charm of the liberal-left-wing Berlin cultural and media scene, the beguiling odour of freedom and petrol. But since optimism had fled from public life, the modernity of Berlin's cultural life seemed to have become less infectious and more exclusive. For those threatened by decline, the modern age felt less like freedom for all and more like pleasure for a few. That intensified into the delusional claim that the modern arts were the destructive work of a corrupt elite that wanted to drive the soul out of the people. Hitler's campaign against 'degenerate art' would later be of prime importance for his success, because it included an assurance that the future *Volksstaat* (People's State) would be geared towards the taste of the people. In this way, he used cultural policy to reinforce the impression that Nazi rule was rule by the people, while democracy had been dominated by a self-infatuated elite, terrorising the people with its minority culture.

In his various calls to arms, Wilhelm Stapel specifically targeted the urban literature of one particular author: Alfred Döblin, author of the novel *Berlin Alexanderplatz*. The doctor and writer replied to Stapel's call for an 'uprising of the land against the city' in the *Vossische Zeitung*, and spoke ironically of the 'art of that very flat country' rebelliously having its say.[40] It sounded controlled and relaxed, but Döblin had been made to feel insecure.

Döblin and Berlin seemed inseparable. The author had always seen the city as the 'topsoil of all his thoughts', and the crowd as his muse, to whose confusion of voices he was only too happy to yield. But now he was finding the crowd unsettling. He had even ended his novel *Berlin Alexanderplatz*, in which over 60 passages contain different walks through the city, with crowds moving past the protagonist Franz Biberkopf with music and song into an open future:

Red dawn, red sunset, lighting us to an early death. [. . .] And keeping pace right and left and right and left, march march, into battle we go, a hundred playmates with us, [. . .] one stops, another falls, one runs on, another lies mute, viddaboom, viddaboom.[41]

The ending of a far-sighted novel of the city.

The mob was the 'white patch on the atlas of your humanity', Döblin wrote in 1931 – 'huge and unformed', the crowd is 'the most striking and the most terrible fact of today'.[42] It was not to be despised – rather one should be shaken by it. This huge, immature mass of people, pushed and shoved hither and thither, would determine everyone's fate, he feared – it would form into a grey army and bring the old world crashing down.

Döblin had taken a letter from the young student Gustav René Hocke, who had written asking him 'out of inner necessity' for 'intelligent words' about the current situation, as an opportunity to write some loose replies and bundle them together into a book of deliberations to which he gave the almost Leninesque title *Know and Change!* The book was hardly likely to satisfy the young man's needs, however. It was a wild, extravagant, distracted treatise, alternately headmasterly, lofty, poetic and naive, but at the same subtle and full of sparkling insights. Döblin had intended nothing less than a 'roll-out of the human problem', and drawn upon everyone who happened to fly through his head, whether as adversaries or slogan makers: Luther, Marx, Goethe, Hegel, the working-class bourgeoisie, the intelligentsia. Throwing around headings like 'Philosophical problems show how the wind blows, or doesn't blow', he threw himself into the fray with an uncontrolled delight in the expression of opinions that was so typical of the Republic.[43]

One notices quickly that the author had no more of a notion about what was going on than the student did. And yet he wrote and wrote, breathlessly contradicting himself, driven onward by the terrible tensions that lay in the air to which he, the man of the crowd, was more sensitive than almost anyone else.

Döblin felt a longing for community and recommended the 'invocation of the private'. He was convinced, he wrote, that 'the public sphere must be dismantled'.[44] A 'powerful intensification of private life' was necessary and a 'weakening of the state impelled by that'. He did not, however, know how this was to be accomplished. There were hardly any real individuals in Germany, only any number of

Crowds and power. In May 1924 a large crowd waited in Potsdamer Platz, Berlin, for the announcement by loudspeaker of the election result. At this Reichstag election the parties of the extreme right and left won an increased share of the vote for the first time.

oddballs. 'But that is not an individual, merely the residue of collectivism.'[45]

He sensed the fateful longing of humanity for leadership, and instead recommended a dialogue with nature: the young man should open himself up to trees, plants, sky and clouds, and sense their 'you'-ness: 'finally face these things as a simple being, no, mingle among them'.[46] He would experience, Döblin argued, how they spoke to him and how he understood their language. Communication between an 'I' and the phenomena of nature was not something new to the medical doctor Döblin. He had repeatedly evoked it in the past and attempted to interpret in it a 'theory of resonance' that was supposed to lead humanity into a new way of feeling about their own biological foundations and fellow creatures.

Were one to outline the content of this overflowingly rich but politically utterly dysfunctional treatise *Know and Change!*, one would have to sum it up like this: embedded in an anarchic programme of dismantling large organisations, in brief passages it takes off and opens up a kind of political-esoteric ecology that radically anticipates postmodern reflections. Döblin steals the agrarian kitsch away from the right and tries to absorb it into a way of thinking compatible with the Republic, one that replaces the materialism of the technological age with a new focus on nature. Döblin's version of the new age looks startlingly green, almost cautious: 'Now one must arrange one-self slowly, slowly, really and entirely on the earth, as human beings in a living nature run through with spirit, whose limbs we are.'[47]

A short time later Döblin abandoned his public medical practice in the proletarian east of Berlin and moved to the elegant west, on Kaiser-damm. There he opened a new practice for only private patients, but hardly anyone came. He, who had always seen the swarming city as the soil in which his thoughts could grow, sat alone in his surgery and wrote. The urban mass had lost one of its most fascinated lovers.

The end of the Charleston

In 1930 a tendency to look backwards appeared in many areas of German life. Senses rearranged themselves and the love of fast-paced living faded. Tastes changed, as did the sense of beauty, the awareness of the body, the feeling of rhythm. The mood plunged, bones went on strike, people began dancing to a different beat. Collective emo-tional states are not the unimportant froth that fashion represents for many people. Emotions are not only indicators of social change, they are often also their medium and their amplifier. Interwoven with hopes, disappointments, bursts of happiness and aversion, they form intricate processes leading to political convictions and ultimately to crosses on ballot papers.

A lot of dancing was also done in 1930, of course, but the way people danced in the big dance palaces, those cheerful, fateful inter-sections of social life, changed fundamentally. Hardly anyone felt like dancing the Charleston, which had so cheerfully powered the 1920s. The thrilling, liberating Charleston, which had shaken off the

conventions of people's souls, made way for the waltz, that measured, brightly rolling dance for couples, which brought the good old
days back to the dancefloor. The driving fury of the Charleston
now seemed impetuous, and there was a tendency to return to the
slightly melancholy rhythm that the waltz provided, swirling, in perfect balance, in a circle: don't let everything get even worse! The
dance teachers' guild was delighted. In 1931 the 'dance chronicler'
F.W. Koebner wrote in the journal *Das Magazin* that the elevated
social dance was back, and that alongside the inevitable waltz people
were now dancing the tango, foxtrot and rumba.[48] The wild freestyle
of jazz, in which everyone danced exactly as they felt like dancing,
was left to the lowest of low dives. Being well trained in the standard
dances again became part of social distinction: 'Dancing badly today
is the same as speaking bad German.'[49] Now, once more, the old, the
overweight and the stiff dared to go back on to the dancefloor.

'The n***** era' was over, *Der Querschnitt* cheered in the article
'The Fashions of 1932', making no attempt to disguise its racism.[50]
There were six waltzes to one tango, and the Charleston was no
longer even mentioned.

> Negro music seems, at least for now, to be pausing its alarming
> advance. [. . .] The radio is drawing tons of waltzes from a thousand
> sources. Whatever may be going on: London, Paris, Amsterdam or
> Berlin: the universe replies with a waltz.[51]

So much conservative self-satisfaction, even in Alfred Flechtheim's
liberal magazine *Querschnitt*! We can only imagine what the mood
was like in more reactionary circles. Still, the anonymous author
noticed a tendency towards a certain 'over-sweetening' and admitted
that it had been the despondency of people during the crisis and not
their good taste that had made them so dependent on comfort and
kitsch:

> The general over-sweetening even feeds into music. Melody is making
> a return. Noise has gone. People are demanding tender songs, pretty

daydreams and freshly blossoming lilac. The chanson, brushed aside
by jazz, is risking a victorious counter-offensive. The street-singers are
awakening to new life. The record of dance music is no longer ousting
the record of song. And even though all trends in this broad field are
asserting themselves, even though there are still realistic and humor-
ous chansons, the sentimental *Schlager* is emerging victorious.[52]

Irony and female confidence were in retreat. In 1932 Fritzi Massary
sang, still entirely in the style of the 1920s:

> Why should a woman not have a relationship?
> She could have a lion hunter
> or a negro from a jazz band
> Heavens, the consumption!
> She's talked about, she's gossiped about
> surely it's the wrong way round!

The singer left Germany the same year. It had become too unsafe
for her.

Most music journalism turned away from 'cultural Bolshevik nihil-
ism' and towards uplifting *Schlager* about old Heidelberg and eternal
love.[53] There was no need for the decree 'Against the Negro Culture'
with which the education minister for the state of Thuringia, Wilhelm
Frick, imposed an absolute ban on jazz in the state in April 1930. The
mainstream was already performing a wide backward curve. The
author Manfred Hausmann complained:

> Those lads have turned us around by one hundred and eighty degrees.
> What we left behind us, they are heading straight towards. And what
> did we leave behind us? The underling, the member of the herd, piety,
> drill, fear for our own lives.[54]

NSDAP minister Frick's prohibition on jazz (the party had had
two ministers in the Thuringian state government since 1930) was

met with scorn and mockery in the liberal circles of Berlin. With his 'Negro Ruling', the *Berliner Volks-Zeitung* wrote, Frick wanted to impose his taste on the people of Thuringia: 'If they put up with that, it's no more than they deserve.'[55] Some democratic reflexes still worked here and there. Even in *Der Stürmer* there was a degree of resistance. In Julius Streicher's paper, one Frida Höft wrote in from Neukölln in Berlin to say that jazz still 'contributed much to the cheerful mood of society', and that she didn't understand what the fuss was all about.[56] The editors of *Der Stürmer* replied that jazz in Germany was not only played by Black musicians and that it had been 'moderated and ennobled' in Germany. It was by no means identical with atonality and disharmony. The melody was phrased and distorted, but 'the rhythm is strictly adhered to', the Nazi paper was happy to note, and advised: 'keep on playing for now!'[57] Today we know: it had run out of steam in any case. Nonetheless, in 1932 Franz von Papen's government introduced a ban on black musicians to improve the chances for white ones. The fact that this was largely accepted shows the extent to which the spirit of freedom had gone on the defensive.

Along with the Charleston, the bob gradually disappeared as well. In the end, bobs were worn only by those who, whether out of political conviction or aesthetic sense, mourned the boom years of liberated lifestyles. Here too there was no need for inflammatory slogans such as 'the braid is Aryan, the bob is Jewish' to motivate women to switch to a more 'feminine' hairstyle. A more conservative appearance now matched the general emotional state. Hair should now look dignified and classical – or else it should be the seductive hair of a cute little blonde like Lilian Harvey, the superstar of the 1930s. Thinness was out; many women now ate Eta-Tragol bonbons to put on weight. 'Unlovely protruding bony cheeks and shoulders are disappearing. You will put on pound after pound, and the extra weight will appear on all parts of the body', the Eta-Tragol advertisements promised. Angularity made way for a flowing silhouette.

And along with the economic crisis, skirt lengths suddenly grew as well. Alert fashion journalists such as Paula von Reznicek interpreted the new style in skirts as a declaration of war against emancipation: 'Have a clear understanding about what you are to give up', she wrote in *Tempo*:

> You are to give up the fashion of the short dress, of sharp lines. And what are you recommended instead? What do they want to force on you? You are to announce a complex, hidden, basically meretricious form of femaleness, at your work in laboratories, offices and factories you are to whirl up the dust with swirling hems. [. . .] There is much more behind all this: a bad, hypocritical reaction against all the gains that we have managed to make over the past ten years.[58]

But many readers did not follow her call. The long skirt – to the disappointment of liberal fashion editors – continued its advance. Editorial departments adapted to the taste of the time and soon abandoned their pedagogical role as guardians of the libertarian Zeitgeist. The bob disappeared from the fashion pages along with the boyish type in general. Instead, the 'modernised Gretchen type' appeared on stage, the ideal of a 'more feminine, more moral but still emotionally independent woman' with classical dignity and imposing stature, who was able to stand up to naive notions of home and hearth, at least for a while.[59]

Inner values corresponded to the external ideal. In *Tempo*, 'Frau Christine', who gave advice about all important female issues, had pleaded for sexual curiosity, self-determination and trial marriage. Now she distanced herself from the 'spiritual costume' of the girls of the 1920s. Young women should not run around in an 'emotional costume from 1928' that was now very much a thing of the past, she wrote in 1932.

> The girl of today thinks too much of herself only to be an object of desire and a 'pal', she no longer wants to endure the terrible emptiness. She wishes and longs for a big, strong, inspiring experience in which one becomes mature as a woman, ripe for marriage.[60]

In 1932 cuddling was the order of the day once more. The woman of today had had enough of 'walking around in an emotional costume from 1928', the advice columnist 'Frau Christine' wrote in Tempo. *'Feminine, modest, and helpless – that is the great fashion in fashion', the magazine wrote a year later. The photograph is by the photographer Yva and was published in 1932 in the* Berliner Illustrirte Zeitung.

So 'Frau Christine' also invoked depth, seriousness, authenticity against the cheeky, frivolous arrogance of the past decade, the 'terrible emptiness' that was suddenly held to be the curse of the time. Many women who had enjoyed sexual generosity now felt more exploited than liberated.

Young women no longer wanted to be a 'pragmatic girl'. The confidence to make it on one's own, the desire to test oneself in different situations before settling down, the wish to question gender roles and curiosity around sexual experiment, seemed largely to have been lost. But their companions in the press had fallen silent. The 'New Woman' had become needy in her worries, like so many others.

The desire of every very modern woman is to look like an old painting. Feminine, modest and helpless – that is the great fashion in
fashion. A little cape, a beret and a muff made of fur or some kind of
curly fur-like fabric make it possible to pursue this line at little
expense.[61]

So wrote Lucy von Jacobi in *Tempo* on 30 January 1933, the day Hitler
became chancellor.

Evening Over Potsdam – the End of a Community of Communication

The supreme law for anyone who does a deal with someone is that he must not put himself in the position of the other person. Empathy is paralysing.

Marieluise Fleisser, 1931

Banquet with easel

It was an exhausting dinner. The painter Lotte Laserstein invited five friends to Potsdam for an evening meal on a friend's roof terrace. They ate, drank, talked a lot about this and that, not least, of course, about the muddled state of the country. After dinner the guests stood or sat as models for a picture. They were posed, re-posed, reorganised, their positions switched, the remains of the meal rearranged – a series of jittery movements, the things we do for art. In the end, Laserstein had everyone in the right posture and in the right place. The important thing now was to endure it and not to move. By the end of the evening the view over Potsdam had been sketched and the outlines of the individual guests painted with a broad brush. Over the coming weeks – the painting, over 2 metres wide, was transported back on the commuter train – each individual sitter had to come to Laserstein's studio in Berlin to sit again for several hours.[1] The end result was *Evening Over Potsdam* (1930), a painting that would later become a symbol for the mood of the declining Republic.

The Jewish artist's large-format painting was the centrepiece of her first solo exhibition at the Gurlitt Gallery in Berlin in 1931. It wasn't sold, and Lotte Laserstein took it with her into her Swedish exile when she left Germany for ever in 1938. The painting was so important to her that she later painted herself standing in front of it. In 1987, six years before her death, she sold it via a gallery to a British collector. It wasn't until 2010, when it was shown as the centrepiece of the exhibition *Modern Times* in the National Gallery in Berlin, that the history of its reception and interpretation over the years could finally be seen as a dark social and political metaphor that had begun in the Gurlitt Gallery in 1931.[2]

The painting shows the end of a little banquet. The five guests are full. Some bread, fruit and wine still lie on the table. In its composition the painting clearly recalls Leonardo's *Last Supper*, not least because of the refined agitation of the essentially calm scene, and the Christ-like pose of the woman in the yellow at the centre of the painting, sitting stiffly, in blank reflection. Two men, three women, each a little lost, inward-looking, tired. Thoughts have been exchanged, all questions are open. A melancholy atmosphere hangs over the scene. These are young, bourgeois people, perhaps artists, obviously

Lotte Laserstein, Evening Over Potsdam, *1930. The dinner scene later became a symbol for the last years of the Republic.*

intellectuals. People committed to ideas, who like talking but have run out of things to say.

One can sense the deep bafflement of a declining class of thoughtful people who have only been relieved for a moment of the growing hatred brewing around them. But what makes the painting so symbolic is something else. It shows a society paused. For a rather sad moment, it has lost its cohesion and broken up into a cluster of isolated individuals. If we take the little group as representative of a wider whole, it reveals many of the attitudes that its enemies criticised in bourgeois society. It was seen as weary and weak, drained, over. Laserstein actually shows an exhausted society – fragile and vulnerable, but also captivatingly beautiful. Every man for himself, and yet all together; what holds them together is extremely delicate. It is a paused moment of frozen emotional body language. The loose bonds of the group are expressively emphasised by the framing bodies of the standing women and the matching postures of the men. The party is captured just at the moment when it has lost its vitality, and the individual members fall back into their silent loneliness. In this ambivalence of distance and proximity, *Evening Over Potsdam* is a tender counter-image to the rowdy, vigorous visions of 'authentic community' with which the NSDAP tormented the public. We could even say that *Evening Over Potsdam* is a declaration of love to a Republic that has just been through a long and noisy party and now has little to say for itself. The 'Roaring Twenties' are over, to be replaced by a melancholy wait for an uncertain future. It is the portrait of a crisis of communication.

*

Germany had moved far from the ideal of a rational bourgeois public sphere. Not that people were silent – outwardly things still ran along orderly, talkative tracks. People chatted in the associations, gossiped in pubs, linked arms in convivial bars. But listening and looking more closely one could discern the gulfs of silence dividing society. People liked to be among their own kind and held the rest in contempt.

Given the muddled state of things, even fewer people than usual were in a position to take anything meaningful from a discussion with people of a different opinion. 'Unity' and 'unanimity' were yearning words on everyone's lips, although there were only two ways of achieving either: through determined silence or brutal violence.

Most Germans had never learned to argue constructively. Under the kaiser, they had been 'patriarchally tended to', without much debate.[3] When they jumped into the icy water of freedom in the November Revolution of 1918, most had been given no opportunity to experience themselves as free citizens. Very few had understood, let alone applauded and experienced on an emotional level, what it meant to take responsibility for oneself and consult with others in the abstract framework of democratic representation. To many, the political parties seemed like the source of all evil, as if it were they who had put the different interest groups in place.

In fact, the parties themselves were ill-prepared for freedom when the 1918 revolution assigned them a central role in the system. In the Kaiserreich they had only played a subsidiary role and had never learned to assume political responsibility, form durable coalitions, and find a middle way between political goals and possible action. Instead, they spoke stridently on behalf of their interests and fought for the preservation of their political identities. They were happy to stab their own ministers in the back when their governmental activities required an attitude of compromise that seemed intolerable to the different factions. The fact that 12 chancellors stood at the head of 20 cabinets over a period of 14 years did not exactly increase trust in the parties. The wider public often learned little about political life beyond slogans, as the newspapers did too little to inform their readers about parliamentary negotiation processes and political compromises. People heard only about 'squabbling' and 'discord'; these two terms were the ones most frequently used to describe politics, much as present-day journalists simplify political issues to cram complicated material into a 90-second slot.

Feuding and squabbling were complained about mainly by those most at odds with the Republic. 'Smash the parties to bits, be German!'

Siegfried Ochs, composer and choir leader, recommended succinctly to his compatriots, and he spoke for many.[4] 'Just think, when everyone could be giving their best for the Fatherland!' the teacher Luise Solmitz complained in her diary about the fruitless disputes of parliamentarians: 'And something so pitiful, such a pile of petty vileness is called "politics", leads a people, chatters, curses, flatters and takes its parliamentary allowances.'[5]

The individual most closely implicated in the decline of political culture was the one who saw himself as its supreme protector: Paul von Hindenburg. Since the president had used emergency decrees to impose a presidential cabinet without a parliamentary majority, the Reichstag had lost even more validity and respect. It had not degenerated into a meaningless shouting match, but its debates had fewer and fewer practical consequences. As they were largely excluded from pragmatic government, the parties gave free rein to their dogmatic tendencies, turning philosophical differences into absolutes and digging their heels in on compromise.

The communication crisis that went hand in hand with the depression devalued all means of promoting social cohesion, public discussions and fairs, but most particularly the press. Readers first withdrew their trust, then their subscriptions. Ullstein alone lost a quarter of its subscribers, and the drop in advertising hit even harder. The newspaper *Germania* cancelled its evening edition, and the *Kreuzzeitung* simply withered away.

There were some 3,300 daily newspapers in Germany, around 140 of those in Berlin, often published twice a day. That sounds like a huge variety, a paradise for critical journalism. And the lively press landscape did produce authors who remain unforgotten – Theodor Wolff and Egen Erwin Kisch, for example, who give their names to the two most important prizes for journalists today.[6] Pugnacious culture sections thrived, encouraging extravagant styles of writing whose ambition eventually alienated the readership. Fred Hildenbrandt, the head of the culture section of the *Berliner Tageblatt*, later recalled: 'Those of us who were part of it all lived among ourselves as if on an island.'[7]

A picture from better days. The communication society takes a lunch break. A view of the MPs' restaurant in the Reichstag, 1928.

Opponents of the Berlin cultural scene had long asserted that it was indeed an island, but every milieu, every newspaper formed an island in itself, with its own opinion makers, whistleblowers and regular readers – an island where the opinions of outsiders were unwelcome. Every political trend, every little party, the tiniest intellectual village had its own newspaper. A form of the infamous 'filter bubble' or 'echo chamber' through which people can become intellectually isolated on digital networks in the present day also existed in Weimar Germany. Reader and newspaper existed in a mutual relationship of confirmation bias; the newspaper wrote what the reader wanted to hear, and the reader stayed loyal as long as the paper didn't trouble him with unwelcome views.[8]

The new medium of radio could have countered this with impartial reporting. Kurt Weill complained of 'the pusillanimity towards the political issues of the day', since radio station administrators had the opportunity to 'remove ignorance of the viewpoint of the opposition'.[9] But radio stayed away from politics – until Goebbels used the instrument for his own ends.

Liberal newspapers from stables such as Mosse or Ullstein, which aimed for a broader spectrum of opinion but were fundamentally committed to the Republic and to parliamentary politics, sensed that an increasing number of people had stopped following them. Even before they cancelled their subscriptions, readers were inwardly quitting. They had lost the feeling that it was their interests that were being discussed. 'Even though our readers remained outwardly loyal to us,' Hermann Ullstein would recall,

> there was little doubt that in their hearts they were no longer on our side. Inwardly, a good half of them who were convinced that 'it can't go on like this' were already in Hitler's camp. Day after day we criticised and attacked their idol, and it didn't have the slightest effect on them.[10]

The liberal press lost trust and credit at first very slowly, then dramatically. The worst hit was the *Berliner Tageblatt*, which was seen as the mouthpiece of the luckless liberal DDP. This brilliant paper lost over 80 per cent of its readers under its editor-in-chief Theodor Wolff. Of 160,000 in 1919, by 1932 only 25,000 were left. The public's lack of interest in democratic business included reports and commentaries on it; the newspapers were perceived as the 'mainstream media' (*Systempressse*), their journalists as 'lackeys of the system' (*Systemlinge*), which is how liberal officials and politicians had already been known for a long time. The term 'lying press' (*Lügenpresse*) was already in general use, but *Systempresse* was even more widespread, and used for anything to the left of the Nazis' own *Völkische Beobachter* or to the right of the Communist *Rote Fahne*.

It was not only politics that lay behind hatred of the liberal press, but also a general dissatisfaction. The Germans could no longer hear one another. On both right and left the phrase-making machine was once again working overtime, incessantly hammering out the old slogans. Unfortunately, the right did so more imaginatively; the KPD sounded like a weary, dull echo chamber of the NSDAP, and even sometimes tried to copy its anti-Semitism.[11] But within the population itself goodwill between the different camps and circles was used up, the willingness to listen had vanished, any desire benignly to consider the arguments of others had been extinguished. The civil art of debate, extremely underdeveloped in any case, had been completely lost in the course of the economic crisis. What 'flour saleswoman Frieda Geier' had said about trade in Marieluise Fleisser's 1931 novel applied to all areas of life: 'The supreme law for anyone who does a deal with someone is that he must not put himself in the position of the other person. Empathy is paralysing.'[12]

On the left *Die Weltbühne*, on the right *Die Tat*

And what about the famous *Weltbühne* (The World Stage)? Wasn't it perfectly suited to a dialogue, at least between the hostile factions of the left-wing political spectrum? The pacifist magazine had emerged from what was originally a theatrical magazine, and was edited first by the gifted hothead Siegfried Jacobsohn, briefly by Kurt Tucholsky after Jacobsohn's death and, from 1927, by Carl von Ossietzky. Devoted to politics and culture and aimed at independent thinkers, it had a strong culture of publishing readers' letters, including those of prominent people. It was the heart and soul of the left-wing intelligentsia, floating between the KPD and the SPD, combative, ironic, always ready for a scrap and open to debate. Its circulation, with a maximum of 15,000 copies sold, was tiny, but because of the indisputable rank of its authors its influence was enormous. Its weakness, however, was its condescending tone. The problem was not its principled pacifism, or its orientation towards Europe and the West, but the arrogance with which *Die Weltbühne* snubbed anyone who wasn't on its wavelength. Sentences like the following by Ossietzky from 1928 were not intended to persuade but to close the ranks of readers with sneering mockery:

Just as some primitive people worship the feeble-minded, the Germans worship political feeble-mindedness and choose their Führer on that basis. In this they doubtless outdo the savages, who limit themselves to worship and timid admiration, but otherwise move neither into war nor peace with their village idiots.[13]

The acidic derision of the political elite struck many chords but could only be enjoyed by those who were not affected by it and who stood with the authors in an intellectual ivory tower.

The extent to which *Die Weltbühne* contributed to the weakening of the Republic with its sometimes scorching disparagement of actual politicians is disputed, but it is true that it was touchingly concerned with its own readership above all else.[14] The Berlin reader's circle met on Wednesday at a quarter past eight in Café Adler on Dönhoff Platz in the centre of the city and listened to lectures from the left-wing university scene. In the second week of 1928, for example, it was the turn of one Louis Gibarti from the 'Anti-Imperialist League'. The article about the meeting of the readers' circle in Berlin was joined by a request to the people of Ludwigshafen, an industrial city in the southwest of the country: 'All readers are politely requested to give their address immediately to the lawyer Dr Ludwig Weil, 16 Kaiser-Wilhelm-Strasse, so that a circle of *Weltbühne* readers can be established in Ludwigshafen.'[15] In the country as a whole, *Die Weltbühne* was little more than a cult rag.

Kurt Tucholsky, the most important author on *Die Weltbühne*, suffered from isolation for which he himself was at least partially responsible. Tucholsky's books sold well, and he knew his way around the newspaper business. Still, not without a degree of egomania, he saw the left's loss of ground to some extent as a personal defeat. The gifted scoffer had strong feelings for his homeland, and he took rejection extremely hard. He cautiously closed his controversial book *Deutschland, Deutschland über alles* – a compendium of his scathing social critiques – with a declaration of love for the country that he had scolded so severely. It was not true that nationalists alone represented a love of Germany.

We are outdone by everyone in terms of patriotism – our emotions are international. In terms of love of our homeland, we are outdone by no one [. . .] We have the right to hate Germany – because we love it. We have to be borne in mind when people speak of Germany, us: Communists, young socialists, pacifists, freedom lovers of every degree. [. . .] Germany is a divided country. We are a part of it. And standing amid all our differences – unshakeable, without flag-waving, without a barrel organ, without sentimentality and without a twitching sabre – is our quiet love of our homeland.[16]

That was a furious conclusion to a succession of polemics, brilliantly formulated but painful to write. Tucholsky's love for his homeland was disappointed, even deeply insulted. He thought the battle was lost very early on, which is why he was much less concerned with persuasion than he was with dishing out the criticism and insisting on being right. He had lived predominantly in Paris since 1924, and in 1929 he moved to Sweden, first to Läggesta near Gripsholm castle, then to the stunning Villa Nedsjöland in Hindås near Gothenburg. From there, he wrote to tell his brother what he really thought of Germany:

You can't believe what the country looks like from outside: a collection of neurasthenic lunatics who are wrong, one and all, in their different ways [. . .] No, my dear brother, that's not why I'm in the world. There's nothing I can do.[17]

*

The right-wing counterpart to the left-wing intellectual Weltbühne was called Die Tat (The Deed), a serious monthly publication since the respected journalist Hans Zehrer had taken over the original 'non-denominational' esoteric magazine in 1929. Zehrer came from the liberal Vossische Zeitung, where he had even been considered for a time as a potential editor-in-chief, and he quickly turned Die Tat into a much-read organ for the 'conservative revolution'. Its circulation reached 30,000, which was, tellingly, twice as high as that of *Die Welt-bühne*. *Die Tat* was in fashion, seemed excitingly new, demonstrated striking similarities with the rising NSDAP and yet was critical towards it – which was exactly how it formed a bridge between intel-lectual readers and National Socialism. No one who wanted to know anything about the new love of myth, the Italian fascists, the strange philosopher Heidegger or the widespread longing for unity could avoid *Die Tat*. It was discussed everywhere; Siegfried Kracauer even wrote two full-page articles about it in the *Frankfurter Zeitung*, giving a detailed examination of the paper's seductive, demanding style.[18]

Die Tat was, of course, unhappy with the 'right-wing' label, since it wanted to appeal to all enemies of the Republic, regardless of whether they were right or left wing, particularly hot-headed young people. The most important ingredients were anti-capitalism, a romantic notion of the *Volk* and a longing for a dictatorship in which 'the best' were in charge.

In brief, the programme of *Die Tat* was more or less this: right and left needed to form a synthesis in the myth of the *Volk*,[19] in a power-ful, religiously charged community, carried by the disappointed middle classes, the intellectually homeless who felt a burning need to belong. But yearning alone would not be enough: however powerful the myth, without violence the strong *Volk* state under the leadership of its elites would be unachievable. If faith was not sufficient, 'the sword and the fist' would help to forge the *Volk* community.[20]

The prospect of violence did not alarm the readers of *Die Tat*, quite the contrary: the authoritarian *Führer* state evoked by Zehrer, without necessarily having Hitler in mind, became more attractive the more muddled the real conditions in the weakened Republic became. The word 'dictatorship', unlike today, when we know the horrors of the gulags and concentration camps, did not necessarily strike a negative chord. The constitutional lawyer and right-wing pioneering thinker Carl Schmitt saw dictatorship as the end of fruit-less discussions and observed: 'Dictatorship is the opposite not of democracy, but of discussion.'[21]

And *Die Tat* was expert at breathing emotion into the cold

functionalism of such theses. Fanatical and haughty, now gentle and idyllic, now gradually rising to a fury like a Wagner crescendo, *Die Tat* painted a picture of the changing times that it promised to help shape. That matched the general mood of the country: the right wing was largely able to reclaim the future for itself. The KPD was also notoriously ready for battle, but its confidence had been eroded by long familiarity, and the Soviet Union only seemed attractive to the most hard-nosed of party members. The independent left beyond the KPD was swathed in bitter pessimism.

Die Tat lived up to its name: it was agile and had a vision of the future. Zehrer painted a detailed picture of the way symptoms of the coming community would form in the apathetic coldness of the modern age. People no longer had any desire for distraction and mere entertainment, for cynical cinema, stale jokes and the old arguments. Instead, in the course of their disillusionment, a new spirit of community was beginning to stir. Here and there, people would start talking to each other again.

> Sometimes a person [. . .] starts talking to his neighbour again. It may be that they will start performing services for one another without being obliged to do so. They may smile resignedly at each other and shake hands. Perhaps many people will sit together in a room and have the feeling: it is good that we are sitting together. Signs and wonders happen. [. . .] One discovers one's neighbour. A street comes to life. It becomes more human. Since one no longer has to be a member of the faithful, since one is in debt, and one's neighbour is too, the boundaries fall. The 'top-down' *Volk* community has not come into being, but the 'bottom-up' one is growing by the day. Anyone whose house of cards has collapsed may not find solid ground, but he will find many others who have collapsed before and with him.[22]

The tricks of this text are simple, the staccato banal, the sentimentality powerful, but one also senses the attraction that it must have exerted in the context of a generally lamented breakdown of society.

The longing for a new community is tangible. Zehrer was enthusiastic about the crisis because he saw in it a chance to overcome democracy in the quiet drama of honesty, modesty, mutual interest, a readiness to talk. 'And there are even people,' he went on, 'who declare with an embarrassed smile: "I really mean what I say."' Here Zehrer was addressing exactly the same crisis of community to which Lotte Laserstein gave a touching face in *Evening Over Potsdam*, and trying to overcome it from the right – with the gruesome consequence that people like Laserstein were killed as a result of this project, although naturally the author could not have known that this would be the case. He was aware, however, that the sweet idyll which he saw germinating here in the form of a new community of communication would involve agitation and violence.

Die Tat tried to give fascism a human face, and an intellectual one. It explicitly supported Mussolini, Hitler only hesitantly. It was suspicious about his fanatical anti-Semitism, and Zehrer himself was married to a Jewish woman. Precisely through this elegant detachment, the *Tat* circle meant that the NSDAP was also welcome in snobbish cultural circles that usually felt little inclination to find common cause with a mass movement and its exhibitionistic, spectacle-organising Führer.

The intellectual aristocrats of the circles around *Die Tat* in fact had sound reasons to be horrified by the brutal mass of people attending Hitler's rallies, which was the grim reality of their notional *Volk*. But in spite of the cautious distance that they put between themselves and the National Socialists, they repeatedly called for Hitler's election. They saw the NSDAP as an opportunity to sweep away hated democracy. Once they had come to power it would be easy to rein them in and guide them on to the proper tracks. But Zehrer wasn't horrified by the prospect of putting up with a small degree of subjugation. For example, he yearned for censorship. 'If the spirit is slowly being placed under the screw of control these days, that is an extremely useful thing'. He quite seriously believed, and consoled his fellow journalists with the notion, that a bit of external discipline did the spirit no harm at all:

The best and deepest thoughts of humanity have seldom been thought in freedom, but have usually come about in oppression. There is no reason for panic. It is only a matter of us really thinking, writing and reading again.[23]

It did not occur to Zehrer that the 'screw of control' might one day torture him as well, indeed that it might forbid him from writing at all. In retrospect, one of his colleagues from *Die Tat*, Wilhelm Eschmann, explained:

We completely misunderstood National Socialism. We knew nothing of the actual power of the movement. We didn't think these people were intelligent enough, and believed that intelligence was what mattered in politics. 1933 was the year of our great awakening.[24]

Many members of the public were also seduced by the feeling that things wouldn't be so bad, and coercion and violence would be kept within bearable limits. The man and woman in the street remained largely unaffected by the brutality with which the NSDAP's gangs of thugs treated their opponents. The only people frightened by the SA's torchlight processions and street demonstrations were those who in their eyes 'had something to fear'. The majority who felt unthreatened, on the other hand, were increasingly fascinated by these marching columns, since they formed an obviously convincing antithesis of a fragmenting society whose 'bickering' was getting so painfully on the nerves of the discouraged population.

Please be as ruthless as possible: arrogance and submission

The crowd in formation – ranked, ordered, cheerfully singing, impressive-looking with their torches – appeared noble rather than brutal to many worried citizens, who perceived National Socialism as a force that would tame the mob and set it to useful purposes. That

seemed better to many than having the masses voting Communist. The NSDAP performed the dubious miracle of attracting both
street thugs and conservative academics with high opinions of themselves. Students, not dull-witted proletarians as the clichés would
have it, spearheaded the SA; in the party, the Hölderlin-loving school-
teacher felt just as much at home as the pharmacist and the
beleaguered civil servant who would never have dreamed of forming
part of the crowd but was desperate to belong to a community.

Devotion to German culture and intense community feeling combined into a mixture that attracted more and more people, even quite
hesitant ones. The NSDAP was a party of brawlers and professors: a
grim bunch whose internal contradictions were cemented only by
the dynamism that they were trying to set in motion. In 1930, attempt-
ing to explain the electoral success of the NSDAP (who had attracted
18.3 per cent of the vote with over 6.4 million votes, eight times more
than in the 1928 election, gaining 107 seats in the Reichstag), Thomas
Mann had already suggested that it had twofold cultural roots: on the
one hand, the irrational, nature-worshipping cult 'which celebrated
the life-giving forces of the unconscious, the dynamic, the darkly creative'. On the other, there was

> a certain philological ideology, German-poets-and-thinkers romanti-
> cism and an unquestioning faith in things Nordic from the academic
> professorial sphere which, in an idiom of mystical respectability and
> high-flown staleness, spoke to the Germans of 1930 with words like
> racial, *völkisch*, *bündisch* [referring to members of the German Youth
> Movement].[25]

In one word – *Bildungsbarbarei* (cultural barbarism).

This essentially bizarre agglomeration was able to work as a unit
as long as it kept coming up with visions of the future and construct-
ing enemies that needed to be kept in check and annihilated. Without
this internal aggression – called things like the '*völkisch* mission' – the
construct of the *Volksgemeinschaft* (the community of the *Volk*) would
have fallen apart immediately. Instead, it drew more and more people

into the maelstrom of a movement that actually seemed capable of uniting left-wing and right-wing elements, plebeian and elitist attitudes. Even though the NSDAP was by some way the most destructive element of the Weimar Republic, it managed to present itself as a party of unity that could shape the madhouse of contradictions into a new community.

The fact that the words 'ruthless' and 'brutal' were constantly on Hitler's lips didn't trouble the people who voted for him. One should use one's own life 'ruthlessly', people should even be 'ruthlessly' trained to use regional products,[26] he was 'brutally' determined to 'fight for' the principle that you shouldn't go after the small criminals before you've hunted down the big ones.[27] People found brutality somehow thrilling – they wanted to be pushed to the edge as if during sports training. Many people weren't alarmed at the prospect of being 'driven up a notch' – in fact, the idea of being relentlessly urged onwards was perceived to be more than enticing after the 'frosts of freedom'.[28]

The teacher Luise Solmitz also sympathised with Hitler because he wanted to rule ruthlessly: 'We are more and more inclined towards the National Socialists because they are promising to be strong, and that is the essential thing', she confided in her diary.[29] She expected Hitler to show the ability to 'force his own people into unity [. . .] to create inward order and cleanliness, outward dignity and firmness'.[30] He needed to clean up 'Jewish, democratic socialist parliamentarism'. This was, by now, how many people thought, but Luise Solmitz's sympathy for Hitler is especially remarkable: she was married to a Jew and had every reason to fear Hitler. Her husband had converted to Protestantism, but they both knew that because of Nazi race theory one's religious denomination was irrelevant. She understood that she and her family would suffer if Hitler came to power. In Nazi terminology, her daughter was considered a half-Jew, even though she had been baptised as a Protestant. 'Nothing in the world is more important to me than my husband and child, but I know that Hitler's racial principles are correct', she wrote in her diary in 1933.[31]

Ernst Jünger, the storm-of-steel fantasist, was also prepared to make sacrifices. The far-right dandy, who published industriously in all kinds of *völkisch* newspapers, had endured enough of the reasoning public sphere and, like Hans Zehrer, demanded 'the draining of that swamp of free opinion that the liberal press has turned into'.[32] Opinions could also be dispensed with. After all, every opinion was immediately followed by a counter-opinion, every news item by its denial. In his grimly utopian, national Bolshevistic vision of the worker's state, published in 1932 under the title *Der Arbeiter* (The Worker), he presented a vision of how he imagined the media of the future: as a technocratic flow of communication in which there was no longer any place for subjective flim-flam, but only for useful information. The future demanded a 'factual, mathematical style, appropriate to the 20th century'. There was no room for the subjective. The press must transform itself from 'an organ of free opinion into the organ of a strict and unambiguous world of work'.[33]

What are we supposed to make of an intellectual for whom opinions no longer meant anything even though he himself was constantly producing them and wasn't capable of any other occupation? What Jünger was demanding was nothing less than the end of the thinking person as known until then. Like Zehrer he longed for censorship. The people who raved about the *Volk* community were the first that wanted it silenced. It didn't occur to them that they might be next in line.

Jünger was also grimly determined to experience the day when freedom of speech was forbidden and the conflict of opinions brought to an end, even though it formed the basis of his own work. He must have been aware that there was no place for someone like him in the society of which he dreamed. With a mixture of pathos and self-pity, he concluded his book about the ant-like workers' state with an impassioned vision of himself: 'One cannot without emotion consider the human being, occupying himself with the toughening of weapons and hearts when trapped in the midst of chaotic zones, and knowing how to renounce happiness as he leaves them.'[34]

Emotion is entirely out of place here, where we are presented with someone who has only had enough of himself. He wants to hand in his freedom at the cloakroom, and his intellect too, like an old hat, so that he can hide in a world of identical far-right mice. His conservative fellow-revolutionary Edgar Jung, author of the *Rule of the Inferior* and speech writer for Vice-Chancellor Franz von Papen, was more honest on the subject. In 1932, feeling once again that the plebeian class with whom he wished to ally himself was too stupid, he wrote furiously in the *Deutsche Rundschau*:

> I respect the primitiveness of a *Volk* movement, the fighting force of victorious Gauleiters and Sturmführers, but their bumptiousness does not give them the right to see themselves as the salt of the earth, and to look down upon their intellectual pioneers.[35]

Unlike Jünger and Zehrer, Jung could not simply submit, and seriously believed that he could issue orders to his Nazi friends: 'It is not acceptable that a revolutionary movement receives its laws from petty bourgeois Party officials rather than from its intellectual representatives.'[36]

Jung should have chosen his friends more carefully. The far-right devotee of Mussolini and Hitler sceptic did not survive his critical friendship with the Nazis for long. The unity of the *Volk* did not tolerate the smallest deviation. In the summer of 1934 Jung was shot by the Gestapo, killed by the dark forces for which he had prepared the ground, to whom he himself had belonged.[37]

Lonely Elites – Cabinet Politics vs Populism

I really didn't feel like exposing myself to the thuggish insults of parliamentary hooligans in this committee, now degraded to the lowest of dives.

Otto Braun, state premier of Prussia, on his regional parliament, 1932

The prelude: coup in Prussia – von Papen drives the regional government out of office

For now, however, the chancellor was not Hitler, but Franz von Papen, a joke figure, at least in the eyes of his many opponents. Caricaturists didn't have to do much to make a mockery of him. The tall top hat on the gaunt, always immaculately attired figure in the tight Sunday coat – 'a bad-tempered billy-goat trying to adopt a pose of great dignity', Harry Graf Kessler wrote, 'a figure out of *Alice in Wonderland*'.[1] Papen came to power on 1 June 1932, in a way typical of Hindenburg's emergency cabinet: at the suggestion of the most powerful behind-the-scenes manipulator among Hindenburg's advisers (known as his '*camarilla*'), Kurt von Schleicher. Hindenburg had lost patience with the unfortunate 'hunger chancellor' Heinrich Brüning, because Brüning had, as we have said, finally managed to commandeer some of the property of the Prussian Junkers – the landowning class from which Hindenburg's own family came. Hindenburg was also unhappy

with the fact that Brüning had banned the SA because of their violent
street battles and the murders they committed. He saw this as a lurch
to the left.

Papen, on the other hand, was the epitome of the *Herrenreiter* – he
had trained as a 'gentleman rider' or 'amateur jockey' – an epithet
that clung to him through his life and beyond. He wasn't the most
intellectual of men, but he was sharp-witted, vain and communicative, a denizen of high-society salons, with exquisite manners when
they were called for. He had married into the wealthy Villeroy and
Boch ceramic dynasty, and had a network of outstanding contacts
with elite businessmen. Papen's taste was very much in line with
his activity for the German Gentlemen's Club, an association of Junkers, large industrialists and bankers, who felt that they were the
country's elite and needed an appropriate figurehead. In the light-
weight Papen they had found it.

Now he was chancellor . . . for a whole six months. Long enough
for Papen and his 'cabinet of barons' – so-called because of the many
aristocrats among the ministers – to do a great deal of mischief. As
previously agreed with Hindenburg, he immediately lifted the ban on
the SA to ensure the cooperation of the NSDAP in the Reichstag.
The SA, by now an organisation of half a million terrifying potential
streetfighters, was almost delirious with joy. They had been forced to
'strip themselves of their garb of honour', as one of their thugs put
it, and 'even in death', referring to the ban, 'treated most vilely'[2] –
now, with equal intensity, they felt that they had been rehabilitated.
Once again a wave of violence crossed the country. In July and August
alone, after the lifting of the SA ban, over 300 people lost their lives in
political clashes.[3] Eighty-six people died in Prussia in July, by no
means only in 'hand to hand' combat. They were attacked in their
apartments and kicked to death, stabbed in the back, beaten up or
thrown into ponds. The Communists gave as good as they got. Of
the 86 July victims, 38 belonged to the NSDAP, 28 to the KPD.[4]

By 20 July 1932 it was plain on which path Papen and his Gentlemen's Club wanted to put Germany. That was the day they held a
putsch of the regional Prussian government, the last in which the

SPD still had a say, and drove it out of office from above. On the morning of what became known as the 'Prussian coup', some representatives of the region – but not State Premier Otto Braun, who was in bed with flu – were summoned to the chancellor's office. There they were handed a decree announcing that they were deposed with immediate effect, and that official Prussian business would henceforth be provisionally conducted by the chancellor until peace and order had been re-established in Prussia. That was it. All that remained was to thank the gentlemen frostily, bid them a curt farewell and usher them out of the door.

The formal reason that Papen gave for this 'Reich execution' was the 'Altona Bloody Sunday' three days previously. On 18 July 1932, after a march by the SA through the working-class district of Altona in the northern city of Hamburg, 18 people had lost their lives. The inevitable disturbances had escalated to such an extent that the overstretched police felt they had no option but to fire at random into the crowd – a tragic failure whose victims were mostly innocent bystanders. Ousting the entire Prussian government in response, however, was made all the more grotesque by the fact that the eruptions of violence had been sparked by Papen lifting the SA ban in the first place.

The disaster of Altona offered a welcome opportunity to put an end to the coalition government between the SPD and the bourgeois parties in the state of Prussia, which had long been a thorn in the side of right-wing conservatives. For months they had spread rumours that Social Democrats and Communists might come together in Prussia and attempt to seize power, even though it was plain to everyone that animosities on the left were unbridgeable. The real motive for stripping the SPD-led state government of power was to bring the 'conservative revolution' a step closer, and clear a potential source of resistance out of the way in the form of the Social Democratic leadership of the biggest state in the Republic.

That same afternoon, Chancellor von Papen carried through the change of government. Prussia's interior minister, Carl Severing, was thrown out of office by his swiftly appointed successor, assisted by two police officers. The Berlin chief of police and his deputy were arrested, as was the commander of the *Schutzpolizei* or *Schupo*, the uniformed branch of the state police. The arrested men were only released the next morning, when the new incumbents swore not to use the *Schupo* to defend their former masters. The last SPD-led regional government was a thing of the past. Some enraged citizens did assemble in front of the Interior Ministry, but the deposed government showed no sign of defending itself. Many SPD members threw their party cards away in fury at the lack of resistance. Could the government not have mustered 90,000 policemen against the army, along with the armed men of the *Reichsbanner* association? 'We will crush them like lice' – the battle-ready Social Democrat supporters were sure of it.[5]

But Braun and Severing stuck to the constitutional path. What else were they supposed to do? Otto Braun's power in the region was almost as shaky as Papen's in the Reich. Since the last election, he had only been a figurehead. Three months previously, in April 1932, the NSDAP had received a sensational 37 per cent in the Federal State Elections, forcing the SPD into second place with 21 per cent. Braun was only still in government because the NSDAP had not been able to form one. And the KPD, which had achieved 13 per cent, would certainly not side with the SPD. Perhaps the situation would improve if there were a new Reichstag election. Braun wanted to wait until then.

The 'Red Tsar' had some depressing months behind him. The son of a railway guard had been given this nickname because he had managed to stay at the top of the Prussian government for 12 years almost without interruption – an astonishingly long time, not only by Weimar standards, during which Prussia, he believed, had been able to consolidate itself as a 'bulwark of democracy'. Not much was left of it. Over the previous few weeks, the Nazis had turned the regional parliament into a farce. At the second session after the election, NSDAP and KPD members had engaged in fistfights and thrown chairs, drawers and ashtrays at one another. A single session had left eight people seriously injured, and the Communists finally left in bitter defeat. But both parties worked together when it came to a motion of no confidence or forcing the government to put up with their mocking laughter. A demoralised Otto Braun had finally taken leave so that he could stay away from state parliament: 'I really didn't feel like exposing myself to the thuggish insults of parliamentary hooligans in this committee, now degraded to the lowest of dives.'[6] The chair of the NSDAP faction, Wilhelm Kube, sneered:

> As long as these gentlemen are receiving their high wages in straitened times like these, they have to put in an appearance. [. . .] That's why we, along with the Communists and the German Nationalists, demand: Braun cabinet, show up for your final inspection![7]

Otto Braun and Carl Severing had insufficient faith that they would receive support from the public to put up any resistance. Rightly so. The population, which had overwhelmingly joined the general strike in defence of the Republic after the 1920 Kapp Putsch, was effectively

After the top-down putsch, 1932: a worried crowd gathers in front of the Interior Ministry of the state of Prussia in Berlin, after their SPD government had been deposed on the orders of the Reich government and after the arrest of the chief of police.

silent. Some parts of the liberal bourgeoisie did protest, but too faintly, because they worried that their position within a Republic-weary society had become rather lonely.

Final offer: networker Kurt von Schleicher and the cross-party front

On 31 July 1932 there were new Reichstag elections. The NSDAP was the strongest party with 37.3 per cent of the vote. The SPD had to settle for second place for the first time since 1890, reaching only 21.6 per cent. With 14.3 per cent of the votes, the Communists were not even half as strong as the National Socialists.

If we sort the result not just according to right or left, but in terms of loyalty towards democracy, it looks even more menacing. De-votees of the anti-Republic parties who backed a dictatorship of the right or the left (NSDAP, KPD and media magnate Hugenberg's DNVP, German National People's Party) together formed a clear majority of almost 60 per cent. Democracy only had support from the voters of the SPD and the two Catholic parties, *Zentrum* (Centre) and the *Bayrische Volkspartei* (Bavarian People's Party). The other bourgeois parties such as the DVP (German People's Party) and the DStP (*Deutsche Staatspartei*, German State Party) had shrunk to insignificance.

Simply carrying on governing under these conditions must have been a difficult task for an elite gentlemen's club without any demo-cratic legitimation apart from the goodwill of the president who had been elected in 1925, even if the gentlemen in question felt predes-tined to rule. Violence in the streets was escalating more and more. 'A constant St Bartholomew's Day', Harry Graf Kessler wrote in his diary, referring to the French massacre of Huguenots in 1572.[8] The SA was furious, because their celebration of Hitler's electoral victory was soon followed by the bitter disappointment that he still didn't become chancellor. Hindenburg did allow the NSDAP to join a coali-tion government under Papen but refused to consider Hitler for the role of chancellor. He did not want to concede to Hitler's demand for the transfer of state power as a whole. In spite of his intensely conservative convictions, Hindenburg felt himself to be the president of all Germans, so much so that he declared himself unwilling to transfer the whole of government responsibility to a party 'that is determined to use this power one-sidedly' – in other words, that it would deal as dictatorially with dissenters as it had always said it would.

Conversely, Hitler was not willing to have his hands tied. As a member of a cabinet under Papen, he would almost inevitably find himself constrained. He was worried that his victory might prove to be pyrrhic, and feared that his aura might be damaged by the sobriety of the inevitable compromises. He also wondered how long his popularity might last in opposition, and knew that much of his persuasive power would be forfeited if he was unable to turn his electoral victories into practical successes. In short, Hitler was in a quandary, and reacted as he always did: by becoming depressed. Meanwhile, frustrated by what would come to be known as his 'legal course', Hitler's impatient troops started displaying even greater brutality, and cost him sympathy among the more hesitant section of his followers.

At this point, in the summer of 1932, social hardship had intensified dramatically once again: there were 6 million unemployed. Alongside those there were 3 million *Kurzarbeiter,* workers who could not satisfy their most urgent needs with their reduced hours and wages so had to rely on state subsidies. Nonetheless, so as not to break the budget, the 'cabinet of barons' drastically cut the amount of support that they issued.

The 'Emergency Decree for the Preservation of Unemployment Benefit', as it was cynically called, reduced benefits by a further 23 per cent. Real hunger broke out in one of the most advanced industrial states on earth, in which at the same time Mercedes cars were getting bigger and bigger, the front pages of the magazines more and more elegant and travel destinations increasingly exotic.

The situation gradually improved, however. Papen eventually backed a reviving investment policy, bringing the numbers of unemployed down slightly, particularly those *Kurzarbeiter* who had depended on state subsidies to top up their wages. Exports grew, albeit hesitantly. The most important thing, however, was that at last Germany was free of the oppressive burden of reparations. After Brüning's protracted preparations, Papen reaped the harvest. At the Lausanne Conference, he reached an agreement with the victorious powers on a remaining balance of only 3 billion Reichsmarks, which was to be paid from 1935 onwards, with the help of an international loan. It was never really paid. The Young Plan that had been accepted by the Reichstag two years earlier in March 1930 had allowed for payments of two billion Marks per year – to be paid regularly until 1966 and then, with a slightly smaller annuity, until 1988. After the collapse of proposed alternative arrangements it was never really paid off.

But what did details matter in this heated atmosphere? When, a good three months later, on 6 November 1932, there was another election, the NSDAP lost 4.2 per cent of votes. That was a considerable setback for it, but it was still not enough to be called a real turnaround. At 33.1 per cent, it was still by some way the strongest party, with the SPD a distant second with 20.4 per cent. What was to be done? The 'cabinet of barons' was in a fix. It could still rely on only 10 per cent of votes; 90 per cent had voted for the various opposition parties.[9] Governing against the majorities in parliament and in the population no longer seemed like a viable option in the long term, given that on the margins the country appeared to be on the brink of civil war. And the Papen cabinet had basically thrown away the tolerant acceptance of the Social Democrats.

When Schleicher understood that Fränzchen, as he called his friend Papen, would not be able to keep Hitler out of power in the long term, he decided to come out of cover and risk going for the top job. He persuaded Hindenburg to drop Papen, and instead try him out as chancellor. In the meantime, Schleicher had come up with the idea of establishing a 'Querfront [cross-party front] of reasonable forces' – from moderate National Socialists to Christian trade unions – to force Hitler into the background. The project has often been mocked in retrospect, but one need only place oneself in

Schleicher's position to understand the logic. He had brought the most unlikely figures together in the past, after all.

Schleicher had been the closest colleague of Quartermaster General Wilhelm Groener, who had concluded the pact for mutual support between the army and the government with Friedrich Ebert at the beginning of the Republic. The post of quartermaster general was not as dusty as it sounds. It involved responsibility, among other things, for the logistical management of the army, including supplies and ordnance for 12 million soldiers.[10] Someone like Schleicher tended to be ridiculed by frontline soldiers as a 'desk-bound soldier', but that derision fails to take into account the importance of logistics in the age of material warfare. And the modernity of Schleicher's position was confirmed after the revolution when he was put in charge of communications, as we would call it today, for Groener and the Reichswehr. He had to establish a basic degree of trust between the generals and the democratic politicians. Schleicher got on with everyone. As a communication strategist he was the ideal candidate for the generally suspicious Reichswehr, even if he did not always fully earn their trust. Convinced that prejudice was pointless, Groener and Schleicher came to terms with the new Social Democratic rulers, without losing sight of their actual goal: the reconquest of the Wehrmacht's supremacy. Schleicher lobbied for the army and gradually strengthened its influence.

Ten years later, his experience in bringing different milieus together persuaded Schleicher that he might be able to tame the NSDAP by making it part of a coalition government and burdening it with responsibility. When that failed because Hitler had no interest in being appointed vice chancellor, he came up with the plan of splitting the NSDAP and establishing an alliance of forces at the left and right ends of the political spectrum and at an angle to the established camps – one last attempt to counter Hitler's claim to total control. The most obvious potential partner within the NSDAP was the party's head of organisation, Gregor Strasser, a pragmatic politician with some charisma, who objected to Joseph Goebbels and Hermann Göring's all-or-nothing approach after the results of the disappointing

November election. Within the narrow range offered by the NSDAP, Strasser was a relatively reasonable man, educated, artistically minded and with contacts in the trade unions. Carl von Ossietzky even described him in *Die Weltbühne* as a 'suave intellectual'.[11] Within the NSDAP, as an arch-enemy of the jealous and competitive Goebbels, he was on the 'left wing', the one more clearly opposed to capitalism. With Strasser as a possible vice chancellor, Schleicher hoped to be able to keep the unpredictable Hitler out of power. Hitler could go on making his speeches as a propagandist. But it never occurred to an arch-manipulator like Schleicher, fixated as he was on the quiet backrooms of power, that Hitler's role as an orator was essential precisely because of its mass impact.

However, Schleicher's *Querfront* concept seemed to have a chance, since it had effective propagandists within right-wing intellectual circles, particularly those around Hans Zehrer's *Die Tat*. The journal's vague and mythically charged vision of a new *Volk* community beyond traditional lines of right and left, to bring about a 'rebirth of the German *Volk* in the spirit of social justice', was related to the combative-sounding notion of the *Querfront* as theory is to practice. And as if to reinforce the concept of the *Querfront*, in November 1932 moderate National Socialists and Communists made common cause in response to Berlin's public transport strike. Red flags and swastikas were seen side by side on 3 November 1932 when workers of the Berlin transport services brought the capital's local transport system to a standstill. The strike was jointly supported and coordinated by the Nazi and Communist parties because it was tacitly directed at the SPD, which had strong influence in the management of Berlin's transport organisation. 'Our reputation among the workforce has risen dazzlingly within only a few days,' Goebbels was pleased to note after the end of the strike.[12] The alarmed bourgeoisie, it was assumed, would get over it in due course.

When von Papen could muster no tolerance for a minority cabinet after the November elections, and agreement was even clearly fading within his own cabinet, with a heavy heart Hindenburg swapped von Papen for von Schleicher on 3 December 1932.[13] The ministers remained the same, apart from two; all of them were independent or had left their parties, in line with Schleicher's concept of a non-ideological pragmatism. The appeal to 'well-intentioned forces' in the country to work together constructively held for a few days, but then unresolved conflicts reopened. The trade unions, which had initially seemed willing to follow Schleicher, could not agree with a policy that excluded the SPD and refused to support a government that refused to reverse the Prussian coup. Schleicher also encountered resistance on the right. The large landowners protested vehemently against his settlement policy, with which he planned to free the cities of unemployed people and deploy them in the east of the Republic instead of cheap Polish seasonal workers. Almost every suggestion was stubbornly blocked. Schleicher's efforts to make everyone happy led to everyone turning away; the opposites that he wanted to bridge in the spirit of goodwill remained bitterly unreconciled. Whether Schleicher was quite as trusting as he appeared remains a mystery even today. The idea of cross-party cooperation under the authoritarian supervision of the supposedly impartial army was defeated by the reality of the fundamental lines of conflict. 'Schleicher's critique of capitalism and socialism at the same time provided few clues to the actual intentions of the cabinet. The general tried to woo everyone and made everyone suspicious', is the concise summary of the historian Karl Dietrich Bracher.[14]

Things continued as before. The Reichstag met under police protection and at every session provided a bleak spectacle of offensive insults, forbidden demonstrations and fistfights. Hermann Göring, president of the Reichstag since August 1932, made every effort to abuse his office. He enjoyed the skirmishes and stirred them up as best he could. Some of the parliamentarians addressed each other as 'ragged mob', 'sub-humans', 'a pack'; Carl Gottfried Gok of the German National People's Party described parliamentarism as a 'hopelessly dead frog'.[15] In the session on 7 December there was a mass brawl in the chamber in which, once again, ashtrays, toilet seats, spittoons and a telephone were used as weapons.[16] A painful tragedy for any parliamentarian who was still even slightly interested in parliamentary democracy.

Schleicher's most glaring error was to have imagined that he could split the National Socialist Party. Strasser was defeated in the battle of power with Hitler, whose reputation had grown once again even among the pragmatic politicians of his own party, after Papen had won him the clear goodwill of some entrepreneurs and industrialists. How serious a challenge Strasser had presented him with is questionable. The fact that Hitler assured him in writing that he would stay out of any kind of political activity was of little use to Strasser: he was arrested in June 1934 and murdered by a group of SS men in Gestapo headquarters.

Schleicher had ultimately misjudged the weakness of 'Fränzchen'. Papen stopped at nothing in his efforts to drive Schleicher back out of the office of chancellor, but he was not about to go easily. Papen approached Hitler. It looked as if the only possible way of attaining the goal of ousting Schleicher would be to have Hitler appointed as chancellor, and himself appointed as vice-chancellor. So he invited Hitler to dinner, and organised a flattering reception with his aristocratic friends at the home of the Cologne banker Kurt Freiherr von Schröder. Behind Schleicher's back, Papen danced attendance around Hindenburg and tried to crack his resistance to Hitler, the 'Bohemian corporal'. It was vital that he succeeded in the end; Hindenburg was besotted with the elegant Papen. In his eyes he was the ideal chancellor, and he could easily imagine him at the top of the party. What if he gritted his teeth and accepted Hitler as chancellor with Papen as vice-chancellor, as a kind of counter-weight? The old man was in a bind. By 30 January 1933 Papen was back in office, this time as vice-chancellor under the new chancellor appointed by Hindenburg: Adolf Hitler.

*

Historians have given minutely detailed accounts of these last days during which the ground was laid for the Weimar Republic to be

handed over to Hitler. The many twists and turns of the ruses of
Papen and Schleicher have been examined in detail. The narrative of
the attempts to rein Hitler in at the last moment and keep him in
check is bitterly exciting and, sometimes in a tragic way, almost comical. The plan by a few dilettante noblemen to employ intrigues and
power-play to guide a society in turmoil, a society that was constantly
holding new elections and discussing its fate in the excitable mass
media, is the story of a quixotic enterprise on a grand scale, narrated
on a tiny stage, with the shouts of the crowd outside breaking through
only very occasionally.

But were Hindenburg, Papen and Schleicher the sole gravediggers
of democracy? If we focus too exclusively on the back rooms of
power, we risk ignoring the role of an equally important protagonist. The crucial part played by the crowd was clearly demonstrated
when it once again expressed its power by voting for a dictator.

Aside from the three aristocratic gentlemen in Berlin, the voters
in Lippe, a tiny state on the edge of North Rhine-Westphalia, would
be of fateful significance to the progress of events. There, on 15 January 1933, the last regional election of the Weimar Republic was held.
The election would have been utterly without importance had it not
followed on from the Nazi Party's election setback on 6 November.
But as things stood it became a test of the water, a landmark election
that attracted national attention. It would decide how much pressure there would be on Hindenburg to give in to Hitler. It was in the
hands of the residents of Lippe to decide whether the Nazis would
see their rise as unstoppable, or whether they would suffer even
greater losses.

The NSDAP went to work even more energetically than usual. It
had set up public-speaking schools across the country in 1928, and by
1930 thousands of trained public speakers were agitating in cities and
villages.[17] In Lippe, however, all of the leading Nazi Party members
engaged in the election, as if the capital were at stake. Hitler himself
delivered 17 speeches in 11 days in the diminutive state, flying in on a
plane in ultra-modern style. He dropped important appointments
with all kinds of influential people and instead solicited the favour of

Hitler on the election trail. He loved flying in by plane. Flight gave him a Germany-wide presence.

each of the 157,000 inhabitants. The most refined cabinet politics was powerless against such populism.

The NSDAP received 39.5 per cent of the vote, an incredible 36.1 per cent more than in the previous regional elections held in Lippe in 1929. From a propaganda point of view this was a triumph, but on closer reflection it was only a modest success given the insane resources that had been put into the election campaign. Six months previously, in July 1932, the party had achieved over 41 per cent of votes in the Reichstag elections here. Still, the NSDAP were able to celebrate their victory energetically, particularly since the SPD had suffered losses of 9 per cent against the elections four years previously, and this time achieved only 30.1 per cent of votes. The outcome of the election was enough to turn the mood of the Nazi Party around, to place Hindenburg and Schleicher under pressure again to set out their claims to power even more clearly, and put an end to their internal power struggles.

Hindenburg and Schleicher might have had a tiny chance of saving Germany by breaking the constitution and putting off the election until the times improved and the enthusiasm of the masses for Hitler had abated. 'In order to preserve the constitutional state, in Weimar's final crisis its defenders would have needed to contravene the letter of a constitution that was neutral towards its own validity', the historian Heinrich August Winkler wrote.[18]

One curious aspect of the undignified end of the Weimar Republic is that things were getting objectively better just as many people lost patience with it. Perhaps if some time had been won through delays and further emergency decrees, indulgence of the weaknesses of the system might actually have returned, and the most feverish radicalism might have subsided. It is much more likely that a considerable number of Germans were no longer willing to engage in a rational examination of their own situation. The awakening of Germany that Hitler had promised held the imagination of his followers in its clutches; it is barely possible to imagine that they would have given up this vision in favour of an acceptance of reality. A new kind of vertigo was on the way, and the portal to a new age, awaited with a religious tremor, had opened wide. 'The time can no longer be understood intellectually, one must bear it within oneself,' the right-wing revolutionary Hans Zehrer wrote in *Die Tat*.[19] An intellectual dismissing his intellect. Emotion was all that mattered.

14

The End: Chancellor Hitler

*I do not need to concern myself with justice. My only mission is to destroy
and exterminate, nothing more.*

Hermann Göring, 1933

Celebration and terror

By 30 January 1933 the time had come. President Hindenburg yielded
to the urging of Franz von Papen, the Junkers, large sections of heavy
industry and the deplorable third of the population that had voted
for the Nazi Party, and appointed Hitler as chancellor. Hitler's water
carrier Franz von Papen became his deputy. Hitler, Papen and Hindenburg, along with Alfred Hugenberg of the German National
People's Party and the *Stahlhelm* association of former frontline soldiers, had been busy sizing up the rest of the cabinet. Apart from the
chancellor, the NSDAP had only two ministers, although those two
were crucial to the party's goals: the former minister for the state of
Thuringia, Wilhelm Frick, was made minister of the interior; Hermann Göring, as 'minister without portfolio', provisionally minister
of the interior for Prussia.

Outwardly it looked as if the three NSDAP cabinet members were
surrounded by rather more moderate forces. With his two interior
ministers, however, Hitler controlled the formulation of laws regarding domestic security and was in command of the police. He had

everything he needed to remodel Germany in such a way that the next election, set for March of that year, would be an even more convincing victory for him.

Three upholstered armchairs had been acquired for the official photographs of the new cabinet. One in the middle for the chancellor, one on either side for Papen and Göring, with the rest of the government gathered awkwardly behind them. Hitler appeared energised; he was the only one who didn't properly fill his chair, half sitting but looking as if he was ready to leap to his feet. Rather than being pleasurably enthroned, he was trying to make a committed impression for the camera, turning now to Göring, now to Papen, as if he were engaged in intense conversation, energetically fulfilling his role from the very first second.

After that brief session, Hitler and his henchmen withdrew to the Kaiserhof Hotel. They were on their own at last, without the tedious

After Hitler's appointment as Chancellor on 30 January 1933 he presented his cabinet. Hitler himself, Göring (left) and Papen (right) were given chairs, while all the others had to settle for being extras.

old gentlemen of the cabinet, whom they would have to put up with for another few weeks. Hitler 'says nothing', Goebbels said later in his diary, 'and we say nothing either. But his eyes are filled with water. The time has come!'[1]

In the evening, Hitler watched the quickly organised, perfectly orchestrated mass procession outside the chancellor's palace. In endless, precisely ordered rows, his major asset passed by in front of him: the masses without whom he would have been nothing. Hitler had understood and defeated democracy. The next day, he set about getting rid of it.

At Hitler's request, President Hindenburg dissolved the Reichstag on 1 February; new elections were set for 5 March. This period without a parliament would be bridged by meetings of the committee for foreign affairs and the supervisory committee – the latter was the only remaining instrument of parliament left to control the government. The first meeting was like a cabinet of horrors. The Nazis did everything they could think of to intimidate the deputies who had assembled on 7 February as they were summoned to do; during the debates, they addressed them using deliberately hateful language – 'swine', 'rogue', 'Jewish pig', 'swinish Jew', 'servant of the Jews'. The SPD member of parliament Wilhelm Hoegner experienced the second session of the committee as follows:

No sooner had Löbe [Paul Löbe, Social Democratic chair of the committee] opened the session than the National Socialists began roaring horribly. Member of parliament Edmund Heines [NSDAP] incessantly brought his fist down on the table. Dr Frank [NSDAP], the deputy chair, walked up to Löbe, shoved him violently aside, grabbed the presidential bell and to the loud applause of his fellow Partymembers declared the session closed. [. . .] As he left the room deputy Morath of the German People's Party was struck in the face by a National Socialist and nudged in the back. We informed the press, but no lawyer dared to request the lifting of immunity for the National Socialist criminals. The President of the Reich and the President of the Reichstag remained silent.[2]

The NSDAP had made no secret of the fact that they would trample the rights and dignity of their opponents as soon as they came to power. Exactly two years before, in February 1931, Joseph Goebbels had declared to the Reichstag that adhering to the Constitution was only a temporary, tactical manoeuvre: 'The National Socialist movement remains in a combative stance towards this system. [. . .] According to the Constitution we are committed to the legality of the way, but not to the legality of the goal. We want to conquer power legally. But what we do with that power once we possess it is up to us.'[3]

No one could have claimed that Hitler had pulled the wool over his voters' eyes. The 1920 party programme had demanded that the Jews be stripped of their citizenship, and that they be 'excluded' from the Volk community. The abolition of a free press and free speech for dissidents had been on the Nazi agenda from the outset. The programme had demanded a 'legal campaign against those who propagate deliberate political lies',[4] a concept that scarcely bothered to conceal its latent tyranny: 'Newspapers transgressing against the common welfare will be suppressed.'[5]

These principles were promptly put into action. The 'President's Emergency Decree for the Protection of the German People', passed on 4 February, legitimised the ban on gatherings for Communists and prohibited KPD and SPD newspapers. Even before, their editors had regularly received 'visits' from the SA, and now the terror was organised by the state. Prussia's new interior minister Göring appointed 50,000 members of the SA, the SS and the Stahlhelm as armed 'auxiliary police' to function alongside the regular police. This put the regular police more immediately under his control. 'Shilly-shalliers' and 'unreliable elements' were promptly reported and suspended. Social Democrats and Communists were declared fair game by the state. Göring's instructions to the police in this matter were unambiguous:

The activities of organisations hostile to the state are to be treated with the greatest harshness. Police officers who make use of firearms in the exercise of their duties will be covered by me without regard for the consequences of that firearm use. Anyone who fails by demonstrating false caution, on the other hand, may expect disciplinary consequences.

That amounted to an order to shoot; almost any kind of despotism against supposed enemies of the state was now sanctioned.

Private individuals also knew that they could, broadly speaking, engage in terrorist activity against the left with impunity. The 17-year-old student who shot the mayor of Stassfurt near Magdeburg in February 1933 was acquitted after a brief hearing. Justice seemed to be blind in its right eye only. Just a few judges, lawyers and police officers objected to state terrorism and insisted on due process.

The managers of city theatres were forced to fire Jewish colleagues and actors, and take politically critical plays off their programmes. The list of forbidden books was constantly growing, and bookshops and libraries were combed for 'disruptive' writing. At Breslau University the legal scholar Ernst Joseph Cohn abandoned a lecture that he was due to give after right-wing students threatened to defenestrate anyone who came to listen.[6]

That spring the Prussian police made 25,000 arrests on the instructions of the new rulers. Those do not include the arrests by the SA and the SS, as their number cannot be established.[7] Soon the regular prisons were not big enough to house the many prisoners. The first assembly camps and torture rooms were set up – often in the middle of residential areas. The fact that neighbours could hear the screams of the victims was in the opinion of many historians intentional. Particularly in working-class districts, it meant that people could be intimidated and further resistance stifled. When the Dutchman Marinus van der Lubbe set fire to the Reichstag on the night of 27 February 1933, it fell into the lap of the new regime like a gift. The claim that Communists had set parliament alight as a signal for a coming uprising was right at hand and provided an opportunity for state terror to be stepped up.

Over the days that followed, more than 5,000 people were arrested in Prussia – Social Democrats, Communists, several artists. In a public speech in Essen on 3 March, Göring announced that the constitutional state was in ruins: 'My measures will not be crippled by any kind of legal concerns. I do not need to concern myself with justice. My only mission is to destroy and exterminate, nothing more.'[8]

Those who had the opportunity to do so slowly began to flee. People who had until recently felt that they were still honoured and respected were bewildered to discover that they were now considered undesirable, fair game. Even Heinrich Mann reluctantly admitted that he had to escape. So as not to arouse suspicion he left his Berlin apartment carrying only his umbrella. His wife Nelly went a different way and brought a small suitcase to his train. The next day he crossed the border at Kehl on the Rhine, creeping stealthily out of the country. One of the most important writers in Germany must for once have been pleased not to be recognised.[9]

Meanwhile his brother Thomas, accompanied by his wife Katia, was on a lecture tour, talking about Wagner. From Paris, the final stage of the tour, he travelled on to Arosa in Switzerland to recover. Once there he received numerous communications warning him not to return to Germany. His daughter Erika arrived, at great speed as usual, in her Ford car and described the menacing situation to her parents. She had brought with her the half-finished manuscript of her father's novel *Joseph and His Brothers* and a considerable amount of research material. Consequently, the decision to remain in Switzerland was an easy one.

Even though very few people were able to rearrange their lives quite as easily and as quickly as the polyglot Nobel laureate, thousands decided to leave Germany as quickly as possible. In those first weeks of Nazi rule, 30,000 people went into exile;[10] about half a million people would go on to leave their homeland, often at the last moment. Most of them, about 85 per cent, were of Jewish descent.

From chancellor to Führer as a result of 'heart-breaking disunity'

The new elections were held on 5 March – overshadowed by an average of five deaths a day from political attacks and clashes, and arrests and bans on newspapers and assemblies. Once again, all the stops had been pulled out for the chancellor's election campaign. Public speakers had moved from village to village, hanging up thousands of posters showing Hitler next to Hindenburg as a way of suggesting continuity. 'Down with the system of permanent discord: one *Volk*, one Führer, one yes!' huge letters roared from the walls of the houses. The evening before the election, the Berlin SA organised torchlight processions. The columns were led by SA men on motorcycles carrying torches. At the rallying points the crowd listened to the speech that Hitler was delivering in Königsberg, broadcast live on all radio stations. Hitler presented himself as a chancellor of unity. For 'reconstruction' to take place, it was crucial that everything divisive be overcome. It was essential 'supreme nationalism' and 'supreme socialism' be investigated to find their common root.[11]

Ullstein's *Berliner Morgenpost*, with the biggest circulation in the city, appeared defiantly on polling Sunday with the pro-Republic headline 'Unity and law and freedom', and the encouraging assurance: 'Electoral freedom is secure!' Anyone who saw the many marching SA men outside the polling stations might have had their doubts about this, but in fact the vote was protected and held in secret. Almost 90 per cent of those eligible to vote turned out. For those who had hoped that some Hitler enthusiasts might have had their eyes opened by the acts of terror, the result was shattering. The NSDAP vote rose once again by 10.8 per cent to almost 44 per cent, allowing the next day's newspapers to carry the headline 'Clear government majority!' – a novelty in what seemed like an eternity.

However, the NSDAP had fallen short of their actual goal of achieving an absolute majority. That would only be achieved by joining forces with the far-right 'Black-White-Red Battle Front', the electoral alliance between the *Stahlhelm* association and Alfred Hugenberg's German National People's Party, which had achieved 8 per cent of the vote.

Despite the massive campaign of intimidation and persecution, the Social Democrat vote remained almost stable at 18.3 per cent, only about 2 per cent down on the vote four months previously. Voters for the KPD proved more disloyal. It lost 4.6 per cent and scraped just over 12 per cent. According to various analyses, many of the new voters for the Nazi Party came from the KPD. Plainly almost a quarter of former KPD voters didn't object to Hitler having Communists persecuted, beaten and murdered.

'A wonderful, unexpected, intoxicating victory! Majority at last!' the teacher Luise Solmitz cheered in her diary.

> The soul of our people is in him, on him, with him. [. . .] Hitler is the son of simple people and barely has a basic education: but what a natural leader he is! Something that cannot be achieved by desire or ability, by education or studiousness, nor yet by rank and class.[12]

It was not economic hardship, nor humiliation by the Versailles Treaty, that made people like Luise Solmitz sink into Hitler's arms, but an intoxicating sense of unity that was open to the greatest variety of expectations and hopes for salvation among those most in need of consolation. Almost any part of his speeches selected at random reveals just how skilfully Hitler was able to play on the keyboard of the collective psyche, to cement his charismatic mastery. Take his governmental declaration 'Appeal to the German People', delivered on 1 February 1933, two days after his appointment, in which he introduced himself as chancellor in a radio address. In a calm voice and without the familiar shouting, he presented himself as the liberator of a nation in a state of discord from which God had withdrawn his blessing because it had forgotten itself. He interpreted political power relations in archaic, emotional categories and combined them with the lament of a lost cultural identity into an emotional mixture of self-pity and sentimentality in which even the hardest of hard cases suddenly seemed in need of salvation. As always, he began his indictment with a reference to the 1918 November Revolution:

> Over fourteen years have passed since that unhappy day when the German people, blinded by promises made by those at home and abroad, forgot the highest values of the past, of the Reich, of its honour and its freedom, and thereby lost everything. Since those days of treason, the Almighty has withdrawn his blessing from our nation. Discord and hatred have moved in. Filled with the deepest distress, millions of the best German men and women from all walks of life see the unity of the nation disintegrating in a welter of egotistical political opinions, economic interests and ideological conflicts.
>
> As so often in our history, Germany, since the day revolution broke out, presents a picture of heart-breaking disunity. We did not receive the equality and fraternity which was promised us; instead we lost our freedom.

He and his comrades-in-arms had been called by the 'venerable World War leader', meaning Hindenburg, 'to fight under him once again, as once we did at the front, but now loyally united for the salvation of the Reich at home'.[13]

These sonorous words were spoken by a wolf in sheep's clothing, who did not balk at the mendacity of arguing for the preservation of peace, the integration of Europe and worldwide disarmament. It isn't hard to imagine how this vision of a united, confident nation might have inspired people who were weighed down by worry, since the new chancellor seemed to possess the magnetic power required to bring a divided nation to its feet and act as its leader. A feeling of joy flowed through them, because 'nothing had left the nation so downcast as its lack of leadership' – as an SA man by the name of Günther Goretzky put it in a report for an American competition in which he was supposed to give an account of why he had become a National Socialist.[14]

Many people voted for Hitler because so many others did. It sounds banal, but it was a fundamental part of his charismatic leadership.

Without seeing himself reflected in the mass, Hitler was nothing. The breathtaking resonance of the crowd, the experience of the euphoric affirmation of his followers, brought Hitler more and more worshippers and his following went viral. Onlookers were thrilled by the sight of marching columns. 'We were intoxicated with enthusiasm, dazzled by the light of the torches right in front of our faces, always in their haze, as if in a sweet cloud of incense', Luise Solmitz wrote in her diary.

> And in front of us were men, men, men, brown, colourful, grey, brown, a flood that lasted for an hour and 20 minutes. In the flickering light of the torches, it was as if one saw only a few recurring types, but there were between 22 and 25,000 different faces.

Torchlight procession in the evening along the Kurfürstendamm after the election of 5 March 1933.

The spectators at the edge saw the march of the united crowd as a real-life metaphor: a way out of the crisis, out of inner and outer disunity, and felt carried along.[15] From that moment of 'awakening' onwards, the opportunity for argument had gone – the dissident was merely a spoilsport, a 'stranger to the *Volk* community', as Luise Solmitz put it, the woman who voted for Hitler even though she had a Jewish husband.

Democracy abolishes itself

Three weeks after the election on 5 March the members of the new Reichstag held their second meeting. Because of the fire damage, it was held directly opposite in the Kroll Opera House in Berlin. On the agenda was Hitler's 'Law to Remedy the Distress of the People and Reich', also known as the Enabling Act. This was intended to give the government the right to make laws independent of parliament and without regard for the constitution and constitutional rights. Because this meant a change to the constitution, a two-thirds majority of the Reichstag was required to pass it.

The KPD was not present; all of their members of parliament had been arrested or murdered, gone into hiding or fled. Twenty-six SPD representatives were in 'protective custody' or on the run, and 94 appeared for the vote in spite of the massive intimidation by thousands of armed brownshirts. They had to walk past hundreds of SA men even to reach the parliamentary session. For Social Democrat MP Wilhelm Hoegner the walk to the building meant running the gauntlet: 'Young lads with swastikas on their chests looked us impudently up and down, blocked our path [. . .] and called out insults like "centrist swine', 'Marxist pig".'[16] SA men stood around in the chamber itself, hissing insults near the SPD members, their hands resting provocatively on their pistols.

In spite of the frightening atmosphere, the SPD voted unanimously against the Enabling Act. The SPD chair Otto Wels stepped bravely forward and explained his party's approach in a lengthy

speech. It ended in the now famous words: 'They can take our freedom and our life, but not our honour.'

That did not apply to the Catholic Centre Party, which voted unanimously for parliament to be stripped of its power. A conscientious
minority of MPs around Heinrich Brüning had spoken out against
the acceptance of the Enabling Act, but in the end they submitted to
party discipline. The Catholics hoped for vague opportunities to play
a part, or at least to be treated sparingly by the new regime, after
Hitler had given an assurance in his address that he was concerned to
ensure a good relationship between church and state. Some MPs
feared for their lives, others didn't want to 'stand aside during the
national upheaval'. The SPD member Fritz Baade recalled 'that
members of the Centre faction [. . .] came to me weeping and said
they had been convinced that they would have been murdered if they
had not voted for the Enabling Act'.[17] They christened this opportun-
ism 'the National Assembly'. That was how the chair of the Catholic
Centre Party, the priest Ludwig Kaas, explained his party's vote with
a clear message of conformity: 'The present hour cannot be governed
by words, its only ruling law is that of the swift, constructive and
redeeming deed. And that deed can be born only in the Assembly.' To
save face, the priest disguised his declaration of submission as a grand
gesture of reconciliation: 'In this way we of the German Centre Party
extend a hand to everyone, including our former opponents, in order
to ensure the continuation of the work towards the rise of the
nation.'[18] The process can be seen as prototypical for the way in which
the Hitler-critical elites made their peace with the new chancellor.
Cobbling together a semblance of self-respect, they put themselves at
the disposal of the 'work towards the rise of the nation' – and they
became experts at dressing up their humiliating genuflections in
fancy language.[19]

With the acquiescence of the Centre and the smaller bourgeois
parties, the Enabling Act was passed with the necessary two-thirds
majority, and democracy was abolished in an apparently democratic
way. 'Now we are also the masters of the Reich in constitutional terms,'
Joseph Goebbels wrote in his diary on the same evening. This was false,

in fact, because the vote had been made under the threat of physical violence and did not therefore conform to the constitution. But duty had been done to the illusion that democracy had willingly abolished itself. Hitler had taken the legal route, which he had pursued to the frustration of many of his party colleagues, right to the end.[20]

As the parliamentary session leading to the Enabling Act progressed, it became clear what the tone of government was going to be like over the coming years. With his usual mixture of self-pity, cynicism and aggression, Göring, leader of the session in his capacity as Reichstag president, railed in his concluding speech against the supposedly libellous press of the Social Democrats and Communists who had gone into exile:

My dear Social Democrats, for the last few days I have been reading the press of your fellow Party members abroad: no press has ever reported more shamelessly, with less humanity; dragged through the mud, pulled through the dirt, the men who are governing the German people today are sullied as disgraceful idiots, as provocateurs, as shabby ne'er-do-wells. You speak of humanity, and your press in Scandinavia is still slandering my own dead wife!

Anyone could travel through Germany, Göring continued, and see:

There are no looted or ruined shops [. . .] not a department store that has been destroyed or robbed or damaged! Go through all the big stores: you will see that those gentlemen are still able to make their profits. [. . .] Look at the prisons, ask Herr Thälmann, Herr Torgler whether anything at all has happened.[21]

Three weeks previously the chair of the KPD, Ernst Thälmann, had been arrested, and throughout the course of the year he was interrogated and tortured many times. Early in 1934 he had several teeth knocked out while being questioned in Gestapo headquarters and was beaten with a rhinoceros whip. The chair of the KPD faction in parliament, Ernst Torgler, who had been in prison since the

Reichstag fire, sat in chains day and night in Moabit remand prison. Meanwhile, Göring continued his speech by mocking the flight of the comrades from the KPD:

> If Herr Thälmann appears depressed about the fact that his followers are running away in their thousands, that is not down to us. In the end I cannot bear any special responsibility for cheering him up. Nothing has happened to those people. If one or other of us should boil over with rage and defend himself at last against the persecution and the attacks – yes, gentlemen, you cannot demand that we put up with being slaughtered, as we would have had to under your system. [. . .] If various of your MPs were taken into protective custody, be grateful to me for doing that, because the people's fury about all that you have done in those fourteen years was so great, so grand, that one might say: if the people had acted according to their sense of justice, you would not be sitting here.[22]

Germany, Göring claimed in conclusion, had never been more peaceful. With those words he ushered the members of parliament into the Third Reich.

*

With the constitutional rights of parliament, the last residue of 'Weimar' had disappeared, even if life in the street looked almost as it always had done, apart from the swastika flags that disfigured the cityscape. Step by step the once diverse society was transformed into a *Volk* community, expelling 'as enemies of the people' those who were needed to hold the insane construct together.

'How long will I remain in office for?' the Jewish professor of Romance languages wrote in his diary on 10 March 1933. 'Complete revolution and party dictatorship', he noted.[23] 'And all the opposing forces appear to have vanished from the earth. This complete collapse of a power that was present only recently, no, its complete disappearance is shattering to me.'[24] Another Jewish colleague's maid handed in her notice, 'Käthe, the good Slav. She has been offered a secure position, she says, and Herr Professor will soon not be in a position to keep staff.'[25] It was the small events that built up into a hopeless situation and, step by step, harassment after harassment, ended in annihilation.

At this point, no one could have imagined that in the coming descent into hell National Socialism would cost the lives of 60 million people, including 6 million murdered European Jews and 12 million murdered Soviet civilians. In spite of the brutality already seen in the interrogation rooms, the terrible crimes of the regime, for which the term 'collapse of civilisation' is an understatement, were still unimaginable. Germans who were not themselves threatened by persecution felt boosted by the 'National Rising' and expected glorious years to come. During the early years of the 'Third Reich', anyone skilled at turning a blind eye and ignoring their conscience saw good times ahead. It was still possible to feel part of a civilised nation if one didn't take the fanatical screeching of the Nazis too seriously. One only had to look the other way when one's Jewish neighbour was being beaten and dragged off, and keep oneself from wondering what would happen to him.

Many of the innovations arising out of the Weimar Republic continued to exist for a time. To outward appearances, even Berlin's exciting nightlife persisted. The dance palaces remained open, although with more boring music. Haus Vaterland, at first still in the 'Jewish ownership' of the Kempinski family, stayed open. The Black and Jewish artists were dismissed, the troupe of girl dancers dissolved. The Kempinski business was gradually 'Aryanised' and incorporated within the 'racially pure' Aschinger company.

Entertainment became simpler, more 'völkisch', which also meant that it became cheaper. The Nazi leisure organisation 'Strength through Joy' turned travel, hitherto a middle-class privilege, into an affordable popular pastime. Those reluctant to take part in this emphatically egalitarian community life, however, could also present themselves as distinguished and ultra-modern, as long as they did not appear 'alien' or socialist. Even the visually advanced lifestyle magazine *Die neue Linie* was still published; its Bauhaus-trained layout artist Herbert Bayer softened its avant-garde look only slightly. In the November issue, the architect Peter Behrens argued for the recognition of modern styles as part of the 'fascist building ethos'. He referred to Mussolini's Italy, where Mies van der Rohe, Erich Mendelsohn and Walter Gropius had been assigned a place of honour at the 1933 Milan Triennale. It was a fact, Behrens wrote, 'that the modern style of building created in Germany – but which still struggles to find recognition here – has been elevated to the official architectural style of fascism in Rome'.[26] Even Mickey Mouse remained a presence, and there were advertisements for Coca-Cola across the whole of Germany. An advertisement for the American drink even appeared in the magazine *Die Wehrmacht* in 1938, recommending that soldiers have 'a refreshing break with ice-cold Coca-Cola'.[27]

In the same year a confident Marlene Dietrich, who had emigrated to Hollywood long before and was consequently subject to frequent attacks in the National Socialist press, appeared on the cover of *Das Magazin*, giving the reader a challenging look.[28]

Despite the official imposition of conformity, there were contradictions in the Nazi aesthetic. Hitler himself favoured a sans-serif font, even the Bauhaus-inspired Futura script; it came closest to his ideal of monumental modernity.[29] He had no time for the gnarly gothic script that harked back to an older Germany; racist ideas were to be conveyed in a plain and ultramodern typeface. And from a practical point of view the sober Futura script was useful in the service of brutal power: people in the occupied territories found it easier to read orders and instructions in Futura than in old German letters.

These may seem like irrelevant details, but they show that the modernity of the Weimar Republic, which so many Nazis hated, was not simply eliminated from one day to the next. National Socialism in fact saw itself as being at the cutting edge and managed to bring the anti-modern, backwoods parts of its following into line with the furious modernism of an authoritarian, achievement-oriented society. The Nazi regime presented itself as a modern welfare state that promised affluence for all *Volksgenossen* (national comrades), pushed

for first-class performance in its technologies, and eradicated snobbish differences of class and social status. Internal contradictions
were blurred by a shared expectation of salvation, which required
everyone to be in permanent combat mode.[30] This temporary reconciliation of agrarian romantics and modern social technocrats was
accomplished on the back of fanatical racial hatred. The despised
qualities of the modern age were attributed to the Jews, who were
then persecuted with the most up-to-date means of bureaucratic
registration and administration. Their ostracism was accompanied
by a horrific dynamic of violence leading ultimately to systematic
murder – the phantom *Volk* community could only mask the real contradictions by feeding its arrogance with constantly growing
aggression. The construction of 'aliens' to be ruthlessly excluded and
persecuted would lead to a campaign of extermination that left few
spots on the earth untouched.

At the same time, the morally bankrupt country basked in the
glow of a nation with a thriving cultural life. The National Socialist
state spent more than a quarter of its culture subsidies on theatre.[31]
Rather than the 'degenerate' excesses of the Weimar era, supposedly
staged only for a decadent cultural elite, most performances now
were plays by Schiller, Goethe and Kleist in edifying productions that
everyone could understand. And the move was successful: between
1938 and 1940 audience numbers rose by a third to 40 million.[32] Joseph
Goebbels was pleased to note: '*Volk* and theatre are now two concepts that complement and condition one another.'[33] In 1940, Hitler
ordered the Wagner festival in Bayreuth to continue even during the
war, and at the same time opened it up to new audience sectors:
'rather than bourgeois listeners in solemn dress, workers and soldiers
brought to the Green Hill [the nickname of Bayreuth Festival Hall] at
the expense of the state'.[34]

*

In 1930 it was still almost impossible to imagine the earth-shaking
scale on which the National Socialists would put their plans for

Germany's awakening into action. In that year, Marlene Dietrich recorded one of the most beautiful songs composed by Friedrich Hollaender, the great Jewish revue and film composer of the 1920s: 'Wenn ich mir was wünschen dürfte' – 'If I Were Granted a Wish'. It is about the joy of ambivalence – a melancholy, deeply anti-utopian, very short song. In a thoughtful voice, almost a whisper, Dietrich sings about the opposite of high-altitude euphoria, the idea of just being 'a bit happy'. In retrospect, what luxury!

> *Wenn ich mir was wünschen dürfte,*
> *Käm ich in Verlegenheit,*
> *Was ich mir den wünschen sollte,*
> *Eine schlimme oder gute Zeit.*
>
> *Wenn if mir was wünschen dürfte,*
> *Möchte ich etwas glücklich sein,*
> *Denn wenn ich gar zu glücklich wär',*
> *Hätt ich Heimweh nach dem Traurigsein.*
>
> If I were granted a wish,
> I would be at a loss,
> About whether I should wish
> For good times or bad.
>
> If I were granted a wish,
> I would like to be a bit happy,
> Because if I were too happy
> I would be homesick for sadness.

That's how wise, how realistic, how coquettish the Weimar Republic could sound.

Epilogue

When Adolf Hitler seized power, some people benefited temporarily, while for others it meant the beginning of hell on earth. Some fled.

The celebrated society photographer *Frieda Riess*, with whom this book began, had already moved to Paris with the former French ambassador Pierre de Margerie. After the German occupation of France, the influential Margerie helped her to conceal her identity. When he died in 1942, she was left unprotected and largely destitute in Paris. Little is known about her last years, not even the exact date of her death. The woman who once enriched the social life of Berlin died alone in Paris some time in 1957.

Philipp Scheidemann, who had proclaimed the Republic on 9 November 1918, fled the SA to Salzburg early in March 1933, before travelling on to Prague. In May 1933 his eldest daughter and his son-in-law escaped the torment of the Nazi authorities by committing suicide. Scheidemann died in November 1939 in Copenhagen, where he had spent the last years of his exile in impoverished circumstances.

Theodor Wolff, the editor-in-chief of the liberal *Berliner Tageblatt*, first went into Swiss exile and later bought a house in Sanary-sur-Mer on the Côte d'Azur, to which many emigrants had fled. In May 1943 he was arrested by Italian civilian police in Nice and handed over to the Gestapo. Seriously ill, he was transferred from Moabit prison in Berlin to the Jewish Hospital, where he died in September 1943.

Waldemar Pabst, involved to a great degree in the murder of Rosa Luxemburg and Karl Liebknecht as an officer of the 'Guards Cavalry

Riflemen Division' Freikorps, was able to make a career in the Nazi defence economy and rearmament office, in spite of the suspicion of having been a devotee of the murdered SA leader Ernst Röhm. In 1940 he founded an import–export firm, SFINDEX, which brokered arms deals between Switzerland and the Wehrmacht. He returned from Switzerland to the Federal Republic in 1955 and went on working as an arms dealer. He died wealthy in 1970, as a sympathiser of the far-right German National Democratic Party (*Nationaldemokratische Partei Deutschlands*, NPD).

At the start of the Second World War, *Ernst Jünger* was recruited into the Wehrmacht and from 1941 he served on the staff of the French Military Commander in Paris. He lived stylishly in the occupied Hôtel Raphael and, in charge of military intelligence and enemy observation, enjoyed life in the elegant circles of French cultural collaborators. He kept his distance from the NSDAP, refusing to allow the *Völkische Beobachter* to reprint his articles. Because of his contacts with resistance circles in the Wehrmacht he was dismissed as 'unworthy to bear arms'. Jünger died, still highly controversial, in 1998 at the age of 102.

Erich Maria Remarque had already been able to lay the foundations for a villa on the western side of Lake Maggiore in the Swiss canton of Ticino. During the war he lived in the USA, mostly depressed, drunk and chain smoking. Women loved him, however; Marlene Dietrich and Greta Garbo had affairs with him, and in 1958 he married the actress Paulette Goddard, the ex-wife of Charlie Chaplin – the poor orphan girl in the film *Modern Times*. He returned with her to his house on Lake Maggiore, where he died in September 1970.

Otto Dix, the fierce hyperrealist, lost his professorship at the Academy of Art in Dresden for 'violation of the moral sensibilities and subversion of the fighting spirit of the German people'. Having been categorised as a 'degenerate artist', he was barely able to earn a living, even though he had switched to uncontroversial landscape painting. Affluent citizens helped him through his difficulties with private commissions. Having joined the Volkssturm militia in 1945, Dix was taken prisoner by the French. After the war, having turned towards

Christian motifs, he followed neither the socialist realism of the GDR nor the abstract artistic currents of the Federal Republic. He died in Singen on Lake Constance in July 1969.

George Grosz emigrated to the USA in January 1933 and stayed there as a successful painter and draughtsman, although his work was stylistically very uneven and lost much of its focus without the direct provocation of the German environment. Despite the recognition of his works in the USA and a home on Long Island, he was plagued by depression, intensified by grim news from Germany. In the final weeks of the war, his mother was killed in a bombing raid on Berlin. His alcoholism worsened, particularly after the community of emigrants thrown together in New York began to fall apart. In 1950 he wrote in a letter to his brother-in-law about his old friend Walter Mehring: 'Mehring? My God, he lives in a coal hole in N.Y. If you want to turn into a basement-dwelling woodlouse there, you can. I barely see him these days.' Grosz, who did not decide to return to Germany until 1959, died on 6 July of the same year, when he fell drunkenly down the stairs.

After 1933 *Friedrich Muck-Lamberty*, probably the best known 'inflation saint' – the pejorative term applied to itinerant preachers during the 1920s and early 1930s – lived apart from the Nazi regime, which viewed his activities with a suspicious eye. He made craft products with his remaining followers in a workshop called the 'Naumburg Factory Brigade', winning clientele from all over Germany. In the late 1940s he moved to the Westerwald because he could find no support for his esoteric vision of applied arts in the GDR.

After the completion of her studies, *Friedl Dicker*, one of the most successful graduates of the Bauhaus, worked as an interior designer, painter and drawing teacher, and opened her own studio in Vienna in 1931. She turned early on to theories of art education and the interior design needs of children. She emigrated to Prague in 1936, was deported with her husband to the camp at Theresienstadt and murdered in Auschwitz on 9 October 1944. After the liberation of Theresienstadt, two suitcases were found containing the drawings of children whom Friedl Dicker had taught in the camp.

Leo Nachtlicht, the Jewish architect of the Haus Gourmenia, was unable to work from 1933 onwards. His request for a work permit in London was rejected. He died in 1942 at the age of 70 in the Jewish Hospital in Berlin, probably after a suicide attempt, while his wife was transported to Riga, where she was murdered.

Alfred Döblin, for whom Berlin was 'the soil of all his thoughts', remained enormously productive in French and American exile. None of his many novels achieved anything like the popularity of *Berlin Alexanderplatz*, however. When Döblin returned to Germany in 1945 in the service of the French miliary authorities to reorganise the country's cultural life, sometimes even appearing as a cultural officer in French uniform, his former admirers reacted with bewilderment. Embittered by the rejection of his compatriots, the author emigrated to Paris for a second time in 1953. He died in 1957 at the age of 78 in a clinic in Emmendingen. His wife took her life two and a half months later in Paris. They were both buried in Housseras in the Vosges, beside their son, who had shot himself there as a French soldier, separated from his comrades, as the German Wehrmacht approached in June 1940.

Joseph Roth left Germany on the day of Hitler's appointment as chancellor. His journey into exile, something of an odyssey, ended in Paris, where he died in 1939 after collapsing in his favourite café. Despite the most adverse conditions, the alcoholic author had managed to remain productive almost to the end. He could have been saved by Irmgard Keun, who met him in 1936 in Ostende. Unfortunately, the author of the novel *The Artificial Silk Girl* was just as dependent on alcohol as he was. Alarmed by his extreme jealousy, and unable to deal with his painful liver condition, she left the man she deeply loved a year before his death.

Irmgard Keun had attempted until 1936 to survive as an author in Germany. In 1935 she bravely brought a case against the Nazi state in a Berlin regional court for the confiscation of her books and demanded compensation. Of course she lost. Her application to the Reich Chamber of Culture, required for a publication permit, was rejected. In 1936 she went to Ostend in Belgium – 'without any

EPILOGUE 383

particular reason, I had to go somewhere'. There she began her passionate, tormented liaison with Joseph Roth. After two years with him, she moved to Amsterdam. When German troops invaded, she acquired a false identity with the help of an SS man who was in love with her and returned to Germany. After the war, she lived there temporarily in a shack on a ruined plot of land in Cologne. Her novel *Ferdinand, the Kind-Hearted Man* was published in 1950. Like her novel written in exile, *After Midnight*, however, it attracted little attention. Irmgard Keun's drinking landed her in a psychiatric hospital in 1966. The stepson of a former boyfriend tracked her down there in 1972 and made her fate public. A short time later she was released. Her 'rediscovery' began in the mid-1970s, and she was able to enjoy the revived popularity of her early works before dying in 1982 at the age of 77.

Egon Erwin Kisch, the 'dashing reporter', arrested immediately after the Reichstag fire, was released from prison on 11 March 1933 after an intervention by the Czechoslovak embassy. His Czechoslovak citizenship saved his life. After some time in Australia, France and the USA, Kisch lived in Mexico, where he co-chaired the Heinrich Heine Club, an emigrants' association, along with the writer Anna Seghers. Having returned to Europe, he died in Prague in 1948.

Arnolt Bronnen, the author who nimbly switched from far left to far right and back again, was subjected to a publishing ban in 1943 in spite of his friendship with Joseph Goebbels. Called up in 1944, he quickly deserted and joined Austrian resistance groups. In the confusion after the war, the Americans appointed him mayor of the village of Goisern in the Salzkammergut in Austria. After failed attempts to find success in Vienna, by now a member of the Austrian Communist Party, he moved to East Berlin in 1955, where his former friend Bertolt Brecht welcomed him into the Berliner Ensemble and won him a few commissions for the *Berliner Zeitung*. He died in 1959.

Louise Ebert, the former label-sticker in a Bremen cigar factory and first lady of the Republic, was left in peace after 1933 apart from two house searches. However, her two remaining sons – the two others had fallen in the First World War – were subject to severe harassment. The elder of the two, Friedrich Ebert Jr, editor of the *Brandenburger Zeitung* and an SPD member of parliament, spent eight months under arrest in 1933, until the London *Times* reported on his case. In 1943 Louise Ebert left Berlin because of the bombing raids and went to stay with relatives of her daughter-in-law in the Black Forest. At the end of 1945 she moved to Heidelberg, her husband's place of birth and also the site of his grave, where she died in 1955. Friedrich Ebert Jr became a member of the East German Socialist Unity Party (*Sozialistische Einheitspartei Deutschlands*, SED) and was, to the lasting annoyance of the West Berlin SPD, mayor of East Berlin from 1948 until 1967. His brother Karl Ebert became an SPD member of parliament in Baden-Württemberg in 1946 and remained so until 1964.

Edwin Redslob, the 'art guardian' of the Weimar Republic, worked under the Nazi regime as a freelance author and cultural historian. In 1940 he wrote the successful book *The Road of the Reich*, an account of the cultural history of the Via Regia Roman road leading from Frankfurt via Leipzig to Berlin. After the war, he became co-founder and publisher of the *Tagesspiegel* in Berlin in 1945. Redslob was one of the most vehement defenders of 'internal emigration', and he delivered a sharp attack against the exile Thomas Mann for considering all the literature published under the Nazi regime 'less than worthless', since it had a 'smell of blood and shame' attached to it. In 1949 Redslob briefly became rector of the Berlin Free University, where he was accused of appointing too many professors with a Nazi past. He died in Berlin in 1973.

Martin Wagner, the Berlin municipal building surveyor, unemployed after his dismissal in March 1933, became a city planning adviser in Istanbul in 1935 and a professor of city planning at Harvard University in 1938. In 1952 he travelled through Germany and was disappointed by the reconstruction and urban planning of the Federal Republic. He died in the USA in 1957.

Bruno Taut, attacked by the Nazis as a 'cultural Bolshevik' and stripped of his professorship, first sought refuge in Switzerland and then travelled to Japan, before becoming professor of architecture at the Academy of Arts in Istanbul. His final commission was the catafalque of Kemal Atatürk in 1938. He died of an asthma attack the same year.

Marcel Breuer, the co-inventor of the cantilever chair, fled to Hungary in 1933, later moved to Great Britain and finally, in 1937, to the USA, where he set up the architectural faculty at Harvard University with Walter Gropius. With his own architectural office, he developed striking buildings such as the Whitney Museum of American Art. He died in New York in 1981.

Paul Schultze-Naumburg, propagandist for the *Heimatschutz* style of architecture and a member of the Reichstag until 1945, came into conflict with the monumental architectural ideas of his Nazi colleagues. His plans for the redesign of Nuremberg Opera House in the *völkisch* style were considered too modest by those in power. Subsequently he was awarded no more significant commissions as an architect. He was still included in Hitler's *Gottbegnadete* ('Blessed by God') list drawn up in 1944. Schultze-Naumburg died in Jena four years after the war.

Christian Schad, the painter of *Sonja* in the Romanische Café, abandoned painting under National Socialism with a few exceptions, instead running a brewery from 1935 onwards. Later, he used his huge gifts in the old-master style to carry out commissioned work: he copied Matthias Grünewald's *Stuppach Madonna* for its original location in the Collegiate Church of St Peter and St Alexander in Aschaffenburg. Schad, whose work was rediscovered in the 1970s, died in Stuttgart in 1982.

Albertine Gimpel, the 'Sonja' of the painting of the same name by Christian Schad, was dismissed from the Berlin oil company Oex in 1933 because of her Jewish origins. In Munich, she became friends with the painter Franz Herda. The German-American rescued her and other Jewish Germans from the threat of deportation. The pair emigrated to New York, where they married in 1948. They returned to Germany in 1962. Albertine Herda died in 1978.

Ruth Landshoff-Yorck went on living as unconventionally in exile as she had in Berlin. In New York, largely without contact with the

German emigrant scene, she made a life for herself as an American author. Apart from the four novels she published in the USA, she also wrote stage plays for New York's off-Broadway scene, including *Lullaby for a Dying Man* in 1963, which addressed themes of homosexuality and the death penalty. She also wrote in German, translated American literature and published some works in Germany, but preferred to stay in New York, where she found an artistic scene that suited her in Greenwich Village. There she also worked for the famous avant-garde theatre La MaMa. She died of a heart attack in the foyer of the Martin Beck Theatre in New York on 19 January 1966.

Clärenore Stinnes, who between 1917 and 1929 became the first person to drive around the world, married the photographer and film maker Carl-Axel Söderström, who had accompanied her on the journey. Until the 1960s she ran a farm in Sweden belonging to the Stinnes families. She also occupied various directorial positions in the Swedish Red Cross and died in Björnlunda in 1990.

Leni Riefenstahl made the propaganda films *Victory of Faith*, *Triumph of the Will* and *Day of Freedom – Our Wehrmacht* for the Nazi regime. Later, with the 'Riefenstahl Special Film Unit', she filmed the invasion of Poland. In spite of her active participation in propaganda, she was ranked as a *Mitläufer*, a 'fellow traveller' who went along with the regime but was not an active participant, in the denazification process. After the war she had a successful career as a photographer. She photographed the Munich Olympic Games for the London *Sunday Times*. The newspaper also included her photographs of Bianca Jagger. Leni Riefenstahl died in 2003 at the age of 101.

Béla Balázs, Leni Riefenstahl's co-writer on the 1932 film *The Blue Light*, was unable, as a Jew and a communist, to return to what was now Nazi Germany after filming in Moscow. In 1945 he moved from Moscow to Budapest. His final film, for which he wrote the script, the 1947 *Somewhere in Europe*, is about a gang of children wandering through the post-war chaos of Hungary. Balázs died in Budapest in 1949.

Siegfried Translateur, who as a 17-year-old composed the *Sport Palace Waltz*, famously played at Berlin's six-day races, lost almost all opportunities to work because of his Jewish descent and had to sell his music publishing company. He was murdered in Theresienstadt in March 1944 at the age of 68.

Bayume Mohamed Husen, the Askari from Haus Vaterland, was dismissed in 1935 because a colleague claimed he had embezzled five marks. He went on to work on a touring exhibition devoted to the restoration of German colonies. At the start of the war in 1939 the former child soldier in the service of the Germans asked in vain to be readmitted to the Wehrmacht. In 1941 he was accused of 'racial shame' (*Rassenschande*) after a woman from Munich had a child by him. He died in Sachsenhausen concentration camp on 24 November 1944 as prisoner no. 39604.

Luise Solmitz, teacher and passionate diarist, for a time continued to worship Hitler even when her husband, the formerly highly decorated Reichswehr Major Friedrich Solmitz, was persecuted and bullied after revealing the Jewish identity that he had kept secret. He was forced to leave his nationalist associations, hand over his weapons and dismiss his maid. From 1943, he was pressed into forced labour. In constant fear that her husband would be deported, even Luise Solmitz eventually became an opponent of Hitler. The whole family survived. After the war, her daughter, raised as an anti-Semite, married a Jew, as her mother had done.

Yva, one of the most successful photographers of the Republic, refused to leave Germany after 1933, in spite of many warnings from her circle of Jewish friends. She went on working until 1938 in her studio, which was run for appearance's sake by an 'Aryan' friend. When she finally had to close the studio, she kept herself afloat as an X-ray assistant in the Jewish Hospital in Berlin. In 1942 she and her husband were arrested and deported to Sobibor extermination camp, where she was murdered on 15 June 1942.

August Sander was unable to continue his work on the documentary photographic project *People of the 20th Century* in the Nazi regime, and the touring exhibition *People of Our Time* was banned. He continued to run his Cologne studio, however, and in 1942 gradually moved it to the Westerwald. Even after the war his major project remained a fragment, but it still won international recognition as such. Sander died in Cologne in 1964.

Hans Zehrer, the head of the young conservative monthly journal *Die Tat*, was given short shrift when he attempted to offer his services to Hitler. *Die Tat* was banned in 1934. But Zehrer's earlier criticism of Hitler did not cost the representative of the concept of the *Querfront* (which was intended to prevent Hitler from becoming chancellor by involving 'moderate' members of the NSDAP) his life. In 1934 Zehrer withdrew to Kampen on the island of Sylt off the north coast of Germany, where he wrote the potboiler *Percy Goes Astray*. On Sylt he later met Axel Springer, who in 1953 made him editor-in-chief of *Die Welt*, which he went on running almost until his death in 1966.

Lotte Laserstein's career as a painter, which had begun promisingly, ended when the Nazis came to power. In 1937 she used an invitation to a solo exhibition in Stockholm as an opportunity to emigrate, taking 60 paintings with her. In Sweden, she made a living by painting commissions, which reveal little of her actual ability. She managed financially, however. At the age of 88, the forgotten artist was astonished to experience her rediscovery. An exhibition at Agnew's Gallery in London in 1987, to rave reviews, marked the beginning of her international recognition. Lotte Laserstein did in 1993 in Kalmar, Sweden.

Kurt von Schleicher, briefly chancellor of the Reich in the winter of 1932–3 and – like Zehrer – an advocate of the concept of the *Querfront*, retreated as an independent gentleman to his villa in Neubabelsberg. There, on 30 June 1934, he and his wife Elisabeth were murdered by six unidentified members of the SA and the SD.

Siegfried Kracauer, editor of the Berlin section of the *Frankfurter Zeitung*, wrote his last article for the paper on 28 February 1933, the morning after the Reichstag fire, before going into exile in Paris two days later. After the invasion by the German Wehrmacht, he fled adventurously to New York, where he wrote the sociological film investigation *From Caligari to Hitler* while working in the curatorial department of the Museum of Modern Art. In the long term he had no wish to return to Germany and ended up working as director of research at the Institute of Applied Social Sciences at Columbia University.

For his last article from Berlin, Kracauer had visited the burned-out Reichstag on the Spree, standing among people who gazed in silence at the ominous spectacle. There were children among them: 'More and more groups of school children mingle among the adults. They smell excitement and are innocently delighted by the sensation. When they grow up, they will learn from history what the Reichstag fire really meant.'

Bibliography

Abel, Theodore, *The Theodore Fred Abel Papers*, Hoover Institution, Stanford University, digitalcollections.hoover.org.

Aly, Götz, *Hitlers Volksstaat. Raub, Rassenkrieg und nationaler Sozialismus* (Frankfurt am Main, 2006)

Aly, Götz, *Unser Kampf 1968. Ein irritierter Blick zurück* (Frankfurt am Main, 2008)

Arenhövel, Alfons (ed.), *Arena der Leidenschaften. Der Berliner Sportpalast und seine Veranstaltungen 1910–1973* (Berlin, 1990)

Asmus, Gesine (ed.), *Hinterhof, Keller und Mansarde. Einblicke in Berliner Wohnungselend 1901–1920* (Reinbek bei Hamburg, 1982)

Austermann, Philipp, *Der Weimarer Reichstag. Die schleichende Ausschaltung, Entmachtung und Zerstörung eines Parlaments* (Vienna / Cologne / Weimar, 2020)

Baedeker, Karl, *Berlin und Umgebung. Handbuch für Reisende*, 20th edition (Leipzig, 1927)

Bahrdt, H.P., *Industriebürokratie* (Stuttgart, 1958).

Balázs, Béla, *Der sichtbare Mensch oder Die Kultur des Films* (Vienna / Leipzig, 1924)

Baum, Vicki, *Menschen im Hotel* (1929; Cologne, 2007)

Baum, Vicki, *Stud. chem. Helene Willfüer* (Berlin, 1928)

Baumunk, Bodo-Michael, 'Rhythmus im Hohlraum – Berlin in den Zwanziger Jahren', in Christian Mothes and Dominik Bartmann (eds), *Tanz auf dem Vulkan. Das Berlin der Zwanziger Jahre im Spiegel der Künste* (Berlin, 2015)

Bechhaus-Gerst, Marianne, *Treu bis in den Tod. Von Deutsch-Ostafrika nach Sachsenhausen. Eine Lebensgeschichte* (Berlin, 2007)

Becker, Frank, 'Autobahnen, Automobilität. Die USA, Italien und Deutschland im Vergleich', in Wolfgang Hardtwig (ed.), *Politische Kulturgeschichte der Zwischenkriegszeit 1918–1939* (Göttingen, 2005)

Becker, Sabina / Christoph Weiß (ed.), *Neue Sachlichkeit im Roman. Neue Interpretationen zum Roman der Weimarer Republik* (Stuttgart, 1995)

Beckers, Marion, Elisabeth Moortgat and Thomas Ehrsam (eds), *Die Riess. Fotografisches Atelier und Salon in Berlin 1918–1932* (Berlin / Tübingen, 2008)

Bellers, Jürgen, 'Radikalisierung und Polarisierung', in Werner Müller (ed.), *Die Welt spielt Roulette. Zur Kultur der Moderne in der Krise 1927 bis 1932* (Frankfurt am Main 2002)

Benjamin, Walter, *Das Kunstwerk im Zeitalter seiner technischen Reproduzierbarkeit. Drei Studien zur Kunstsoziologie* (Frankfurt am Main, 1970)

Benjamin, Walter, *Illuminationen. Ausgewählte Schriften 1* (Frankfurt am Main, 1977). English translation: *Illuminations*, trans. Harry Zohn with an introduction by Hannah Arendt, (London, 1973)

Benz, Wolfgang (ed.), *Dimension des Völkermords: die Zahl der jüdischen Opfer des National-sozialismus* (Munich, 1991)

Berger, John, *Understanding a Photograph. Essays*, ed. and with an introduction by Geoff Dyer (London, 2013)

Bergmann, Klaus, *Agrarromantik und Großstadtfeindschaft* (Meisenheim am Glan, 1970)

Biebl, Sabine, *Betriebsgeräusch Normalität. Angestelltendiskurs und Gesellschaft um 1930* (Berlin, 2013)

Biebl, Sabine, Verena Mund and Heide Volkening (eds), *Working Girls: Zur Ökonomie von Liebe und Arbeit* (Berlin, 2008)

Bienert, Michael (ed.), *Joseph Roth in Berlin. Ein Lesebuch für Spaziergänger* (Cologne, 1996)

Bienert, Michael and Elke Linda Buchholz, *Die Zwanziger Jahre in Berlin. Ein Wegweiser durch die Stadt* (Berlin, 2015)

Bisky, Jens, *Berlin. Biographie einer großen Stadt* (Berlin, 2019)

Bleitner, Thomas, *Frauen der 1920er Jahre. Glamour, Stil und Avantgarde* (Berlin, 2017)

Bliven, Jr, Bruce, *The Wonderful Writing Machine* (New York, 1954)

Blom, Philipp, *Die zerrissenen Jahre. 1918–1933* (Munich, 2016)

Bösch, Frank, 'Militante Geselligkeit. Formierungsformen der bürgerlichen Vereinswelt zwischen Revolution und Nationalsozialismus', in Wolfgang Hardtwig (ed.), *Politische Kulturgeschichte der Zwischenkriegszeit 1919–1939* (Göttingen, 2005)

Boveri, Margret, *Wir lügen alle. Eine Hauptstadtzeitung unter Hitler* (Olten, 1965)

Bracher, Karl Dietrich, *Die Auflösung der Weimarer Republik. Eine Studie zum Problem des Machtzerfalls in der Weimarer Republik* (Stuttgart/Düsseldorf, 1955)

Braune, Rudolf, *Das Mädchen an der Orga Privat. Ein kleiner Roman aus Berlin* (Frankfurt am Main, 1930)

Braune, Rudolf, *Junge Leute in der Stadt* (1932; Hanover, 2019)

Brecht, Bertolt, *Der Kinnhaken und andere Box- und Sportgeschichten*, ed. Günter Berg (Frankfurt am Main, 1995)

Brecht, Bertolt, *Nordseekrabben. Geschichten und Gespräche*, ed. Gerhard Seidel (Berlin, 1987)

Briesen, Detlef, *Warenhaus, Massenkonsum und Sozialmoral. Zur Geschichte der Konsumkritik im 20. Jahrhundert* (Frankfurt am Main / New York, 2001)

Broch, Hermann, *Die Schlafwandler. Ein Romantrilogie (1930–1932). Kommentierte Werkausgabe*, vol. 1, ed. Paul Michael Lützeler (Frankfurt am Main, 1994)

Broch, Hermann, *Die Schuldlosen. Roman in elf Erzählungen* (1950, Frankfurt am Main, 1974)

Bronnen, Arnolt, *O.S.* (1929; Klagenfurt/Vienna, 1995)

Brück, Christa Anita, *Schicksale hinter Schreibmaschinen* (Berlin, 1930)

Brückle, Wolfgang, 'Kein Porträt mehr? Physiognomik in der deutschen Bildnisphotographie um 1930', in Claudia Schmölders and Sander Gilman (eds), *Gesichter der Weimarer Republik. Eine physiognomische Kulturgeschichte* (Cologne, 2000)

Bud, Elsa Maria, *Bravo Musch!* (Berlin, 1931)

Bude, Heinz, *Das Gefühl der Welt. Über die Macht von Stimmungen* (Munich, 2016)

Buggeln, Marc and Michael Wildt (eds), *Arbeit im Nationalsozialismus* (Munich, 2014)

Bürger, Jan, *Im Schattenreich der wilden Zwanziger. Fotografien von Karl Vollmoeller aus dem Nachlass von Ruth Landshoff-Yorck* (Marbach, 2018)

Büttner, Ursula, *Weimar. Die überforderte Republik, 1918–1933. Leistung und Versagen in Staat, Gesellschaft, Wirtschaft und Kultur* (Stuttgart, 2008)

Conze, Vanessa, *Haus Vaterland. Der große Vergnügungspalast im Herzen Berlins* (Berlin, 2021)

Cowan, Michael and Kai Marcel Sicks (eds), *Leibhaftige Moderne. Körper in Kunst und Massenmedien 1918–1933* (Bielefeld, 2005)

Cziffra, Géza von, *Kauf dir einen bunten Luftballon. Erinnerungen an Götter und Halbgötter* (Munich/Berlin, 1975)

Dalbajewa, Birgit (ed.), *Neue Sachlichkeit in Dresden. Malerei der Zwanziger Jahre von Dix bis Querner* (Dresden, 2011)

Delabar, Walter, *Klassische Moderne. Deutschsprachige Literatur 1918–1933* (Berlin, 2010)

Derenthal, Ludger, Evelin Förster and Enno Kaufhold (eds), *Berlin in der Revolution 1918/1919. Fotografie, Film, Unterhaltungskultur* (Dortmund, 2018)

Döblin, Alfred, *Berlin Alexanderplatz* (1929; Frankfurt am Main, 1999). English translation: *Berlin Alexanderplatz*, trans. Michael Hofmann (London, 2019)

Döblin, Alfred, *Der deutsche Maskenball von Linke Poot. Wissen und Verändern!* (Olten/Freiburg im Breisgau, 1972)

Döblin, Alfred, *Kleine Schriften*, vol. 1 (Olten/Freiburg im Breisgau, 1985)

Döblin, Alfred, *November 1918. Eine deutsche Revolution* (1948; Munich, 1978)

Döblin, Alfred, *Schriften zu Leben und Werk* (Olten/Freiburg im Breisgau, 1986)

Dogramaci, Burcu, '"Frauen, die ihr Geld selbst verdienen", Lieselotte Friedlaender, der "Moden-Spiegel" und das Bild der großstädtischen Frau', *Querelles. Jahrbuch für Frauen- und Geschlechterforschung* 11: 'Garçonnes à la mode im Berlin und Paris der zwanziger Jahre' (2006)

Dogramaci, Burcu, 'Mode-Körper. Zur Inszenierung von Weiblichkeit in Modegrafik und -fotografie der Weimarer Republik', in Michael Cowan and Kai Marcel Sicks (eds), *Leibhaftige Moderne. Körper in Kunst und Massenmedien 1918–1933* (Bielefeld, 2005)

Donat, Helmut, 'Rebell in Uniform', *Die Zeit* 22 (2020)

Dreyer, Michael and Andreas Braune (eds), *Weimar als Herausforderung. Die Weimarer Republik und die Demokratie im 21. Jahrhundert* (Stuttgart, 2016)

Dreyfuss, Carl, *Beruf und Ideologie der Angestellten* (Munich/Leipzig, 1933)

Drommer, Günther, *Die Wahrheit der Bilder. Zeitgenössische Fotografien vom Leben des deutschen Volkes*, vol. 2: *Die ruhelose Republik. Alltag zwischen Gewalt und Hoffnung 1918–1933* (Berlin, 2004)

Eberhard, Erhard F.W. (ed.), *Geschlechtscharakter und Volkskraft. Grundprobleme des Feminismus* (Darmstadt/Leipzig, 1930)

Eckert, Georg, *Die Zwanziger Jahre. Das Jahrzehnt der Moderne* (Münster, 2020)

Ehmen, Sönke, *Nordwolle Delmenhorst. Nordwestdeutsches Museum für Industriekultur* (Oldenburg, 2010)

Ehrenburg, Ilja, *Das Leben der Autos* (Berlin, 1930)

Eichstedt, Astrid and Bernd Polster, *Wie die Wilden. Tänze auf der Höhe ihrer Zeit* (Berlin, 1985)

Eilenberger, Wolfram, *Zeit der Zauberer. Das große Jahrzehnt der Philosophie 1919–1929* (Stuttgart, 2018); English translation: *Time of the Magicians: The great century of philosophy 1919–1929*, trans. Shaun Whiteside (London/New York, 2020)

Encke, Julia, *Augenblicke der Gefahr. Der Krieg und die Sinne, 1914–1934* (Munich, 2006)

Enzensberger, Hans Magnus, *Hammerstein oder der Eigensinn* (Frankfurt am Main, 2008)

Evangelista, Stefano and Gesa Stedman (eds), *Happy in Berlin? Englische Autor*innen der 1920er und 30er Jahre* (Göttingen, 2021)

Fallada, Hans, *Kleiner Mann – was nun?* (1932; unabridged new edition Berlin, 2016). English translation: *Little Man, What Now?*, trans. Michael Hofmann, (London, 2019)

Fallada, Hans, *Wolf unter Wölfen* (1937; Berlin, 2011)

Falter, Jürgen W., *Hitlers Wähler. Die Anhänger der NSDAP 1924–1933* (Frankfurt am Main/New York, 2020)

Faulstich, Werner (ed.), *Die Kultur der 20er Jahre* (Munich, 2008)

Feilchenfeldt Breslauer, Marianne, *Bilder meines Lebens. Erinnerungen* (Wädenswil, 2009)

Ferber, Christian (ed.), *Berliner Illustrirte Zeitung. Zeitbild, Chronik, Moritat für jedermann 1892–1945* (Berlin, 1982)

Fest, Joachim, *Hitler. Eine Biographie* (Frankfurt am Main, 1973)

Feuchtwanger, Lion, *Erfolg* (1930; Berlin/Weimar, 1974)

Fiedler, Jeannine and Peter Feierabend (eds), *Bauhaus* (Potsdam, 2016)

Fischer, Joachim and Michael Makropoulos (eds), *Potsdamer Platz. Soziologische Theorien zu einem Ort der Moderne* (Munich, 2004)

Fleißer, Marieluise, 'Avantgarde', in *Fleißer, Gesammelte Werke*, vol. 3: *Gesammelte Erzählungen*, ed. Günther Rühle (Frankfurt am Main, 1972)

Fleißer, Marieluise, *Mehlreisende Friede Geier. Roman vom Rauchen, Sporteln, Lieben und Verkaufen* (Berlin, 1931); revised under the title *Eine Zierde für den Verein. Roman vom Rauchen, Sporteln, Lieben und Verkaufen* (1972; Frankfurt am Main, 1975)

Flierl, Thomas and Philipp Oswalt (eds), *Hannes Meyer und das Bauhaus. Im Streit der Deutungen* (Leipzig, 2019)

Fogt, Helmut, *Politische Generationen. Empirische Bedeutung und theoretisches Modell* (Wiesbaden, 1982)

Follmann, Sigrid, *Wenn Frauen sich entblößen . . . Mode als Ausdrucksmittel der Frau der zwanziger Jahre* (Weimar, 2010)

Föllmer, Moritz, 'Auf der Suche nach dem eigenen Leben. Junge Frauen und Individualität in der Weimarer Republik', in Moritz Föllmer and Rüdiger Graf (eds), *Die 'Krise' der Weimarer Republik. Zur Kritik eines Deutungsmusters* (Frankfurt am Main, 2005)

Föllmer, Moritz, *Die Verteidigung der bürgerlichen Nation. Industrielle und hohe Beamte in Deutschland und Frankreich 1900–1930* (Göttingen, 2002)

Föllmer, Moritz (ed.), *Sehnsucht nach Nähe. Interpersonelle Kommunikation in Deutschland seit dem 19. Jahrhundert* (Stuttgart, 2004)

Föllmer, Moritz and Rüdiger Graf (eds), *Die 'Krise' der Weimarer Republik. Zur Kritik eines Deutungsmusters* (Frankfurt am Main, 2005).

Förster, Evelin, *Die Frau im Dunkeln. Autorinnen und Komponistinnen des Kabaretts und der Unterhaltung von 1901 bis 1935. Eine Kulturgeschichte* (Berlin, 2013)

Frevert; Ute, 'Traditionale Weiblichkeit und moderne Interessenorganisation. Frauen im Angestelltenberuf 1918–1933', *Geschichte und Gesellschaft* 7/3–4, 'Frauen in der Geschichte des 19. und 20. Jahrhunderts' (1981)

Friedrich, Otto, *Morgen ist Weltuntergang. Berlin in den Zwanziger Jahren* (Berlin, 1998)

Fritz, Georg, 'Das Zeitalter der Verweiberung und Entartung', in Erhard F.W. Eberhard (ed.), *Geschlechtscharakter und Volkskraft. Grundprobleme des Feminismus* (Darmstadt/Leipzig, 1930)

Fritzsche, Peter, *Wie aus Deutschen Nazis wurden* (Zurich, 1999)

Führer, Daniel, *Alltagssorgen und Gemeinschaftssehnsüchte. Tagebücher der Weimarer Republik (1913–1934)* (Stuttgart, 2020)

Gall, Lothar, *Die Deutsche Bank 1870–1995. 125 Jahre deutsche Finanz- und Wirtschaftsgeschichte* (Munich, 1995)

Gallus, Alexander (ed.), *Die vergessene Revolution von 1918/19* (Göttingen 2010)

Gay, Peter, *Weimar Culture: The Outsider as Insider* (Harmondsworth, 1974)

Gerlinger, Dieter, 'Louis Haeusser, der Bönnigheimer Heiland. Facetten aus seinem Leben', Stadt Bönnigheim, https://www.boennigheim.de/website/ de/stadt_boennigheim/geschichte_und_wappen/louis_haeusser

Gert, Valeska, *Ich bin eine Hexe. Kaleidoskop meines Lebens* (Munich, 1989)

Geyer, Martin H., *Verkehrte Welt. Revolution, Inflation und Moderne: Munich 1914–1924* (Göttingen, 1998)

Glaeser, Ernst, *Jahrgang 1902* (1928), ed. Christian Klein (Göttingen, 2013)

Gordon, Mel, *Voluptuous Panic: The Erotic World of Weimar Berlin* (Los Angeles, 2000)

Görtemaker, Manfred/Bildarchiv Preußischer Kulturbesitz, *Weimar in Berlin. Porträt einer Epoche* (Berlin, 2002)

Graf, Rüdiger, *Die Zukunft der Weimarer Republik. Krisen und Zukunftsaneignungen in Deutschland 1918–1933* (Munich, 2008)

Graml, Hermann, 'Präsidialsystem und Außenpolitik', *Vierteljahrshefte für Zeitgeschichte* 21 (1973), H. 2.

Gropius, Walter, *Bauhaus-Manifest* (Weimar, 1919)

Gropius, Walter, 'Baukunst im freien Volksstaat', *Deutscher Revolutionsalmanach* (1919)

Gumbel, Emil Julius, *Vier Jahre politischer Mord. Reprint der Originalausgabe von 1922* (Heidelberg, 1980)

Gumbrecht, Hans Ulrich, *1926. Ein Jahr am Rand der Zeit* (Frankfurt am Main, 2003)

Guratzsch, Dankwart, 'Architekt Ernst May, der Vater der Trabantenstädte', *Die Welt*, 9 August 2011

Gurk, Paul, *Die Wege des teelschen Hans* (Trier, 1922)

Haffner, Ernst, *Blutsbrüder. Ein Berliner Cliquenroman* (1932; Berlin, 2013)

Haffner, Sebastian, *Die deutsche Revolution 1918/19* (Reinbek bei Hamburg, 2018)

Haffner, Sebastian, *Geschichte eines Deutschen. Die Erinnerungen 1914–1933* (Munich, 2006)

Hagen, Wolfgang, '"Kulturinstrument Radio". Zur Genealogie der medialen Katastrophe der Weimarer Republik', in Jessica Nitsche and Nadine Werner (eds), *Populärkultur, Massenmedien, Avantgarde 1919–1933* (Munich, 2012)

Hardtwig, Wolfgang (ed.), *Ordnungen in der Krise. Zur politischen Kulturgeschichte Deutschlands 1900–1933* (Munich, 2007)

Hardtwig, Wolfgang (ed.), *Politische Kulturgeschichte der Zwischenkriegszeit 1918–1939* (Göttingen, 2005)

Haustedt, Birgit, *Die wilden Jahre in Berlin. Eine Klatsch- und Kulturgeschichte der Frauen* (Berlin, 2013)

Heidegger, Martin, *Zollikoner Seminare. Protokolle – Zwiegespräche – Briefe*, ed. Medard Boss (Frankfurt am Main, 1994)

Hepp, Michael, *Kurt Tucholsky* (Reinbek bei Hamburg, 1993)

Herbert, Ulrich, *Geschichte Deutschlands im 20. Jahrhundert* (Munich, 2017)

Hertling, Anke, *Eroberung der Männerdomäne Automobil. Die Selbstfahrerinnen Ruth Landshoff-Yorck, Erika Mann und Annemarie Schwarzenbach* (Bielefeld, 2013)

Herzig, Arno, '1815–1933: Emanzipation und Akkulturation', in *Jüdisches Leben in Deutschland. Informationen zur politischen Bildung* 307 (2010)

Hesse, Jan-Otmar, Roman Köster and Werner Plumpe, *Die große Depression. Die Weltwirtschaftskrise 1929–1939* (Frankfurt am Main / New York, 2014)

Hessel, Franz, *Ein Flaneur in Berlin* (Berlin, 2007)

Hessel, Franz, *Spazieren in Berlin. Sonderausgabe* (1929; Berlin, 2007)

Hildenbrandt, Fred, *. . . ich soll dich grüßen von Berlin. 1922–1932. Berliner Erinnerungen ganz und gar unpolitisch* (Berlin, 1966)

Hitler, Adolf, *Hitler. Sämtliche Aufzeichnungen 1905–1924*, ed. Eberhard Jäckel with Axel Kuhn (Stuttgart, 1980)

Hoegner, Wilhelm, *Der schwierige Außenseiter. Erinnerungen eines Abgeordneten, Emigranten und Ministerpräsidenten* (Munich, 1959)

Hoffmann, Tobias, *Deutschland gegen Frankreich. Der Kampf um den Stil 1900–1930* (Cologne, 2016)

Holzach, Cornelie, *Art déco – Schmuck und Accessoires. Ein neuer Stil für eine neue Welt* (Stuttgart, 2008)

Homann, Klaus et al. (eds), *Martin Wagner. 1885–1957. Wohnungsbau und Weltstadtplanung. Die Rationalisierung des Glücks. Ausstellung der Akademie der Künste* (Berlin, 1985)

Hoppé, E.O., *Deutsche Arbeit. Bilder vom Wiederaufstieg Deutschlands. 92 Aufnahmen*, with a foreword by Bruno H. Bürgel (Berlin, 1930)

Huebner, Friedrich Markus (ed.), *Die Frau von morgen, wie wir sie wünschen* (Leipzig, 1929)

Hung, Jochen. 'Das veränderliche "Gesicht der weiblichen Generation". Ein Beitrag zur politischen Kulturgeschichte der späten Weimarer Republik', in Gabriele Metzler and Dirk Schumann (eds), *Geschlechter(un)ordnung und Politik in der späten Weimarer Republik* (Bonn, 2016)

Hung, Jochen: '"Die Zeitung der Zeit". Die Tageszeitung Tempo und das Ende der Weimarer Republik', in David Oels and Ute Schneider (eds), *'Der ganze Verlag ist einfach eine Bonboniere'. Ullstein in der ersten Hälfte des 20. Jahrhunderts* (Berlin / Munich / Boston, 2015)

Hürten, Heinz (ed.), *Deutsche Geschichte in Quellen und Darstellung*, vol. 9: *Weimarer Republik und Drittes Reich 1918–1945* (Stuttgart, 1995)

Illies, Florian, *Liebe in Zeiten des Hasses. Chronik eines Gefühls 1929–1939* (Frankfurt am Main, 2021)

Jäger, Joachim et al. (eds), *Die Kunst der Gesellschaft. 1900–1945. Ausstellungskatalog Neue Nationalgalerie* (Berlin, 2021)

Jähner, Harald, *Erzählter, montierter, soufflierter Text. Zur Konstruktion des Romans 'Berlin Alexanderplatz' von Alfred Döblin* (Frankfurt am Main, 1984)

Jahoda, Marie, Paul F. Lazarsfeld and Hans Zeisel, *Die Arbeitslosen von Marienthal. Ein soziographischer Versuch* (1933; Berlin, 2020)

James, Harold, *Deutschland in der Weltwirtschaftskrise 1924–1936* (Darmstadt, 1988)

Jansen, Wolfgang, *Glanzrevuen der zwanziger Jahre* (Berlin, 1987)

Jasper, Gotthard, *Die gescheiterte Zähmung. Wege zur Machtergreifung Hitlers 1930–1934* (Frankfurt am Main, 1986)

Jaspers, Karl, *Die geistige Situation der Zeit* (Berlin, 1933)

Jelavich, Peter, *Berlin Cabaret* (Cambridge, MA, 1996)

Jentsch, Ralph, *Alfred Flechtheim und George Grosz. Zwei deutsche Schicksale* (Bonn, 2008)

John, Wolfgang, *. . . ohne festen Wohnsitz . . . Ursache und Geschichte der Nichtseßhaftigkeit und die Möglichkeiten der Hilfe* (Bielefeld, 1988)

Jones, Mark, *Founding Weimar: Violence and the German Revolution of 1918-1919* (Cambridge, 2016)

Josting, Petra and Walter Fähnders, *'Laboratorium Vielseitigkeit'. Zur Literatur der Weimarer Republik* (Bielefeld, 2005)

Judin, Juerg M. (ed.), *George Grosz. Die Jahre in Amerika 1933–1958* (Ostfildern, 2009)

Jung, Edgar Julius, *Die Herrschaft der Minderwertigen. Ihr Zerfall und ihre Ablösung durch ein neues Reich* (Berlin, 1930)

Jünger, Ernst, *Das Abenteuerliche Herz. Aufzeichnungen bei Tag und Nacht* (Berlin, 1929)

Jünger, Ernst, *Der Arbeiter. Herrschaft und Gestalt* (1932; Stuttgart, 2014)

Jünger, Ernst, *In Stahlgewittern. Aus dem Tagebuch eines Stoßtruppführers* (1920), in *idem*, *Stahlgewittern. Historisch-kritische Ausgabe*, vol. 1: *Die gedruckten Fassungen unter Berücksichtigung der Korrekturbücher*, ed. Helmuth Kiesel (Stuttgart, 2013). English translation: *Storm of Steel*, Trans. Michael Hofmann (London, 2016)

Kandinsky, Wassily, *Über das Geistige in der Kunst* (1911; Bern, 2004). English translation: *Concerning the Spiritual in Art*, trans. Michael Sadleir (New York, 1977)

Käppner, Joachim, *1918. Aufstand für die Freiheit. Die Revolution der Besonnenen* (Munich, 2017)

Karasek, Hellmuth, *Billy Wilder. Eine Nahaufnahme* (Hamburg, 1992)

Kästner, Erich, *Fabian. Die Geschichte eines Moralisten* (1931; Munich, 2003)

Kaufhold, Enno, *Berliner Interieurs 1910–1930. Fotografien von Waldema Titzenthaler* (Berlin, 2013)

Kaufmann, Doris, *'"Primitivismus". Zur Geschichte eines semantischen Feldes 1900–1930'*, in Wolfgang Hardtwig (ed.), *Ordnungen in der Krise. Zur politischen Kulturgeschichte Deutschlands 1900–1933* (Munich, 2007)

Kessel, Martin, *Herrn Brechers Fiasko* (1932; Frankfurt am Main. 1978)

Kessemeier, Gesa, *Sportlich, sachlich, männlich: Das Bild der 'Neuen Frau' in den Zwanziger Jahren. Zur Konstruktion geschlechtsspezifischer Körperbilder in der Mode der Jahre 1920 bis 1929* (Dortmund, 2000)

Kessler, Harry Graf, *Tagebücher 1918–1937*, ed. Wolfgang Pfeiffer-Belli (Frankfurt am Main/Leipzig, 1996)

Keun, Irmgard, *Das kunstseidene Mädchen* (1932; Berlin, 2005)

Keun, Irmgard, *Gilgi, eine von uns* (1931), in *idem*, *Das Werk*, vol. 1: *Texte aus der Weimarer Republik. 1931–1933*, ed. Heinrich Detering and Beate Kennedy (Göttingen, 2018)

Kindt, Werner (ed.), *Dokumentation der Jugendbewegung*, vol. 1: *Grundschriften der deutschen Jugendbewegung* (Düsseldorf/Cologne, 1963)

Kisch, Egon Erwin, *Aus dem Café Größenwahn. Berliner Reportagen* (Berlin, 2014)

Klemperer, Victor, *Ich will Zeugnis ablegen bis zum letzten. Tagebücher 1933–1945*, vol. 1: *Tagebücher 1933–1941*, ed. Walter Nowojski in collaboration with Hadwig Klemperer (Berlin, 1995). English translation: *I Shall Bear Witness: The Diaries of Victor Klemperer*, trans. Martin Chalmers (London, 1999)

Knickerbocker, Hubert Renfro, *Deutschland so oder so?* (Berlin, 1932)

Kocka, Jürgen, *Die Angestellten in der deutschen Geschichte: 1850–1980. Vom Privatbeamten zum angestellten Arbeitnehmer* (Göttingen, 1981)

Koebner, F.W. (ed.), *Jazz und Shimmy. Brevier der neuesten Tänze* (Berlin, 1921)

Kolb, Eberhard, *Gustav Stresemann* (Munich, 2003)

Koller, Christian, 'Die "Schwarze Schmach". Wahrnehmungen der Besatzungssoldaten im Rheinland nach dem Ersten Weltkrieg in deutscher und französischer Perspektive', in Rosmarie Beier-de Haan and Jan Werquet (eds), *Fremde? Bilder von den 'Anderen' in Deutschland und Frankreich seit 1871* (Dresden, 2009)

Kollwitz, Käthe, *Die Tagebücher* (Berlin, 1989)

Konyševa, Evgenija and Mark Meerovič, *Linkes Ufer, rechtes Ufer. Ernst May und die Planungsgeschichte von Magnitogorsk (1930–1933)*, ed. Thomas Flierl (Berlin, 2014)

Koslowsky, Friedrich (ed.), *Deutschlands Köpfe der Gegenwart über Deutschlands Zukunft*, with a foreword by Graf Rüdiger von der Goltz (Berlin, 1928)

Kracauer, Siegfried, *Das Ornament der Masse. Essays* (Frankfurt am Main, 1977)

Kracauer, Siegfried, *Die Angestellten. Aus dem neuesten Deutschland* (1930; Frankfurt am Main, 1980)

Kracauer, Siegfried, *Georg* (Frankfurt am Main, 1973)

Kracauer, Siegfried, *Kino. Essays, Studien, Glossen zum Film* (Frankfurt am Main, 1974)

Kracauer, Siegfried, *Straßen in Berlin und anderswo* (Berlin, 1987)

Krause, Ulrike, *Realität der Weimarer Republik. Gewalt und Kriminalität in deutschen Filmen der 'Goldenen Zwanziger'* (Saarbrücken, 2012)

Krausse, Anna-Carola, *Lotte Laserstein. Meine einzige Wirklichkeit* (Berlin/Munich, 2018)

Krumeich, Gerd, *Die unbewältigte Niederlage. Das Trauma des Ersten Weltkriegs und die Weimarer Republik* (Freiburg im Breisgau/Basel/Vienna, 2018)

Küenzlen, Gottfried, *Der Neue Mensch. Zur säkularen Religionsgeschichte der Moderne* (Munich, 1994)

Künkel, Fritz, *Krisenbriefe. Über den Zusammenhang von Wirtschaftskrise und Charakterkrise* (1932; Tübingen, 1977)

Landsberger, Artur, *Raffke & Cie. Die neue Gesellschaft* (Hanover, 1924)

Landshoff, Rut, *Die Vielen und der Eine* (1930; Hamburg, 2020)

Laqueur, Walter, *Weimar, A Cultural History* (Somerset, N.J, 2011)

Lau, Dirk, *Wahlkämpfe der Weimarer Republik. Propaganda und Programme der politischen Parteien bei den Wahlen zum Deutschen Reichstag von 1924 bis 1930* (Marburg, 2008)

Lederer, Joe, *Das Mädchen George* (Berlin, 1928)

Leidinger, Armin, *Hure Babylon. Großstadtsymphonie oder Angriff auf die Landschaft? Alfred Döblins Roman 'Berlin Alexanderplatz' und die Großstadt Berlin. Eine Annäherung aus kulturgeschichtlicher Perspektive* (Würzburg, 2010)

Leo, Per, *Der Wille zum Wesen. Weltanschauungskultur, charakterologisches Denken und Judenfeindschaft in Deutschland 1890–1940* (Berlin, 2013)

Lerski, Helmar, *Köpfe des Alltags. Unbekannte Menschen gesehen von Helmar Lerski* (Berlin, 1931)

Lessing, Theodor, *Der Lärm. Eine Kampfschrift gegen die Geräusche unseres Lebens* (Wiesbaden, 1908)

Lessing, Theodor, *Haarmann. Die Geschichte eines Werwolfs* (1925), ed. Rainer Marwedel (Frankfurt am Main, 1989)

Lethen, Helmut, *Verhaltenslehren der Kälte. Lebensversuche zwischen den Kriegen* (Frankfurt am Main, 1994)

Liebknecht, Karl, *Reden und Aufsätze*, ed. Julian Gumperz (Hamburg, 1921)

Longerich, Peter (ed.), *Die erste Republik. Dokumente zur Geschichte des Weimarer Staates* (Munich/Zurich, 1992)

Lüdtke, Helga, *Der Bubikopf. Männlicher Blick, weiblicher Eigen-Sinn* (Göttingen, 2021)

Luks, Timo, *Der Betrieb als Ort der Moderne. Zur Geschichte von Industriearbeit, Ordnungsdenken und Social Engineering im 20. Jahrhundert* (Bielefeld, 2010)

Lusk, Irene-Charlotte, *Montagen ins Blaue. Laszlo Moholy-Nagy. Fotomontagen und -collagen 1922–1943* (Berlin, 1980)

Luxemburg, Rosa, *Gesammelte Werke*, vol. 4: *August 1914 bis Januar 1919* (Berlin, 1974)

Makropoulos, Michael, 'Ein Mythos massenkultureller Urbanität. Der Potsdamer Platz aus der Perspektive von Diskursanalyse und Semiologie', in Joachim Fischer and Michael Makropoulos (eds), *Potsdamer Platz. Soziologische Theorien zu einem Ort der Moderne* (Munich, 2004)

Makropoulos, Michael, 'Krise und Kontingenz. Zwei Kategorien im Modernitätsdiskurs der Klassischen Moderne', in Moritz Föllmer and Rüdiger Graf (eds), *Die 'Krise' der Weimarer Republik. Zur Kritik eines Deutungsmusters* (Frankfurt am Main, 2005)

Mann, Erika, *Blitze überm Ozean. Aufsätze, Reden, Reportagen*, eds Irmela von der Lühe and Uwe Naumann (Reinbek bei Hamburg, 2001)

Mann, Erika and Klaus Mann, *Das Buch von der Riviera* (1931; Munich, 2019)

Mann, Heinrich, *Ein Zeitalter wird besichtigt. Erinnerungen* (Berlin, 1947)

Mann, Klaus, *Der Wendepunkt. Ein Lebensbericht* (1952; Reinbek bei Hamburg, 1985)

Mann, Thomas, 'Brief über Ebert', in idem, *Große kommentierte Frankfurter Ausgabe*, vol. 15.1: *Essays II. 1914–1926*, ed. and annotated by Hermann Kurzke (Frankfurt am Main, 2002)

Mann, Thomas, *Der Zauberberg* (1924; Frankfurt am Main, 2002). English translation: *The Magic Mountain*, trans. John E. Woods (New York, 2005)

Mann, Thomas, 'Deutsche Ansprache. Ein Appell an die Vernunft', in idem, *Gesammelte Werke in Einzelbänden. Frankfurter Ausgabe. Von Deutscher Republik. Politische Schriften und Reden in Deutschland*, ed. Peter de Mendelssohn (Frankfurt am Main, 1984)

Mann, Thomas, 'Unordnung und frühes Leid', in idem, *Gesammelte Werke*, vol. 8: *Erzählungen* (Frankfurt am Main, 1960)

Mann, Thomas, 'Von deutscher Republik', in idem, *Große kommentierte Frankfurter Ausgabe*, vol. 15.1: *Essays II. 1914–1926*, ed. and annotated by Hermann Kurzke (Frankfurt am Main, 2002)

Marchlewitz, Ingrid, *Irmgard Keun. Leben und Werk* (Würzburg, 1999)

Martin, Peter and Christine Alonzo (eds), *Zwischen Charleston und Stechschritt. Schwarze im Nationalsozialismus* (Munich, 2004)

Martus, Steffen, *Ernst Jünger* (Stuttgart/Weimar, 2001)

Martynkewicz, Wolfgang, *1920. Am Nullpunkt des Sinns* (Berlin, 2019)

Maser, Werner, *Friedrich Ebert, der erste deutsche Reichspräsident. Eine politische Biographie* (Munich, 1987)

Matzke, Frank, *Jugend bekennt: So sind wir!* (Leipzig, 1930)

Mendelssohn, Peter de, *Fertig mit Berlin?* (1930), with an afterword by Katharina Rutschky (Frankfurt am Main, 2004)

Mendelssohn, Peter de, *Zeitungsstadt Berlin. Menschen und Mächte in der Geschichte der deutschen Presse*, revised edition (Berlin, 1982)

Mergel, Thomas, *Parlamentarische Kultur in der Weimarer Republik. Politische Kommunikation, symbolische Öffnung und Öffentlichkeit im Reichstag* (Düsseldorf, 2002)

Merz, Kai-Uwe, *Der AGA-Wagen. Eine Automobilgeschichte aus Berlin* (Berlin, 2011)

Merz, Kai-Uwe, *Vulkan Berlin. Eine Kulturgeschichte der 1920er Jahre* (Berlin, 2020)

Metzger, Rainer, *Die Stadt. Vom antiken Athen bis zu den Megacitys. Eine Weltgeschichte in Geschichten* (Vienna, 2015)

Metzler, Gabriele and Dirk Schumann (eds), *Geschlechter(un)ordnung und Politik in der späten Weimarer Republik* (Bonn, 2016)

Michalka, Wolfgang and Gottfried Niedhart, *Deutsche Geschichte 1918–1933. Dokumente zur Innen- und Außenpolitik* (Frankfurt am Main, 2002)

Mikat, Paul, 'Zur Kundgebung der Fuldaer Bischofskonferenz über die nationalsozialistische Bewegung vom 28. März 1933', *Jahrbuch für christliche Sozialwissenschaften* 3 (1962)

Mills, C. Wright, *Menschen im Büro* (Frankfurt am Main, 1955)

Mohler, Armin, *Die Konservative Revolution in Deutschland 1918–1932. Ein Handbuch* (Graz / Stuttgart, 1999)

Mohr, Max, *Frau ohne Reue* (1933; Bonn, 2020)

Mohr, Max, *Venus in den Fischen* (1927; Hanover, 2014)

Molderings, Herbert, *Umbo. Otto Umbehr. 1902–1980* (Düsseldorf, 1996)

Morsey, Rudolf, *Das 'Ermächtigungsgesetz' vom 24. März 1933. Quellen zur Geschichte und Interpretation des 'Gesetzes zur Behebung der Not von Volk und Reich'* (Düsseldorf, 1992)

Mothes, Christian and Dominik Bartmann (eds), *Tanz auf dem Vulkan. Das Berlin der Zwanziger Jahre im Spiegel der Künste* (Berlin, 2015)

Mühland, Rudolf, 'Die vergessene Revolution', in FAU Duisburg (ed.), *März 1920. Die vergessene Revolution im Ruhrgebiet* (Moers, 2019)

Mühlhausen, Walter, 'Der Typus Ebert. Anmerkungen zur Biographie des Parteiführers im Staatsamt der Weimarer Republik', *Mitteilungsblatt des Instituts für Soziale Bewegungen* 45 (2011)

Mühlhausen, Walter, *Friedrich Ebert. Sein Leben in Bildern* (Ostfildern, 2019)

Mühlhausen, Walter, *Friedrich Ebert 1871–1925. Reichspräsident der Weimarer Republik* (Bonn, 2006)

Müller, Corinna, 'Übergang zum Tonfilm. Wandel der kulturellen Öffentlichkeit insbesondere am Beispiel Hamburgs', *Jahrbuch für Kommunikationsgeschichte* 4 (2002)

Müller, Tim B., 'Die Weimarer Republik und die europäische Demokratie', in Michael Dreyer and Andreas Braune (eds), *Weimar als Herausforderung. Die Weimarer Republik und die Demokratie im 21. Jahrhundert* (Stuttgart, 2016)

Müller, Tim B. and Adam Tooze (eds), *Normalität und Fragilität. Demokratie nach dem Ersten Weltkrieg* (Hamburg, 2015)

Müller, Werner (ed.), *Die Welt spielt Roulette. Zur Kultur der Moderne in der Krise 1927 bis 1932* (Frankfurt am Main, 2002)

Musil, Robert, *Der Mann ohne Eigenschaften*, in idem, *Gesammelte Werke*, ed. Adolf Frisé (Reinbek bei Hamburg, 1978). English translation: *The Man Without Qualities*, trans. Sophie Wilkins and Burton Pike (New York, 1995)

Niedbalski, Johanna, *Die ganze Welt des Vergnügens. Berliner Vergnügungsparks der 1880er bis 1930er Jahre* (Berlin, 2018)

Nielsen, Asta, *Die schweigende Muse. Lebenserinnerung* (1945; Berlin, 1979)

Nielsen, Philipp, 'Verantwortung und Kompromiss. Die Deutschnationalen auf der Suche nach einer konservativen Demokratie', in Tim B. Müller and Adam Tooze (eds), *Normalität und Fragilität. Demokratie nach dem Ersten Weltkrieg* (Hamburg, 2015)

Niess, Wolfgang, *Die Revolution von 1918/19. Der wahre Beginn unserer Demokratie* (Berlin / Munich / Zurich, 2017)

Niess, Wolfgang. *Die Revolution von 1918/19 in der deutschen Geschichtsschreibung. Deutungen von der Weimarer Republik bis ins 21. Jahrhundert* (Berlin / Boston, 2013)

Nippoldt, Robert and Boris Pofalla, *Es wird Nacht im Berlin der Wilden Zwanziger* (Cologne, 2018)

Nitsche, Jessica and Nadine Werner (eds), *Populärkultur, Massenmedien, Avantgarde 1919–1933* (Munich, 2012)

Oels, David and Ute Schneider (eds), *'Der ganze Verlag ist einfach eine Bonboniere'. Ullstein in der ersten Hälfte des 20. Jahrhunderts* (Berlin / Munich / Boston, 2015)

Ostwald, Hans, *Sittengeschichte der Inflation. Ein Kulturdokument aus den Jahren des Marktsturzes* (Berlin, 1931)

Paasche, Hans, *Das verlorene Afrika. Ansichten vom Lebensweg eines Kolonialoffiziers zum Pazifisten und Revolutionär*, ed. P. Werner Lange with the participation of Helga Paasche (Berlin, 2008)

Paasche, Hans, *Die Forschungsreise des Afrikaners Lukanga Mukara ins innerste Deutschland. Geschildert in Briefen Lukanga Mukuras an den König Ruoma von Kitara* (1922; Berlin, 2017)

Peukert, Detlev J.K., *Die Weimarer Republik. Krisenjahre der Klassischen Moderne* (Frankfurt am Main, 1987)

Peukert, Detlev J.K., *Volksgenossen und Gemeinschaftsfremde. Anpassung, Ausmerze und Aufbegehren unter dem Nationalsozialismus* (Cologne, 1982)

Pfahl-Traughber, Armin, *'Konservative Revolution' und 'Neue Rechte'. Rechtsextremistische Intellektuelle gegen den demokratischen Verfassungsstaat* (Opladen, 1998)

Pfeiffer, Ingrid (ed.), *Glanz und Elend der Weimarer Republik* (Frankfurt am Main, 2017)

Pieken, Gorch and Cornelia Kruse, *Preußisches Liebesglück. Eine deutsche Familie aus Afrika* (Berlin, 2007)

Pinthus, Kurt (ed.), *Menschheitsdämmerung. Symphonie jüngster Dichtung* (Berlin, 1920)

Piper, Ernst, *Rosa Luxemburg. Ein Leben* (Munich, 2019)

Pirker, Theo, *Büro und Maschine. Zur Geschichte und Soziologie der Mechanisierung der Büroarbeit, der Maschinisierung des Büros und der Büroautomation* (Basel/Tübingen, 1962)

Planert, Ute, 'Kulturkritik und Geschlechterverhältnis. Zur Krise der Geschlechterordnung zwischen Jahrhundertwende und "Drittem Reich"', in Wolfgang Hardtwig (ed.), *Ordnungen in der Krise. Zur politischen Kulturgeschichte Deutschlands 1900–1933* (Munich, 2007)

Plarre, Stefanie, *Die Kochenhofsiedlung – das Gegenmodell zur Weißenhofsiedlung. Paul Schmitthenners Siedlungsprojekt in Stuttgart von 1927 bis 1933* (Stuttgart, 2001)

Plessner, Helmuth, *Grenzen der Gemeinschaft: Eine Kritik des sozialen Radikalismus* (1924; Frankfurt am Main, 2001)

Polaschegg, Andrea and Michael Weichenhain (eds), *Berlin – Babylon. Eine deutsche Faszination* (Berlin, 2017)

Polgar, Alfred, *Hinterland* (Berlin, 1929)

Pörtner, Rudolf (ed.), *Alltag in der Weimarer Republik. Kindheit und Jugend in unruhiger Zeit* (Düsseldorf/Vienna/New York, 1990)

Posener, Julius, *Aufsätze und Vorträge 1931–1980* (Braunschweig/Wiesbaden, 1981)

Postert, André, *Von der Kritik der Parteien zur außerparlamentarischen Opposition. Die jungkonservative Klub-Bewegung und ihre Auflösung im Nationalsozialismus* (Baden-Baden, 2014)

Praesent, Hans (ed.), *Der Weg voran! Eine Bildschau deutscher Höchstleistungen* (Leipzig, 1931)

Pressler, Florian, *Die erste Weltwirtschaftskrise. Eine kleine Geschichte der großen Depression* (Munich, 2013)

Prinzler, Hans Helmut, *Licht und Schatten. Die großen Stumm- und Tonfilme der Weimarer Republik* (Munich, 2012)

Puttkammer, Claudia and Sacha Szabo, *Gruß aus dem Luna-Park. Eine Archäologie des Vergnügens. Freizeit- und Vergnügungsparks Anfang des zwanzigsten Jahrhunderts* (Berlin, 2007)

Rasche, Adelheid, 'Der männliche Blick. Das Bild der "Neuen Frau" in Männerzeitschriften', *Querelles. Jahrbuch für Frauen- und Geschlechterforschung* 11: 'Garçonnes à la mode im Berlin und Paris der zwanziger Jahre' (2006)

Reger, Erik, *Union der festen Hand* (1931; Essen, 2007)

Reichardt, Sven, 'Gewalt, Körper, Politik. Paradoxien in der deutschen Kulturgeschichte der Zwischenkriegszeit', in Wolfgang Hardtwig (ed.), *Politische Kulturgeschichte der Zwischenkriegszeit 1918–1939* (Göttingen, 2005)

Reichert, Martin (David Chipperfield Architects), 'Indienstnahme einer historisch nobilitierten Szenografie', *Bauwelt* 22 (2020).

Reick, Philipp, 'A Poor People's Movement? Erwerbslosenproteste in Berlin und New York in den frühen 1930er Jahren', *Jahrbuch für Forschungen zur Geschichte der Arbeiterbewegung* I (2015)

Remarque, Erich Maria, *Im Westen nichts Neues* (1929; Cologne, 2014). English translation: *All Quiet on the Western Front*, trans. Brian Murdoch (London, 1994)

Retzlaff, Erich, *Die von der Scholle. Sechsundfünfzig photographische Bildnisse bodenständiger Menschen*, with a foreword by Hans Friedrich Blunck (Göttingen, 1931)

Richter, Thomas, *Christian Schad. Künstler im 20. Jahrhundert. Bausteine zur Biographie* (Petersberg, 2020)

Riess, Curt, *Das war mein Leben! Erinnerungen* (Frankfurt am Main/Berlin, 1990)

Rosenberg, Arthur, *Geschichte der Weimarer Republik* (Frankfurt am Main, 1961)

Rössler, Patrick, *Bauhausmädels: A Tribute to Pioneering Women Artists* (Cologne, 2019)

Rössler, Patrick and Elizabeth Otto, *Frauen am Bauhaus. Wegweisende Künstlerinnen der Moderne* (Munich, 2019)

Rossol, Nadine and Benjamin Ziemann (eds), *Aufbruch und Abgründe. Das Handbuch der Weimarer Republik* (Darmstadt, 2021)

Roth, Joseph, *Berliner Saisonbericht. Unbekannte Reportagen und journalistische Arbeiten 1920–1939*, ed. Klaus Westermann (Cologne, 1984)

Roth, Joseph, *Trübsal einer Straßenbahn. Stadtfeuilletons*, ed. and with an afterword by Wiebke Porombka (Salzburg/Vienna, 2012)

Rüther, Martin et al., *Jugend in Deutschland 1918–1945*, website with documents from NS- Dokumentationszentrum der Stadt Cologne, https://jugend1918-1945.de/portal/jugend/thema.aspx?bereich=- projekt&root=25004&id=26857&redir=

Sack, Heidi, *Moderne Jugend vor Gericht. Sensationsprozesse, "Sexualtragödien" und die Krise der Jugend in der Weimarer Republik* (Bielefeld, 2016)

Sack, Manfred, 'Weißenhofsiedlung. Noch jetzt hallt das Drama nach', *Die Zeit* 18 (1968)

Saekel, Ursula, *Der US-Film in der Weimarer Republik – ein Medium der 'Amerikanisierung'? Deutsche Filmwirtschaft, Kulturpolitik und mediale Globalisierung im Fokus transatlantischer Interessen* (Paderborn, 2011)

Sander, August, *Antlitz der Zeit. Sechzig Aufnahmen deutscher Menschen des 19 Jahrhunderts* (1929), with an introduction by Alfred Döblin (Munich, 1976)

Schäche, Wolfgang, 'Das "Neue Berlin". Architektur und Städtebau', in Manfred Görtemaker and Bildarchiv Preußischer Kulturbesitz, *Weimar in Berlin. Porträt einer Epoche* (Berlin, 2002)

Schäfer, Hans Dieter, *Das gespaltene Bewußtsein: Über deutsche Kultur und Lebenswirklichkeit 1933–1945* (Munich/Vienna, 1983)

Schalansky, Judith, 'Hitler mochte Futura', *Der Freitag*, 1 June 2007

Schär, Christian, *Der Schlager und seine Tänze im Deutschland der 20er Jahre. Sozialgeschichtliche Aspekte zum Wandel in der Musik- und Tanzkultur während der Weimarer Republik* (Zurich, 1991)

Schauwecker, Franz, *Deutsche allein. Schnitt durch die Zeit* (Berlin, 1931)

Schivelbusch, Wolfgang, *Die Kultur der Niederlage. Der amerikanische Süden 1865 – Frankreich 1871 – Deutschland 1918* (Reinbek bei Hamburg, 2012)

Schmitt, Carl, *Politische Theologie. Vier Kapitel zur Lehre von der Souveränität* (1922; Berlin, 1993)

Schmölders, Claudia and Sander Gilman (eds), *Gesichter der Weimarer Republik. Eine physiognomische Kulturgeschichte* (Cologne, 2000)

Schneede, Uwe M. (ed.), *Die Zwanziger Jahre. Manifeste und Dokumente deutscher Künstler* (Cologne, 1979)

Schönpflug, Daniel, *Kometenjahre. 1918: Die Welt im Aufbruch* (Frankfurt am Main, 2017)

Schube, Inka (ed.), *Umbo – Fotograf* (Cologne, 2019)

Schultz, Edmund (ed.), *Das Gesicht der Demokratie. Ein Bildwerk zur Geschichte der Nachkriegszeit*, with an introduction by Friedrich Georg Jünger (Leipzig, 1931)

Schulz, Günther, 'Wohnungspolitik in Deutschland und England 1900–1939. Generelle Linien und ausgewählte Beispiele', in Clemens Zimmermann (ed.), *Europäische Wohnungspolitik in vergleichender Perspektive 1900–1939* (Stuttgart, 1997)

Schütze, Silke, *Henny Walden. Memoiren einer vergessenen Soubrette* (Reinbek bei Hamburg, 2014)

Schützinger, Hermann, *Bürgerkrieg* (Leipzig, 1924)

Schwarzenbach, Annemarie, *Lyrische Novelle* (Berlin, 1933)

Sicks, Kai Marcel, ' "Der Querschnitt" oder: Die Kunst des Sporttreibens', in Michael Cowan and Kai Marcel Sicks (eds), *Leibhaftige Moderne. Körper in Kunst und Massenmedien 1918–1933* (Bielefeld, 2005)

Sildatke, Arne, *Dekorative Moderne. Das Art Déco in der Raumkunst der Weimarer Republik* (Münster, 2013)

Soden, Kristine von and Maruta Schmidt (eds), *Neue Frauen. Die Zwanziger Jahre* (Berlin, 1988)

Söll, Änne, *Der neue Mann? Männerporträts von Otto Dix, Christian Schad und Anton Räderscheidt 1914–1930* (Munich, 2016)

Sombart, Werner, *Die Juden und das Wirtschaftsleben* (Leipzig, 1911)

Sontheimer, Kurt, 'Der Tatkreis', *Vierteljahrshefte für Zeitgeschichte* 7/3 (1959)

Später, Jörg, 'Die goldenen Zwanziger Jahre? Zur Lage der Intelligenz am Beispiel Adorno, Benjamin, Bloch, Kracauer', *Jahrbuch zur Kultur und Literatur der Weimarer Republik* 20/21 (2019/20)

Spengler, Oswald, *Der Untergang des Abendlandes. Umrisse einer Morphologie der Weltgeschichte* (1918; Munich, 1989)

Speyer, Wilhelm, *Ich geh aus und du bleibst da. Roman eines Mannequins* (1930; Coesfeld, 2011)

Spiekermann, Uwe, '1932 – das Jahr des Jo-Jos' (13 August 2020), https://uwe-spiekermann.com/2020/08/13/1932-das-jahr-des-jo-jos/

Stegmann, Dirk, 'Angestelltenkultur in der Weimarer Republik', in Werner Faulstich (ed.), *Die Kultur der 20er Jahre* (Munich, 2008)

Sternburg, Wilhelm von, *Gustav Stresemann* (Frankfurt am Main, 1990)

Stinnes, Clärenore, *Im Auto durch zwei Welten. Die erste Autofahrt einer Frau um die Welt 1927 bis 1929*, ed. and with a foreword by Gabriele Habinger (Vienna, 2007).

Strohmeyer, Klaus (ed.), *Berlin in Bewegung. Literarischer Spaziergang*, vol. 2: *Die Stadt* (Reinbek bei Hamburg, 1987)

Taut, Bruno, *Frühlicht. Beilage zur Stadtbaukunst aus alter und neuer Zeit* (Berlin, 1920)

Taylor, Frederick, *The Downfall of Money: Germany's Hyperinflation and the Destruction of the Middle Class* (London, 2013)

Tergit, Gabriele, *Blüten der zwanziger Jahre. Gerichtsreportagen und Feuilletons 1923–1933*, ed. Jens Brüning (Berlin, 1984)

Tergit, Gabriele, *Käsebier erobert den Kurfürstendamm* (1931; Berlin, 1988)

Theweleit, Klaus, *Männerphantasien*, vol. 1: *Frauen, Fluten, Körper, Geschichte* (Frankfurt am Main, 1977). English translation: *Male Fantasies*, trans. Stephen Conway with Erica Carter and Chris Turner (Cambridge, 1988)

Torp, Claudius, *Konsum und Politik in der Weimarer Republik* (Göttingen, 2011)

Tucholsky, Kurt, *Deutschland, Deutschland über alles. Ein Bilderbuch von Kurt Tucholsky und vielen Fotografen. Montiert von John Heartfield* (1929; Reinbek bei Hamburg, 1973)

Uhlig, Heinrich, *Die Warenhäuser im Dritten Reich* (Cologne/Opladen, 1956)

Ulmer, Manfred and Jörg Kurz, *Die Weißenhofsiedlung. Geschichte und Gegenwart* (Stuttgart, 2006)

Ulrich, Bernd and Benjamin Ziemann (eds), *Frontalltag im Ersten Weltkrieg. Ein historisches Lesebuch* (Essen, 2008)

Vierkandt, Alfred (ed.), *Handwörterbuch der Soziologie* (Stuttgart, 1931)

Waetzoldt, Stephan and Verena Haas (eds), *Tendenzen der Zwanziger Jahre. Katalog zur Europaratsausstellung* (Berlin, 1977)

Waggerl, Karl Heinrich, *Brot* (Frankfurt am Main 1930)

Walther, Peter, *Fieber. Universum Berlin 1930–1933* (Berlin, 2020)

Wangenheim, Inge von, *Mein Haus Vaterland. Erinnerungen einer jungen Frau* (Halle an der Saale, 1976)

Wechssler, Eduard, *Esprit und Geist. Versuch einer Wesenskunde des Deutschen und des Franzosen* (Leipzig/Bielefeld, 1927)

Wedemeyer-Kolwe, Bernd, '"Ein Ereignis für den ganzen Westen". Körperkultur in Weimar zwischen Öffentlichkeit, Kunst und Kultur', in Michael Cowan and Kai Marcel Sicks (eds), *Leibhaftige Moderne. Körper in Kunst und Massenmedien 1918–1933* (Bielefeld, 2005)

Wehler, Hans-Ulrich, *Deutsche Gesellschaftsgeschichte*, vol. 4: *1914–1949. Vom Beginn des Ersten Weltkriegs bis zur Gründung der beiden deutschen Staaten* (Munich, 2008)

Wehler, Hans-Ulrich, *Preußen ist wieder chic . . . Politik und Polemik in zwanzig Essays* (Frankfurt am Main, 1983)

Weidermann, Volker, *Träumer. Als die Dichter die Macht übernahmen* (Cologne, 2017)

Wette, Wolfram (ed.), *Pazifistische Offiziere in Deutschland 1871–1933* (Bremen, 1999)

Wilder, Billy, *Der Prinz von Wales geht auf Urlaub. Berliner Reportagen, Feuilletons und Kritiken der zwanziger Jahre*, ed. Klaus Siebenhaar (Berlin, 1996)

Wildt, Michael, 'Der Begriff der Arbeit bei Hitler', in Marc Buggeln and Michael Wildt (eds), *Arbeit im Nationalsozialismus* (Munich, 2014)

Wildt, Michael, 'Machteroberung 1933', *Nationalsozialismus: Aufstieg und Herrschaft. Informationen zur politischen Bildung* 314 (2012)

Wildt, Michael, *Zerborstene Zeit. Deutsche Geschichte von 1918–1945* (Munich, 2022)

Willett, John, *Explosion der Mitte. Kunst und Politik 1917–1933* (Munich, 1981)

Winkler, Heinrich August, *Weimar 1918–1933. Die Geschichte der ersten deutschen Demokratie* (Munich, 2018)

Witt, Peter-Christian, *Friedrich Ebert. Parteiführer, Reichskanzler, Volksbeauftragter, Reichspräsident* (Bonn, 1992)

Witte, Karsten (ed.), *Theorie des Kinos. Ideologiekritik der Traumfabrik* (Frankfurt am Main, 1972)

Wittstock, Uwe, *Februar 33. Der Winter der Literatur* (Munich, 2021)

Wolfe, Thomas, *Eine Deutschlandreise. Literarische Zeitbilder 1926–1936* (Munich, 2020)

Wolfram, Knud, *Tanzdielen und Vergnügungspaläste. Berliner Nachtleben in den dreißiger und vierziger Jahren* (Berlin, 1992)

Worringer, Wilhelm, *Abstraktion und Einfühlung. Ein Beitrag zur Stilpsychologie* (Munich, 1908)

Wünsche, Konrad, *Bauhaus. Versuche, das Leben zu ordnen* (Berlin, 1997)

Xammar, Eugeni, *Das Schlangenei. Berichte aus dem Deutschland der Inflationsjahre 1922–1924* (Berlin, 2007)

Ziemann, Benjamin, 'Landwirtschaft und ländliche Gesellschaft', in Nadine Rossol and Benjamin Ziemann (eds), *Aufbruch und Abgründe. Das Handbuch der Weimarer Republik* (Darmstadt, 2021)

Ziemann, Benjamin, *Veteranen der Republik. Kriegserinnerung und demokratische Republik 1918–1933* (Bonn, 2014)

Zitzmann, Marc, 'Unorthodoxer geht es hier gar nicht. Joséphine Baker ins Pantheon', *Frankfurter Allgemeine Zeitung*, 25 August 2021

Zuckmayer, Carl, *Als wär's ein Stück von mir. Horen der Freundschaft* (Frankfurt am Main, 1969)

Newspapers and Magazines

Arbeiter-Illustrierte-Zeitung
Berliner Börsen-Zeitung
Berliner Illustrirte Zeitung
Berliner Tageblatt
Berliner Volks-Zeitung
Blau-Rot. Eine Monatsschrift für den Herrn Das Kunstblatt

Das Leben
Das Magazin
Das Neue Frankfurt. Monatsschrift für die Fragen der Großstadt-Gestaltung
Der Angriff
Der Stürmer
Deutsche Rundschau
Die Dame. Illustrierte Mode-Zeitschrift
Die Erde
Die LichtBildBühne. Illustrierte Tageszeitung des Films
Die neue linie
Die Rote Fahne. Zentralorgan des Spartacusbundes
Die Tat
Die Weltbühne
Frankfurter Zeitung Illustrierter Film-Kurier
Kunst und Künstler. Illustrierte Monatsschrift für bildende Kunst und Kunstgewerbe
Kulturwille. Zeitschrift für Minderheitenkultur und -politik
Neue Berliner Zeitung
Proletarische Sozialpolitik. Organ der Arbeitsgemeinschaft Sozialpolitische Organisationen
Revue des Monats
Sport im Bild
Tempo. Berliner Abend-Zeitung
Tempo. Das Magazin für Fortschritt und Kultur
Uhu. Das neue Ullsteinmagazin
Vossische Zeitung
Vorwärts. Central-Organ der Sozialdemokratie Deutschlands

Endnotes

Preface: The New Life

1 Valeska Gert, *Ich bin eine Hexe. Kaleidoskop meines Lebens* (Munich, 1989), p. 38. • 2 Bruno Taut, 'Nieder der Seriosismus!', in *Frühlicht. Beilage zur Stadtbaukunst aus alter und neuer Zeit* (Berlin, 1920), quoted in Stephan Waetzoldt and Verena Haas (eds), *Tendenzen der Zwanziger Jahre. Katalog zur Europaratsausstellung* (Berlin, 1977), vol. 2, p. 64. • 3 Ibid. • 4 Detlev J.K. Peukert, *Die Weimarer Republik. Krisenjahre der Klassischen Moderne* (Frankfurt am Main, 1987), p. 268.

Chapter 1: When the War Came Home

1 *Berliner Tageblatt*, 2 December 1918. • 2 *Berliner Tageblatt*, 16 December 1918. • 3 Karl Liebknecht, 'Was will der Spartakusbund? Rede in der Berliner Hasenheide', 23 December 1918, in *idem, Reden und Aufsätze*, ed. Julian Gumperz (Hamburg, 1921), p. 338. • 4 Cf. *Berliner Tageblatt*, 1 January 1919, p. 3. • 5 Cf. Mark Jones, *Founding Weimar: Violence and the German Revolution of 1918–1919* (Cambridge, 2016), p. 108. • 6 Quoted in: Volker Weidermann, *Träumer. Als die Dichter die Macht übernahmen* (Cologne, 2017), p. 222. • 7 Quoted in ibid., p. 247. • 8 Quoted in Jones, *Founding Weimar*, p. 120. • 9 Cf. ibid., p. 154. Jones sees the interview with Lequis as 'one of the morning's most important political outcomes' for the entire history of violence in the Weimar Republic. • 10 Cf. Klaus Theweleit, *Male Fantasies*, vol. 1: *Women, Floods, Bodies, History* (Cambridge, 1987), p. 65. • 11 Ernst von Salomon, *Die Geächteten* (The Outlaws) (Berlin, 1935), quoted in Theweleit, *Male Fantasies*, vol. 1, p. 65. • 12 Quoted in Theweleit, *Male Fantasies*, vol. 1, p. 174. • 13 Quoted in Ernst Piper, *Rosa Luxemburg. Ein Leben* (Munich, 2019), p. 45. • 14 Rosa Luxemburg, *Gesammelte Werke*, vol. 4: *August 1914 bis Januar 1919* (Berlin, 1974), p. 460. • 15 Ibid., p. 461. • 16 Jones, *Founding Weimar*, p. 5. • 17 Cf. Wolfgang Niess, *Die Revolution von 1918/19. Der wahre Beginn unserer Demokratie* (Berlin/Munich/Zurich/Vienna, 2017), p. 315. • 18 Quoted in Jones, *Founding Weimar*, p. 182. • 19 Noske's tacit consent is now also conceded by the SPD. Tilman Ficther wrote in *Vorwärts* on 10 January 2020: 'The political responsibility for this momentous double murder clearly rests with Gustav Noske. That much has already been admitted by Ottmar Schreiner, Federal Business Leader of the SPD, and the Social Democratic historian Helga Grebing in an SPD panel discussion in the Willy Brandt House, Berlin, on 14 January 1999. Where Noske's actual behaviour on the night of the murder, 15 to 16 January, is concerned, given the account given by Klaus Gietinger we can now definitively rule out the possibility that Gustav Noske issued a secret or official instruction to Captain Pabst to commit

murder. On the other hand in 1962 Pabst hinted in *Der Spiegel* that Noske had no objection to Luxemburg and Liebknecht being shot.' Klaus Gietinger, mentioned above, is a television director who has spent 30 years investigating what happened that night. • 20 This is what Alfred Döblin noted during the Christmas shootings at Marstall in Berlin; Alfred Döblin, 'Ruinen, neues Leben', in *idem, Kleine Schriften*, vol. 1 (Olten/Freiburg im Breisgau, 1985), p. 240. • 21 Harry Graf Kessler, *Tagebücher 1918–1937*, ed. Wolfgang Pfeiffer-Belli (Frankfurt am Main/Leipzig, 1996), p. 101. • 22 *Berliner Tageblatt*, 1 January 1919, p. 5. • 23 The background to the poster's history is perhaps just as interesting as the poster itself. The lines come from the poem by the Expressionist author Paul Zech, 'Pause, Berlin . . .' written in 1914/1916. The poster was largely believed to have been printed as a warning against the many irresponsible strikes and demonstrations that were taking place. It might, however, also be a reference to the consequences of the rising wave of influenza, as a call to social distancing. The possibility of an artistic action is also not impossible to rule out. Even among contemporaries the poster was seen as a puzzle. The author Silke Schütze has her fictitious but precisely researched singer Henriette Walden write in her diary: 'What a poster. Completely mad. Berolina in the arms of a skeleton. Underneath, the words: "Pause, Berlin. Reflect. Your dance partner is death." Horrific. Herr Kressin says death is the Communists. Do Communists wear patent shoes like death in the poster? Well, rather die than not dance.' Silke Schütze, *Henny Walden. Memoiren einer vergessen Soubrette* (Henny Walden: Memoirs of a Forgotten Soubrette) (Reinbek bei Hamburg, 2014), p. 53. • 24 Alfred Döblin, 'Kannibalisches', in *idem, Der deutsche Maskenball von Linke Poot. Wissen und Verändern!* (Olten/Freiburg im Breisgau, 1972), pp. 20–3. • 25 Hermann Schützinger, *Bürgerkrieg. Leipzig 1924*, quoted in Wolfram Wette (ed.), *Pazifistische Offiziere in Deutschland 1871–1933* (Bremen, 1999), p. 292. • 26 Ibid. • 27 Quoted in Rudolf Mühland, 'Die vergessene Revolution', in FAU Duisburg (ed.), *März 1920. Die vergessene Revolution im Ruhrgebiet* (Moers, 2019), http://www.syndikalismusforschung.info/marz1920.htm (accessed 21 May 2022). • 28 Ibid. • 29 *Berliner Volks-Zeitung*, 27 March 1920. • 30 Quoted in Günther Drommer, *Die Wahrheit der Bilder. Zeitgenössische Fotografien vom Leben des deutschen Volkes*, vol. 2: *Die ruhelose Republik. Alltag zwischen Gewalt und Hoffnung 1918–1933* (Berlin, 2004). • 31 By now worldwide sales – the book was translated into 50 languages – run to over 20 million. • 32 Erich Maria Remarque, *Im Westen nichts Neues* (1929; Cologne, 2014), p. 258. English translation: *All Quiet on the Western Front*, trans. Brian Murdoch (London, 1994). The German title literally means 'Nothing new in the West'. • 33 Remarque, *All Quiet on the Western Front*, p. 83. • 34 Ibid., p. 192. • 35 Ibid., p. 87. • 36 Cf. Benjamin Ziemann, *Veteranen der Republik. Kriegserinnerung und demokratische Republik 1918–1933* (Bonn, 2014). Ziemann uses the term 'patriotic pacifism' to describe the fundamental values of the biggest veterans' association. 'They abhorred war, criticised rearmament projects and were convinced that the Republic embodied a better Germany by leaving behind the legacy of Prussian militarism.' • 37 Remarque, *All Quiet on the Western Front*, p. 167. • 38 Ernst Jünger, *In Stahlgewittern. Aus dem Tagebuch eines Stoßtruppführers* (1920), in *idem, In Stahlgewittern. Historisch-kritische Ausgabe*, vol. 1: *Die gedruckten Fassungen unter Berücksichtigung der Korrekturbücher*, ed. Helmuth Kiesel (Stuttgart, 2013, p. 20). • 39 Jünger, *In Stahlgewittern*, p. 18. • 40 Ibid., p. 19. • 41 Ibid. • 42 Cf. Gerd Krumeich, *Die unbewältigte Niederlage. Das Trauma des Ersten Weltkriegs und die Weimarer Republik* (Freiburg im Breisgau/Basel/Vienna, 2018), p. 230. • 43 Quoted in Ludwig Laibacher, 'Auf dem Rathaus wehte die Rote Fahne', *Stuttgarter Zeitung*, 12 November 2018. • 44 Franz Schauwecker, *Deutsche allein. Schnitt durch die Zeit* (Berlin, 1931), p. 14. It is worth quoting the whole of this passage from the far-right novel, in which the main character, with his returning comrades, passes by the mayor of a small town who is eager to greet them in the market square: 'The fat man on the wooden podium that looked like a scaffold, began to talk, words of thanks, words of praise, words of complete lack of understanding. He emptied upon them buckets of swollen phrases from his manly chest that had safely survived the war; he dared to call them "heroes", he ascribed all fame to them; he praised their silent, upright suffering and patience for the new Germany of freedom and happiness; and so he spattered them from top to bottom until they were covered with melodrama and falsity. He did it all with dignified comedy, and with the busy confidence of a successful grocer. He too had been washed to the top by the Revolution and stood now at the top of a town, convinced to the tips of his walrus moustache of his mission of international brotherhood and private prosperity. And they came from those fields! They had to put up with this! After the battles in France, it felt like an unbloody and hence an entirely repellent form of mockery' (ibid.). • 45 Jünger, *In Stahlgewittern*, p. 19. • 46 Arnolt Bronnen, *O.S.* (1929; Klagenfurt/Vienna, 1995), p. 114. • 47 Emil Julius Gumbel, *Vier Jahre politischer Mord* (1922; Heidelberg, 1980). • 48 The Landvolkbewegung (Rural People's Movement) was an agrarian protest movement originating in Schleswig-Holstein against the consequences of the agricultural crisis of 1927, which had led to numerous compulsory auctions of bankrupt farms. • 49 Quoted in Helmut Donat, 'Rebell in Uniform', *Die Zeit* 22 (20 May 2020). • 50 Kessler, *Tagebücher 1918–1937*, p. 231. • 51 Quoted in Walter Mühlhausen, *Friedrich Ebert 1871–1925. Reichspräsident der Weimarer Republik* (Bonn, 2006), p. 48. • 52 This would make Louise Ebert the successor to Maria-Luise von Hannover-Cumberland, the wife of Max von Baden. • 53 Cf. Peter-Christian Witt, *Friedrich Ebert. Parteiführer, Reichskanzler, Volks beauftragter, Reichspräsident* (Bonn, 1992). • 54 Quoted in Werner Maser, *Friedrich Ebert, der erste deutsche Reichspräsident. Eine politische Biographie* (Munich, 1987), p. 270. • 55 Peter Panter (Kurt Tucholsky), 'Auf dem Nachttisch. Friedrich Ebert, "Kämpfe und Ziele" ', *Die Weltbühne* 23/49 (1927): 863. • 56 Cf. Sebastian Haffner, *Die deutsche Revolution 1918/19* (Reinbek bei Hamburg, 2018), ch. 15. • 57 Ibid., p. 240. • 58 Walter Mühlhausen, 'Der Typus Ebert. Anmerkungen zur Biographie des Parteiführers im Staatsamt der Weimarer Republik', *Mitteilungsblatt des Instituts für Soziale Bewegungen* 45 (2011): 104. • 59 Thomas Mann, 'Brief über Ebert', in idem, *Große kommentierte Frankfurter Ausgabe*, vol. 15.1: *Essays II. 1914–1926*, ed. and annotated by Hermann Kurzke (Frankfurt am Main, 2002), p. 949. • 60 Mann, 'Von deutscher Republik', *Essays II*, p. 531.

Chapter 2: When Money Dies

1 Cf. Frederick Taylor, Taylor, Frederick, *The Downfall of Money: Germany's Hyperinflation and the Destruction of the Middle Class* (London, 2013), p. 122. • 2 Ibid., p. 31. • 3 Ibid., p. 199. • 4 Cf. Joseph Roth, 'Berlin im Taumel der Verzweiflung', in idem, *Trübsal einer Straßenbahn. Stadtfeuilletons*, ed. and with an afterword by Wiebke Porombka (Salzburg/Vienna, 2012), p. 180. • 5 Between 1907 and 1925 in Munich the number of those working in domestic service fell from 3.8 per cent of all employed to 1.82 per cent. Cf. Martin H. Geyer, *Verkehrte Welt. Revolution, Inflation und Moderne: München 1914–1924* (Göttingen, 1998), p. 136. • 6 Cf. Kai-Uwe Mer, *Vulkan Berlin. Eine Kulturgeschichte der 1920er Jahre* (Berlin, 2020), p. 150. • 7 Cf. Taylor, *Inflation*, p. 181. • 8 Artur Landsberger, *Raffke & Cie. Die neue Gesellschaft* (Hanover, 1924), p. 233. • 9 Egon Erwin Kisch, *Café Größenwahn. Berliner Reportagen* (Berlin, 2014), p. 53. • 10 Joseph Roth, 'In der Region des Hungers', in idem, *Trübsal einer Straßenbahn*, p. 183. • 11 Geyer, *Verkehrte Welt*, p. 266. • 12 Cf. Otto Friedrich, *Morgen ist Weltuntergang. Berlin in den Zwanziger Jahren* (Berlin, 1998), p. 157. • 13 Sebastian Haffner, *Geschichte eines Deutschen. Die Erinnerungen 1914–1933* (Munich, 2006), p. 64. • 14 Ibid. • 15 *Vossische Zeitung*, 11 November 1924. • 16 Hans Fallada, *Wolf unter Wölfen* (1937; Berlin, 2011), p. 7. • 17 Haffner, *Geschichte eines Deutschen*, p. 64. • 18 Klaus Mann, *Der Wendepunkt. Ein Lebensbericht* (1952; Reinbek bei Hamburg, 1985), p. 125. • 19 Geyer, *Verkehrte Welt*, p. 73. • 20 Irmgard Keun, *Das kunstseidene Mädchen* (1932; Berlin, 2005), p. 79. • 21 Egon Erwin Kisch, *Aus dem Café Größenwahn. Berliner Reportagen* (Berlin, 2013), p. 50. • 22 Mel Gordon, *Voluptuous Panic: The Erotic World of Weimar Berlin* (Los Angeles, 2000), p. 28. • 23 Hans Ostwald, *Sittengeschichte der Inflation. Ein Kulturdokument aus den Jahren des Marktsturzes* (Berlin, 1931), p. 126. • 24 Ibid. • 25 Cf. *Die*

Weltbühne, quoted in Ostwald, *Sittengeschichte der Inflation*, p. 99. • 26 Alfred Polgar, *Hinterland* (Berlin, 1929). • 27 On 10 September 1926 Germany joined the League of Nations. Three years later, shortly before his death, Stresemann delivered a speech to the League in which he argued for an intensification of the European currency system and, in passing, for the euro: 'Where in Europe is the European coin, the European stamp?' Cf. Stresemann to the League of Nations on 9 September 1929, in Wolfgang Michalka and Gottfried Niedhart (eds), *Deutsche Geschichte 1918–1933. Dokumente zur Innen- und Außenpolitik* (Frankfurt am Main, 2002), p. 144. • 28 Cf. 'Dokumentation einer Rede Stresemanns über seine Locarnopolitik vor dem Zentralvorstand der Deutschen Volkspartei am 22. November 1925', *Vierteljahrshefte für Zeitgeschichte* 15/4 (1967): 426. • 29 The rotor ship was a modern invention of the 1920s that could be reintroduced today for energy-saving purposes. The ship is propelled by a cylinder, standing upright on deck, which also acts as a sail. • 30 Erich Dombrowski, 'Am Jahresende', *Berliner Tageblatt*, 31 December 1934 (evening edition). • 31 Ibid. • 32 In his novel *Venus in den Fischen* (Venus Among the Fishes), published by Ullstein in 1927, the very popular author Max Mohr devoted himself to the then current abundance of crazes that were developing among the well-to-do: the Dostoyevsky craze, the English craze, the country-house craze, the communist craze, the fascist craze, the closing-time craze or the sensible craze that followed on from the English one. Max Mohr, *Venus in den Fischen* (1927; Hanover, 2014), p. 45. • 33 Quoted in Dieter Gerlinger, 'Louis Haeusser, der Bönnigheimer Heiland. Facetten aus seinem Leben', Stadt Bönnigheim, www.boennigheim.de/website/de/kultur-tourismus/stadt_boennigheim/geschichte_und_wappen/louis_haeusser (accessed 5 November 2023). • 34 Robert Musil, *Der Mann ohne Eigenschaften*, in *idem*, *Gesammelte Werke*, ed. Adolf Frisé, vol. 1 (Reinbek bei Hamburg, 1978), p. 56 (English: *The Man Without Qualities*, trans. Sophie Wilkins and Burton Pike, New York, 1995). Here Musil is describing the revolutionary period leading up to the Revolution of 1848, but at the same time creating a projection of his own contemporary world, which he portrays on several different time levels. *Der Mann ohne Eigenschaften* was published in three volumes from 1930 onwards. • 35 Cf. Peukert, *Die Weimarer Republik*, p. 187: 'Characteristically, representatives of both approaches, progressive optimists and cultural critics, adopted the approach of being able to achieve the total solution of all of humanity's problems. These could rarely be anything less than a "New World: and a "New Man".' Rüdiger Graf undertakes a sophisticated analysis of the expectations of the long-term and the immediate future in the Weimar Republic. He warns against an exaggeration and absolute acceptance of Peukert's theory with reference to some pragmatic voices of contemporaries warning against 'utopian thinking', but agrees with him that the idea of a 'new world' and a 'new man' were very popular after the First World War. Rüdiger Graf, *Die Zukunft der Weimarer Republik. Krisen und Zukunftsaneignungen in Deutschland 1918–1933* (Munich, 2008). • 36 Gert, *Ich bin eine Hexe*, p. 46. • 37 Stoep, 'Tanz-Elfen', *Sport im Bild*, 9 January 1920, p. 32. • 38 Wolfram Eilenberger, *Zeit der Zauberer. Das große Jahrzehnt der Philosophie 1919–1929* (Stuttgart, 2018), p. 144 (*Time of the Magicians: The Great Century of Philosophy 1919–1929*, trans. Shaun Whiteside, London and New York, 2020, p. 122). • 39 Walter Benjamin, 'Erfahrung und Armut' (1933), in *idem*., *Illuminationen. Ausgewählte Schriften 1* (Frankfurt am Main, 1977), p. 291 (*Illuminations*, ed. and with an introduction by Hannah Arendt, trans. Harry Zohn, London, 1970, p. 84).

Chapter 3: Extreme Living

1 Taut, 'Nieder der Seriosismus!', quoted in Waetzoldt and Haas (eds), *Tendenzen der Zwanziger Jahre*, vol. 2, p. 64. • 2 Ibid. • 3 Ibid. • 4 Walter Gropius, 'Bauhaus-Manifest', four-page flyer, quoted in Uwe M. Schneede (ed.), *Die Zwanziger Jahre. Manifeste und Dokumente deutscher Künstler* (Cologne, 1979), p. 165. • 5 Walter Gropius, 'Baukunst im freien Volksstaat',

in *Deutscher Revolutionsalmanach für das Jahr 1919*, quoted in Jeannine Fiedler and Peter Feierabend (eds), *Bauhaus* (Potsdam, 2016), p. 17. • 6 Gropius, 'Baukunst im freien Volksstaat',
p. 136. • 7 *Uhu* 4/6 (1927/8): 49. • 8 *Uhu* 2/7 (1925/6): 34. • 9 Cf. Fiedler and Feierabend (eds),
Bauhaus, p. 466. • 10 In 2007. Cf. Patrick Rössler and Elizabeth Otto, *Frauen am Bauhaus.
Wegweisende Künstlerinnen der Moderne* (Munich, 2019), p. 80. • 11 Cf. the illustrated volume
by Patrick Rössler, *Bauhausmädels: A Tribute to Pioneering Women Artists* (Cologne, 2019). •
12 Cf. Tobias Hoffmann, *Deutschland gegen Frankreich. Der Kampf um den Stil 1900–1930*
(Cologne, 2016), p. 199. The poster was designed by Willi Baumeister for the 1927 Werkbund exhibition in Stuttgart. • 13 Cf. Enno Kaufhold, *Berliner Interieurs 1910–1930. Fotografien
von Waldemar Titzenthaler* (Berlin, 2013), p. 84 ff. • 14 *Uhu* 3/1 (1926/7): 33. • 15 Ibid. • 16 Bertolt Brecht, *Nordseekrabben. Geschichten und Gespräche*, ed. Gerhard Seidel (Berlin, 1987),
p. 34. • 17 Ibid., p. 44. • 18 It began with a series of experiments featuring a structure of
wooden struts, which Marcel Breuer submitted as an apprentice piece to the Bauhaus. This
was followed in 1925 by experiments in steel. Breuer exhibited a club chair made from steel
tubes screwed into one another, stretched with an extremely tough material from the Bauhaus weaving mill. 'Wassily', as the model – still commercially available – is called today,
seemed almost to float in comparison to a massive armchair. Two years later the Dutch-
born Mart Stam developed a cantilever chair out of rigid gas pipes, which decorated a
number of buildings in Stuttgart's Weissenhof Estate. But the chair didn't rock because the
tubes were too inflexible. It was only after material studies were conducted at Mannes-
mann, which produced seamlessly made steel pipes in every strength, that Breuer
developed the significantly more elegant 'B32' and offered it to the Thonet furniture company. In parallel, Mies van der Rohe constructed a free-swinging chair, still called
'Kragstuhl', and registered it as a patent. • 19 Theodor Lessing, *Haarmann. Die Geschichte
eines Werwolfs* (1925), ed. Rainer Marwedel (Frankfurt am Main, 1989), p. 54. • 20 Ibid., p. 55.
• 21 Cf. Wolfgang John, . . . *ohne festen Wohnsitz . . . Ursache und Geschichte der Nichtseßhaftigkeit und die Möglichkeiten der Hilfe* (Bielefeld, 1988), p. 279. John gives figure of 428,900
homeless people, or 0.7 per cent of the population, in 1930. • 22 Cf. Günther Schulz, 'Wohnungspolitik in Deutschland und England 1900–1939. Generelle Linien und ausgewählte
Beispiele', in Clemens Zimmermann (ed.), *Europäische Wohnungspolitik in vergleichender
Perspektive 1900–1939* (Stuttgart, 1997), pp. 153–65. • 23 Cf. https://de.statista.com/statistik/
daten/studie/259681/umfrage/fertiggestellte-wohnungen-in-berlin/ (accessed 21 May 2022).
• 24 Ernst May listed his planning tasks according to place and number. '"Magnitogorsk
200,000 people, Kusnetsk 150,000 people, Leninsk 200,000 people. Chcheklovsk 135,000
people, Orsk 50,000 people, Karaganda 250,000 people, Kashira 100,000 people, Makievka
150,000 people, Leninakan 120,000 people"– these were the figures he gave in the *Neueste
Zeitung* for 8.8.1932. Pioneering thinker, architect, city and society planner for 1.4 million
people – that was the role in which this reinventor of traditional living habits in the Soviet
Union saw himself, and the message that he wanted to convey to those who remained at
home.' Dankwart Guratzsch, 'Architekt Ernst May, der Vater der Trabantenstädte', *Die
Welt*, 9 August 2011. • 25 Quoted in Knud Wolffram, *Tanzdielen und Vergnügungspaläste.
Berliner Nachtleben in den dreißiger und vierziger Jahren* (Berlin, 1995), p. 41. • 26 Cf. Arne Sildatke, *Dekorative Moderne. Das Art Déco in der Raumkunst der Weimarer Republik* (Münster,
2013), p. 360 ff. • 27 The description is from the advertising brochure for Gourmenia, quoted
in Wolffram, *Tanzdielen und Vergnügungspaläste*, p. 44. • 28 Ibid., p. 456. • 29 Ibid. • 30 Cf.
Martin Reichert (David Chipperfield Architects), 'Indienstnahme einer historisch nobilitierten Szenografie', *Bauwelt* 22 (2020): 21: 'Die Straßenansicht erscheint im mesopotamischen
Metropolis-Gewand.' • 31 Hoffmann, *Deutschland gegen Frankreich*, p. 142. • 32 Prof. Schultze-
Naumburg and Walter Gropius, 'Wer hat Recht: traditionelle Baukunst oder Bauen in
neuen Formen? Zwei sich widersprechende Ansichten', *Uhu* 2/7 (1925/6): 30 ff. • 33 Ibid.,
p. 38. • 34 Ibid. • 35 Ibid. • 36 Ibid., p. 34. • 37 Against this Plessner set the art of tact: 'It is in
applying a sophisticated approach towards suggestion, a culture of reticence, that the

mature person shows his full mastery. [. . .] A person demonstrates his full inimitability in indirectness.' Helmut Plessner, *Grenzen der Gemeinschaft. Eine Kritik des sozialen Radikalismus* (1924; Frankfurt am Main, 2001), p. 106. • 38 Franz Hessel, *Ein Flaneur in Berlin* (Berlin, 2007), p. 103. • 39 This barbarism, known as *Entstuckung* or *Abstuckung*, would continue over two generations. Under National Socialism the process was also known as *Entschandeln* (de-shaming), and in the young Federal Republic as 'purification'. It reached a peak in the 1950s and early 1960s when in Berlin's Kreuzberg district alone 1,400 decorated houses were turned back into raw brick buildings before being plastered smooth. The fact that the ornamentation of the Kaiserreich could fall victim to this monstrosity over several generations and under almost all political regimes is one of the peculiarities of the history of taste. • 40 Geyer, *Verkehrte Welt*, p. 271. • 41 Theo van Doesburg, 'Die Verkehrsstadt' (1929), in Waetzoldt and Haas (eds), *Tendenzen der Zwanziger Jahre*, vol. 22, p. 102. • 42 Cf. Wolfgang Schäche, 'Das "Neue Berlin". Architektur und Städtebau', in Manfred Görtemaker and Bildarchiv Preußischer Kulturbesitz, *Weimar in Berlin. Porträt einer Epoche* (Berlin, 2002), p. 6. • 43 *Uhu* 2/7 (1925/6): 40. • 44 Paul Bonatz, 'Noch einmal die Werkbundsiedlung', *Schwäbischer Merkur*, 5 May 1926, evening edition, quoted in Stefanie Plarre, *Die Kochenhofsiedlung – das Gegenmodell zur Weißenhofsiedlung. Paul Schmitthenners Siedlungsprojekt in Stuttgart von 1927 bis 1933* (Stuttgart, 2001), p. 88. • 45 Cf. Adolf Behne, 'Zur Ästhetik des flachen Daches', *Das Neue Frankfurt* 1/7 (1926/7), quoted in Manfred Ulmer and Jörg Kurz, *Die Weißenhofsiedlung. Geschichte und Gegenwart* (Stuttgart, 2006), p. 230. • 46 Karl Scheffler, 'Dächerkrieg und Universum', *Kunst und Künstler. Illustrierte Monatsschrift für bildende Kunst und Kunstgewerbe* 27/2 (1929): 78. • 47 Manfred Sack, 'Weißenhofsiedlung. Noch jetzt hallt das Drama nach', *Die Zeit* 18 (1968). • 48 Cf. Ibid. • 49 A similar conflict between two different architectural camps arose in Berlin in the context of what became known as the 'Zehlendorf Roof War'. Here, from 1926 under the direction of Bruno Taut, the city's GEHAG (public housing association) erected the modern 'Uncle Tom's Cottage' estate. The affluent middle class of Zehlendorf feared that the SPD would fill it with workers. They were almost as suspicious of the planned flat roofs as they were about the future residents. Directly opposite, GAGFAH (a non-profit organisation building homes for office workers) raised an opposing flag: an estate for senior office workers in a moderated reform style – obviously with a pointed roof. Today both estates have protected status, complement one another charmingly and get on extremely well. • 50 Quoted in Ulmer and Kurz, *Die Weißenhofsiedlung*, p. 182.

Chapter 4: 'Destinies Behind Typewriters' – The Supporting Class of the New Age

1 In the larger exchanges, lines were connected not directly but via a second operator who was responsible for the desired network. Over time the flaps were replaced by small lights. • 2 The lifts that circulated constantly within these winding administrative labyrinths were known tellingly as 'paternosters'. These were cabins suspended on an endlessly moving belt, which passed vertically through the floors without stopping and switched direction over a big roller at the top and the bottom, in the basement and under the roof. People had to step into or out of the cabin at exactly the right moment as it floated by, and hence fit in with the rhythm of an anxiety-inducing sequence that was determined by some unknown factor. They were called paternosters because they resembled the rosary, the chain of counting beads used when reciting the Lord's prayer. According to Hans Ulrich the name refers 'to the ceaseless rhythm of collective prayer; to trust in an invisible and independent [. . .] cause of the movement and to the anxiety prompted by these lifts. [. . .] Between the departure of one cabin and the arrival of the next there was nothing in the shaft but a black abyss.' Hans Ulrich Gumbrecht, *1926. Ein Jahr am Rand der Zeit* (Frankfurt am Main, 2003),

p. 108. • 3 The novel *Herr Brechers Fiasko* by Martin Kessel, published in 1932, describes the inner life of the factionary Berlin company Uvag, the mighty Universale Vermittlungs Aktien Gesellschaft ('Universal Food Company Ltd') freely based on the Hugenberg food company. Uvag was 'helpfulness itself', a symbolic enterprise for nothing and everything, the epitome of an all-encompassing office in which no one really knew what they were working on, which meant that the boundaries between working life and private life blurred all the more easily. Martin Kessel, *Herrn Brechers Fiasko* (Frankfurt am Main, 1978), p. 19. • 4 Ibid. • 5 Cf. Ute Frevert, 'Traditionale Weiblichkeit und moderne Interessenorganisation. Frauen im Angestelltenberuf 1918–1933', *Geschichte und Gesellschaft* 7/3–4, 'Frauen in der Geschichte des 19. und 20. Jahrhunderts' (1981): 514. Cf. also Dirk Stegmann, 'Angestellten-kultur in der Weimarer Republik', in Werner Faulstich (ed.), *Die Kultur der 20er Jahre* (Munich, 2008), p. 21 ff. • 6 Siegfried Kracauer, *Die Angestellten. Aus dem neuesten Deutschland* (1930; Frankfurt am Main, 1980), p. 11. • 7 Incidentally, Walter Benjamin worked as an adviser on the novel *Ich geh aus und du bleibst da* (I Go Out and You Stay Here) for 5 per cent of the royalties. Cf. the afterword by Sophia Ebert in Wilhelm Speyer, *Ich geh aus und du bleibst da. Roman eines Mannequins* (Coesfeld, 2011). • 8 Quoted in Robert Nippoldt and Boris Pofalla, *Es wird Nacht im Berlin der Wilden Zwanziger* (Cologne, 2018), p. 82. • 9 Peter Kaprun, 'Zoologie der Stenotypistin. Mit neun Spezialaufnahmen', in *Das Leben* 7/1 (1929/30): 73 ff. • 10 Peter Panter (Kurt Tucholsky), 'Die Dame im Vorzimmer. Die Priva sekretärin als Gouvernante', *Uhu* 5/3 (1928/9): 67. • 11 Alfred Vierkandt (ed.), *Handwörterbuch der Soziologie* (Stuttgart, 1931), p. 457. • 12 H. Bahrdt, *Industriebürokratie* (Stuttgart, 1958), quoted in Theo Pirker, *Büro und Maschine. Zur Geschichte und Soziologie der Mechanisierung der Büroarbeit, der Maschinisierung des Büros und der Büroautomation* (Basel/Tübingen, 1962), p. 97. • 13 Kessel, *Herrn Brechers Fiasko*, p. 24. • 14 Pirker, *Büro und Maschine*, p. 50. • 15 Bruce Bliven, Jr, *The Wonderful Writing Machine* (New York, 1954), quoted in Pirker, *Büro und Maschine*, p. 53. • 16 Cf. Pirker, *Büro und Maschine*, p. 55. • 17 Kracauer, *Die Angestellten*, p. 44. • 18 Ibid., p. 51. Siegfried Kracauer himself was not free of a certain recklessness with regard to age. For example, he lays some of the blame for women who are facing an increasing threat of dismissal on the women themselves: 'However the misfortune of the girls is often down to their own foolishness. Since they can save quite considerably with the increased income they have from their office work, they balk at a marriage that would leave them materially worse off. Then, if they are dismissed, they end up with neither a new position nor a husband' (ibid., p. 46). • 19 Christa Anita Brück, *Schicksale hinter Schreib-maschinen* (Berlin, 1930), p. 13. • 20 Pirker, *Büro und Maschine*, p. 82. • 21 C. Wright Mills, *White Collar: The American Middle Classes* (1951; Frankfurt am Main, 1955), p. 213, quoted in Pirker, *Büro und Maschine*, p. 81. • 22 Paul Gurk, *Die Wege des teelschen Hans* (Trier, 1922), quoted in Sabine Biebl, *Betriebsgeräusch Normalität. Angestelltendiskurs und Gesellschaft* (1930; Berlin, 2013), p. 162. • 23 Cf. Biebl, *Betriebsgeräusch Normalität*, p. 193 ff. • 24 Cf. *Das Leben* 7/1 (1929/30): 77. • 25 Rudolf Braune, *Das Mädchen an der Orga Privat. Ein kleiner Roman aus Berlin* (Frankfurt am Main, 1930), p. 125. • 26 Brück, *Schicksale hinter Schreibmaschinen*, p. 164. • 27 The 'nimbleness of the fingers of the young things', Siegfried Kracauer wrote, was fabulous. 'When the middle class was doing better, many girls who are now typing prac-tised Etudes on the pianos at home.' Kracauer, *Die Angestellten*, p. 29. • 28 Kessel, *Herrn Brechers Fiasko*, p. 19. • 29 Ibid., p. 34. • 30 Cf. Frevert, *Traditionale Weiblichkeit*, p. 515: 'Of the salesgirls in trade, a quarter rose to be the wife of an independent businessman, in most cases the owner of the shop himself.' • 31 Cf. Hans-Ulrich Wehler, *Deutsche Gesellschaftsge-schichte*, vol 4: *1914–1949. Vom Beginn des Ersten Weltkriegs bis zur Gründung der beiden deutschen Staaten* (Munich, 2008), p. 304: 'In accordance with the self-image of the office workers as a bourgeois social formation, they took their bearings from the values of the social behav-iour which they saw as bourgeois and modern. Indirectly this can be read from the reliable test case of marriage. While marriages with manual workers declined starkly, those with the middle classes strikingly increased but were exceeded still further by endogamy within the office-working class. In Berlin and Bielefeld, for example, this form of social bonding rose from 3 per cent to 40 per cent between 1907 and 1925.' • 32 Irmgard Keun, *Gilgi, eine von uns* (1931), in idem, *Das Werk*, vol. 1: *Texte aus der Weimarer Republik. 1931–1933*, ed. Heinrich Detering and Beate Kennedy (Göttingen, 2018), p. 107. • 33 Brück, *Schicksale hinter Schreibmaschinen*. The blurb for the book, published in 1930 by the Sieben-Stäbe-Verlag, sums up the content very well: 'This ground-breaking book is the world of countless thousands of women who fulfil their duty day after day at the typewriter, oppressed, shoved aside, abused and humiliated in many ways. They are fighting on *three* fronts: male sexuality, the false ambition of their co-workers and their own economic and spiritual adversity. Many succumb in this desperate struggle for recognition and advancement, in their fear of growing old, of unemployment and illness, in their fear of demotion and pursuit or worldly pleasure. The heroine of his book, herself spiritually broken, homeless and unemployed, finds her way back to herself in desperation and loneliness and, in this work without histrionics, with a deep sense of responsibility, with the unambiguity of the unvarnished truth, shapes the "destinies behind typewriters" which, while it acknowledges genuine delight in work, is also an accusation and a cry for help.' • 34 Ibid., p. 11. • 35 Keun, *Gilgi*, p. 107. • 36 Ibid., p. 85. • 37 Ibid., p. 94. • 38 *Uhu* 6/11 (1929/30): 17 ff. • 39 Kracauer, *Die Angestellten*, p. 75. • 40 Ibid., p. 76. • 41 Cf. Gumbrecht, *1926*, p. 32. • 42 Frevert, *Traditionale Weiblichkeit*, p. 517. • 43 Kracauer, *Die Angestellten*, p. 69. • 44 Ibid., p. 70. • 45 Ibid., p. 69. • 46 In the 'Zoology of the Shorthand Typist' from the magazine *Das Leben*, 'Fräulein Doktor', or 'the intellectual', appears as a typical office phenomenon: 'Wears tortoiseshell glasses and is "a lady". She lets all the other members of the office know that she speaks English, French and Italian, and that she carries around her a hint of university education. She reads *Die Fackel* or *Das Tagebuch*, and frequents the Romanische Café. [. . .] The boss thinks she is a creature from a higher, albeit less solid world, which she exploits by treating him like a servant: for him he is "the bourgeois". At the age of thirty she usually marries the chief buyer and becomes a misunderstood lady.' *Das Leben* 7/1 (1929/30): 76. • 47 'One perfect example of this genre is the nice factory-owner's daughter from West Germany, who often spends her time at the Romanische Café. She likes it better there than she does with her family, whom she escaped one day wearing her beret with the little tab; better too than in the big company where she works on the adding machine for 150 Marks a month. What is one supposed to do if one wants to live, really live, and doesn't get the slightest support from home? Certainly, she wants to achieve a more elevated position, but office work is still only the indispensable condition of the freedom that she wants to try. After the close of business she drinks a strong coffee that freshens her up, and then off she goes, into the midst of life, to the students and artists with whom she can chat, smoke and paddle around in boats. Probably much else besides. Just a short while, and she's been seen. But her colleagues in the office stay.' Kracauer, *Die Angestellten*, p. 72. • 48 Ibid. • 49 On 'Sonja's' real name, cf. Thomas Richter: *Christian Schad. Künstler im 20. Jahrhundert. Bausteine zur Biographie* (Petersberg, 2020), p. 156, and Joachim Jäger et al. (eds), *Die Kunst der Gesellschaft. 1900–1945. Ausstellungskatalog Neue Nationalgalerie* (Berlin, 2021), p. 17. • 50 Wehler, *Deutsche Gesellschaftsgeschichte*, vol. 4, p. 304.

Chapter 5: Precarious Balance: The Death of Ebert, the Arrival of Hindenburg

1 *Vossische Zeitung*, 2 March 1925, p. 1. • 2 Ibid. • 3 *Berliner Tageblatt*, 4 March 1925, p. 2. • 4 *Spandauer Zeitung*, 5 March 1925, p. 1. • 5 In the second election 48.3 per cent of those eligible had voted for Hindenburg, three points more than for the opposing candidate of the *Volksblock*, the centrist politician Wilhelm Marx, who was also supported by the SPD and the DDP. • 6 *Berliner Volkszeitung*, 27 April 1925, p. 1. Since the Communists had refused to

join the republican block and put up their own candidate, the victorious Hindenburg was only a 'minority president'. • 7 *Berliner Börsen-Zeitung*, 27 April 1925, p. 1. • 8 Cf. Heinrich August Winkler, *Weimar 1918–1933. Die Geschichte der ersten deutschen Demokratie* (Munich, 2018), p. 283: 'The fact that Hindenburg promised to respect the Republic constitution made it hard for some who had previously despised the Republic to maintain their irreconcilable hostility to the new state.' • 9 *Vossische Zeitung*, 21 May 1928, p. 1. • 10 *Berliner Tageblatt*, 21 May 1928, p. 1. • 11 Cf. Ursula Büttner, *Weimar. Die überfordete Republik 1918–1933. Leistung und Versagen in Staat, Gesellschaft, Wirtschaft und Kultur* (Stuttgart, 2008), p. 385. • 12 Philipp Nielsen, 'Verantwortung und Kompromiss. Die Deutschnationalen auf der Suche nach einer konservativen Demokratie', in Tim B. Müller and Adam Tooze (eds), *Normalität und Fragilität. Demokratie nach dem Ersten Weltkrieg* (Hamburg, 2015), p. 298. • 13 Cf. Büttner, *Weimar*, p. 383 ff. • 14 Friedrich Koslowsky (ed.), *Deutschlands Köpfe der Gegenwart über Deutschlands Zukunft*, with a foreword by Graf Rüdiger von der Goltz (Berlin, 1928), p. 204. • 15 Letter from the Ahrenshoop spa administration, in *Vossische Zeitung*, 31 July 1928, p. 3. • 16 Cf. Petra Josting and Walter Fähnders, *Laboratorium Vielseitigkeit. Zur Literatur der Weimarer Republik* (Bielefeld, 2005). • 17 Walter Laqueur, *Weimar: A Cultural History* (London, 1974), p. 42. • 18 Ibid. • 19 Siegfried Kracauer, *Georg* (Berlin, 2013), p. 31. The novel, completed in 1934, was not brought out until 1973; Kracauer published the first chapter in the *Frankfurter Zeitung* in 1928. • 20 Erich Kästner, *Fabian. Die Geschichte eines Moralisten* (1931; Munich, 2003), p. 186. • 21 'We live in a great time, he said, and it is becoming greater by the day' (ibid., p. 87).

Chapter 6: Traffic as the Art of Citizenship

1 Theodor Lessing, *Der Lärm. Eine Kampfschrift gegen die Geräusche unseres Lebens* (Wiesbaden, 1908), p. 45. • 2 Martin Wagner, 'Deutsche Städtebauausstellung 1930 gegen 1900', *Die Baugilde* 11/19 (1929), quoted in Klaus Homann et al. (eds), *Martin Wagner. 1885–1957. Wohnungsbau und Weltstadtplanung. Diee Rationalisierung des Glücks. Ausstellung der Akademie der Künste* (Berlin, 1985), p. 10. • 3 Martin Wagner, 'Städtebauliche Probleme der Großstadt'. Lecture from the cycle 'Berlin', delivered on 18 March 1929. Quoted in Homann et al. (eds), *Martin Wagner*, p. 105. • 4 In Wagner's defence we should mention that his own suggestion for a roundabout in Alexanderplatz allowed for a much denser construction, ten storeys in a semicircle adjacent to the traffic lanes, ending as a triangle in two tall towers to the west. Mies van der Rohe, on the other hand, proposed a comparatively large area, loosely surrounded by cubic buildings, which looked as if they had been dropped there at random. First prize went to the architects Luckhardt Brothers & Anker with a design that looked like a synthesis of American and Soviet avant-gardes. After discussions with the investor, building finally began with a design by Peter Behrens, who came second. But only half of the project was completed; his Alexanderhaus and Berolinahaus still stand on the square today as important testimony to *Neue Sachlichkeit*. • 5 Martin Wagner, 'Zivilisation, Kultur, Kunst', *Wohnungswirtschaft* 3/20–21 (1926): 165. • 6 Ibid., p. 106. • 7 Wagner, *Städtebuliche Problleme der Grossstadt*, p. 104. • 8 Cf. Oswald Spengler, *Der Untergang des Abendlandes. Umrisse einer Morphologie der Weltgeschichte* (1918; Munich, 1989), p. 43 ff. • 9 Joseph Roth, *Berliner Saisonbericht. Unbekannte Reportagen und journalistische Arbeiten 1920–1939*, ed. Klaus Westermann (Cologne, 1984), quoted in Klaus Strohmeyer (ed.), *Berlin in Bewegung. Literarischer Spaziergang*, vol. 2: *Die Stadt* (Reinbek bei Hamburg, 1987), p. 139. • 10 Ibid., p. 141. • 11 Alfred Döblin, 'Berlin und seine Künstler', in *idem, Schriften zu Leben und Werk* (Olten/Freiburg im Breisgau, 1986), p. 38. • 12 The title of a book by Helmut Lethen, who made Plessner a valuable source for the self-interpretation of the Weimar Republic: *Verhaltenslehren der Kälte. Lebensversuche zwischen den Kriegen* (Frankfurt am Main, 1994). • 13 Plessner, *Grenzen der Gemeinschaft*, p. 109. • 14 Ibid., p. 108. • 15 Siegfried Kracauer, 'Kleine

Signale', *Frankfurter Zeitung*, 10 October 1930. • 16 The standard work of the novelist Eduard Wechssler has been cited as an example of the current national stereotype on the right: *Esprit und Geist. Versuch einer Wesenskunde des Deutschen und des Franzosen* (Leipzig/Bielefeld, 1927). Wechssler maintains that 'an emotion of great universal unity and secret essential unity' stirs the mind of the German 'and ennobles his thoughts', while 'the Frenchman' is only capable of splitting hairs. 'The essential German is impelled by a desire to observe, illuminate, envision, notice, explain and grasp' (ibid., p. 111). Wechssler contrasts this introspective ponderer with the notoriously social Frenchman, who remains entirely superficial in his cheerful existence. The French 'people of city-dwellers', which pursues the urban lifestyle even in the smallest village, nurtures the cult of sociability even in its spoken sentence construction: 'Every word and every syllable is arranged within a sociable association in whose evenly advancing sequence the single concept is integrated as a link and must abandon all right to special individual status' (ibid., p. 91). • 17 Lethen, *Verhaltenslehren der Kälte*, p. 48. • 18 Ignaz Wrobel (Kurt Tucholsky), 'Berliner Verkehr', *Die Weltbühne* 22/45 (1926): 741. • 19 Ibid., p. 739. • 20 Ibid. • 21 Ibid. • 22 If Potsdamer Platz, even more than Alexanderplatz, was able to become the epitome of urbanity, it was down not only to the prettily designed traffic-light tower, but to the fact that it was a 'square without qualities', as the sociologist Michael Makropoulos observed: it was perceived 'as a swirling, surging, noisy, cubistly splintering structure, but never as a square. It was, one might say, the non-square par excellence, and by virtue of that very fact so significant and fascinating, ideally placed for promotion to the embodiment of the "beautiful new age".' Michael Makropoulos, 'Ein Mythos massenkultureller Urbanität. Der Potsdamer Platz aus der Perspektive von Diskursanalyse und Semiologie', in Joachim Fischer and Michael Makropoulos (eds), *Potsdamer Platz. Soziologische Theorien zu einem Ort der Moderne* (Munich, 2004), p. 162. • 23 Karl Baedeker, *Berlin und Umgebung. Handbuch für Reisende*, 20th edition (Leipzig, 1927), p. 164. • 24 For example, *Dresdner Bahnüberführung*, 1922, Hermitage, St Petersburg, or *Haus im Gewitter*, 1922, Staatliche Kunstsammlungen Dresden. Both in: Birgit Dalbajewa (ed.), *Neue Sachlichkeit in Dresden. Malerei von Dix bis Querner* (Dresden, 2011). • 25 For example, *Abbrucharbeiten am alten Stuttgarter Bahnhof*, 1924, Kunstmuseum Stuttgart, or *Neubau des Tagblattturms*, 1930, Kunstmuseum Stuttgart. • 26 For example, *Stiglmaierplatz in München bei Nacht*, 1935, Stadtmuseum München. • 27 Alfred Wolfenstein, 'Städter', in Kurt Pinthus (ed.), *Menschheitsdämmerung. Symphonie jüngster Dichtung* (Berlin, 1920), p. 10. • 28 Kurt Tucholsky, 'Augen in der Großstadt'. The poem was first published under the pseudonym Theobald Tiger in: *Arbeiter-Illustrierte-Zeitung* 9/11 (1930): 217.

> When you go to work
> in the early morning
> when you stand at the station
> with all your worries:
> then the city shows itself
> to you asphalt-smooth
> in the human funnel
> millions of faces:
> Two strange eyes, a brief glance,
> The eyebrows, pupils, eyelids –
> What was that? perhaps your life's happiness . . .
> Gone, vanished, never again.
> You walk your whole life long
> on a thousand streets;
> along the way you see
> the ones who forgot you.
> An eye beckons,

your soul echoes;
you've found it,
only for seconds . . .
Two strange eyes, a brief glance,
the eyebrows, pupils, eyelids –
What was that? perhaps your life's happiness . . .
Gone, vanished, never again.
As you walk you must
Wander through cities;
see for a pulse-beat
the strange other.
It may be a foe,
it may be a friend,
in battle it may be
your comrade.
It looks over
and moves past.
Two strange eyes, a brief glance,
the eyebrows, pupils, eyelids –
What was that?
A piece of great humanity!
Gone, vanished, never again.

• 29 Franz Hessel, *Spazieren in Berlin. Sonderausgabe* (1929; Berlin, 2007), p. 8. • 30 Quoted in Bodo-Michael Baumunk, 'Rhythmus im Hohlraum – Berlin in den Zwanziger Jahren', in Christian Mothes and Dominik Bartmann (eds), *Tanz auf dem Vulkan. Das Berlin der Zwanziger Jahre im Spiegel der Künste* (Berlin, 2015), p. 13. • 31 Ibid., p. 103. • 32 Siegfried Kracauer, 'Aus dem Fenster gesehen', in *idem, Straßen in Berlin und anderswo* (Berlin, 1987), p. 50 f. • 33 *Uhu* 6/2 (1929/30): 65. • 34 Ilja Ehrenburg, *Das Leben der Autos* (Berlin, 1930), p. 235. (*10 PS* was published in Germany under the title *Das Leben der Autos* by Malik Verlag.) • 35 Ernst Jünger: *Der Arbeiter. Herrschaft und Gestalt* (1932; Stuttgart, 2014), p. 100. • 36 Ibid. • 37 Erika Mann, 'Verflixtes Regenwetter!', *Tempo*, 10 July 1929. Quoted in Anke Hertling, *Eroberung der Männerdomäne Automobil. Die Selbstfahrerinnen Ruth Landshoff-Yorck, Erika Mann und Annemarie Schwarzenbach* (Bielefeld, 2013), p. 173. • 38 Quoted in Jens Bisky, *Berlin. Biographie einer großen Stadt* (Berlin, 2019), p. 468. • 39 Cf. Clärenore Stinnes, *Im Auto durch zwei Welten. Die erste Autofahrt einer Frau um die Welt 1927 bis 1929*, ed. and with a foreword by Gabriele Habinger (Vienna, 2007); Thomas Bleitner, *Frauen der 1920er Jahre. Glamour, Stil und Avantgarde* (Berlin, 2017), p. 189 ff. • 40 Cf. Hertling, *Eroberung der Männerdomäne Automobil*, p. 184: 'They have to drive up to 1,200 kilometres a day. There's hardly time for sleep, meals or grooming. "Ideas," Erika Mann continues, "change curiously on a trip like this. Sleep is the most valuable thing, the only valuable thing, in fact." ' The quotation is from an article by Erika Mann in the magazine *Ford im Bild* in 1931. • 41 Erika Mann, 'Rom? – nur eine Waschgelegenheit', in *idem, Blitze überm Ozean. Aufsätze, Reden, Reportagen*, ed. Irmela von der Lühe and Uwe Naumann (Reinbek bei Hamburg, 2001), pp. 90–2. • 42 Quoted in *Der Spiegel* 39 (1963): 90. • 43 Jan Bürger, *Im Schattenreich der wilden Zwanziger. Fotografien von Karl Vollmoeller aus dem Nachlass von Ruth Landshoff-Yorck* (Marbach, 2018), p. 9. • 44 Ibid., p. 8. • 45 Géza von Cziffra, *Kauf dir einen bunten Luftballon. Erinnerungen an Götter und Halbgötter* (Munich/Berlin, 1975), quoted in Bürger, *Im Schattenreich der wilden Zwanziger*, p. 9. • 46 Kessler, *Tagebücher 1918–1937*, p. 479. • 47 Ibid. • 48 Rut Landshoff, *Die Vielen und der Eine* (1930; Hamburg, 2020), p. 5. (Around this time Ruth Landshoff spelled her first name without an 'h'.) • 49 *Sport im Bild* 35 (1929), p. 845, quoted in Hertling, *Eroberung der Männerdomäne Automobil*. • 50 Ibid., p. 844. • 51 Cf. Hertling, *Eroberung der Männerdomäne Automobil*, p. 154.

• 52 Karl Vollmoeller, 'Auto und junges Mädchen', *Der Querschnitt* 12/4 (1932): 244. Other quotations from the text are from the same passage. • 53 In 1972 Marieluise Fleisser revised the novel, originally from 1931, and republished it under the title *Eine Zierde für den Verein* (A Credit for the Club). It is from this version that quotations are taken. • 54 Cf Marieluise Fleißer, *Eine Zierde für den Verein. Roman vom Rauchen, Sporteln, Lieben und Verkaufen* (Frankfurt am Main, 1975), p. 109. • 55 Ibid., p. 31. • 56 Martin Kessel, 'Hymne auf den Verkehr', in idem, *Gebändigte Kurven. Gedichte* (1925), quoted in Armin Leidinger, *Hure Babylon. Großstadtsymphonie oder Angriff auf die Landschaft? Alfred Döblins Roman "Berlin Alexanderplatz" und die Großstadt Berlin. Eine Annäherung aus kulturgeschichtlicher Perspektive* (Würzburg, 2010), p. 131. • 57 Kessel, *Herrn Brechers Fiasko*, p. 167.

Chapter 7: The Charleston Years

1 Cf. *Revue des Monats* 1/7 (1926/7): 737. • 2 Billy Wilder, 'Herr Ober, bitte einen Tänzer. Aus dem Leben eines Eintänzers', *B.Z. am Mittag*, 19, 20, 22 and 24 January 1927, quoted in idem, *Der Prinz von Wales geht auf Urlaub. Berliner Reportagen, Feuilletons und Kritiken der zwanziger Jahre*, ed. Klaus Siebenhaar (Berlin, 1996), p. 23. • 3 Hellmuth Karasek, *Billy Wilder. Eine Nahaufnahme* (Hamburg, 1992). • 4 Ibid. • 5 Wilder, *Der Prinz von Wales geht auf Urlaub*, p. 10. • 6 Thomas Mann, 'Unordnung und frühes Leid', in idem, *Gesammelte Werke*, vol. 8: *Erzählungen* (Frankfurt am Main, 1960), p. 647. • 7 Quoted in Astrid Eichstedt and Bernd Polster, *Wie die Wilden. Tänze auf der Höhe ihrer Zeit* (Berlin, 1985), p. 47. • 8 Cf. ibid. • 9 F.W. Koebner (ed.), *Jazz und Shimmy. Brevier der neuesten Tänze* (Berlin, 1921), p. 58. • 10 Eichstedt and Polster, *Wie die Wilden*, p. 49. • 11 Klaus Mann, *Der Wendepunkt*, p. 126. • 12 Quoted in Eichstedt and Polster, *Wie die Wilden*, p. 39. • 13 R.L. Leonard, 'Jazz – Shimmy – Steinach & Co', in Koebner (ed.), *Jazz und Shimmy*, p. 122. • 14 Hans Siemsen, 'Jazz-Band', in Koebner (ed.), *Jazz und Shimmy*, p. 18. • 15 Peter Panter (Kurt Tucholsky), 'Die neuen Troubadoure', *Die Weltbühne* 17/12 (1921): 342; also under the title 'Jazzband' in Koebner (ed.), *Jazz und Shimmy*, p. 107. • 16 Helmut Günther, *Die Tänze und Riten der Afroamerikaner* (Bonn, 1982), quoted in Eichstedt and Polster, *Wie die Wilden*, p. 56. • 17 Eichstedt and Polster, *Wie die Wilden*, p. 57. • 18 Quoted in Marc Zitzmann, 'Unorthodoxer geht es hier gar nicht. Joséphine Baker ins Pantheon', *Frankfurter Allgemeine Zeitung*, 25 August 2021. • 19 Ibid. • 20 *Berliner Börsen-Zeitung*, 7 January 1926. • 21 Ibid. • 22 Quoted in Eichstedt and Polster, *Wie die Wilden*, p. 65. • 23 Ottomar Starke, 'Revue nègre', *Der Querschnitt* 6/2 (1926): 119. • 24 On the biography of Bayume Husen cf. Vanessa Conze, *Haus Vaterland. Der große Vergnügungspalast im Herzen Berlins* (Berlin, 2021), p. 96 ff., and Marianne Bechhaus-Gerst, *Treu bis in den Tod. Von Deutsch-Ostafrika nach Sachsenhausen. Eine Lebensgeschichte* (Berlin, 2007). • 25 Carl Zuckmayer, 'Franzosenzeit', quoted in Christian Koller: 'Die "Schwarze Schmach". Wahrnehmungen der Besatzungssoldaten im Rheinland nach dem Ersten Weltkrieg in deutscher und französischer Perspektive', in Rosmarie Beier-de Haan and Jan Werquet (eds), *Fremde? Bilder von den "Anderen" in Deutschland und Frankreich seit 1871* (Dresden, 2009). • 26 Tucholsky, 'Jazzband', in Koebner (ed.), *Jazz und Shimmy*, p. 107. • 27 Carl Zuckmayer, 'Franzosenzeit am Oberrhein', *Vossische Zeitung* 4, supplement (29 June 1930). • 28 *B.Z. am Mittag*, 24 May 1921. • 29 Even beyond showbusiness it was at least imaginable that African origins and professional success were not mutually exclusive. Max Mohr's popular novel *Venus in den Fischen* (1927) centred on a fashionable African doctor, the head of an expensive sanatorium, who treated the overstimulated nerves of his wealthy Berlin clientele with great psychological sensitivity. • 30 Cf. Gorch Pieken and Cornelia Kruse, *Preußisches Liebesglück. Eine deutsche Familie aus Afrika* (Berlin, 2007), p. 150. The book tells the story of the Sabac el Cher family from 1836 until the present. • 31 Wassily Kandinsky, *Über das Geistige in der Kunst* (1911; Bern, 2004), p. 25. • 32 Wilhelm Worringer, *Abstraktion und Einfühlung*.

Ein Beitrag zur Stilpsychologie (Munich, 1908), quoted in Doris Kaufmann: ' "Primitivismus". Zur Geschichte eines semantischen Feldes 1900–1930', in Wolfgang Hardtwig (ed.), *Ordnungen in der Krise. Zur politischen Kulturgeschichte Deutschlands 1900–1933* (Munich, 2007), p. 431. • 33 Manfred von Killinger, 'SA-Männer – Landsknechte', *Der SA-Mann* 5 (February 1932), quoted in Sven Reichardt, 'Gewalt, Körper, Politik. Paradoxien in der deutschen Kulturgeschichte der Zwischenkriegszeit', in Wolfgang Hardtwig (ed.), *Politische Kulturgeschichte der Zwischenkriegszeit 1918–1939* (Göttingen, 2005), p. 228. • 34 Not to be confused with the daily newspaper of the same name published by Ullstein. The illustrated magazine *Tempo – Das Magazin für Fortschritt und Kultur* was similar in themes to *Uhu* and *Querschnitt*, but distinguished by an avant-garde, extremely playful layout. • 35 *Tempo* 1/2 (1928): 5. • 36 Ibid., p. 6. • 37 Ibid., p. 36. • 38 Ibid., p. 37. • 39 Kracauer, *Die Angestellten*, p. 96. • 40 Wolffram, *Tanzdielen und Vergnügungspaläste*, p. 44. • 41 Keun, *Das kunstseidene Mädchen*, p. 88. • 42 Ibid., p. 87. • 43 Inge von Wangenheim, *Mein Haus Vaterland* (Halle an der Saale, 1976), p. 304. • 44 Ibid. • 45 Yvan Goll, 'Ode an Berlin', *Die Erde* 2/1 (1920): 62. • 46 Karl Vetter, *Die Revue im Weltstadtprogramm*, quoted in Wolfgang Jansen, *Glanzrevuen der zwanziger Jahre* (Berlin, 1987), p. 91. • 47 Joseph Roth, 'Berliner Vergnügungsindustrie', *Münchner Neueste Nachrichten*, 1 May 1930, quoted in Michael Bienert (ed.), *Joseph Roth in Berlin. Ein Lesebuch für Spaziergänger* (Cologne, 1996), p. 209 ff. Also the following quotations. • 48 Ibid., p. 212. • 49 Ibid. • 50 Kracauer, *Die Angestellten*, p. 96. • 51 Ibid., p. 97. • 52 Cornelie Holzach, *Art déco – Schmuck und Accessoires. Ein neuer Stil für eine neue Welt* (Stuttgart, 2008). • 53 Siegfried Kracauer, *Das Ornament der Masse. Essays* (Frankfurt am Main, 1977), p. 280. • 54 Ibid., p. 97. • 55 *Das Leben* 8/1 (1930/1): 39.

Chapter 8: Self-optimisation: Perfecting Leisure and the Body

1 *Uhu* 3/8 (1926/7): 101. • 2 *Uhu* 2/12 (1925/6): 6. The text advocates driving out to lakes and the seaside and camping out. 'During the week many of us switch ourselves off and turn into machine-people, then they can spend a day and a half chasing after us to catch up with themselves, to overtake and recover themselves. For three days we hurry back to ourselves, to our childhood days and those of humanity. On Sundays we flood the lakes and let the shores stretch far inland.' • 3 Cf. ibid., p. 107. • 4 Fabian Tobias, 'Anglomanisches Brevier', *Der Querschnitt* 16/10 (1936): 585. • 5 Cf. Johanna Niedbalski, *Die ganze Welt des Vergnügens. Berliner Vergnü gungsparks der 1880er bis 1930er Jahre* (Berlin, 2018). • 6 Joseph Roth, 'Berlin Lunapark', *Der Artist*, 3 June 1920, quoted in Niedbalski, *Die ganze Welt des Vergnügens*, p. 135. • 7 Cf. Niedbalski, *Die ganze Welt des Vergnügens*, pp. 13 ff. and 402 ff. • 8 Cf. Conze, *Haus Vaterland*, p. 31. • 9 *Die Rote Fahne*, 7 July 1922. • 10 Siegfried Kracauer, 'Wochenschau-Theater' (1931), in *idem, Kino. Essays, Studien, Glossen zum Film* (Frankfurt am Main, 1974), p. 15. • 11 Cf. Siegfried Kracauer, 'Kult der Zerstreuung. Über die Berliner Lichtspielhäuser', in Karsten Witte (ed.), *Theorie des Kinos. Ideologiekritik der Traumfabrik* (Frankfurt am Main, 1972), p. 234. • 12 Cf. Béla Balázs, *Der sichtbare Mensch oder Die Kultur des Films* (Vienna/Leipzig, 1924), p. 33 ff. • 13 Cf. Siegfried Kracauer, 'Lichter der Großstadt' (1931), in *idem, Kino*, p. 15. • 14 Rudolf Arnheim, 'Stumme Schönheit und tönender Unfug. Ein Abenteuer mit dem Tonfilm', *Die Weltbühne* 25/41 (1929), quoted in Corinna Müller, 'Übergang zum Tonfilm. Wandel der kulturellen Öffentlichkeit insbesondere am Beispiel Hamburgs', *Jahrbuch für Kommunikationsgeschichte* 4 (2002): 139. • 15 Ibid., p. 140. • 16 *Film-Kurier* 65 (17 March 1925). • 17 Siegfried Kracauer, 'Wege zu Kraft und Schönheit', *Frankfurter Zeitung*, 21 May 1921. • 18 Kessel, *Herrn Brechers Fiasko*, p. 19. • 19 Kracauer, 'Wege zu Kraft und Schönheit'. • 20 *LichtBildBühne* 23 (17 March 1925). • 21 *Illustrierter Film-Kurier* 159 (1925). • 22 Cf. Heidegger's notes on his thoughts regarding *'Leiblichkeit'* (corporality) as set out in 1927 in *Being and Time*: 'Everything that we now call corporality, to the last muscle fibre,

the most hidden hormone molecule, is hence not fundamentally lifeless material, but a sphere of that non-reifiable, not optically visible ability to perceive the significances of that which one encounters, of which the whole of Dasein consists.' Martin Heidegger, *Zollikoner Seminare. Protokolle – Zwiegespräche – Briefe*, ed. Medard Boss (Frankfurt am Main, 1994), p. 293. • 23 Devastatingly influential in this regard was the leading eugenicist Alfred Ploetz who, with his book *Die Tüchtigkeit unserer Rasse und der Schutz der Schwachen* (The Excellence of Our Race and the Protection of the Weak), published in 1895, tirelessly advocated euthanasia. • 24 Quoted in Graf, *Die Zukunft der Weimarer Republik*, p. 19. • 25 Bernd Wedemeyer-Kolwe, '"Ein Ereignis für den ganzen Westen". Körper-kultur in Weimar zwischen Öffentlichkeit, Kunst und Kultur', in Michael Cowan and Kai Marcel Sicks (eds), *Leibhaftige Moderne. Körper in Kunst und Massenmedien 1918–1933* (Bielefeld, 2005), p. 194. • 26 Egon Erwin Kisch, 'Elliptische Tretmühle' (1925), in idem, *Aus dem Café Größenwahn*, p. 91. • 27 Cf. Gumbrecht, 1926, p. 221 ff. • 28 Herbert Obscherningkat, 'Was fällt, das soll man stoßen', *Angriff*, 23 November 1933, quoted in Alfons Arenhövel (ed.), *Arena der Leidenschaften. Der Berliner Sportpalast und seine Veranstaltungen 1910–1973* (Berlin, 1990), p. 76. • 29 Curt Riess, *Das war mein Leben! Erinnerungen* (Frankfurt am Main/Berlin, 1990), p. 120. • 30 Bertolt Brecht, 'Das Theater als Sport' (1920), in idem, *Der Kinnhaken und andere Box- und Sportgeschichten*, ed. Günter Berg (Frankfurt am Main, 1995), p. 23. • 31 *Uhu* 3/1 (1926/7): 68. • 32 Ibid., p. 72. • 33 Bertolt Brecht, 'Sport und geistiges Schaffen,' in idem, *Der Kinnhaken*, p. 35. • 34 Brecht, *Der Kinnhaken*, p. 99. • 35 *Der Querschnitt* 1/6 (1921): 221. • 36 *Der Querschnitt* 6/1 (1926): 49. • 37 Kai Marcel Sick, '"Der Querschnitt" oder: Die Kunst des Sporttreibens', in Cowan and Sicks (eds), *Leibhaftige Moderne*, p. 44. • 38 Hans von Wedderkop, quoted in: Cowan and Sicks (eds), *Leibhaftige Moderne*, p. 44. • 39 *Film-Kurier* 73 (26 March 1932). • 40 Theobald Tiger (Kurt Tucholsky), 'Das Mitglied', *Die Weltbühne* 22 (1926): 865. • 41 Cf. Martin Rüther et al., *Jugend in Deutschland 1918–1945*, website with documents from NS-Dokumentationszentrum der Stadt Cologne, https://jugend1918-1945.de/portal/jugend/thema. aspx?bereich=projekt&root=25004&id=26857&redir= (accessed 24 May 2022). • 42 Quoted in ibid. • 43 Cf. Frank Bösch, 'Militante Geselligkeit. Formierungsformen der bürgerlichen Vereinswelt zwischen Revolution und Nationalsozialismus', in Hartwig (ed.), *Politische Kulturgeschichte der Zwischenkriegszeit*, p. 151 ff. 'The small businessmen and manual workers who assembled in the urban fire services were not only practised in extinguishing fires. They were also influenced by their experience of revolution and were preparing measures to be taken against strikes' (ibid., p. 160). • 44 Ibid., p. 151 ff. • 45 Ibid., p. 170. • 46 Cf. Tim B. Müller, 'Die Weimarer Republik und die europäische Demokratie', in Michael Dreyer and Andreas Braune (eds), *Weimar als Herausforderung. Die Weimarer Republik und die Demokratie im 21. Jahrhundert* (Stuttgart, 2016), p. 64. • 47 Martin Voelkel, 'Hie Ritter und Reich!', *Der Weiße Ritter* 6, 'Sedung' special issue (1921), quoted in Werner Kindt (ed.), *Dokumentation der Jugendbewegung*, vol. 1: *Grundschriften der deutschen Jugendbewegung* (Düsseldorf/Cologne, 1963), p. 372. • 48 Romano Guardini, *Quickborn. Tatsachen und Grundsätze* (1921), quoted in Gottfried Küenzlen, *Der Neue Mensch. Eine Untersuchung zur säkularen Religionsgeschichte der Moderne* (Munich, 1994), p. 160. • 49 Reichardt, *Gewalt, Körper, Politik*, p, 219. • 50 Ibid., p. 217. • 51 Ernst Jünger, *Das Abenteuerliche Herz. Aufzeichnungen bei Tag und Nacht* (Berlin, 1929), p. 155, quoted in Armin Mohler, *Die Konservative Revolution in Deutschland 1918–1932. Ein Handbuch* (Graz/Stuttgart, 1999), p. 39. • 52 *Arbeiter-Illustrierte-Zeitung* 31 (1932), quoted in Reichardt, *Gewalt, Körper, Politik*, p. 219. Sven Reichardt shows that the communist 'critique of the sabre-rattling of our grandfathers' was shared by the far right: 'The National Socialists took a stand against military tomfoolery by presenting themselves as a movement renewed by the First World War, and which was assembled from young and dynamic, uncompromising, dangerous male bodies that were ready to engage in violence' (ibid.). • 53 Frank Fischer, *Wandern ein Traum. Epilog eines Wandervogelführers* (1909), quoted in Küenzlen, *Der Neue Mensch*, p. 161.

Chapter 9: Between Woman and Man – Gender Doubts

1 Stefan Zweig, 'Zutrauen zur Zukunft', in Friedrich Markus Huebner (ed.), *Die Frau von morgen, wie wir sie wünschen* (Leipzig, 1929), p. 7. • 2 Ibid., p. 9. • 3 Robert Musil, 'Die Frau gestern und morgen', in Huebner (ed.), *Die Frau von morgen, wie wir sie wünschen*, p. 101. • 4 Paula von Reznicek, *Die perfekte Dame* (1928), quoted in Burcu Dogramaci, 'Mode-Körper. Zur Inszenierung von Weiblichkeit in Modegrafik und -fotografie der Weimarer Republik', in Cowan and Sicks (eds), *Leibhaftige Moderne*, p. 128. • 5 Ilse Reicke, *Das Junge Mädchen* (Berlin, 1927), p. 70. • 6 Elsa Maria Bud, *Bravo Musch!* (Berlin, 1931), p. 45. • 7 Quoted in Helga Lüdtke, *Der Bubikopf. Männlicher Blick, weiblicher Eigen-Sinn* (Göttingen, 2021), p. 256. • 8 Cf. ibid., p. 243. • 9 Cf. ibid., p. 234. • 10 *Die Dame* 57 (1929/30): 24, quoted in Lüdtke, *Der Bubikopf*, p. 143. • 11 Stephanie Kaul, 'Schwarze Kappen mit heller Garnitur', *Die Dame* 58 (1930): 67. • 12 Marianne Feilchenfeldt Breslauer, *Bilder meines Lebens. Erinnerungen* (Wädenswil, 2009), quoted in Lüdtke, *Der Bubikopf*, p. 280. • 13 Peter Huchel, 'Die Knäbin', *Der Querschnitt* 12/4 (1932): 245. There it is identified as having been written in 1927. • 14 Emil Lucka, 'Verwandlung der Frau', in Huebner (ed.): *Die Frau von morgen, wie wir sie wünschen*, p. 83. • 15 Joseph Roth, 'Der Herr mit dem Monokel', in *Vorwärts*, 23 March 1924, in *idem*, *Trübsal einer Straßenbahn*, p. 204. • 16 Quoted in Theweleit, *Male Fantasies*, vol. 1, p. 72. • 17 Ibid. • 18 Cf. Christian Ferber (ed.), *Berliner Illustrirte Zeitung. Zeitbild, Chronik, Moritat für jedermann 1892–1945* (Berlin, 1982), p. 264. • 19 Franz Blei, 'Mode und Erotik', *Blau-Rot* 1/2 (1928), quoted in Adelheid Rasche, 'Der männliche Blick. Das Bild der "Neuen Frau" in Männerzeitschriften', *Querelles. Jahrbuch für Frauen- und Geschlechterforschung* 11, 'Garçonnes à la mode im Berlin und Paris der zwanziger Jahre' (2006): 126. • 20 Lucka, 'Verwandlung der Frau', p. 82. • 21 Quoted in Stefano Evangelista and Gesa Stedman (eds), *Happy in Berlin? Englische Autor*innen der 1920er und 30er Jahre* (Göttingen, 2021), p. 63. • 22 Quoted in Rasche, 'Der männliche Blick', p. 126. • 23 Ibid., p. 83. • 24 Ibid., p. 82. • 25 Cf. Burcu Dogramaci: '"Frauen, die ihr Geld selbst verdienen". Lieselotte Friedlaender, der "Moden-Spiegel" und das Bild der großstädtischen Frau', *Querelles. Jahrbuch für Frauen- und Geschlechterforschung* 11: 'Garçonnes à la mode im Berlin und Paris der zwanziger Jahre' (2006). • 26 Gret Gottschalk to Walter Arndt, quoted in Moritz Föllmer, 'Auf der Suche nach dem eigenen Leben. Junge Frauen und Individualität in der Weimarer Republik', in Moritz Föllmer and Rüdiger Graf (eds), *Die "Krise" der Weimarer Republik. Zur Kritik eines Deutungsmusters* (Frankfurt am Main, 2005), p. 296. • 27 Fritz Künke, *Krisenbriefe. Über den Zusammenhang von Wirtschaftskrise und Charakterkrise* (1932; Tübingen, 1977), p. 67 f. • 28 Axel Eggebrecht, 'Machen wir uns nichts vor', in Huebner (ed.), *Die Frau von morgen, wie wir sie wünschen*, p. 121. • 29 Kästner, *Fabian*, p. 150. • 30 Ibid., p. 20. • 31 Ibid., p. 235. • 32 Friedrich Georg Jünger, 'Introduction', in *Das Gesicht der Demokratie. Ein Bildwerk zur Geschichte der Nachkriegszeit*, ed. Edmund Schultz (Leipzig, 1931), p. 22. Jünger, like his brother Ernst, hoped that the paramilitary men's leagues would bring a violent end to liberal democracy: 'The important thing is that a resolute male in the form of a community with military discipline should begin to rise up against the socially organised parties. The state is male in gender. The path from the ideal of these fighting associations to an authoritarian state that organises the nation's struggle for life and power is a very predictable one' (ibid.). • 33 Georg Fritz, 'Das Zeitalter der Verweiberung und Entartung', in Erhard F.W. Eberhard (ed.), *Geschlechtscharakter und Volkskraft. Grund probleme des Feminismus* (Darmstadt/Leipzig, 1930). • 34 Quoted in Ute Planert, 'Kulturkritik und Geschlechterverhältnis. Zur Krise der Geschlechterordnung zwischen Jahrhundertwende und "Drittem Reich"', in Hardtwig (ed.), *Ordnungen in der Krise*, p. 202. • 35 Arnolt Bronnen, 'Die weibliche Kriegs Generation', in Huebner (ed.), *Die Frau von morgen, wie wir sie uns wünschen*, p. 69. • 36 Ibid., p. 72. • 37 Ibid., p. 76. • 38 Ibid. • 39 Ibid. • 40 Thomas Wolfe, *Eine Deutschlandreise. Literarische Zeitbilder 1926–1936* (Munich, 2020), p. 38. • 41 Lion Feuchtwanger, *Erfolg* (1930; Berlin/Weimar, 1974), p. 533. • 42 Alfred Döblin, 'Von Gesichtern, Bildern und ihrer Wahrheit', in August

Sander, *Antlitz der Zeit. Sechzig Aufnahmen deutscher Menschen des 20. Jahrhunderts* (1929), with an introduction by Alfred Döblin (Munich, 1976), p. 13. • 43 Walter Benjamin used the expression for Sander's work in his 1931 'Kleine Geschichte der Photographie' in *idem, Das Kunstwerk im Zeitalter seiner technischen Reproduzierbarkeit. Drei Studien zur Kunstsoziologie* (Frankfurt am Main, 1970), p. 86. • 44 The art critic and author John Berger put forward an opposite thesis in 1979. He interpreted the many suits in Sander's photographs as the expression of a class hegemony in the sense of the communist theorist Antonio Gramsci. Farmers and workers, 'persuaded' by advertising, mass media, shop assistants, etc., had submitted to the fashion ideal of the bourgeoisie and now wore tight, ill-fitting clothes, more appropriate to the exercise of 'sedentary power' than physical labour, and which made their bodies look misshapen and distorted. In their ill-fitting bourgeois suits, for example, the musicians of a peasant band in Sander's book *Menschen des 20. Jahrhunderts* 'give the impression of being uncoordinated, bandy-legged, barrel chested, low-arsed, twisted or scalene' (John Berger, 'The Suit and the Photograph', in *idem, Understanding a Photograph*, ed. and with an introduction by Geoff Dyer, New York, 2013, pp. 36–41). Berger's thesis is a fascinating example of how the politically motivated taste of the time guides perception. From a present-day perspective, probably no more justified in assuming timeless validity, Berger's vision is simply not true: while the efforts of the band to look perfect may not have been 100 per cent successful, no one here looks 'twisted'. The post-1968 distaste for suits and bow ties has run wild in Berger. One does not see any foolish consequences of 'class betrayal', but a well-dressed band, perfect for a village ball, that thinks highly of itself. • 45 Cf. Wolfgang Brückle, 'Kein Porträt mehr? Physiognomik in der deutschen Bildnisphotographie um 1930', in Claudia Schmölderls and Sander Gilman (eds), *Gesichter der Weimarer Republik. Eine physiognomische Kulturgeschichte* (Cologne, 2000), p. 147. • 46 Curt Glaser, 'Introduction', in Helmar Lerski, *Köpfe des Alltags. Unbekannte Menschen gesehen von Helmar Lerski* (Berlin, 1931), p. ix. • 47 Ibid., p. xiii.

Chapter 10: The Work Runs Out

1 On the European debt carousel and international currency policy, cf. Florian Pressler, *Die erste Weltwirtschaftskrise. Eine kleine Geschichte der großen Depression* (Munich, 2013), p. 27–50. • 2 Gustav Stresemann to Dr Jarres on 24 November 1927, quoted in Arthur Rosenberg, *Geschichte der Weimarer Republik* (Frankfurt am Main, 1961), p. 168. • 3 Cf. Harold James, *Deutschland in der Weltwirtschaftskrise 1924–1936* (Darmstadt, 1988), pp. 275–311. • 4 On Ivar Kreuger, cf. Pressler, *Die erste Weltwirtschaftskrise*, p. 126 ff. • 5 This oft-quoted remark from Brüning's memoirs corresponds to several similar-sounding statements by the chancellor, to the effect that the bad state of the German economy was 'the strongest and most penetrating weapon' that the Reich government had with regard to the question of reparations. Cf. Hermann Graml, 'Präsidialsystem und Außenpolitik', *Vierteljahrshefte für Zeitgeschichte* 21/2 (1973): 137 ff. • 6 Cf. Büttner, *Weimar*, p. 439: 'In December 1932, of almost 5.9 million registered unemployed 13.7% received insurance payments, 22.2% crisis support, and 41.7% welfare support; 22.4% received no help at all. Unemployment insurance [*Arbeitslosenversicherung*], one of the great achievements of the Weimar Republic, was largely replaced by unemployment assistance [*Erserbslosenfürsorge*].' • 7 Quoted in Lothar Gall, *Die Deutsche Bank 1870–1995. 125 Jahre deutsche Finanz- und Wirtschaftsgeschichte* (Munich, 1995), p. 294. • 8 *Vossische Zeitung*, 15 July 1931, p. 2. • 9 Ibid. • 10 Quoted in Joachim Fest, *Hitler. Eine Biographie* (Frankfurt am Main, 1973), p. 425. • 11 Jan-Otmar Hesse, Roman Köster and Werner Plumpe, *Die große Depression. Die Weltwirtschaftskrise 1929–1939* (Frankfurt am Main/New York, 2014), p. 56. • 12 Ernst Haffner, *Blutsbrüder. Ein Berliner Cliquenroman* (1932; Berlin, 2013), p. 104. • 13 Ibid., p. 105. • 14 Cf. Hubert Renfro Knickerbocker, *Deutschland so oder so?* (Berlin, 1932), quoted in Strohmeyer (ed.), *Berlin in Bewegung*, vol. 2, p. 132. • 15 Quoted in

Alexander Jung, 'Sturz in den Ruin', *Spiegel Special Geschicthe* 1 (2008): 27. • 16 Bienert (ed.), *Joseph Roth in Berlin*, p. 106. • 17 Haffner, *Blutsbrüder*, p. 111. • 18 Bruno H. Bürgel, 'Das Hohelied der Arbeit', in *Deutsche Arbeit. Bilder vom Wiederaufstieg Deutschlands. 92 Aufnahmen von E.O. Hoppé*, with a foreword by Bruno H. Bürgel (Berlin, 1930), p. 7. • 19 Jünger, *Der Arbeiter*, p. 273. • 20 Cf. Philipp Reick, 'A Poor People's Movement? Erwerbslosenproteste in Berlin und New York in den frühen 1930er Jahren', *Jahrbuch für Forschungen zur Geschichte der Arbeiterbewegung* 1 (2015): 20 ff. • 21 Cf. similar descriptions in the novel by Rudolf Braune, *Junge Leute in der Stadt* (1932; Hanover, 2019), chapter titled 'Das Arbeitsamt' (The labour exchange). • 22 *Proletarische Sozialpolitik* 7 (1928): 195. • 23 Ibid. • 24 *Rote Fahne*, 24 August 1930, p. 1. • 25 Ibid. • 26 Marie Jahoda, Paul F. Lazarsfeld and Hans Zeisel, *Die Arbeitslosen von Marienthal. Ein soziographischer Versuch* (1933; Berlin, 2020), p. 58. • 27 Ibid., p. 59. • 28 Cf. Otto Voß and Herbert Schön, *Die Cliquen jugendlicher Verwahrloster als sozialpädagogisches Problem* (1930), quoted in Peter Longerich (ed.), *Die Erste Republik. Dokumente zur Geschichte des Weimarer Staates* (Munich/Zurich, 1992), pp. 205–11. • 29 Cf. Jürgen W. Falter, *Hitlers Wähler. Die Anhänger der NSDAP 1924–1933* (Frankfurt am main/New York, 2020), p. 354: 'According to the results of ecological regression analysis, above-average numbers of unemployed turned to the KPD during the global economic crisis, while in 1932 and 1933 the NSDAP had low levels of support among them. Unemployed workers seem particularly often to have voted for the Communists and rather more rarely for the SPD.' • 30 Hans Fallada, *Kleiner Mann – was nun?* (1932; unabridged edition, Berlin, 2016), p. 394. • 31 This was the description by the 22-year-old Peter de Mendelssohn, who worked as a volunteer for the *Berliner Tageblatt* (although he does not name the newspaper) after his end-of-school exams, in his debut novel *Fertig mit Berlin?* (Done with Berlin?). The novel was published in 1930, and apart from youthful adventures in friendship and love, it deals with the everyday reality of editorial life and chronic financial worries. Peter de Mendelssohn, *Fertig mit Berlin?* (1930), with an afterword by Katharina Rutschky (Frankfurt am Main, 2004). • 32 Jörg Später, 'Die goldenen Zwanziger Jahre? Zur Lage der Intelligenz am Beispiel Adorno, Benjamin, Bloch, Kracauer', *Jahrbuch zur Kultur und Literatur der Weimarer Republik* 20/21 (2019/20): 41. • 33 Cf. Helmut Fogt, *Politische Generationen. Empirische Bedeutung und theoretisches Modell* (Wiesbaden, 1982), p. 131. • 34 James, *Deutschland in der Weltwirtschaftskrise*, p. 35. • 35 https://www.bundesarchiv.de/aktenreichskanzlei/1919-1933/0000/vsc/vsc1p/kap1_2/para2_25.html (accessed 11 September 2023). • 36 Cf. Michael Wildt, 'Der Begriff der Arbeit bei Hitler', in Marc Buggeln and Michael Wildt (eds), *Arbeit im Nationalsozialismus* (Munich, 2014), p. 5. • 37 Cf. Hitler in the speech 'Why are we Anti-Semites?', delivered on 13 August 1920 in the Hofbräuhaus, Munich. In Adolf Hitler, *Sämtliche Aufzeichnungen 1905–1924*, ed. Eberhard Jäckel with Axel Kuhn (Stuttgart, 1980), pp. 184–204. • 38 Quoted in Wildt, *Der Begriff der Arbeit bei Hitler*, p. 5. • 39 Cf. Arno Herzig, '1815–1933: Emanzipation und Akkulturation', *Jüdisches Leben in Deutschland. Informationen zur politischen Bildung* 307 (2010). • 40 In Germany, in 1925 there were 564,000 'faith Jews' who belonged to Jewish communities. The number of people of Jewish descent who had no religion or had converted was notoriously overestimated by the National Socialists in their racial delusion. Rather than the expected 300,000, in May 1939 the Nazi authorities counted 19,716 'Jews of other or no religion' who had not been included in earlier surveys, since they were not based on the racist terminology of the National Socialists. Cf. Wolfgang Benz (ed.), *Dimension des Völkermords. Die Zahl der jüdischen Opfer des Nationalsozialismus* (Munich, 1991), p. 32. • 41 Quoted in Heinrich Uhlig, *Die Warenhäuser im Dritten Reich* (Cologne/Opladen, 1956), p. 64. • 42 *Der Stürmer* 16/17 (1930), quoted in ibid., p. 65. • 43 Quoted in Uhlig, *Die Warenhäuser im Dritten Reich*, p. 36. • 44 Ibid., p. 37. • 45 Ibid., p. 38. • 46 *Vossische Zeitung*, 1 January 1930, p. 13. • 47 *Berliner Börsen-Zeitung*, 31 December 1929, p. 5.

Chapter 11: The Mood Plummets, Taste
Adapts – Cultural Conflicts in a Time of Depression

1 Julius Posener, 'Erich Mendelsohn', in *idem*, *Aufsätze und Vorträge 1931–1980* (Brauns-
chweig/Wiesbaden, 1981), p. 184. • 2 For example, at Berlin Radio, called Funk-Stunde AG,
Vox Records and Gramophones was involved; at Ostmarken-Rundfunk AG, based in
Königsberg, it was Elektrohandel Walter Zabel; and in the city of Königsberg, at Mitteldeutsche Rundfunk, it was newspaper publisher Edgar Herfurth and the Leipzig Fair
Office. Fifty-one per cent of shares had to be kept by the Post Office. • 3 Cf. Wolfgang
Hagen's account of legal radio censorship: 'Surveillance committees and cultural advisory
boards liked to interfere in advance in broadcast planning, banned planned programmes,
censored manuscripts and only allowed live discussions on the condition that contents
were made available in great detail before broadcast. For that reason most directors preferred to avoid political subjects.' Wolfgang Hagen, ' "Kulturinstrument Radio". Zur
Genealogie der medialen Katastrophe der Weimarer Republik', in Jessica Nitsche and
Nadine Werner (eds), *Populärkultur, Massenmedien, Avantgarde 1919–1933* (Munich, 2012),
p. 70. • 4 Pem (Paul Marcus), 'Charell, Wien und der Kongreß tanzen', *Neue Berliner Zeitung –
Das 12 Uhr Blatt*, 30 September 1931. • 5 These are the words of Schauwecker's hero and alter
ego Friedrich in Schauwecker, *Deutsche allein*, p. 55. The former frontline soldier Friedrich
is sitting on the train to Berlin, dreaming of destruction: 'One must live in his time in order
to overcome it. Because this time is only worth destroying. But in order to destroy it, you
must first know it very well. Otherwise you will succumb to it. [. . .] And so he travelled
with the tender love that only hatred can give, into that cackling city, to live in it so that he
would bring about its end' (ibid.). • 6 Heinrich Mann, *Ein Zeitalter wird besichtigt* (Berlin,
1947), p. 341. • 7 Ibid., p. 342. • 8 Herbert Ihering, *Ufa und Buster Keaton* (1926), quoted in
Ursula Saekel, *Der US-Film in der Weimarer Republik – ein Medium der "Amerikanisierung"?
Deutsche Filmwirtschaft, Kulturpolitik und mediale Globalisierung im Fokus transatlantischer
Interessen* (Paderborn, 2011), p. 20. • 9 In Koslowsky (ed.), *Deutschlands Köpfe*, p. 255. •
10 Luise Solmitz, *Tagebuch*, quoted in Daniel Führer, *Alltagssorgen und Gemeinschaftssehnsüchte.
Tagebücher der Weimarer Republik (1913–1934)* (Stuttgart, 2020), p. 194. • 11 Ibid. • 12 Cf. Uwe
Spiekermann, '1932 – das Jahr des Jo-Jos', online text posted 13 August 2020, https://uwe-
spiekermann.com/2020/08/13/1932-das-jahr-des-jo-jos/ (accessed 24 May 2022). References
to most of the sources quoted on the yo-yo come from this text. • 13 Siegfried Kracauer,
'Aus einem französischen Seebad', *Frankfurter Zeitung*, 14 September 1932. • 14 Cf. 'Die Yo-
Yo-Stadt', *Vorwärts*, 2 December 1932, p. 3. • 15 *Vossische Zeitung*, 2 October 1932, p. 21. •
16 George Grosz, 'Unter anderem ein Wort für deutsche Tradition', *Das Kunstblatt* 15/3 (1931),
quoted in Schneede (ed.), *Die Zwanziger Jahre*, p. 280. • 17 Ibid., p. 278. • 18 Ibid., p. 279. •
19 Ibid., p. 280. • 20 H. Reiser, quoted in Peukert, *Die Weimarer Republik*, p. 169. • 21 H. Günther,
Die Kunst von morgen (1939), quoted in Peukert, *Die Weimarer Republik*, p. 175. • 22 Hitler's
radio address, 'Proclamation from the Reich Government to the German People', 1 February 1933. • 23 Cf. Mohler, (ed.), *Die konservative Revolution*, p. 142. • 24 Quoted in ibid., p. 143.
• 25 Speech by Alfred Hugenberg at the rally at the Harzburg Front on 11 October 1931,
quoted in Michalka and Niedhart (eds), *Deutsche Geschichte 1918–1933*, p. 201. • 26 Hans
Praesent (ed.), *Der Weg voran! Eine Bildschau deutscher Höchstleistungen* (Leipzig, 1931). •
27 The publishing house – a music publisher, in fact, which sold musical scores – had a right-
wing management and quickly radicalised in the course of the 1930s. While *Der Weg voran!*
also celebrated the achievements of Social Democratic and left-liberal elites, even though
the achievements of the right greatly outnumbered them, the volume of photographs *Das
Gesicht der Demokratie*, also published in 1931 by Breitkopf & Härtel, was distinctly far right
in tone. The face of democracy is shown as extremely ugly; in the preface Friedrich Georg
Jünger pleads vehemently for it to be replaced by an authoritarian state that would be

better at organising the 'nation's struggle for life and power'. Cf. Schulz (ed.), *Das Gesicht der Demokratie*, p. 21. • 28 Praesent, *Der Weg voran!*, p. xv. • 29 Quoted in Jochen Hung, '"Die Zeitung der Zeit". Die Tageszeitung Tempo und das Ende der Weimarer Republik', in David Oles and Ute Schneider (eds), *'Der ganze Verlag ist einfach eine Bonboniere'. Ullstein in der ersten Hälfte des 20. Jahrhunderts* (Berlin/Munich/Boston, 2015), p. 152. • 30 Quoted in ibid., p. 153. • 31 Quoted in ibid., p. 150. • 32 Cf. Benjamin Ziemann, 'Landwirtschaft und ländliche Gesellschaft', in Nadine Rossol and Benjamin Ziemann (eds), *Aufbruch und Abgründe. Das Handbuch der Weimarer Republik* (Darmstadt, 2021), p. 570. • 33 Bruno Tanzmann, 'Das deutsche Leid als Geburtsstunde des schöpferischen Menschen', quoted in Klaus Bergmann, *Agrarromantik und Großstadtfeindschaft* (Meisenheim am Glan, 1970), p. 234. • 34 Cf. ibid., p. 265. • 35 In this they followed the influential theses of Oswald Spengler. The topic of the connection between the city and nomadic life had been running through many people's heads since the turn of the century. It was summed up particularly pithily by Werner Sombart: 'The city, however, is the immediate continuation of the desert' (*Die Juden und das Wirtschaftsleben*, Leipzig, 1911, p. 427). • 36 Hans Friedrich Blunck, 'Preface', in Erich Retzlaff, *Die von der Scholle. Sechsundfünfzig photographische Bildnisse bodenständiger Menschen* (Göttingen, 1931), p. vii. • 37 In passing, and almost unnoticed, it is mentioned that the main character has been released from prison. This makes him a 'colleague' of Franz Biberkopf, who came into the world a year previously in Alfred Döblin's novel *Berlin Alexanderplatz*. One of them ends up in the wilderness, the other in the bustling cosmopolitan city. • 38 Wilhelm Stapel, 'Der Geistige und sein Volk', *Deutsches Volkstum* 12 (1930), quoted in Walter Delabar, *Klassische Moderne. Deutschsprachige Literatur 1918–1933* (Berlin, 2010), p. 183 • 39 Ibid. • 40 Alfred Döblin, 'Bilanz der Dichterakademie', *Vossische Zeitung*, 25 January 1931, arts supplement. • 41 Alfred Döblin, *Berlin Alexanderplatz*, 489. • 42 Alfred Döblin, 'Wissen und Verändern!' (1931), in idem, *Der deutsche Maskenball von Linke Poot*, p. 250. • 43 Ibid., p. 187. • 44 Ibid., p. 263. • 45 Ibid., p. 265. • 46 Ibid., p. 241. • 47 Ibid., p. 242. • 48 F.W. Koebner, 'Was tanzt man diesen Winter?', *Das Magazin* 8 (December 1931/2): 6627. • 49 Ibid. • 50 *Der Querschnitt* 12/7 (1932): 509. • 51 Ibid., p. 511. • 52 Ibid. • 53 The counterpart to this in painting was called *Neue Romantik* (New Romanticism) or *beschauliche Sachlichkeit* (tranquil functionalism). Hidden behind this was *Neue Sachlichkeit*, stripped of its earlier focus and ruthlessness. Franz Lenk, Frank Radziwill, Carlo Mense, Georg Schrumpf and Wilhelm Heise were now presented as neo-romantics, for the first time in 1929 in the Duisburg exhibition *Neue Sachlichkeit – Neue Romantik*, then in quick succession in various shows in Ulm, Frankfurt, Dessau, Cologne and Hanover, finishing with *Deutsche Provinz – Beschauliche Sachlichkeit* in Mannheim. The journal *Die Kunst* greeted the emotional turn in realism as 'the expression of a deeply felt necessity for the development of a new spirituality', while the critic Paul Westheim mocked: 'You could say decaffeinated *Sachlichkeit*.' Quoted in Anna-Carola Krausse, *Lotte Laserstein. Meine einzige Wirklichkeit* (Berlin/Munich, 2018), pp. 213 and 112. • 54 Manfred Hausmann, 'Was mir in dieser Zeit als Wichtigstes am Herzen liegt', *Uhu* 8 (February 1932): 9. • 55 *Berliner Volks-Zeitung*, 18 April 1930. • 56 Quoted in ibid. • 57 Quoted in ibid. • 58 Paula von Reznicek, 'Wir wollen nicht! Eine Kriegserklärung', *Tempo*, 12 October 1929, quoted in Jochen Hung, 'Das veränderliche "Gesicht der weiblichen Generation". Ein Beitrag zur politischen Kulturgeschichte der späten Weimarer Republik', in Gabriele Metzler and Dirk Schumann (eds), *Geschlechter(un)ordnung und Politik in der Weimarer Republik* (Bonn, 2016), p. 238. My account broadly follows Jochen Hung's enlightening analyses of the history of the newspaper *Tempo*. • 59 Ibid., p. 242. • 60 Frau Christine, 'Die Sachliche', *Tempo*, 9 April 1932, quoted in Hung, 'Das veränderliche "Gesicht der weiblichen Generation"', p. 249. • 61 Quoted in Hung, 'Das veränderliche "Gesicht der weiblichen Generation"', p. 251.

Chapter 12: *Evening Over Potsdam* – the End of a Community of Communication

1 Traute Rose, the painter's friend, muse and favourite model, later remembered the complicated process by which the painting was made: 'The friends came together for the first sketches. They took their seats, and the decision was made about where they were going to sit and stand. The figures were only sketched, because the background was going to be painted first. After that had happened, the painter transported the wooden panel back to her studio with its high windows, where the light conditions were the same as they were on the terrace. Now the long work with the various models began. My position on the far right in front of the parapet was unchanged, and so was my husband's (the second seated figure on the left), with our dog at his feet. The middle figure was originally a girl in a red pullover, although she didn't last long and was replaced in the end by the girl in the yellow blouse. The man sitting next to her also had a predecessor. To his great regret he was eliminated. The standing girl in green in the background was suitable, but she couldn't stay on her feet for very long, so I modelled for her legs. My husband Ernst, resting his thrown-back head on his hand, had the greatest difficulty holding his pose. After a while the dog was replaced by an old fur, because he clearly didn't like Ernst's feet.' Quoted in Krausse, *Lotte Laserstein*, p. 110. • 2 Lotte Laserstein had previously been rediscovered by a gallery in London, but above all through the exhibition *Lotte Lasterstein – My Only Reality* in Das Verborgene Museum, Berlin, 2003. • 3 Jürgen Bellers, 'Radikalisierung und Polarisierung', in Werner Müller (ed.), *Die Welt spielt Roulette. Zur Kultur der Moderne in der Krise 1927 bis 1932* (Frankfurt am Main, 2002), p. 139. • 4 In Koslowsky (ed.), *Deutschlands Köpfe*, p. 206. • 5 Führer, *Alltagssorgen und Gemeinschaftssehnsüchte*, p. 308. • 6 The Egon-Erwin-Kisch-Preis changed to the Henri-Nannen-Preis in 2005. • 7 Fred Hildenbrand, . . . *ich soll dich grüßen von Berlin. 1922–1932. Berliner Erinnerungen ganz und gar unpolitisch* (Berlin, 1966), p. 26. • 8 The subscription system meant that this kind of narrow way of reading was further intensified. While in America or England readers usually bought a newspaper from a kiosk and chose now one, now another, depending on which was offered first, Germans usually only read their regular paper. Georg Bernhard, editor-in-chief of the *Vossische Zeitung*, saw kiosk sales as a more democratic variation from the perspective of public education: 'The reader will find the depiction of the situation of the world interpreted now from this party direction and now from that. He is consequently trained to get used to the relativity of all points of view.' The subscriber, on the other hand, saw his prejudiced confirmed day after day. Cf. Peter de Mendelssohn, *Zeitungsstadt Berlin. Menschen und Mächte in der Geschichte der deutschen Presse*, revised edition (Berlin, 1982), p. 379. • 9 Kurt Weill, '1929', quoted in Hagen, 'Kulturinstrument Radio', p. 71. • 10 Quoted in Mendelssohn, *Zeitungsstadt Berlin*, p. 378. • 11 In the early summer of 1923, the KPD was able to use the nationalistic mood for its own ends by declaring the radical activist Albert Leo Schlageter, sentenced to death by the French, as a martyr. Ruth Fischer, the leading member of the Berlin KPD, at first violently criticised the strategy, but then, even though she was herself 'half-Jewish', allowed herself to be swept up in an anti-Semitic attack that the Nazis confirmed as hatred of the Jews, and also accused her of not going far enough in her anti-capitalism: 'You are against Jewish capital and want to defeat the stock-market traders. Quite right. Kick down the Jewish capitalists, hang them from street-lights, trample them. But gentlemen, what are your views on the large-scale capitalists, like Stinnes and Klöckner? Only in an alliance with Russia, my gentlemen on the *völkisch* side, can the German *Volk* expel French capitalism from the Ruhr.' Quoted in Winkler, *Weimar 1918–1933*, p. 196. • 12 Marieluise Fleißer, *Mehlreisende Frieda Geier. Roman vom Rauchen, Sporteln, Lieben und Verkaufen*, first version (Berlin, 1931), p. 52. • 13 *Die Weltbühne* 24/45 (1928): 690. • 14 Cf. Hans-Ulrich Wehler: 'Any democracy must also be able to cope with radical journalistic criticism. But within the ethic of responsibility of democratic journalists it must not be allowed to cross the boundary of hostility to the state in principle. In his own way,

however, with *Die Weltbühne* Carl von Ossietzky actively contributed still further to the weakening of the already deeply wounded Republic, actively and unapologetically discrediting it with his criticism from the left. Even though von Ossietzky might have believed that he was always fighting for the Republic, the effect was that he had tended in the end towards the destructive.' Hans-Ulrich Wehler, 'Leopold Schwarzschild contra Carl von Ossietzky. Politische Vernunft für die Verteidigung der Republik gegen ultralinke Systemkritik und Volksfront-Illusionen', in idem, *Preußen ist wieder chic . . . Politik und Polemik in zwanzig Essays* (Frankfurt am Main, 1983), p. 82. • 15 Ibid., p. 464. • 16 Kurt Tucholsky, *Deutschland, Deutschland über alles. Ein Bilderbuch von Kurt Tucholsky und vielen Fotografen. Montiert von John Heartfield* (1929; Reinbek bei Hamburg, 1973), p. 231. • 17 Quoted in Michael Hepp, *Kurt Tucholsky* (Reinbek bei Hamburg, 1993), chapter 'Deutschenspiegel' (Mirrors of the Germans). • 18 Siegfried Kracauer, 'Aufruhr der Mittelschichten. Eine Auseinandersetzung mit dem "Tat"-Kreis', in Kracauer, *Das Ornament der Masse*, p. 81 ff. • 19 Cf. Hans Zehrer, 'Rechts oder links?', *Die Tat* 23 (1932): 505. • 20 Ibid., p. 510. • 21 Carl Schmitt, *Politische Theologie. Vier Kapitel zur Lehre von der Souveränität* (1922; Berlin, 1993), p. 67. • 22 Erwin Ritter (Hans Zehrer), 'Die große Stadt', *Die Tat* 23 (1931): 637. • 23 Quoted in ibid., p. 257. • 24 Cf. Kurt Sontheimer, 'Der Tatkreis', *Vierteljahrshefte für Zeitgeschichte* 7/3 (1959): 256. • 25 Thomas Mann, 'Deutsche Ansprache. Ein Appell an die Vernunft' in idem, *Gesammelte Werke in Einzelbänden. Frankfurter Ausgabe. Von Deutscher Republik. Politische Schriften und Reden in Deutschland*, ed. Peter de Mendelssohn (Frankfurt am Main, 1984), p. 312. • 26 Cf. NSDAP Manifesto, 10 September 1930: 'The National Socialist Movement, when victorious, will protect the peasants by ruthlessly training the *Volk* in the use of our own products', in Michalka and Niedhart (eds), *Deutsche Geschichte 1918–1933*, p. 184. • 27 Ibid.: the National Socialist movement 'will return to the German *Volk* its violated right by brutally advocating the principle that petty criminals may not be hanged as long as the largest criminals remain unpunished and scot-free.' • 28 Marieluise Fleißer, 'Avantgarde', in idem, *Gesammelte Werke*, vol. 3: *Gesammelte Erzählungen*, ed. Günther Rühle (Frankfurt am Main, 1972), p. 120. • 29 Quoted in Führer, *Alltagssorgen und Gemeinschaftssehnsüchte*, p. 309. • 30 Ibid., p. 310. • 31 Ibid., p. 89. • 32 Jünger, *Der Arbeiter*, p. 276. • 33 Ibid., p. 278. • 34 Ibid., p. 309. • 35 Edgar Julius Jung, 'Neubelebung von Weimar?', *Deutsche Rundschau* 58 (1932): 158 f. • 36 Ibid. • 37 Jung himself was one of the pioneers of National Socialism: 'The intellectual preconditions for the German revolution are created outside of National Socialism. To some extent National Socialism has taken over the role "Volk movement" in this grand labour community. It has expanded it magnificently and become a proud power. Not only are we pleased with this, but we have made our own contribution to this growth. In a huge amount of detailed work, particularly among the educated classes, we created the preconditions for the day when the German *Volk* gave its vote to the National Socialist candidates. This work was heroic, because it dispensed with an external resonance' (ibid.).

Chapter 13: Lonely Elites – Cabinet Politics vs Populism

1 Kessler, *Tagebücher 1918–1937*, p. 712. • 2 Cf. The Theodore Fred Abel Papers, Hoover Institution, Stanford University, digitalcollections.hoover.org (accessed 31 May 2022). • 3 Cf. Büttner, *Weimar*, p. 173. • 4 Ibid., p. 470. • 5 Cf. Peter Walther, *Fieber. Universum Berlin 1930– 1933* (Berlin, 2020), p. 191. • 6 Otto Braun, *Von Weimar zu Hitler* (1939), quoted in Walther, *Fieber*, p. 187. • 7 Quoted in ibid. • 8 Kessler, *Tagebücher 1918–1937*, p. 717, entry for 12 July 1932. • 9 Cf. Michael Wildt, *Zerborstene Zeit. Deutsche Geschichte von 1918–1945* (Munich, 2022), p. 341. • 10 Groener only became quartermaster general in 1918, so along with his protégé Schleicher he was dealing mostly with the logistics of retreat. But even prior to that, Groener and his underling were entrusted with organisational tasks in a managerial capacity. At the start of the war, Groener had run the railway division of the General Staff, and

had been in charge of the transportation of millions of soldiers to the front. Schleicher was also in his staff at this time. • 11 Cf. Walther, *Fieber*, p. 213. • 12 Quoted in Winkler, *Weimar 1918–1933*, p. 534. • 13 Cf. Büttner, *Weimar*, p. 195. • 14 Karl Dietrich Bracher, *Die Auflösung der Weimarer Republik. Eine Studie zum Problem des Machtverfalls in der Demokratie* (Stuttgart/Düsseldorf, 1955), p. 687. • 15 Cf. Philipp Austermann, *Der Weimarer Reichstag. Die schleichende Ausschaltung, Entmachtung und Zerstörung eines Parlaments* (Vienna/Cologne/Weimar, 2020), p. 205. • 16 Ibid. • 17 Cf. Wildt, *Zerborstene Zeit*, p. 334. • 18 Winkler, *Weimar 1918–1933*, p. 594. • 19 Quoted in Sontheimer, *Der Tatkreis*, p. 237.

Chapter 14: The End: Chancellor Hitler

1 Joseph Goebbels, 'Tagebücher', entry for 30 January 1933, quoted in Michalka and Niedhart (eds), *Deutsche Geschichte 1918–1933*, p. 240. • 2 Wilhelm Hoegner, *Der schwierige Außenseiter. Erinnerungen eines Abgeordneten, Emigranten und Ministerpräsidenten* (Munich, 1959), quoted in Austermann, *Der Weimarer Reichstag*, p. 218. • 3 *Reichstagsprotokolle*, vol. 444, 5th parliament 1930/31, 17th session, 5 February 1931, p. 692, www.reichstagsprotokolle.de/Blatt2_w5_bsb00000128_00700.html (accessed 24 May 2022). • 4 NSDAP programme, 24 February 1920, quoted in Heinz Hürten (ed.), *Deutsche Geschichte in Quellen und Darstellung*, vol. 9: *Weimarer Republik und Drittes Reich 1918–1945* (Stuttgart, 1995), p. 70. • 5 Ibid. • 6 Cf. *Berliner Morgenpost*, 2 February 1933, p. 3. • 7 Cf. Austermann, *Der Weimarer Reichstag*, p. 221. • 8 Quoted in Michael Wildt, 'Machteroberung 1933', in *Nationalsozialismus: Aufstieg und Herrschaft. Informationen zur politischen Bildung* 314 (2012). • 9 Cf. Uwe Wittstock, *Februar 33. Der Winter der Literatur* (Munich, 2021), p. 251. • 10 Cf. Austermann, *Der Weimarer Reichstag*, p. 222. • 11 Cf. *Berliner Morgenpost*, 5 May 1933, p. 3. • 12 Quoted in Führer, *Alltagssorgen und Gemeinschaftssehnsüchte*, p. 327. • 13 J. Noakes and G. Pridham, *Documents on Nazism 1919–1945* (London, 1973), pp. 162–4. • 14 The American sociologist Theodore Abel organised a competition for NSDAP members for which they were to write a report over several pages setting out why they became National Socialists. He received 584 reports, a total of around 3,700 pages, which have now been posted on the internet as the *Abel Papers*. • 15 Ulrich Herbert provides a very good description of the magnetic attraction of the 'unity' promised and embodied by Hitler: 'In fact the basic idea of "national revolution", the elimination of plural political, social and cultural forces to establish national "unity" met with agreement even among many of those who lost their voice and their influence in consequence; after all, along with the "splintering" and "disunity" of the German people, the supposed causes of Germany's defeat had been removed. A communality of intellectual and manual work, men and women, rich and poor, South Germans and Prussians, Catholics and Protestants, liberals and socialists: the "re-establishment of unity" and the overcoming of the "calamitous division of the German people" were, along with the "destruction of Marxism", the most-used slogans of these weeks and months and far more than mere propaganda. Expressed in this was the whole unease with the complicated play of political forces, the interaction and counteraction of social and political interests and the difficult quest for long-term compromises and coalitions which found expression in the separation of powers, parties, economic connections and not least the multivocal public, and made life in a modern industrial society so difficult and incomprehensible to many. From this perspective the refusal of plurality and the system of institutionalised clashes of interest that the Nazi government was now putting into practical effect was perceived less as a usurpation of power by a single party and more as the implementation of the natural, national unity of a people against the artificial social and political splintering that happens in a modern state of parties and associations.' Ulrich Herbert, *Geschichte Deutschlands in 20. Jahrhundert* (Munich, 2017), p. 317. • 16 W. Hoegner, *Flucht vor Hitler* (Frankfurt, 1979), p. 98. • 17 Quoted in Rudolf Morsey, *Das 'Ermächtigungsgesetz' vom 24. März 1933. Quellen zur*

Geschichte und Interpretation des 'Gesetzes zur Behebung der Not von Volk und Reich' (Düsseldorf, 1992), p. 163 f. • 18 Ibid. • 19 A fine example of such linguistic inventiveness occurred a few days later, when the Fulda Catholic bishops' conference abandoned their reservations against the NSDAP in an official resolution, after Hitler had assured them that the churches would play an important part in the necessary 'detoxification' of the country. The bishops also discussed the question of allowing large formations of SA men to attend holy mass. In a circular, Cardinal Bertram, the chair of the bishops' conference, set out the following solicitous recommendation: 'Members of the National Socialist movement and Party should not worry about their membership in the context of receiving the sacrament, as long as they do not prevail against their dignity in other respects, and as long as they are determined never to agree to views or actions hostile to faith or the Church.' Suggestions for instruction to the clergy, supplement to the circular of 25 March 1933. Quoted in Paul Mikat, 'Zur Kundgebung der Fuldaer Bischofskonferenz über die nationalsozialistische Bewegung vom 28. März 1933', *Jahrbuch für christliche Sozialwissenschaften* 3 (1962): 229. The 'bringing in of flags' was to be prohibited by friendly exhortation. If this was of no avail, a public furore was to be avoided. Behind the admission of armed Nazis to mass there was also the consideration that they might otherwise fill the churches of the Protestant competition in their hordes on Sunday. The Protestant church was known to have numerous connections with the NSDAP, while the Catholic congregations were significantly more reserved towards it. Unfortunately, the individual faithful had been abandoned by their priests, and from now on they had to rely on their private consciences in their rejection of the Nazis. • 20 *Reichstagsprotokolle*, vol. 457, 8th parliament 1933, 2nd session, 23 March 1933, p. 39, www.reichstagsprotokolle.de/Blatt2_w8_bsb00000141_00041.html (accessed 24 May 2022). • 21 Ibid. • 22 Ibid. • 23 Victor Klemperer, *Ich will Zeugnis ablegen bis zum letzten. Tagebücher 1933–1945*, vol. 1: *Tagebücher 1933–1941*, ed. Walter Nowojski with the collaboration of Hadwig Klemperer (Berlin, 1995), p. 9. • 24 Ibid. • 25 Ibid., p. 14. • 26 Peter Behrens, 'Die Baugesinnung des Faschismus', *Die neue linie* 5/3 (1933/4): 11. • 27 Cf. Hans Dieter Schäfer, *Das gespaltene Bewußtsein. Über deutsche Kultur und Lebenswirklichkeit 1933–1945* (Munich/Vienna, 1983), p. 118. • 28 *Das Magazin* 14 (May 1938). • 29 Cf. Judith Schalansky, 'Hitler mochte Futura', *Der Freitag*, 1 June 2007. • 30 Detlev J.K. Peukert speaks of the 'pathological form of development of the modern age'. Cf. Peukert, *Volksgenossen und Gemeinschaftsfremde. Anpassung, Ausmerze und Aufbegehren unter dem Nationalsozialismus* (Cologne, 1982), p. 296. • 31 Cf. Herbert, *Geschichte Deutschlands im 20. Jahrhundert*, p. 505. • 32 Cf. ibid. • 33 Quoted in ibid. • 34 Ibid.

Acknowledgements

Books are social beings; where there is one, there will be others. This book is also unthinkable without the many that came before. I am grateful to the authors who gripped, stimulated, informed, annoyed and even sometimes entertained me, starting with the oldest, Arthur Rosenberg, who finished his *History of the German Republic* in exile in Liverpool in 1935. It was the first book I read at the start of my studies, over 50 years ago. To list all the authors who have influenced me would take far too long: there are many references in the bibliography. 'Weimar research' is a vital spring from which new surprises are constantly spilling forth.

I am grateful that I was able to read newspapers and magazines from the period between the wars at home. That was made possible by online portals such as Zefys, the newspaper information system of the Staatsbiobliothek Berlin, and the online collection 'Illustrierte Magazine der Klassischen Moderne' of the Sächsische Landesbibliothek – Staats- und Universtätsbibliothek Dresden (SLUB).

I am deeply grateful to Birgit Lübbert Jähner. She is the best checker anyone could imagine. My publisher Gunnar Schmidt believed in the book from the beginning; being edited and improved by him is the purest pleasure.

Picture credits

Text credits

Index

Page references in *italics* indicate images.

ABOUT THE AUTHOR

Harald Jähner is a cultural journalist and former editor of the *Berliner Zeitung*. He was also an honorary professor of cultural journalism at the Berlin University of the Arts. His book *Aftermath: Life in the Fallout of the Third Reich* was shortlisted for the 2021 Baillie Gifford Prize for Non-Fiction, the British Academy Book Prize and the Cundill History Prize, and won the Leipzig Book Fair Prize for Non-Fiction in his native Germany.

ABOUT THE TRANSLATOR

Shaun Whiteside is an award-winning translator from French, German, Italian and Dutch. His most recent translations from German include *Aftermath* by Harald Jähner, *To Die in Spring* by Ralf Rothmann, *Swansong 1945* by Walter Kempowski, *Berlin Finale* by Heinz Rein and *The Broken House* by Horst Krüger.